The History of
MOTION
PICTURES

by

MAURICE BARDÈCHE

and

ROBERT BRASILLACH

TRANSLATED AND EDITED BY IRIS BARRY

New York

W · W · NORTON & COMPANY · INC ·

and

THE MUSEUM OF MODERN ART

PRINTED IN THE UNITED STATES OF AMERICA
FOR THE PUBLISHERS BY THE VAIL-BALLOU PRESS

D. W. Griffith directing The Birth of a Nation *(1915). G. W. Bitzer at the camera, Lillian Gish and Wallace Reid seated.* (CULVER SERVICE)

Contents

v

List of Illustrations

ix

Foreword

THIS *History of Motion Pictures* has the merit of approaching its subject in a form which hitherto has not been available to the large public interested in the film. It very properly attempts to survey the entire history of film making in Europe and in America and to describe the exchange of influences to which the film as a whole has been subject. That it surveys the field from a European angle, even from a distinctly French angle, rather than from our own native viewpoint, makes it a useful check on other accounts of this art-industry, today so predominantly and characteristically American. France was once, if she is no longer, a major producing country, and she was as early as Germany and far quicker than we were in recognizing the intrinsic merits of the new invention.

For more than forty years films have been produced in large numbers in many countries and, after being seen by millions of people, have vanished from view. Although they were made for the purpose of entertaining the largest possible public, those films unquestionably had enormous influence in forming the taste and affecting the attitude to life of that public. At the same time these films were unconsciously reflecting the changing ideas and customs, moral and physical characteristics of the twentieth century.

Only quite recently has there been a move to preserve this unique testimony from destruction, or to re-examine the films of the past with a view to discovering what they reflect of the cultures and societies that created and enjoyed them and what, on the other hand, were the steps through which this new and pervasive art has developed. The Museum of Modern Art Film Library was founded in 1935 for this purpose. It has collected and preserved characteristic films of all periods and all countries, has made these films available for study and has registered their history and that of the men and women who created them.

Today a study of the motion picture, its aesthetic and its social content, is being actively pursued in many of our colleges and by cultural and educational groups throughout the United States. Moreover, the re-examination of outstanding films of the past has also been undertaken by other institutions and groups abroad. An international exchange of knowledge and opinion about the past of this liveliest of the contemporary arts is the order of the day.

The tale which Messieurs Bardèche and Brasillach have to tell is a fascinating one. It recalls how France, England and Sweden, Italy, Germany and the U.S.S.R. in turn contributed much to the growing film, while America furnished so many technical discoveries as well as so much new subject matter and now today provides the lion's share of this universal entertainment. Only after a prolonged and complete re-examination of the films of the past will a wholly authoritative analysis of the film come to be recorded; in the meantime this animated (if often controversial) account is most welcome.

The text has been translated as closely as possible to retain the attitudes and opinions of its authors, which are extremely revealing; it is worth noting how exactly they estimate most of the best American product. Their conclusions do not necessarily coincide with those of the Film Library.

John E. Abbott
DIRECTOR, MUSEUM OF MODERN ART
FILM LIBRARY

Translator's Note

MANY foreign films appear here not under their original titles, nor under their French names, but under their American release titles; e. g., the Swedish film *Korkarlen*, called *La Charrette Fantôme* in France, appears in the text as *The Stroke of Midnight*.

Some omissions and corrections have been made.

PART ONE

The Birth of the Film

1895–1908

AUDIENCES nowadays streaming into sumptuous movie theaters to see Greta Garbo or the Marx Brothers have quite forgotten, if they ever knew, the "heroic age" of the cinema. They seem to think that films came into existence with the cowboys, with Fairbanks and Tom Mix or with the old serials and *The Clutching Hand*. As children, they used to see Fatty Arbuckle, imperturbable Buster Keaton and the little man in oversized trousers whom no one at that date yet spoke of as Mr. Chaplin. Consequently, they regard the films of these men as the "primitives" of what was once known as the silent art, and continues to be the seventh art.

Everyone probably knows, nevertheless, that the origins of the film lie much further back, and that movies date from the era of President Faure and President Cleveland and of Bourget's first novels. They date, in fact, from a time when the boy Proust used to admire Mme. Swann in the Bois de Boulogne, and woo Gilberte in the Champs Elysées. A Jewish army captain was arrested and tried then, but nobody foresaw that a year or two later the name of Dreyfus would convulse the whole French nation. The bicycle was still a velocipede. The automobile had just appeared, but older people insisted that it would never be as much use as the horse. Boldini was the fashionable painter. It was at such a moment that the film appeared.

THE FIRST STEPS

It is one of the peculiarities of this particular art that we can set the date of its birth.

The history of those discoveries which finally led to the invention of cinematography has given rise to many disputes, into which there is little point in entering. Animated pictures of one kind or another are very ancient and, for a while, the magic lantern had attempted to cater to the public liking for them. The law of the persistence of images, on which the film is based, was known in antiquity and utilized ever since the eighteenth century

3

in toys such as the Dazzling Top of Abbé Nollet. Magic lanterns, optical toys, Chinese shadow shows and the whole repertory of the conjurer and the illusionist are all common sources of inspiration which culminated finally in the film.

As soon as the principles of photography had been discovered by Niépce and Daguerre, there were various attempts to add movement to these new and wonderfully accurate pictures. In 1882, Etienne Marey invented a photographic gun with which to record the flight of birds. In 1888, Emile Reynaud patented his praxinoscope, which attempted to give the illusion of movement; he also perfected the perforation of film. He organized a Théâtre Optique which for many years gave shows at the Musée Grévin. It is worth noting that, at first, the pictures which he animated were paintings, and that it was only later that he used photographs. Then, in 1893, Demeny invented chronophotography, while in America Edison, following Muybridge, applied himself to similar problems and produced the kinetoscope or peep show.

The task of co-ordinating all these different experiments (Marey's was especially important) fell upon the brothers Louis and Auguste Lumière. On February 13, 1895 * they patented their first projection machine. On March 28, 1895 the first film— *Lunch Hour at the Lumière Factory*—was shown before the Société d'Encouragement de L'Industrie Nationale. It was fifty feet long. Nine months later, the cinema came into existence.

/The first public or paying performance was given, actually, on December 28, 1895 at the Grand Café, Boulevard des Capucines, in a basement christened the Salon Indien. Here the film was born, in distinctly humble circumstances. The proprietor of the Grand Café, somewhat skeptical, had preferred to charge a rental of thirty francs a day in lieu of the customary twenty

* For the sake of convenience, it is customary to regard the first *public* exhibition of motion pictures projected on a screen (in contradistinction to Edison's motion pictures shown in a peep show box or kinetoscope) as the beginning of the film's history. Lumière's exhibition at the Grand Café in this sense followed Latham's exhibition in New York in April and May 1895 and Armat's exhibition in Atlanta in September 1895, but preceded Paul's exhibition in London in February 1896.

per cent of the takings. Admission was one franc. For this sum, audiences saw ten films, each fifty feet long and lasting one or two minutes. The first day's takings were thirty-five francs. The organizers were rather discouraged. Three weeks later, without a single line of advertising, the profits had risen to two thousand francs a day. Of what did this famous initial show consist? First, *Lunch Hour at the Lumière Factory* with its crowd of respectably dressed working girls in ample blouses and ornate hats like characters from a novel by Zola. There was also the famous *Arrival of a Train at the Station*, whose engine is said to have terrified the spectators; the *Rue de la République* in Lyons; a shot of *Blacksmiths;* and, last of all, a *Bathing Beach*. This delighted everybody by the "marvelous realism of an unmistakably genuine ocean in all its immensity and restlessness," as the paper *Le Radical* wrote next day in reporting on the new invention, to which, it added, "has been given the somewhat harsh name of cinematograph." *Teasing the Gardener*, which afterwards became famous as the first comic film, was not made until later. It was on topical and scenic films that the first success of the cinema was established.

The films shown at the Grand Café then and later were much like those which amateur cinematographers still turn out today. The Lumière family's factory and house provided backgrounds for many brief pictures of domestic life. In one, a little girl sits on Mme. Lumière's lap, somewhat messily eating cereal; they called that one *Baby's Breakfast*. Beside a pool in the garden, Mme. Lumière, in a tussore dress with a polka dot bodice and a sailor hat tilted over her forehead, fishes for goldfish with a roguish air. Under an arbor at the end of the garden, Auguste Lumière and his friend Mr. Trewey play piquet and drink their beer.

Such were the masterpieces shown in the basement of the Grand Café, in the salon of the Café de la Paix, in the arcade of the Opéra where Edison's films were given, in the Musée Grévin's rival establishment, the Porte-Saint-Martin Museum, at the *Petit Journal*, at Dufayel's. Admission was fifty centimes and entitled one to from twenty to thirty minutes of entertainment.

There was a piano to accompany the films, and outside barkers yelled at the top of their lungs. Such were the first movie theaters.

On May 4, 1897 so many people * lost their lives in the disastrous fire which broke out at the Bazar de la Charité that the career of the infant industry was almost cut short forever. The calamity was laid—incorrectly, as it seems—to the celluloid film's catching fire. For years afterwards, the hazard of fire bulked largest among all the worries of producers and of exhibitors alike. Early film journals almost invariably carried a regular feature on the fire problem.

Meanwhile, it was time to do something more ambitious than filming one's most recent grandchild. Photography may be a domestic art, like charades and embroidery, but it is also a public art; and it can furnish material for a magazine just as well as for the family album. Thus, many of the first efforts at production were directed towards providing animated pictures similar to the still pictures in *L'Illustration*. The Lumières were all prepared. Their principal agent, Promio, while traveling through Europe to exploit their invention, also took along a camera with which to furnish the firm with new pictures. He photographed artillerymen in Spain and, in London, filmed the funeral of Queen Victoria from a balcony. As film in those days was manufactured in very short lengths, in order to be able to shoot uninterruptedly he now provided himself with two cameras, so that one could be reloaded while he was using the other.

His work was not without its difficulties. Once at Bremen, as all the photographic shops were closed, he only managed to reload his camera by persuading an undertaker to lend him a coffin which he could use as a darkroom. In Geneva it was an empty beer barrel which served the same purpose. This free-and-easy production method was not to last. The first serious difficulty was encountered when Edison, after a vigorous fight, succeeded in closing the American market to the Lumière product and the Lumière representatives left New York secretly in a

* One hundred and eighty dead, of whom 130 were members of the nobility or persons of eminence.

small boat, and hung about in the Bay waiting for a liner to pick them up and take them back home. This picaresque incident might almost have been invented for use in some future film.

It was natural enough that the cinema should start with scenic views, since scenic views are really a logical development from picture postcards, just as films of domestic life are a logical step from the family photograph album. Each producing firm turned out a series much like one another's. To Lumière's *Lunch Hour at the Lumière Factory*, Gaumont retorted with a *Lunch Hour at the Panhard and Levassor Factories*. Promio had photographed policemen, but Charles Pathé came back with a *Troop of Hussars*. Gaumont filmed *The Fountains of Versailles*, Méliès filmed the *Boulevard des Italiens*, Pathé had *The Czar's Arrival in Paris*. In addition, there were also such picturesque items as *Masons at Work*, *Divers*, *A Canoe Trip*, *At the Barber's*, *A Cabinet-maker at His Bench*. All of these were about fifty feet in length and could be obtained either in black and white or in color. They were sold outright to the exhibitors, most of whom were traveling showmen. The average price was twelve cents a foot for black-and-white films, and from twenty-four to thirty cents for colored films.

All the big producers of the time began by making much the same subjects: they turned out ten different versions of *Teasing the Gardener*, twenty of a *Policeman's Patrol* and then attempted simple fairground farces like Gaumont's first film, with Alice Guy, *The Misadventures of a Piece of Veal*. The actress thought it would be a good idea to play the scene against an artificial instead of a real background. A journeyman-painter consequently prepared a backdrop representing the Rue de Belleville with its funicular railway, an employee and an apprentice were pressed into service as actors and the first narrative film of Léon Gaumont was created.

Abroad it was much the same story. But it is interesting, today, to see one of the first films made in Germany, about 1898. It is an *Excursion*, with young men and girls bicycling along a road. On the face of it, nothing could be more similar to the material being turned out in France and in America at the same date. Yet there is one great difference. The scene opens in longshot, then in a much closer shot we are shown the long line of bicycles snaking along the road, then the faces of the young people, then their legs (that famous shot of legs which was to become one of the standbys of the cinema!). We see these legs, encased in button boots, going up and down; then we again see the cyclists full length. In this simple little film the whole pictorial sense of the Germans, their attention to detail, their propensity for using the camera's eye to show us things our own eyes would never seek out, are already to be detected. There is also a rudiment of sex appeal. In how many films made before 1900 can one detect an ethnic and national * character? Otherwise, everywhere else the films being made ·were scenic views of no great interest, or records of current political and social events.

Denmark was one of the first countries to adopt the new invention. The first Danish film, a documentary, was made as early as 1898 by a court photographer, P. Elfelt, who had a camera similar to that of the Lumières constructed by the village carpenter. During the summer of 1898, instead of photographing the Royal Family he filmed them. It is delightful and even touching to recognize in this black-clad group, with their ill-fitting coats and countrified felt hats, Queen Alexandra of England, the Danish princes and the Czar of all the Russias with the Czarina holding the pale Czarevitch in her arms. In front of them, seated on the ground, are four little boys in sailor suits and five little girls in white frocks, obediently motionless as they wait for the "birdie to come out of the black box." The whole group is surrounded by potted fuchsias adorning a terrace much like any terrace in a middle-class garden anywhere.

Alas, this prehistoric period of the cinema was shortly to draw to a close. The Lumières were soon to cease exploiting their discovery. "After 1900," Louis Lumière says, "films turned more and more towards the theater and towards the use of staged

---

* The authors do not realize how beautifully French are the Lumière films like *Pastime in the Family Circle!*

scenes, compelling us to abandon production since we were not equipped to do this kind of thing."

The cinema was through with exclusively straightforward photography. Other men were appearing who foresaw what else the film could do: men like Léon Gaumont and, still more important, Charles Pathé.

Charles Pathé at the age of thirty possessed a thousand francs. He bought a phonograph and a light van, and began traveling to fairs. Customers paid two sous to hear one record, or ten to hear six. Often enough, they left without paying. Yet, by nightfall, the takings would be as high as two hundred francs. After a few months of this arduous work, Pathé set up shop in the square at Vincennes, discovered the cinema through Edison's films, went into partnership with the inventor Joly, and manufactured a camera to go into competition with Lumière. His first film was *Arrival of a Train at Vincennes Station*. Quite a number of trains arrived and departed in the early films, but Pathé's train was to carry him far.

Shortly afterwards, Pathé built a studio, went into partnership with his brothers but afterwards parted with two of them, and (when he managed to obtain a million francs from M. Grivolas) launched the firm on an ambitious venture which was to turn out very fortunately for him. Without ever having had one really original idea, yet gifted with much perspicacity and remarkable intuition, well able to take advantage of the public's changing taste, Charles Pathé is one of the real pioneers of the film, of its good and bad qualities alike. Yet the title of creator belongs properly to another man, a genuine inventor, Georges Méliès.

AN EARLY MASTER

There is no knowing how long the film might have continued to be pure reportage and newsreel had it not been for the one man who brought to this new technical invention an immense number of really original ideas, and who finally made of the film something other than a mere offshoot of photography. Georges Méliès, born in 1861, was thirty-four years old when the Lumières produced their invention. To him, their first film show seemed a sort of miracle. "Long before it was over," he relates, "I rushed up to Auguste Lumière and offered to buy his invention. I offered ten thousand, twenty thousand, fifty thousand francs. I would gladly have given him my fortune, my house, my family in exchange for it. Lumière would not listen to me. 'Young man,' said he, 'you should be grateful, since although my invention is not for sale, it would undoubtedly ruin you. It can be exploited for a certain time as a scientific curiosity but, apart from that, it has no commercial future whatsoever.'"

Lumière was perfectly sincere in saying this. But Méliès would not listen to him. This young man had been a manufacturer, a mechanic, a cabinetmaker, a draughtsman, a painter, a caricaturist on *La Griffe*, which he ran and illustrated almost entirely himself throughout the Boulangist period. For the last eight years he had been the manager and proprietor of the Théâtre Robert-Houdin at 16, Passage de l'Opéra, where he gave shows of magic and prestidigitation, produced puppet shows and devised various pieces of electrical apparatus by means of which to present tableaux and transformations like *The Marvelous Wreath*. Even at school at Louis-le-Grand he had constructed a Punch-and-Judy show in his desk.

He brought to the films wide experience and interests, and the resourcefulness of a Jack-of-all-trades which enabled him to make anything he wanted at lightning speed, a robust and unspoilt talent much like that of the early painters, an imagination as rich and all-embracing as that of a child. He had a curious Protean quality in a world which is both changeable and deceptive. "I was at one and the same time," he said one day in his delightfully simple way, "an intellectual worker and a manual worker. That explains why I loved the cinema so passionately."

This prestidigitator was just what the cinema needed. As he knew how to do everything, how to make anything, how to devise all sorts of tricks, the Lumières' invention gave him a chance to unleash all his gifts. He began by showing Edison's films on the Boulevard des Italiens, then, realizing the possibilities of this new medium, soon became a producer and made a first *Trip to the Moon* at Montreuil. Films of marching regiments and of trains puffing into stations were not enough to satisfy him.

Almost immediately he attempted to apply to the new invention what he had learned in the Théâtre Robert-Houdin. *The Vanishing Lady* was his first tentative attempt in this direction. Success gave him confidence. He produced *The Bewitched Inn*, then in 1896 *The Devil's Castle*, a film nearly a reel long, and *The Laboratory of Mephistopheles*.

Chance played its usual jocular role in his development. One day when he was filming the traffic on the Place de l'Opéra, his camera jammed. It took him all of a minute to readjust it. He continued to crank and finished his picture, but when he came to develop it he perceived that while his camera had been out of gear the scene had undergone a change, and that a passing omnibus had suddenly been metamorphosed into a hearse—as unexpectedly as, twenty years later, another hearse also surprisingly appeared in *Entr'acte*. From this mishap, Méliès learned something extremely important—that in the realm of the cinema there is no such thing as fair play, that the hand of the director can control everything in a film and that, above all, the film's chief purpose is to entertain the public by tricks like this one which accident had just fortuitously discovered for him.

Méliès soon afterwards produced his *One Man Band* in which he, as the one and only actor, appeared in numerous roles simultaneously. Besides multiple exposure, he also introduced stop-motion photography, taken frame by frame, so that inanimate objects appear to move on the screen as, in 1925, we saw the furniture scuttling from the house in René Clair's *Italian Straw Hat*.

To these innovations another important one was shortly to be added. Early in 1897, the singer Paulus came to Méliès and asked him to make movies of him singing his songs.* At the last moment Paulus, made up as for the stage, refused to perform in the daylight. Faced with this problem, Méliès hurriedly painted

* To be shown with phonograph accompaniment.

some scenery, fixed up adequate illumination, and made the films indoors. The results were satisfactory, and thus the idea of a studio was born.*

MAKING A FILM IN 1900

The success of such novelties as these gave the improvised or manufactured film an advantage over the straightforward photography of everyday events. It was now that Méliès' gifts really came into play: he became the general factotum of the new art and turned out a fresh film each week (though of course the longest of them was at first only two hundred feet). The work entailed in production was huge. First, scenery had to be prepared as a background in the form of a large painted canvas hung at the end of the studio, like a back cloth in an old-fashioned photographic studio. The desired scenery was depicted in grays and blacks, for if colors were used they created false photographic values. Once the background was ready, the producer then manufactured whatever furniture or stage properties he thought fit to introduce. This was the work that Méliès loved best. He has preserved to this day enormous portfolios full of his sketches. "Film production is interesting because it is first and foremost manual work," he declared some years later. At times quite complicated sets were used. For instance, if a factory were to be shown in the distance, this had to be constructed in miniature (much as a child might laboriously make one out of toy bricks, rather than in the highly scientific manner used by Fritz Lang in *Metropolis*). All these contrivances were executed in a workmanlike studio, "the first in the world," which Méliès had built to his own design behind his house at Montreuil. "In a word," he said, "it is a combination of an immense photographic studio and the stage of a theater." This gigantic building was all of fifty feet long by thirty feet wide. The backdrops hung at one end as in the theater. Often there

* The Edison "studio," the Black Maria, existed from 1893, but many Edison films, such as *The Execution of Mary Queen of Scots*, were made in the open air outside the Black Maria.

were also wings and set pieces in the foreground as well. Light came in through the glass roof and sides, and the actual filming had to be done promptly, since "if time were wasted, the daylight began to fade and made it impossible to shoot." The really original thing about the place was the number of trap doors, holes, chutes, ropes, capstans, revolving drums and winches used for making characters appear or vanish, and for creating "apparitions." Actually the building looked much more like a torture chamber than like a modern studio, though it retained the glass panes of the old-fashioned photographer.

When the setting was all ready, two strings were attached to the foot of the camera, carried thence to the extreme right and left edges of the background and there secured. These marked the limits of the photographic field of vision. Next the cameraman fixed another string across, parallel to the back cloth, to delimit the area beyond which a player must not advance if he were to appear full length. Now, closer to the camera, he fixed yet another string parallel to the first to mark the point at which an actor would be photographed down to the knees and yet another at the point where he would be visible only to the waist. One director, Robert Péguy, has related how once, when he wanted to use these medium shots, his producer objected. "Are you crazy?" he cried. "What are all these individuals of whom one sees only the upper half? Audiences are going to think that we have hired a lot of cripples!" *

In all of Léon Gaumont's first films the star, Alice Guy, was supported by two leading men, one of whom was a studio mechanic and the other an apprentice at the factory. Carpenters, electricians and engineers working in the studio frequently played starring roles. Everybody took part. Zecca, Pathé's collaborator, acted drunks, and just before the war Léonce Perret was more often occupied as a comedian than as a director, particularly in the series of *Léonce* comedies. When an attempt was made to employ professional actors, unexpected difficulties arose. They opened their mouths wide, threw back their heads and thumped

* A similar anecdote is told of D. W. Griffith's earliest films using medium shots and close-ups.

their chests but failed to register anything comprehensible in this unfamiliar medium. Besides, they heartily despised the cinema, which they regarded as a proper field only for jugglers and acrobats. Rather than struggle with such artists, the producers preferred to do their own acting or to employ their relatives and friends. This is what Méliès did, and so did Pathé.

After the film had been photographed, it had to be edited and often colored, too. Editing was a complicated job at first because it was necessary to cut up the film into six-foot lengths in order to develop it. Coloring was carried out in two special workrooms in Paris, run by a Mme. Thuilier and Mlle. Chaumont, both employing about fifty colorists, each of whom was entrusted with a single color, like the rabbits in Walt Disney's *Funny Little Bunnies*. The work was done entirely by hand, which accounts for the freshness, the naïveté and accuracy of the color in the early films. A few years later, Pathé invented stencil coloring: this put an end to hand coloring but it also shortly put an end to colored film.

MUSÉE GRÉVIN

From now on, films became more diversified. It would be impossible to understand the real nature of this radically *popular* art without considering certain very important influences * which it absorbed. The film originally derived much of its character from the picture postcard, from the Musée Grévin † and from the colored pages of the *Petit Journal*. Thirty years ago in any little village you could find (and sometimes still find today) one of those small stores smelling of licorice, flypapers, barley sugar and coffee. Inside, a little old woman as placid as a cabbage sits among reels of thread and jars of candy. At her right on a re-

---

* Dr. Erwin Panofsky has illuminatingly defined the three principal ingredients of the motion picture in his article "Style and Medium in the Motion Picture," *Transition*, No. 26, 1937, pp. 121–133. They are "Melodramatic incidents, preferably of a sanguinary kind . . . crudely comical incidents as illustrated in the cheapest kind of funny cartoons . . . mildly pornographic postcards . . ." This important article deserves close study.
† Similar to the Eden Musée and Mme. Tussaud's.

volving stand are displayed faded picture postcards, of Czar Nicholas with President Loubet, a train puffing into a station and sweethearts gazing at each other across a pink fence. On her left hang illustrations from the *Petit Journal*, such as have excited the dramatic instincts of the local rustics by their melodramatic style and violent colors in presenting the Assassination of President Carnot, the Fire at the Bazar de la Charité or the Execution of Bolo Pacha. Such were the models on which the film based itself, as it became self-conscious and realized its power to deceive the eye.

One of Méliès' earliest successes, late in 1898, was a series of films in which he reconstructed (in little incidents barely sixty feet long) the principal events in the Dreyfus case. Among them were "Dreyfus' Court-Martial—Arrest of Dreyfus," "Devil's Island—Within the Palisade," "Suicide of Colonel Henry," "Dreyfus Meets His Wife at Rennes" and "The Degradation of Dreyfus."

This admirable series of primitives, a sort of animated waxworks, somehow reminds one of the character in Pabst's *Dreigroschenoper* who sings of the various adventures of Mackie Messer to the music of a hand organ.*

A prototype of Mackie himself was about to appear in Zecca's *Story of a Crime*, issued by Pathé and one of that firm's biggest successes. It showed an apache with peaked cap and sinister forelock, engaged upon nefarious tasks in a dark street; then the night patrol and the discovery of the crime; magistrates in frock coats, and the medical officer with his precise gestures; witnesses giving evidence; the arrest in a wretched bar; and, finally, an early-morning scene at the guillotine. It was thought necessary to ban this final tableau. Censorship came into action almost before the film was out of its cradle.

A few months later, Pathé produced a series of *Capital Punishments in Various European Countries*—by the ax, by hanging,

---

* Actually the Dreyfus film "reminds" one much more appropriately of the magic lantern slides which were so popular before the invention of the motion picture: there is a definite relationship between them and primitive films of this sort.

garroting, etc., each thirty feet long. Simultaneously, the magazine *Lectures Pour Tous* ran some copiously illustrated articles on the same topic: public taste at the time ran very much in this direction. A similar source of inspiration gave us the film *Underworld of Paris* in 1906 and *The Exploits of Elaine* in 1915. For films of this type any current event might furnish a fresh subject.

An *Assassination of President McKinley* was re-enacted in one studio and followed suitably enough by *The Execution of His Murderer*, by *The Death of Pope Leo XIII*, *The Assassination of the Serbian Royal Family* and *The Eruption of Mont-Pélé*. Foremost among reconstructed events, however, was the film of *Edward VII's Coronation* which Méliès made for the English firm, Warwick Trading Company. It was produced at Montreuil and provided the monarch himself with considerable amusement when he eventually saw it.

"ART" FILMS

There was yet another traditional source upon which the films were to draw, and here too the influence of the picture postcard is to be traced, though with a difference, for they were a rather special type of postcard. They were those which in catalogues are rather prettily described as "piquant." These "piquant scenes" had been popularized by Piron, the famous Parisian photographer, known as the "Royal Photographer," who conceived the idea of producing an album of "art" photographs; they included some very seductive studies of Mlle. Louise Milly. One of his friends thought the cinema might as well profit by his success in this direction and, under his supervision and that of Léar, the album was translated to the screen in a film christened *Bedtime for the Bride*. Two new halls had to be opened to cope with the demand for this. Today most films of this type appeal to us, if at all, by their ridiculous coyness, but at that time they struck the public imagination in quite another way. There is no more astonishing document for us today on the morals of the era of the Paris Exposition than the films like *The Indiscreet Maid*, or a childish and reticent *Flirting on the Train,* in which gentlemen in morn-ing coats with immensely high starched collars sway amorously towards ladies in satin waists and button boots, all nonchalance and prudery. There is, for instance, a *Judgment of Paris* of this period in which the roles are enacted by acrobats with carefully curled hair, in flesh-colored tights from the ends of which toes and fingers of a darker tone protrude; the whole thing takes place in a grotto straight out of comic opera. An *Awakening of Chry-sis* is lyrically described in a catalogue of the time: "Chrysis wakes in an atmosphere redolent of Oriental perfumes. A negress tends her respectfully, as languorously she raises from her couch her slumbrous body." This film cost forty francs outright.

If you had the price, you could see Mlle. Milly smoking a ciga-rette in the sumptuous boudoir of a demimondaine, or vainly hunting for a flea in her tussore petticoat. A *Fashionable Lady at Her Bath* was shown receiving visitors in a bathroom decked in silken draperies and a Japanese screen on which exotic birds sported among bamboos. But let us draw a veil here. It is an exag-geration to say, as some have, that the film was born in ques-tionable surroundings. That it obtained some of its education there cannot be denied.

COMEDIES AND ANIMATED CARTOONS

The era of the short film persisted for a long time. We must remember that most of the first exhibitors were fairground peo-ple. In their eyes, a film had to provide a substitute for an acrobatic turn or a parade, and the films they liked best were comedies from sixty to a hundred and twenty feet long. The comedian Dranem in his first films appeared now as a baker's man, now as an old soldier, an elderly hag or a man smitten with the colic. The elderly dude, the policeman, the detective, the lady's maid, the pastry cook, the drunk and the porter were the principal characters in these comedies, which varied very little and were all based on the inexhaustible material drawn from cir-cuses and pantomimes. Trick photography added ludicrous novel-ties—garments disappeared or flung themselves onto human torsos with unbelievable rapidity, beefsteaks vanished, pots of paint flew about, furniture executed a wild dance.

Then animated cartoons made their appearance. The first cartoon-on-film was made by Emile Cohl in 1908 with the appropriate title of *Phantasmagoria*. It was composed of two thousand drawings and was one hundred feet long. The essential technique of animated cartoons was exhibited in it, though the drawings themselves were crude. *Le Fétard* of 1908, for instance, is little more than schoolboy scribbling. Curiously enough, when the Russians began making animated cartoons in 1934 * they used the same rather infantile fashion of drawing faces and bodies, just as if thirty years of technical improvement had not elapsed. Emile Cohl made many cartoons—such as *When Matches Struck, Merry Microbes* and his parody on *Chantecler*—but later on turned to the production of popular-scientific films.

FAIRY TALES AND TRANSFORMATIONS

The contribution of all these early producers cannot be overlooked. Despite the founding of American or Italian firms, the film throughout its first years was predominantly French—Gaumont, Pathé, Léar. Also, one must not overlook the part played by Mesguich †—one of Lumière's first projectionists and cameramen, who opened movie shows in the United States and all over the world. He traveled as far afield as Tibet and China, was the first man to photograph Lhasa and explored the country of the Tuaregs and the Far West. It was he who suggested having *A Trip to the Moon* accompanied by appropriate music. But the greatest creative worker was still Méliès.

His earliest fantastic films, such as *The Devil's Castle*, were much to the liking of the youthful audiences at the Théâtre Robert-Houdin. Partly out of a desire to please them, partly

* An error, perhaps a misprint for 1914. The first Russian animated cartoons were made by Starevich in 1913. After the Revolution, production was resumed in 1923.

† Mesguich has recounted his experiences in *Tours de Manivelle*, Grasset, Paris, 1933.

An early French film, Louis Lumière's Pastime in the Family
Circle *(1896)*.

The May Irwin–John C. Rice Kiss, *a popular American film*
of 1896.

An Impossible Voyage (*1904*), *one of the many trick-films*
produced, designed and directed by Georges Méliès.

The studio in which Georges Méliès made his films.

out of a personal predilection for the sumptuous settings, the diverse and fairylike flora of imaginary worlds, Méliès made films of adventures such as a child might dream. During the Exposition of 1900 he began work on his first superfilms, all nearly a whole reel long—*Cinderella, Red Riding Hood, Bluebeard.* The first one, *Cinderella,* set the type for them all. It was distributed by Pathé, and Méliès was vexed when Zecca cut it down from two thousand to nine hundred feet, thus sacrificing many of the trick scenes. After this, Méliès broke with Pathé. Among these lizards that turn into lackeys, rats that turn into coachmen without sacrificing their long whiskers, amid all this complicated and childish fairyland, Méliès had hit upon something. Out of his past experience, he discovered how to produce trick scenes and thus become quite independent of "reality." He was to turn all the fairy tales into films: and even they were not enough. The miracles of science, of speed, must be drawn upon, too. He concocted this new recipe for entertainment out of a droll and delightful combination in which monstrous machines from *La Science et la Vie* were allied to Jules Verne's plots. It was as though, in 1900, Méliès himself had been a twelve-year-old boy.

He turned out *A Trip to the Moon, An Adventurous Automobile Trip, Under the Sea, Rip Van Winkle, Robinson Crusoe, An Impossible Voyage, The Merry Frolics of Satan.* These films defied both technical limitations and current fashion. They were made for a public such as filled the Théâtre du Châtelet and were probably none the worse for that. With their good-humored air, their rough-and-ready cutting, their stilted acting, their settings which put one in mind of the opera at its worst, and their restricted movement, they display all the faults of the infant film. Yet from many points of view they are exceedingly rich and suggestive. A technical audacity which grew constantly bolder, an unflagging inventiveness and the virtuosity of an intellectual juggler earned for his work a special place and led him to open new paths for the motion picture. His prodigious fertility, his habit of disregarding obstacles and even of inviting them, and the ability of this Paganini of the film to juggle with décor, was what particularly struck his contemporaries and gave him a front place in their ranks. But his films as a whole would seem to us little better than ingenious mechanical contrivances today were they not redeemed by more important elements. What we love in Méliès is a poetical quality, somewhat painstaking and clumsily archaic, but full of unexpected and sincere lovableness.

Castles copied from old missals, landscapes such as only fairyland knows, meticulous and primitive perspectives, a rather acid color, settings and characters straight out of Mme. Tussaud's, all surge up in the thick of incredible adventures, reminding us sometimes of a valentine and sometimes of the little Tuscan villages in Lorenzetti's paintings—and all in bad taste so ingenuous that it is transformed in some strange way into the most elegant poetry. It is elements like these which combine to make his early masterpieces so precious.

This Jules Verne of the screen was not merely a gifted prestidigitator: he happened also to be the first poet of the cinema. There have not been many of them since. The nearest thing to these laboriously tinted films, with their deliberately unreal settings and infinite repertory of tricks, is the animated cartoons of today. The heir to Méliès is Walt Disney. But others, too, learned much from him. Otherwise, should we ever have had that ascension scene in *Liliom*, where Lang so charmingly created a paradise out of fairgrounds and merry-go-rounds? When we look at one of Méliès' exquisite scenes—some little seaport with its dainty fleet straight out of Gozzoli—we can readily forgive the heavy make-up and frenzied gesturing of the actors (who are the weakest part of his films). He has only to show us a gilded coach drawn by one old skeleton of a horse to put us in the frame of mind to set forth too, in fancy, with this quixotic steed, to realize that the Milky Way is a pretty girl in a 1900 costume, that the stars know how to play the lyre, or to accept the existence of a whole miraculous cosmogony such as we see at the end of *The Merry Frolics of Satan*. It seems quite natural that men should walk upside down on the ceiling, evil spirits spring out of clocks, Aurora and the Great Bear engage in a swimming contest, an umbrella turn into a giant mushroom, Saturn appear in the midst of his own rings and ten women come tumbling out of a parasol.

A BUSINESS ANECDOTE OF 1898

Méliès was going full blast. His firm, Star-Films, was pre-eminent in the French market and his product was widely circulated abroad. His competitors—Charles Pathé and Léon Gaumont in France, Urban and Warwick Trading Company in England, Ambrosio and Cines in Italy—followed his recipes and imitated his methods. In 1904, despite Edison's opposition, he opened a branch in the United States. In 1908, Méliès presided over the International Congress of Film Producers, at which all the most important film makers gathered. It was on this occasion that he succeeded, despite opposition, in getting a standard perforation of film stock adopted, a step which finally made possible a really international motion-picture industry. President of the Chambre Syndicale du Cinéma which he had founded in 1897, he was the undisputed leader of the new industry. At the same time he was its most creative technician. To the innumerable trick effects he invented, which his fellow producers sought unavailingly to imitate, he had just added the "dissolve" which rendered unnecessary abrupt cuts between scenes. Here again a lucky accident helped him.

In his studio it had become customary gradually to diminish the aperture of the lens while shooting the last few feet of each scene, in order not to fog the film. When the work of editing followed, this portion was eliminated as being no part of the footage proper. One day someone forgot to cut it, and, when the film was projected, Méliès realized that a much smoother transition from one scene to the next could thus be achieved. He experimented with repeating the process inversely, commencing each new scene with the diaphragm almost closed, then opening the aperture gradually as the new scene started. By doing this at the beginning and end of each scene he effected a rough dissolve. Méliès also discovered the use of masking, double-exposure, slow-motion and rapid-motion photography.

His prosperity concealed one serious weakness, which was the financial organization of his firm, Star-Films. At the beginning of 1898, when Méliès' business was beginning to expand, an agent came to him to propose putting him in touch with important silent partners. Méliès agreed. A few days later, the agent called again with a Mr. W., who introduced himself as director of the Société d'Etudes Industrielles et Commerciales. Méliès explained how his business operated: they listened with interest. Next came an expert, then an engineer, then another expert. Each of them declared that the firm seemed extremely sound and that the Société d'Etudes would willingly undertake to find capital to invest in it. Only, there were certain steps to be taken first, they would probably have to sound out various parties and, in short, they asked Méliès to pay down twenty-five thousand francs. Méliès paid. Several months passed: Méliès waited. The Société d'Etudes gave no sign of life. Méliès became worried and finally reached the point where he should have started: he began investigations. They were sadly conclusive. The Société d'Etudes had engaged in various financial operations about which numerous firms in the entertainment business had little to report that was pleasant. Méliès wanted to bring suit. He was asked to lay out sixty thousand francs before he could appear against Mr. W. He felt disinclined to do so and left Mr. W. to pursue his course untroubled. This incident gave Méliès little liking for investments or for partners.

Some time later another man came to see Méliès. "I am M. Grivolas. I am in the electrical supply business and the films interest me." "I see," said Méliès. "Are you doing well?" "Not badly," said he. "And are you breaking into the foreign markets?" "Here and there," said Méliès. "M. Méliès," continued M. Grivolas, "it has occurred to me that the capital at my disposal (here Méliès pricked up his ears) might be of considerable service to some sound firm in the motion-picture business able to offer me suitable inducements to invest in it." Méliès had now reared up in alarming fashion, but the unsuspecting M. Grivolas continued: "If you are willing to let my experts come and see you and also to give me security, I am willing to invest the sum of . . ." M. Grivolas was unable to complete his sentence. Méliès had risen and in silent fury showed him the door.

M. Grivolas was much mystified but little disposed to argue. He went to see M. Pathé instead and enabled him to form a limited liability company with a capital of 2,600,000 francs. When Grivolas meets Méliès he never fails to say: "If you had listened to me, today you would own the firm of Méliès-Natan." When Méliès tells the anecdote, he sighs.

The situation generally was about to undergo a change. At first, producers sold their films outright to the exhibitors, a system which made it possible for independents like Méliès to compete with more extensively financed producers. In 1904, however, three of Méliès' assistants, Michaux, Astaix and Lallement, opened a film-renting agency. This enterprise, after initial difficulties, was so successful that in 1907 Pathé decided to abandon the sale of films and to organize instead a chain of renting offices all over France. Méliès, feeling that he was ill-equipped for this method of operation, stuck to outright sales. From that time on his position became that of a lively and colorful pioneer, more interesting by reason of the variety and originality of his output than any of his competitors, but destined to defeat at their hands in the field of commerce. Thenceforward he specialized. He made a domain of the fantastic and trick film, in which his superiority remained incontestable, but he stood aside from the main avenues along which the motion picture was now to progress.

NARRATIVE FILMS

The chief of these avenues, as was inevitable once the first superfilms of six hundred to twelve hundred feet had appeared, was that of the narrative film. There was at first a sort of instinctive repugnance to the construction of motion pictures around a unified and set plot. The idea of a scenario developed slowly. Méliès himself regarded his own films as a series of gags and of diverting trick effects: each single incident or scene which of-

fered him the opportunity to create a startling or comical pictorial effect interested him far more than the main plot of his
films.

Again it was the Musée Grévin, that repository of undeviating
tradition, which inspired the coming change. The first ambitious
films had consisted of a series of *tableaux vivants* rather than of
coherent plots. Someone had the idea of translating famous paintings to the screen—Millet's "Angelus," for instance, or "Les Dernières Cartouches" and "La Défense du Drapeau." * Next, a
whole sequence of illustrations was used as the basis for an early
Life of Christ, a sort of photographic Stations of the Cross which
bore more resemblance to cheap religious chromos than to the
famous paintings they affected to represent.

A long lineage of films was founded by Zecca's *Story of a
Crime*, a picture of real importance. Here for the first time was
tapped the whole repertory of sanguinary crime as illustrated
in the daily papers. From *The Story of a Crime* sprang a posterity of violence which is still with us. In 1906 Pathé produced a
"dramatic and realistic" *Underworld of Paris*, half a reel in length.
Here is the plot of this ancestor of *The Exploits of Elaine*:

This film offers us an authentic study of the lower depths of
the city and reveals the operations of the fearsome apaches, so
much dreaded by the inhabitants of Paris. In eight strikingly realistic scenes we are offered a complete survey of the Paris underworld and its sinister denizens.

Two o'clock in the morning: The bold robbers under cover of
darkness pry up the heavy cover of a sewer and disappear into
the bowels of the earth. The gang proceeds to the cellars of a
bank and breaks in through a wall. We see the floor give way beneath their repeated blows and the thieves climbing through one
by one. They seize the safe, lower it into the street and carry it
off.

At dawn near the fortifications: Near the fortifications, meeting place for all the most dangerous of Paris' human vermin, the

* "Les Dernières Cartouches" by Alphonse de Neuville, "La Défense
du Drapeau" by Paul Alexandre Protais exhibited respectively at the Salons
of 1873 and 1876. The first depicts an incident during the battle of Sedan
and the other an incident at Metz.

bandits gather to divide the spoils. The empty safe lies abandoned in the grass: the bags of gold it once contained are being passed from hand to hand. Vagrant women, the pitiful companions of these thieves, lend their aid. But now the police, hot on the trail, arrive on the scene and by an ingenious maneuver, every detail of which can be followed, encircle the gang. After a stubborn resistance the bandits are captured, save one of the fiercest who engages the police sergeant in a hand-to-hand contest.

This extremely lively film will delight all with its vivid realism, depicting as it does one of the depredations carried out daily by these bold thieves who are the terror of the merchants of Paris and the despair of its police.

As this dramatic genre proved popular, each firm now started to issue quantities of story films. Pathé began with *The School of Adversity*, ancestor of many psychological pictures. In 1904 his firm produced *Roman d'Amour: A Drama Relived*, in seven scenes: The Seduction—From Toil to a Life of Pleasure—Abandoned—Dying of Hunger—A Letter to Her Parents—The Dreadful Expiation—In the Hospital. This film was issued with a colored poster and with illustrated handbills. A little later came *A Fair Spy*, *A Woman in Despair*, *A Venetian Drama*. This was a rich era of plots from Henry Bataille, of velvet gowns *à la* Worth, of bicycles and of last-minute reconciliations. There was nothing to prevent the movies from progressing from plots inspired by the penny novelette to the full splendor of the psychological drama; and Pathé produced *The Age for Love*. About this the Pathé catalogue grows lyrical:

She had married out of ignorance, or fear, or obedience, or indifference, as young girls do.

He was an elderly general, gallant and covered with medals, decorations and glory. . . .

She was everything in the world to him, the one great love in the life of a man already growing old.

Her days were long, meaningless and gay, filled up with a round of engagements and visits where everyone ate and drank and laughed without knowing why. She had no child. She lived without cares, without hope, without anchorage.

A young acquaintance of her husband's who came often to the house brought new interest into her life. She felt happy, suffused with a quick and radiant joy under the influence of a dawning sympathy for him. They went for walks together, talking as they strolled slowly side by side. She drank in his every word, gazing entranced as he spoke of things often disturbing to hear but delicious to listen to.

He became her lover. . . . How should it happen otherwise when two human beings are drawn together by a mutual love?

The husband, warned by an anonymous letter, surprises them in a hunting lodge. Yet in his troubled soul pity arises and, maybe, a realization of the helplessness of two such young and ardent lovers, and he turns against himself the weapon with which he had thought to reap revenge. 250 feet,* price 170 francs.

In 1902 Pathé also produced an ancestor of many a screen adaptation by offering the first *Quo Vadis*, a film that lasted all of twenty minutes and which, apparently, caused audiences to roar with laughter.

TALKING FILMS AT THE PARIS EXPOSITION

Only the spoken word was needed to make these masterpieces the equal of Henry Bataille's and Henri Lavédan's plays but, happily, at that time speech was reserved for other uses. Talking films, however, were not unknown and before the war Léon Gaumont gave a talkie each week in his theaters. In 1900 he had effected a combination between the phonograph and the movie; in 1902 he put the Chronophone on the market. Synchronized films were also given under the name of Phonos-Scènes. In 1912, even colored talkies were to appear.

Here again Méliès had led the way. When Paulus had inspired him to create a studio, he had also given him the idea of allying the old-fashioned cylindrical phonograph record to the movie projection machine. Paulus sang on the screen every evening thereafter.

Others were not slow to take the hint. Various kinds of spe-

* Two hundred and fifty feet of film last four minutes.

cial phonographs for synchronization were manufactured. Several
Duos from Carmen (film and record, 120 francs) and the like
were issued. Sketches by Galipaux, songs by Yvette Guilbert
were recorded; and in 1902—for the delectation of those sensitive
souls in love with high-class poetry—they produced a talkie of
The Dress by Eugène Manuel, with the sound of a distant noc-
turne apparently drifting in through a window and a double-
exposure angel floating around: film and record, 120 francs.

At the Paris Exposition of 1900, talkies of recitations by famous actors, of songs and of snatches of opera enacted before
shaky scenery, in fact everything from Little Tich to Coquelin
and Rostand was shown, though only with relative success. Today these early talkies strike one as extraordinary, for, despite
their imperfections, one can observe the gestures, catch the in-
flections and study the postures of the famous performers of yes-
terday. The duel scene from *Cyrano*, a fragment from *Les Précieuses Ridicules* has the power to amaze and disconcert us. Was
that what they called great acting in 1900? Can they actually
have admired such barefaced mugging, such winks and nods to
the audience, such poses, such an extraordinary style of delivery?
The really astonishing thing is that the film, deriving in part from
a theatrical tradition such as this, should ever have developed a
style of its own.

At times the primitive talkies have power to move us, ridiculous though they be. Yet they were hardly more effective in
their way than the old cinema noise machines, borrowed from
the Châtelet, from which, by means of a complicated system of
cranks and rolls, emanated the sound of hoofbeats, trains, automobiles and the smashing of china. These reproduced sounds
about as well as the early sound films of 1928.

As recording for the phonograph was a tricky business at best,
and as it was necessary to speak close to the recording apparatus,
these early talkies were made by two separate operations. The
actors sang first, then acted afterwards. An ingenious device
roughly synchronized lip movements and sound. Thus from the
very birth of the talking film, sound-synchronization has been
used, and from the very birth of cinematography the films have

talked. Understandably enough, it was announced in 1907 that "the cinema has now attained its climax."

THE AMERICAN FILM *

What was happening in America all this time? The early years of the American film resemble in many ways those of the French film. Events were perhaps more excessive and frenzied, and there was an almost terrifying amount of invention, of wild experiments, of crazy ideas and of fortunes made in a few weeks and lost in a day. A horde of adventurers of every description—cattlemen and plumbers, furriers, secondhand furniture dealers and fairground proprietors—hurled themselves upon the new amusement, engaged in epic struggles with one another and finally from out of chaos created the foundations of a great industry.

Edison had invented, at about the same time as Lumière, a machine called the kinetoscope.† In 1895, Armat and Jenkins had also perfected a machine much better adapted for projection, which they called the vitascope. The first private exhibitions with the vitascope were given during the summer of 1895. Edison invited Armat to join the firm he had already founded for the exploitation of the kinetoscope, and to use a projector which would combine the features of both machines.‡ This was done and, in April 1896, Edison gave a first public performance at Koster and Bial's in New York, which proved as much of a success as had Lumière's first exhibition in December 1895. A few weeks later the Lumière company and B. F. Keith also gave exhibitions in New York, the former at the Eden Musée and the latter in a theater on Union Square. These first shows were received well enough, though with a certain suspicion. The Ameri-

* Much of this and of subsequent sections devoted to the American film is based on Hampton's *A History of the Movies*, Covici Friede, New York, 1930. *q.v.*

† Edison had invented the kinetoscope or peep show in 1889; it was this which inspired Lumière to make motion pictures which could be projected, in 1895. The first kinetoscope parlor opened on Broadway in 1894.

‡ Actually the sequence of events was not as simple as this. The facts can be found in *A Million and One Nights*, by Terry Ramsaye, Simon & Schuster, New York, 1926, 2 vols.

cans had recently been familiarized with all sorts of new marvels by Barnum and others, and had encountered various good reasons for mistrusting dark halls. There seemed something odd about this novelty which offered so much in the way of entertainment for a few cents; and the public remained so obstinately suspicious of a trick of some kind that one enterprising exhibitor cut a hole in the back wall of his hall so that prospective customers might peep in before buying a ticket and convince themselves that there really would be something inside worth seeing. There was also the danger of pickpockets but, as people gradually discovered that darkness provided certain compensations as well as dangers, they finally got used to the idea.

By some common instinct, the first American films were very much like those being turned out by Pathé or Gaumont or Méliès. In any case, the Americans did not insist upon originality. As late as 1905 their films, broadly speaking, followed the lines indicated by the French. Their studios painstakingly imitated the brief farces and the love scenes made in France. During those early years the producers cared little enough about what they turned out, though they were firmly convinced that the public would accept only films lasting no more than two or three minutes and that anything longer would prove bewildering or incomprehensible. As they themselves made up both the plot and the incidents of their films it is easy to imagine the sort of things they were.

They did produce, however, a certain amount of characteristically American material. Topical films and newsreels were among their earliest successes. In 1897, a patriotic superfilm was made one night on top of the Morse Building only a few hours after the declaration of war with Spain; its title, *Tearing Down the Spanish Flag!* This early effort of the Vitagraph Company (afterwards merged in Warner Brothers) proved a tremendous hit. Other producers sought to go one better and film the actual fighting in Cuba. They were not permitted to get anywhere near the scene of actual hostilities, for the unfamiliar cameras they brought with them were suspected of sinister uses and the cameramen were sent packing. Nothing daunted, one of them named

Amet, on his return to New York, launched in his bathtub a
flotilla of little boats made of cork, or wood, or paper, and so
filmed the sinking of Cernera's fleet before Santiago. According
to M. Ferri-Pisani * the Spaniards purchased a print of this naval
epic and placed it in their national archives as a record of their
stubborn and heroic resistance.

Having set a fashion in this simple manner, American producers proceeded to film, at a safe distance, episodes of the Boer
War: audiences vigorously booed the English troops. At other
times, however, they went to the actual scene, as when in 1899
gold was discovered in Alaska and propaganda films financed by
railroad and steamship companies were made to show the public
(much after the fashion described in Jules Romains' *Donogoo-
Tonka*) the attractions of life in the Far North.

Quite as typically American and even more revealing of American temperament was the first superfilm, two reels long and
consecrated to religious propaganda. It was estimated that the
piety of the public would admit of a film of such extraordinary
length, and no expense was spared in the making of it. Hurd, the
American representative of Lumière, was accordingly sent abroad
to film the Oberammergau *Passion Play*. So popular was it that
the manager of the Eden Musée decided to film another *Passion
Play*, but without incurring any traveling expenses. He assembled
a group of actors on the roof of an office building and made
the film there in deep secrecy. Though the secret of its origin
leaked out, this film too earned great success.

The first genuine expression of the national spirit did not make
its appearance until 1903, when Edwin S. Porter furnished new
inspiration with his *Great Train Robbery*. This was the first
genuine narrative film in America, lasting twelve minutes and
having a real if crude plot. *The Great Train Robbery* holds the
same place in the history of the American film as the *Arrival of
a Train* held in that of the French film.† Its success established

---

* Who borrowed it from Terry Ramsaye.
† This is surely an error. *The Black Diamond Express* made by Edison
in 1897 was the equivalent of *Arrival of a Train*, and *The Great Train
Robbery* of Zecca's *Story of a Crime*.

a whole school: burglaries and criminal assaults were to be the order of the day. *The Great Bank Robbery* followed, then a host of others whose success was reinforced if not inspired by French films of the same sort, such as *Story of a Crime* and *Underworld of Paris*. By 1905, Vitagraph was making *Raffles, the Gentleman Crook*.

Meanwhile a queer crowd of people had been drawn into the new industry and were fighting ferociously with one another for pre-eminence. From Chicago, New York and St. Louis they came, a host of bold and crafty businessmen hot on the scent of something new. The firstcomers were the most picturesque. Marcus Loew, a furrier, bought a projector and traveled around the fairs with it; he made money and rented two or three halls. He then took one of his friends as partner, Adolph Zukor, also a furrier, and was shortly followed by a secondhand clothes dealer called William Fox. Carl Laemmle, a clothier, left a town in Wisconsin in order to rent a hall in Chicago, after long debating whether there really were people crazy enough to pay money for something they couldn't carry away with them. A fireman in Kansas City made a fortune by giving shows in a simulated railway coach across the end of which shimmered movies of faraway lands.* In 1905 an ingenious Pittsburgh businessman had the happy idea of renting a store, outside which he erected a glittering and many-hued façade. Here he provided a show lasting twenty minutes with piano accompaniment, all for five cents; he remained open from 8 A. M. to midnight. This emporium of elegance combined with cheapness was baptized a nickelodeon, a name which hit the public fancy and also indicated exactly what the cinema was to be for years to come. Nickelodeons opened in towns everywhere, attracted a large public and made it difficult for the producers to keep up with the demand for film.

The producers were not well organized. In 1895 † Edison had taken out a patent on his kinetoscope, and again for the vitascope

---

*These were shown similarly all over the world and were known as "Hale's Tours."

† Edison applied for his first patent on the kinetoscope on August 24, 1891. *See* Terry Ramsaye.

when he went into business with Armat. But, like Lumière, he regarded the films as a mere toy, interesting as a scientific problem but due for a vogue of a few months only. When he was urged to take out international patents he replied that he would not lay out so much as a dollar on any such foolery. He was an obstinate man and a genius: no one argued with him. But a few years later, when Edison saw how the film industry was developing, he became anxious to protect his patents in the United States and thus to exercise an absolute monopoly over the whole American industry.

As early as 1897 he started to fight by putting his affairs in the hands of a celebrated firm of lawyers, Dyer and Dyer, and instituting suits against all existing producers. It was the beginning of a protracted battle. Edison employed private detectives to ferret out all unauthorized copies of his machines. The old inventor at that time cut a singular figure, and a harsh one. Passionately intent on protecting his own interests, he actually bore little resemblance to the idyllic savant whom we were taught to admire in our childhood. Litigious, rapacious, he became a positive menace to film businessmen, who never knew when the sheriff would serve a subpoena of Edison's on them next. As a matter of fact, the other producers themselves were no better, and it is rather significant that the industry in America developed as a series of guerrilla wars between gangs armed literally as well as figuratively. Pathé had founded an American branch and attempted in 1907 to interpose in the endless series of lawsuits, but without success. All the talent of the best American lawyers barely sufficed to deliver the other producers from Edison's domination. Peace was signed in 1908 at a great and solemn banquet at which, in the presence of his rivals, the artful old fellow—faced with the threat of a relentless war against him waged by all of them in concert—finally came to terms.

It was only after this that the industry could go ahead and begin to make films seriously, though the earliest years are not without interest. America had no Méliès, but already in her first efforts, so full of movement and action, it is possible to foresee what she was to develop. It is possible also to foresee in what light America was to regard the cinema as a whole: as a rich and entertaining *industry*.

After 1900 the film was to enter upon a new phase, but in its first years it most singularly recorded the death throes of an epoch. More clearly even than in the advertisements of the magazines of the period one may discern in the earliest films what the character of the era was, the secret history of its fashions, its bad taste, its aspirations and illusions. In the topical films and newsreels, in the buffooneries of the vulgar little comedies and farces, one catches the very flavor of the period when dining rooms, to be elegant, had to be furnished with Tudor reproductions, when the *art-nouveau* entrances to the Paris subway stations were erected, when automobiles first chugged along the highways and melodramas were all the rage. It is not a full photographic likeness of the time, but the cross references are unmistakable and not very flattering. An involuntary gesture can sometimes tell us more than a whole volume of memoirs, and the films with their abrupt and unstudied imagery really reveal the age. When the history of manners of 1897–1905 comes to be written the historians must not neglect to refer to these documents, for the authentic *look* of the epoch is there.

In all those first years, Méliès stood apart. Very much a man of his time, he was greatly impressed by "the marvels of science." As the Jules Verne of the cinema, he stems from the same impulses as produced the Eiffel Tower, the switchback railway and the novels of H. G. Wells. His predilection for make-believe was his salvation. He saw clearly that the cinema is not vowed to honesty and mere representation, that it knows no compulsion to logic or probability and that, above all else, it is a machine for creating illusions. Stamped all over his work is the first great law of the cinema: "Thou shalt deceive," and thus he invented an art and forged far ahead of his rivals.

He was one of the first to love his work genuinely, to realize its potential richness and greatness. "The art of cinematography," he wrote, "calls for so much experiment, necessitates so many different kinds of activity and requires so much sustained attention that I do not hesitate to say in all sincerity that it is the most alluring and the most interesting of all the arts, for it makes use of virtually all of them: drawing, painting, the drama, sculpture, architecture, mechanics and manual labor of every sort are all called into play in pursuing this extraordinary profession."

It was only much later that some extraordinary results of this attitude of his were to be seen, and they were to appear in another land. Using quite different methods from his, the animated cartoon was later to reveal what absolute freedom the moving image enjoys. The laws that govern the elements, the law of gravity, even life and death itself were to be suspended in favor of Mickey Mouse when trickery again became the inspiration of the cinema. But that was far ahead. When the champion in *Million Dollar Legs* flashed fifteen times around the stadium at the speed of a motorcycle, when the trees in the garden shed their bark to reveal cautious spies, when the dictator's palace proved to be a positive nest of trap doors and false panels, who could fail to recognize in this film a younger brother of *An Impossible Voyage* and *The Merry Frolics of Satan?*

Even if it had not been destined to constitute the first tentative step towards an original development of the film, the work of Méliès would still have been valuable. It can only be studied today in sadly few examples. In 1914 Star-Films was already insolvent when the government commandeered its offices and studios for military uses. There were several hundred kilograms of film there, the product of twenty years of work. In order to remove them, money was needed both for transportation and for new storage room. Méliès had lost most of his customers, his affairs were in bad shape, all entertainments had momentarily been closed and so he accepted an offer from a junk merchant, who melted his four hundred films down into a substance used in the manufacture of footwear. M. Mauclères, founder of Studio 28, has since unearthed a few reels in an attic. They are the best-known ones—*A Trip to the Moon, The Merry Frolics of Satan, The Conquest of the Pole,* and one or two others. Caroly, a well-known prestidigitator, owns a few others, and that is all that remains in France of the work of this pioneer. There is some consolation, however, in the knowledge that Star-Films had a New York branch which prospered not at all: Vitagraph bought it out in 1913. An almost complete collection of Méliès' films is now owned by a Mr. S. . . . He will neither sell them nor show them, presumably believing that some day they may have a value.

In 1928 M. Druhot, of the *Ciné-Journal*, discovered Méliès selling candy and toys in a booth at the Gare Montparnasse. He was given a banquet, and much lauded; he was even given some sort of decoration. Today he lives at Orly.* The Chambre Syndicale, which he founded and of which for ten years he was president, offered him quarters in its Home for the Aged there. One would imagine that something more might have been managed, in recognition of the role he played and of his own eminence as well as that which he conferred on the French film internationally. He was the only one of the first producers who did not make a fortune.

* Georges Méliès died after a short illness in January, 1938.

PART TWO

The Prewar Film

1908-1914

THE film was not to abandon the sideshows and fairgrounds all at once. Several years were to elapse before it broke off relations with these childhood sweethearts, into whose arms chance as well as affection had thrown it. In the French provinces and the small towns of America *The Story of a Crime* and *The Great Train Robbery* continued for years to be projected in tents and barns with a sheet for screen, on which the bandits appeared in an aura of spots and "rain."

However, the early cinema men gradually became sophisticated, learning to wear stiff collars, groom their nails and be interviewed by journalists. They gave up roaming through Ohio or Normandy. Soon they were to be intimate with ladies from the Comédie Française and their politician-sweethearts, with investors and their girl friends, with town councilors and subsidies, with editors of independent journals and their advertising space-rates.

At the Congress of Film Producers, February 2, 1908, it was decided to stop renting films to the little cafés that showed them without charge to their customers. There was a general desire to raise the prestige of the cinema and erase the memory of its lowly past. The cinema, last-born of the arts, was becoming respectable. Pathé was to be its leader.

TRADITIONS ESTABLISHED

The primitive films did not die out immediately. Méliès continued to make films right up to the war, and in 1912, for instance, produced a *Conquest of the Pole*, slightly heavy-handed but charming in detail, with a monstrous bearded old Father Pole who devoured travelers and looked as though he had escaped from a pantomime of the *Odyssey*. Many of his imitators, both American and French, also continued to exploit the fantastic film with its transformation scenes, magicians in conical hats and men metamorphosed into animals or monsters. Even during the war films of his were still current and appealed to children almost as

39

much as *Fantomas* and Miss Pearl White. *Fairy Bell, The En-chanted Lake, The Good Little Shepherdess and the Wicked Princess, The Spirit of the Chimes*, all by Méliès, were in fact shown exclusively for children, something to be remembered when considering them. But by 1908 the film was ceasing to be a mere childish entertainment: adults had acquired a steady taste for it. It was for them that films of quite another kind were developed.

America had early and successfully essayed the religious film, also popular in France. Before the war, producing firms evinced a startling degree of piety every Easter and Christmas, which rose to frenzied heights when the Italian film began to develop. In the "for sale and wanted" columns of the movie magazines of 1908 there was a lively demand for secondhand copies of a twelve-hundred-foot *Passion* * of Pathé's, a three-reel *Life of Christ* in color, side by side with offers for *Operations by Dr. Doyen.* In 1911 Jacques Guilhène was featured in a *Jesus,* and in 1914 Pathé produced yet another *Passion.*

The bishops, somewhat skeptical of the real motives of the producers, were rather alarmed by this invasion of the territory of religion with its queer blend of commerce and piety, and they quickly took measures. In 1913, His Holiness Pius X very wisely forbade the use of films for religious instruction, and formally condemned the representation on the screen of scenes from the Gospel and sacred themes generally. This somewhat, but not entirely, damped the fervor of the film people.

In another direction, the film continued throughout the decisive years to be what it had originally set out to be: a sort of magazine. In 1909 the first newsreel theater opened on the boulevards.

News was still frequently faked, as in the earlier days. When scenes from the Russo-Japanese War were made, the producer forgot to disguise his backgrounds, and audiences watched with some amazement the soldiers of the Mikado engaged in blood-thirsty battle with the troops of the Czar in front of the grand-stand at Chantilly. Not all producers erred so flagrantly, but at

* Made by Zecca.

the time of the Steinheil case one of them reconstructed its principal episodes before the trial, including those as yet wholly unpredictable, such as the course justice would eventually take, the acquittal and the crowd outside Saint-Lazare lynching the culprit as he came out.

Newsreels of a sensational kind enjoyed a field day at the time of the Messina earthquake. "A film so moving that audiences weep . . . ! The Russian sailors! The ruins! Terrifying scenes! Rescue work! Etc! Etc!—387 copies sold in two days." A week later a second film appeared: "After Three Days Under the Ruins —Taking the Wounded on Board—Night in a Living Tomb— Burying the Dead." This description of the film was followed by the following practical information: "700 feet, price 150 francs. Telegraphic code word: EPOUVANTE." *

Celebrities of the day now began to appear on the screen; audiences could hiss Caillaux, applaud Barthou and thrill at the army maneuvers: "Audiences cheer this to the echo, enraptured with the gaiety, courage and endurance of our brave troops."

These old reels are fascinating. Since 1925 the little cinemas and newsreel theaters have often revived them, and they delight us with their outmoded dresses and vanished celebrities. Sometimes pathos as well as pleasure is provided, as when we see, in a sky of long ago, Pégoud's † airplane gradually disappear from sight. Documentary films are not the whole of the cinema, but they are an important feature of it. Gradually the screen journalists learned how to handle their material better and, no longer content merely to photograph, began to compose. There is much of interest and beauty—an unintentional beauty—in some of these reels which often are useful to incorporate into current productions. It would be an excellent idea to compile a prewar history from this old material, but the work would have to be done by an artist, not a hack, by someone who understood their real charm, someone with a feeling for rhythm, able to do with them

* At that time the producers issued catalogues of their films, each one of which was identified by a code word so that exhibitors could wire for them inexpensively.
† Pégoud was the first to loop the loop.

what Walter Ruttmann attempted in *Melody of the World*. Why not Jean Cocteau?

At times these accidental compositions have a more intrinsic interest. There is a *Tolstoy at Home* of 1908 which registers all the Christlike mummery of this false prophet, pseudo-great man and very great writer. There is a *Poincaré's Visit to Russia*, with the whole Royal Family magnificent in this composition in black and white, the women saluting the flag with a little jerk of the chin but no other movement of the body, the pallid Czar, the tough little Frenchman and—deployed on the plain of Tsarskoye-Selo—a superb military review photographed with a sense of the dramatic and a feeling for movement which is quite extraordinary.

The first scientific films were also made at this period. Dr. Doyen's surgical operations were recorded, Pathé made a picture of ant life in 1912 and Eclair an *Entomological Studies*, after Fabre, in 1913. All these pictures from real life were prime favorites with the public from 1910 to 1914—and rightly so.

THE FILM D'ART

Films were becoming longer: from two reels they were increasing to four and even more. As the length of their films increased, so did the ambition of the producers to set foot on the rocky but honorable path of "real art." On November 17, 1908 the first production of a new firm, the Film d'Art, saw the light —the famous *Assassination of the Duc de Guise*. This historic event has sometimes erroneously been given as of 1903, when in fact an earlier *Assassination* had been produced from a scenario by Jules Lemaître, who also wrote the scenario for the very popular *Return of Ulysses*. But it was the second *Assassination* from a scenario by Henri Lavédan, well-known Academician, which made history.

The brothers Lafitte had financed it; they insisted on its being directed by Le Bargy, who lost no time in summoning his friends from the Comédie Française to come and confer distinction on the new medium. A replica of the great staircase of the Château de Blois was constructed out of wood and painted canvas. Down this structure the body of the murdered duke (in the person of Albert Lambert) was borne. At each step, the whole staircase shook and the scenery quivered. Spectators must have been surprised to find Renaissance architecture so fragile. But the film caused a sensation. Its opening was a solemn affair. Le Bargy recited poetry by Rostand, Regina Badet made an appearance, and a special musical accompaniment by Saint-Saëns had been provided. It was the first time that eminent actors had condescended to act for the films: * the cinema was bidding farewell to tents and circuses in order to woo a buskined Muse. Confronted by this everlasting monument to bombast and stupidity, M. Charles Pathé turned to the Lafitte brothers with tears in his eyes and cried aloud: "Ah, gentlemen, you are our masters!" Highly flattered, the two gentlemen bowed in response, while Le Bargy and his co-director André Calmettes almost burst with pride.

The film industry as a whole was anything but cordial to the new producing firm or its output. Severe articles appeared, reproaching the producers for having been "too artistic." They compared this literary monstrosity very unfavorably with current Italian films and especially with Ambrosio's *Last Days of Pompeii.* The public, however, lapped up the new film. Dramatic critics like Adolphe Brisson and Claretie were wildly enthusiastic. Even the Academy acknowledged the existence of the cinema, which almost made November 17, 1908 as memorable a date as December 28, 1895.

As a result, the S.C.A.G.L. (Société Cinématographique des Auteurs et Gens de Lettres) was founded, in which literature was represented by those eminent masters of the serial, Eugène Gugenheim and Pierre Decourcelle. Pathé became affiliated with an Italian Film d'Art, and launched a Série d'Art Pathé. Gaumont launched a Film Esthétique. Eclair organized the Association Cinématographique des Auteurs Dramatiques. A Film d'Auteurs was founded independently, and a Théatro-Film founded by

---

* That is, in narrative films. Bernhardt, Coquelin, etc., had made records of their stage performances in 1900. In America, Jefferson had appeared for Mutoscope in a scene from *Rip van Winkle* as early as 1895.

Féraudy, but this was short-lived. By 1909, a sea of artistic pretentiousness threatened to swamp the film. Everything was pressed into service—prose and poetry, tragedies, novels, light comedies, history, Georges Ohnet and Brieux, François Coppée and Michelet and, of course, Lavédan and Sardou. The Film d'Art produced *Theodora*, *For the Crown*, *Madame Sans-Gêne*, *The Abbé Constantin*, *Louis XI*, *The Red Robe*, *The Iron-Master*, *Oliver Twist*, *La Tosca* and even *Werther* with André Brûlé. France, Italy and Denmark all flung themselves into adaptations from the stage or from books. The art of the film suffers to this day from the results.

No venture was too daring. Edmond Rostand wrote scenarios in which the gods descended from Olympus only to get involved in automobile accidents. Someone asked permission of Anatole France to film *The Red Lily*. As he had never seen a film at that time he was a little surprised: "Can it really be done?" he asked. They assured him it could, he gave the necessary consent and, shortly afterwards (for it did not take long to make a film in those days), they came to fetch him to see his masterpiece in its new dress. When the film was over, France was full of admiration and praise. "How very interesting," he said, "how really extraordinary!" And then he added, quietly: "But are you quite sure that it is really *The Red Lily*?"

The original impulse provided by Le Bargy continued its influence, no matter what fate befell the producing companies or even the Film d'Art, which went bankrupt, was reorganized, changed hands and passed into the control of a newcomer, Ben-Kaled (otherwise known as Charles Delac, who made an immense fortune out of the cinema and drew unto himself Louis Nalpas and others). Le Bargy and Calmettes had made the basic error of approaching the new medium in terms of the theater. They wanted to elevate the film, an excellent motive certainly, but it might have been better had they left it to the tender mercies of the clowns and the prestidigitators. It was Méliès and Max Linder who developed the film, not the Comédie Française.

It was a heyday for stage actors. Of course, they were disconcerted by the film's lack of words. When Mounet-Sully appeared in a film *Oedipus*, he refused to omit a single word of the great speeches and the film showed him grotesquely mouthing and gesticulating as he strode in silence up and down the papier-mâché scenery, quite unable to realize that all his talent counted for nothing in face of his refusal to submit to the demands of a new medium. This nowise prevented the entire Comédie Française and countless other actors from following his unfortunate example. Albert Lambert and Robinne appeared in the *Assassination of the Duc de Guise*, Grétillat in *The Man with White Gloves* (made in 1906 under Capellani's direction); Madeleine Roch, Mme. Delvair, Napierkowska, Alexandre, Jean Worms and Berthe Bovy (who was Pathé's leading lady for years) all followed suit. Réjane made *Madame Sans-Gêne* and even Sarah Bernhardt made a screen debut in *La Tosca*.* Her greatest triumph, however, was in Mercanton's *Queen Elizabeth* (1912), presented in a sort of imaginary Renaissance style. Her pale face, large gestures and sumptuous costumes (but alas not her glorious voice) continued to astound the public for years to come; the film had a big success abroad and especially in America. Finally de Max himself ventured *The Mask of Horror* under the direction of a young man from the Film d'Art called Abel Gance.

Gance was born in Paris on October 25, 1889. He had acted a little, had written a book of poems entitled *Un Doigt sur le Clavier* and even a volume of metaphysical essays (unpublished), besides *The Samothracian Victory*, a five-act tragedy in verse and prose intended for Bernhardt. He entered the films as an actor, played several leading roles and appeared with Max Linder. The screen provided an outlet for his poetic leanings. He sold his first scenario—about Paganini—for thirty-five francs to Gaumont, who later paid him forty-five francs for another, *The Crime of a Grandfather*, for Séverin-Mars. Launched as a scenarist, he now wrote *Cyrano and d'Assoucy, Moonlight Under Richelieu, The Tragic Love of Mona Lisa* which Capellani directed, *The Nurse* which Pouctal directed for the Film d'Art. A few months later, Louis Nalpas paid him five thousand francs to make *Drama at the Château d'Acre* in a week. Next, inventing

* Not a debut; she had made a scene from *Hamlet* in 1900.

Caligarism long before *Caligari*, he directed *The Folly of Doctor Tube*, the story of a madman who succeeded in breaking up light rays and creating a strange world of deformities. He so greatly abused the use of distorting lenses and out-of-focus photography that it was considered inadvisable to release the film.

Gance was to go far. Not even his worst errors—as monumental as his talents—can erase the memory of what the cinema owes him for *La Roue* of 1922 or *Napoleon* of 1926. In 1906, however, nobody really understood the proper function of a director. The films of some of the really original directors are, it is true, unmistakable, such as those of Méliès. But Méliès was also a producer. Otherwise, it was only towards the end of the period under review that the names of directors were even credited. It must be said in favor of Film d'Art—which did in certain ways contribute something to the development of the film—that it also gave more importance to the director.

One of the outstanding directors was Zecca, who worked with Pathé from the very beginning. He had been hired by Charles Pathé in 1895—but for his voice! It was he, in fact, who delivered the speeches of famous people for phonograph recordings, such as the sermons of Père Olivier, and Carnot's last address at Lyons. When Pathé began to make films, he employed Zecca as *compère* or commentator, to explain the action on the screen, for there were no subtitles in those days. Next, Zecca turned director of films, at first after Méliès' recipe as in his *Seven Castles of the Devil*, and finally of all sorts and kinds. He was one of the real giants of that era of glorious absurdities. One remark of his gives the measure of the man. Michel Carré went to see him. Zecca was busily blue-penciling a manuscript. Zecca barely paused long enough to greet him and growled out: "I'm rewriting Shakespeare. The wretched fellow has left out the most marvelous things."

The whole story of the Film d'Art is in that cry. Now that the film had mastered its technical problems, it began to look upon art just as a nouveau riche might. Ten years of horrors were to result. Camille de Morlhon, author of numerous melodramas, was the most important figure. Gaumont one day asked him for a scenario: he wrote the story of an army officer turned thief, but the Dreyfus affair was too recent and Gaumont turned it down. Morlhon, disgusted, was only reconciled to the cinema by Edmond Benoit-Lévy and Pathé, and thereupon turned out a succession of sentimental dramas: *Twenty Years of Hate, A Superhuman Sacrifice, The Orphan's Secret* and—his biggest success—*A Beast in Human Shape.* André Heuzé, author of *The Age for Love*, directed *The Hunchback;* Albert Capellani made *The Arlesienne, Notre Dame de Paris,* and *The Wild Ass' Skin* with Napierkowska, *The Two Orphans, Athalie* and *L'Assommoir* with de Max, *The Lyons Mail* and *Les Misérables.* "We now enter a new era," wrote the film journals of the period, "of accurate settings, of admirable reconstructions of history, of adaptations from the masterpieces which are the glory of our race and of our language."

Michel Carré in 1907 filmed his pantomime *The Prodigal Child,* in three parts of fifteen hundred feet each. It introduced something new, in the form of a musical score by Wormser fitted exactly to the action. The adaptation itself had been carefully prepared by Benoit-Lévy and the roles were entrusted to professional actors. It opened at the Variétés on June 15, 1907, and ran for more than a hundred performances—one of the biggest successes up to that time. The special musical score was clearly an improvement but proved too expensive for general use. It was reintroduced by Gaumont in 1911.

The most important names of the period were unquestionably those of Capellani, Daniel Riche, the fecund author of so many popular novels, Camille de Morlhon and—above all—Louis Feuillade, who worked for Gaumont from 1906 on, became his art director and, just before the war, directed the famous series of *Fantomas* films. We shall meet him again later in the company of Louis Nalpas, former general secretary of the Film d'Art.

Such were the men and such the birth of a new movement which wasted all the prewar years in misdirected energy and efforts doomed to come to naught. It remains to consider the influence of the Italian films, which, with the Film d'Art, constituted the most characteristic production of the period.

THE ITALIAN FILM

The firm of Ambrosio, which began by making short comedies, had been founded in 1908, and was followed by the firms Pasquali and Itala. With Cines, these constituted the Italian film, which was of real importance before the war. The Ambrosio films featuring Mme. Tarlarini and Alberto Capozzi included a series, known as the Golden Series, which reached the limits of unintentional humor: *Perjury, Grandmother's Lamp, The Mysterious Piano* carried to extreme lengths the worst excesses of melodrama, of theatrical gesturing and of the contortions customary in *bel canto.* The Italian films went in heavily for history and pseudohistory. Pasquali produced several about the French Revolution, the most important of which was *Citoyen Simon.* Among the numerous companies founded in Rome was, inevitably, a Film d'Arte. The first of its productions featuring famous Italian actors were *Othello, The Rape of the Sabines* and *Phèdre;* these were distributed in France by Pathé and thus exercised considerable influence on the French film. This firm specialized in antiquity. One of the greatest successes in America was enjoyed by the Italian *Quo Vadis,* which, in 1912, completely revolutionized methods of film production with its vast crowds of extras and its emphasis on grandiose spectacle. It came at the end of a long line of historical dramas on subjects that ranged from the French Revolution to the fourteenth century and the early Christians.

The most important film of the period, not generally released in France until 1916, was the superproduction *Cabiria,* based on an original scenario by Gabriele d'Annunzio. It is a real document of the period, cost two hundred and fifty thousand dollars and—begun in 1912—was not finished until 1914. Audiences stared in amazement at its statue of Moloch, one hundred and twenty-five feet high, at the army crossing the Alps in the snow. In imitation of *Quo Vadis* and *Salammbô,* it included all the customary spectacles and also a siege, with the besieged raining stones and pepper on the besiegers, advancing under a roof of their own shields and in siege towers. The assault by a pyramid of soldiers, standing on one another's shoulders with their shields over their heads, made audiences gasp. But best of all was Maciste. For everyone who was young in 1914, Maciste as the giant slave will ever remain an imperishable memory of heroism. It is said that the actor had been a furniture-mover, whom they had painstakingly taught to act a little. He was an astounding creature, as gentle as he appeared fearsome, with unbelievable muscle. He picked up women as though they were feathers, tore chains apart with his bare hands, threw walls down. He instinctively translated his role of the Avenger of Wrongs into terms of the circus and the variety stage; he was like some great natural force in the splendor of his unconscious strength. Louis Delluc has called him "the Guitry of the biceps."

Maciste and the other sensational elements of the film earned it a success such as even *Ben Hur* never surpassed. Nothing else was talked of in France for years: the film opened at the Vaudeville Theatre in 1915 and ran for months. The great naval battle, the meeting of Hasdrubal and Massinissa in a Carthaginian palace whose roof was supported by two golden elephants, the setting on fire of the fleet by the aid of Archimedes' mirrors—all combined to create a "masterpiece" such as no one imagined could ever be outrivaled. People especially enjoyed qualities in this film which were not theatrical but visual, and consequently cinematographic. The eruption of Etna was admired as though it had been an etching or a painting, and the critics ran out of adjectives in expressing their delight. "M. d'Annunzio," *Le Cinéma* wrote, "seems to have laid the foundation here for a new art which is perfectly in the spirit and to the taste of our times." *L'Opinion* hailed him (for d'Annunzio was given all the credit, the director Pastrone was quite overlooked) as "the early master of a new art, the Giotto of the cinema." The film made a lasting impression. No one thought it absurd when, as late as 1920, Harry Baur in describing the closing scenes of the film wrote in *Le Crapouillot* as follows:

Abstract poetry has never been better made concrete, thought itself has never more admirably been made tangible.

On a calm evening, a trireme glides over a calm ocean leaving a sprinkling of stars in its wake: hills loom in the distance. Sheltered by a sail, a young couple in simple linen tunics whisper of their love. Maciste, herculean and childlike guardian out of some old legend, plays on the pipes of Pan.

Above the hilltops, mingling with the stars in the infinite heavens, we discern living shapes: they grow more clearly visible as human beings in filmy veils that drift like mists as they move into a dance such as Botticelli might have painted, and then slowly vanish.

Cabiria, that series of colossal picture postcards, inspired much cheap but lyrical praise for years to come. Though it was the most celebrated it was not the only one of its kind. Italy attempted to dazzle the masses with a hundred historical spectacles. In 1908 *The Last Days of Pompeii* had appeared to compete with the first *films d'art*. In June 1912, the firm Artistica Gloria advertised widely throughout France a *Nero and Agrippina*. This was a favorite subject: Ambrosio had made a *Nero* in 1908 and Cines an *Agrippina* in 1912. The inevitable lavish spectacles —pagan orgy, imperial trireme, Christians with lions, human torches, Rome burning—were advertised as unheard-of marvels:

Every exhibitor will hasten to show this film, for which a whole city was rebuilt at a cost of more than a million francs, with its reconstructed palaces and forums, its Coliseum and its armored fleet. . . . Never before has anything so artistic been attempted, never has such brilliant success attended an effort of this kind. It puts everything heretofore attempted into the shade. Here is the Rome of the Caesars. . . . Neither words nor illustrations can convey any real idea of the lavishness of this cinematographic *tour de force.* . . .

Tacitus, Suetonius, Racine, Sienkiewicz and Bulwer-Lytton had all been pillaged to provide this strange medley produced under Mario Caserini's direction. Pathé bought the French rights for a hundred and fifty thousand francs. It seems a pity that, almost before there had been time to show it in a few first-run theaters in the biggest cities, the war came to change public taste for spectacles of this type.

These spectacles were impressive. Portly operatic tenors in

The Great Train Robbery (*1903*), *directed by Edwin S. Porter.*

Rescued from an Eagle's Nest (*1907*), *directed by Edwin S. Porter.*
The actor is D. W. Griffith.

The famous actress Réjane in Madame Sans-Gène *(1911), made at the time France was producing many films of stage plays with stage celebrities.*

The Last Days of Pompeii *(1913), one of the Italian costume dramas widely circulated before the war.*

togas, stout matrons waving olive branches or giving the Roman salute, little legionaries running at a trot, howling mobs raising or lowering their thumbs provided the constant ingredients. Roman orgies, a positive rain of blossoms, and the games were but a prelude to the inevitable splendors of the finale in which a whole cardboard city blazed merrily under the calm gaze of a paunchy and bemonocled emperor as dignified as a bishop.

While historical spectacles, and especially classical ones, were a specialty of the Italians, they sometimes explored the modern soul too. Cines came to it late under the influence of Danish and French films. The Film d'Arte had launched Paola Monti in *The Kiss of Glory*, which proved popular. After *Quo Vadis* and *Mark Antony and Cleopatra*, Cines announced *The Vow of Hatred*, its first modern film, which appeared in 1914. "Cines," wrote the critics, "comes through the ordeal even greater than before." The film was based on an original story about a young girl who, after taking part in some amateur theatricals, ran away from home. "Romantic and anxious to live a life of her own, the young girl took seriously the part she had been playing and left the paternal roof to follow the actor Steno, who had been coaching her. Heedless of the tears and entreaties of her sister, she consented finally, so as to avoid scandal, to simulate death." Maria was then abandoned by the actor, became a singer in a tavern, then a celebrated artiste. Misfortunes of every sort overtake both the heroine and her sister. This tear-jerker made a name for the actress who played the leading role—Maria Carmi. There followed an avalanche of melodramas and of adaptations from novels.

The most extraordinary subjects found producers and backing. Dante and Homer were not spared, nor Shakespeare, Racine and the Bible. Cines made several *Lives of Christ* and *The Maccabees*. *The Inferno*, *Purgatorio* and *Paradiso* were each made into half-hour films. Ambitious directors hurled themselves on Francesca da Rimini and Virgil. What is more, the Americans had replied to Cines' *Hamlet* with a *Romeo*, a *Richard III* and another *Hamlet*. When Ambrosio's *Priestess of Tanit* modeled itself too freely on *Salammbô*, the French were outraged. "For shame, MM. the Italians," they screamed. As for Spain, which had also discovered the cinema by now, there emanated from the short-lived Hispano-Film a *Carmen* (naturally) and *Don Juan de Serra-longa*. It was a universal disease.

DRAMAS

Meanwhile the *Assassination of the Duc de Guise* had given birth to a host of historical romances—*The Queen's Necklace, Escape from the Tuileries* ("based on the erudite studies of M. Georges Cain, curator of the Musée Carnavalet"), *The Death of Robespierre, The Chevalier of Maison Rouge, Camille Desmoulins*, with Dehelly and Mlle. Lara. The Duc de Reichstadt, Henry VIII and his wives, Charles V and Theodora likewise provided subjects for plots drawn indifferently from Michelet, Dumas or Sardou.

From history it was an easy step to costume pictures: fiction and the drama were drained, as the example of Italy and of the Film d'Arte suggested what treasures lay ready to hand. The *Roman d'un Spahi* was screened. Bernhardt appeared in an adaptation of her own production, *Adrienne Lecouvreur*. Pathé ventured into prehistory with *La Guerre du Feu* and into Biblical history with *David and Goliath*. In a magazine of 1914 one learns with astonishment that, according to report, M. André Gide's *Lafcadio's Adventures* was to be filmed (but the rumor proved false). Pathé provided *The Children of Edward*, "based on Shakespeare and M. Casimir Delavigne, adapted by M. Paul d'Ivoi, directed by M. Andreani, featuring Mme. Delvair of the Comédie Française." Robinne and Alexandre appeared in *The Queen of Sheba* and—an effort at modernism—Pathé produced Bernstein's *The Thief, The Assault* and *The Claw*, as Pathé-Natan were to do again twenty years later.

These dramas which overburdened the screen with speechless suffering from 1908 to 1912 were not essentially very different from those which Pathé had turned out in 1904, but they were longer and played by better-known actors and they strove valiantly after psychological profundity. Most of the themes which

the cinema was later to develop with so much unintentional absurdity were already in existence in those half-hour or hour-long
films, that whole romantic repertory of the unbelievable and the
ridiculous—deserted wives, illegitimate offspring, society ladies,
wicked sirens and good-hearted crooks. The public loved them.
In 1912 Pathé engaged Alexandre and Dehelly and summoned
all the Comédie Française to create the first monument to the
"vamp," and gave her her proper name in a film called *Femme
Fatale*. It was a story about one Juliet, a servant who bewitches
her employer's son. She tempts him to steal, then runs off to
Paris with him. There she makes the acquaintance of a baron
and the young man commits suicide. Juliet becomes an actress
and seduces a grand duke. In the end, she is laid low by an illness that disfigures her. An object of horror, she dies haunted
by the specters of her victims. In this superfilm, which ran for
a whole hour, Madeleine Roch represented the *femme fatale* with
a rich repertory of sweeping gestures and expressions.

Though it is possible sincerely to admire the films of Méliès
and of Max Linder on other than purely archaeological grounds,
the huge flood of prewar dramas merely bore or convulse one
today. Yet through their medium a style of acting less and less
theatrical and more and more simple was developed. Mimes like
Wague or Paul Franck and above all Séverin-Mars brought to
the screen the expressive gestures and rounded technique of a
noble and ancient art. Their films today may look as meaningless as those of their contemporaries, but if we examine them
closely we realize how much these men contributed to screen
acting. Pantomime is not, perhaps, the language of the film:
pantomime seeks to express everything in symbolical gestures,
whereas the cinema can manage without symbols. But it was
pantomime that pointed the way to the proper method of screen
acting as a purely theatrical style could never have done.

The art of telling a story was slowly being discovered as the
actors adapted themselves to the medium, and paths now opened
that were to lead to *The Cheat* and *Broken Blossoms*—so important historically because they mark a real development. Yet even
for the historian the prewar dramas themselves are dull stuff, and

the best use to be made of them is to show never more than brief excerpts from them and simply to enjoy their utter absurdity. René Clair in his most ironical moments has never made anything funnier than these "thrilling dramas of modern life," which today hardly seem to us like films at all, for all that they were so much admired at the time.

Meanwhile Gaumont had improved its talking films, synchronized with phonograph records. Edison in New York had also, though less successfully, run synchronized film-and-phonograph talkies. Léon Gaumont showed one of his before the Académie des Sciences: a M. d'Arsonval was both seen and heard from the screen. "A moment later," wrote *L'Illustration*, "the illustrious Academician vanished and in his place appeared a magnificent rooster, crowing lustily." By 1912 many synchronizing machines were on the market. One of them, called *Le Chantant*, had for its slogan: "A film without Mendel synchronization is like a beautiful woman who is unable to speak."

The "wonderful dramas from modern life" were to expire unexpectedly in a blaze of patriotism. In the troubled conditions of 1913 and under the influence of the new conscription laws, the cinema discovered a new vein. *1870–1871* extolled the heroism of the French armies. *The Old Sergeant* recalled the internment of Bourbaki's army in Switzerland. Even better was *A Soldier's Honor*, while *Hands off the Flag* stirred the crowd to its depths. The very titles of its scenes were eloquent: The Revenge of a Wretch—At the Maneuvers—Theft of the Sacred Emblem—Salute to the French Flag.

Thus through the inspiration of Dumas and Hervieu and Bataille a new patriotic trend was developed, and, in imitation of Balzac (whose works as adapted to the screen bore a curious resemblance to those of Eugène Sue), the cinema slowly progressed towards a new prewar development—that of the serial film and the adventure film. Far removed from the pomposities of the Film d'Art, they were of real importance. Our popular fare of this type was to undergo the influence of the American films, as our historical films had undergone that of the Italian. The most typically French of films—the love drama and sob stuff—were themselves a model for three other nations about to become important in the realm of film production.

THE RUSSIAN FILM

In other countries, film dramas were much the same as in France. The Russians, particularly, specialized in this type of production, though with the difference that the theatrical tradition they brought to the screen was of a different kind, that they took more care for pictorial composition and were more genuinely pessimistic in their tragedies. Russia exported little but exceedingly somber dramas, which were admired and esteemed above their French prototypes. Russian society and Russian national traditions provided picturesque material for films such as *The Alchemist* and *What the Forest Said*. There was novelty in the Russian product generally and in the adaptations of Tolstoy and other writers, which were produced in considerable numbers. In a film like *The Suicide Club* audiences detected a sort of Russian essence—the Little Father, *nitchevo* and intellectual nihilism. The prewar Russian films were not negligible, and, later on, Russian directors who emigrated to France and to Germany made competent and attractive pictures—Volkov, Tourjanski, Mosjoukine and Buchovetski.

Russian cinemas at that time showed many French films, but original work was also being done. Ladislas Starevich, director for Khanjonkov, produced his first puppet film, *The Grasshopper and the Ant*, which was shown before the Czar, in 1913. Tourjanski, former stage actor, directed *Mozart and Salieri* in 1913, then *The Brothers Karamazov* with actors from the Moscow Art Theatre. This revealed the influence of Stanislavsky and of those scenic artists of the ballet—Alexander Benois and Léon Bakst. We shall meet Tourjanski again, with Volkov and Mosjoukine.

It seemed to French audiences that the Russian films they saw were more intelligent than similar productions made elsewhere, and this of course conferred on the Russian film a certain snobbish appeal. There was also a certain snobbism about the Danish and the Swedish film. With certain characteristics in common, the films of these three countries revealed a particular attention to pictorial composition, an impressive melancholy, a dramatic power rendered more effective by its foreign accent, and an appealing exoticism which earned them popularity. In the case of the Danish film it was a quite considerable popularity.

THE DANISH AND GERMAN FILM

It was not until 1906 that the first Danish film-producing company, Nordisk Films, was founded by the resourceful Ole Olsen. He purchased an aged horse, a rheumatic lion which the Zoo had decided to have destroyed, and some shrubs. These he carried off to a small island and there produced a picture of a lion hunt, much to the annoyance of the aged lion. Thus Nordisk was born.

One can only judge of these early Danish films by hearsay today, but they were very popular before the war. In 1913 more than two hundred and fifty copies of *At the Prison Gates* were sold. In Denmark, as elsewhere, films at that time were commonly based on novels such as Hermann Bang's *Four Devils*, and plays such as *A Marriage Under the Revolution*, both of which were used several times. This does not sound as though the Danish film were very different from the general output of the period, or of particular originality. Nevertheless, it was highly esteemed: Nordisk flooded the French market with pictures which were admired for their dramatic intensity and their artistic qualities. Among them must be noted the work of Urban Gad, for he discovered a really great actress whom Germany afterwards acquired—Asta Nielsen. The future star of *The Joyless Street* * and *The Tragedy of the Street* faced the camera for the first time in 1910 in *The Abyss* for Urban Gad, under whose direction she worked for many years. Even as a girl her face was already a tragic mask, almost impassive yet strangely

* *The Joyless Street* (1925) was also Greta Garbo's second picture.

expressive with great burning eyes: it earned for her later the title of "the Duse of the screen." It is instructive to read the articles about her in the early movie magazines. She was "the uncontested sovereign of the screen," the "artist who best knew how to adapt herself to its requirements"; her "oblique, austere and restrained style of acting" was "infinitely more impressive and more intelligent than that of the Italian stars." Through a whole succession of films far more realistic and much more carefully made than the current product, Asta Nielsen developed a screen character—the somewhat artificial and even conventional character of a beautiful and intelligent woman in the clutches of destiny. In *The General's Children*, *The Black Dream*, *The Strange Bird*, *Vertigo*, *The Power of Gold* and *Poor Jenny* she displayed to the public all the romanticism of the northern countries, full of Ibsen and of the suffering but conscientious character of the Nordic writers and dramatists of the eighteen-eighties. (The cinema is always a few years behind the reigning intellectual fashions.) In Asta Nielsen, the Danish film gave us an artist of real merit whose sphinxlike appeal was to last for many years.

Germany was Nordisk's best market, and several films were made by the firm specifically for German distributors. The German firms—Messter, Union, Biograph, Bioscop—were of quite secondary importance in comparison with Nordisk, for at that time Germany was, as regards the cinema, simply a tributary of Copenhagen.

THE SWEDISH FILM

The Swedish film also merits attention. The first film was produced there in 1909 by Charles Magnusson, head of the film industry until 1928. Oddly enough, most of the first films were songs or talkies such as Méliès and Gaumont had introduced. Yet from the beginning there were also attempts at basing films on purely national themes, from which the Swedish film derived its essential originality. We meet this trend already in *Men of Varmland*, after a famous opera which was to serve again on several occasions and even as a talkie. There was also *The Emigrant*, from an original screen story by the novelist Henning Burger, directed by Muck Linden of the Royal Theatre.

As censorship already existed and as this film included a rape scene, the banned portion was replaced with a subtitle, "Interval of Two Minutes," which caused a sensation.

The industry developed slowly. Magnusson's Svenska Biografteatern built the first studio and, in 1912, engaged the two men who were to carry the Swedish film to its full development —Sjöström and Stiller. Both of them were former stage actors, but they brought to the cinema a quite original if literary "conception." At first they worked together, Sjöström as actor and Stiller as director. In *The Black Masks* there was a scene with Sjöström crossing a street on a wire, five stories up in the air. In 1913 Sjöström directed *Ingeborg Holm*, in which he discovered the actress Hilda Borgström, while Stiller made *Gränsfolken*. Pathé imported into France a Swedish film based on a sensational novel, *The Spy of Oesterland* by Georges de Klercker.

By the time war broke out, Sweden had already developed some of her best actors—Hilda Borgström, who was to play the heroine of *The Stroke of Midnight*, and Lars Hanson—as well as her two great directors, Sjöström and Stiller, and had discovered her typical themes and characteristic atmosphere. Elsewhere in Europe at that time only the Italian film had any real national flavor, and even so it was of an exaggerated and uncinematic kind. While it would not be true to say that the Swedish film was in full possession of its powers (for, as in other countries, many sacrifices were made to the popular idols of farce and of stage drama), there was already in Sweden a complete realization of the function that national legends and the national character were to play, as material fitting for translation into visual imagery and rhythm. The cinema finds it difficult and will continue to find it difficult to build out of nothing. When it has done so, the original plots provided have often been written by such nincompoops and ignoramuses that the result has been deplorable. And so, while other countries were also to furnish films of increasing merit, it was Sweden which first made the world realize that there really is an art of the motion picture and that it is worthy of respect.

All these developments so far considered were European. In America, they regarded pictures such as those of the Film d'Art with suspicion. As a consequence of the innumerable difficulties that surrounded the industry in its early years, the Americans sought chiefly to please the greatest number of people. At the same time, they developed in a very special way both movement and a purely visual drama. Though the French industry was extremely prosperous, and her producers well and happily entrenched in the error of their ways, nevertheless France began to look towards the United States with envy and alarm.

THE AMERICAN FILM *

Hampered in its infancy in an infinite number of ways, the American industry had barely escaped out of Edison's hands when it fell a prey to the attack of much more redoubtable enemies—the puritans. This war has never entirely ended. On January 10, 1909 the Chicago *Tribune* denounced the cinema as a corrupter of youth, and cited the somewhat unfortunate titles of films being shown that very week: *An Old Man's Darling, Underworld of Paris, Raffles,* etc. The producers, much upset, protested through the newspapers that an art which had already given the world *Ben Hur* (the first one) and a *Passion* was hardly an immoral one at heart. This nowise deterred the Society for the Protection of Children from raiding any cinema that showed a film not to its liking; the municipal board of Chicago gave the chief of police full authority to ban immoral films. It was in that gangsterland that American censorship was really born.

Another danger lurked at the very heart of the film industry itself. Though Edison had virtually retired from the scene, a more formidable power had arisen in the producers' Trust, the Motion Picture Patents Company, a dictatorship as dangerous as that of the inventor himself.

* Most of this section is based on Benjamin Hampton's *A History of the Movies,* Covici Friede, New York, 1930. *q.v.*

The Trust consisted of the ten biggest producers, each of whom paid Edison royalties in exchange for the right to use his apparatus. Peace had thus been secured: by rights the American industry should have gone ahead undisturbed. Actually an even more picturesque war was about to open.

The Trust had in fact created a joint renting business and intended to dominate the market. It counted on rigorously exercising its monopoly. Its members were men of considerable influence, or their lawyers were, and they despised the countless small proprietors of cinemas whom they regarded as so many junk merchants and circus proprietors, entirely under their thumbs. They were in error. The exhibitors had not the slightest respect for the bigwigs of the Trust and cared not a rap for the jurisprudence of chambers of commerce. Besides which, they were ably backed up by fifty or more small producers too modest for the Trust to bother about, who were therefore at war with the Trust. These independent producers or "outlaws" thought nothing of using cameras that bore no Trust stamp, or of distributing films made with such cameras. Thousands of suits were entered against them. The outlaws were unimpressed. They bought foreign cameras which had the advantage of being independent of Edison's patent but also the disadvantage of working very badly. So they took the works out of them, and replaced them with Edison machinery. At the same time they took direct action by hiring away technicians from the Trust and offering them twice as much pay; for if you employ only one cameraman you can afford to pay him well, whereas the Trust had fifty and did not want to raise their wages. By these methods the outlaws produced some excellent films which the cinemas accepted all the more readily since to do so was to injure the Trust further.

Meanwhile the lawsuits piled up, the lawyers were working busily and the Trust won a lot of injunctions but lost a lot of time. From the due process of law they now proceeded to hire private detectives, who realized immediately that though an injunction will not stop a man from making films, a broken camera will. The fight was on in earnest. On the pretext of taking affidavits, they gained admittance to the studios and then seized and smashed the cameras. Each sally of this kind led to a pitched battle. The small producers migrated to the suburbs of New York or Chicago: the private detectives followed them. Armed guards were organized at the studios, but the detectives, become burglars, still managed to break in. There were new conflicts, battles and chases every day. It was with difficulty that the film continued to mature and grow longer under such conditions. Some of the incidents that occurred were really epic, in genuine movie style, and might have been imagined by a scenarist of adventure films.

Carl Laemmle, one of the most formidable of the independent producers, carried Mary Pickford off to work under the direction of Ince, whom he had put in charge of his studio and who, later, was to direct one of the first really important silent films— *The Aryan.* The Trust set all its detectives and all its bailiffs on his tracks. Laemmle fled with his cameras and his company to Cuba, much in the manner of L'Illustre Théâtre, Molière's theatrical company, on its peregrinations along the roads of France. Mary Pickford's mother followed in hot pursuit on a steamer chartered by the Trust, accompanied by a police guard and armed with a fistful of warrants. Happily, Mary Pickford and her fortune were beyond the jurisdiction of the United States. Production was carried on in Cuba without interruption, Mary married Owen Moore and peaceful overtures were made to the venerable Mrs. Pickford.

For all their audacity and their ruses, the outlaws faced defeat when salvation suddenly opened before them. At the most critical moment, they remembered that Selig, one of the original members of the Trust, had formerly escaped from Edison's process-servers by moving off to the California coast. This was a ray of hope in the darkness. They quickly gathered together their cameras, their painted scenery and their make-up boxes and set forth on an exodus to the West. San Francisco tempted them for a while. But their attention shortly turned to a nice little town which, in their eyes, had one inestimable advantage— it was only a few miles from the Mexican frontier. Los Angeles thereupon became the headquarters of the Independents. Here were sunny skies which made elaborate studio buildings unnecessary. A few planks, some trees, a bungalow to sleep in, a café for leisure moments were sufficient. If detectives turned up, they could pile actors, scenery and cameras into a car and disappear across the border for a few days. It was under these conditions that an era of commercial stability dawned for the American film.

The rivalry between the Trust and the outlaws was now transferred to another sphere. The ambitions of the Trust were simple: they had discovered that a lot of money was to be made by providing the nickelodeons with short films of one reel each, turned out cheaply by a formula. They were quite content to market their goods as though they had been boots or bananas. The Independents, who could not hope to compete with the Trust on such grounds, found it expedient to compete with this kind of stuff, turned out like sausages, by providing films of another style and attempting to develop the public's taste for something different.

They began by luring the best actors away from the Trust and acquired George Anderson, otherwise Broncho Billy, Tom Mix and—most important—the sixteen-year-old Canadian girl who was to become famous as Mary Pickford. Meanwhile, she was known as "little Mary." She had made her debut on the stage as a child in order to supplement the family income, and then appeared on Broadway. In 1909 she went to see Griffith at the Biograph studio. Griffith was making *The Lonely Villa*, based on André de Lorde's well-known play, *At the Telephone*. He gave her a small part and paid her five dollars. Three days afterwards she played Giannina in *The Violin Maker of Cremona* (for in America, too, "artistic" films were looming). Later, she joined the Independents.

It was with her help that the Independents were able to wage a war of *quality* against the Trust, who turned out films in undifferentiated bulk. Europe had already set the example. While the cinemas in America were still showing much the same sort of movies that had made Pathé's fortune in 1903, the Italians and the French—stimulated by the Film d'Art—were producing spectacles which both in length and in content far surpassed the current American product. The better-informed Independents knew what was going on in Europe and what success had attended it. The method of American distribution did not, however, lend itself readily to the importation of these films. The theater owners were accustomed to rent a complete program each day, but with a daily change of program it was not possible to show these much more expensive foreign movies, which were profitable only where a run of many days was feasible.

All the same, in 1908 and 1909 a considerable number of more ambitious films were made in America. A *Faust* appeared, then a *Carmen*. The Italian successes had given Hobart Bosworth the idea of introducing Roman togas and peplums to the Californian scenery. The French films, too, found their imitators. The same Hobart Bosworth produced dramas inspired by Henry Bataille against backgrounds worthy of the Théâtre-Français itself, with officers and gentlemen of fashion strolling through them, gesticulating and looking extremely grand. Ladies with elaborate lace waists and stuffed birds on their hats fainted on Louis XV sofas. Disgraced businessmen blew out their brains at Empire desks. *The Roman, The Code of Honor, The Evil Men Do* appeared as two-reel films, advertised as "first class" in order to embarrass the Trust, whose films thus automatically became "second class." One of the best directors of that time was already making films that displayed genuine emotions and were stamped with a certain originality. It was Griffith. He had called one day on Edison to propose a film adaptation of *La Tosca*. Instead, he was invited to play the role of a mountaineer in a film entitled *Rescued from an Eagle's Nest*. As the eagle with which he had to do battle was a stuffed one, he accepted, and earned the sum—large for those days—of twenty dollars. That was his first contact with the screen. Soon afterwards he directed his first film, *The Adventures of Dolly*, over half a reel long. His wife acted in it. Soon he was regularly making films for Biograph. He brought some new ideas along with him, and began by replacing professional actors by very young people whom he could mold as he wished and whom he instructed in a simple, direct and expressive style of acting quite at variance with the customary methods employed. He made an important discovery in Mary Pickford. At the same time he abandoned the customary conventions of the screen and tried to create a new method of presenting characters. He placed them differently in the scene and was just as likely to show his actors in profile or from the back as face on; he evolved more complex situations and a more convincing action. Eventually he found how to make the camera itself into an actor, gradually discovering how to move it about, how to make it *see* from different points of view and, in a word, to give it a creative role in the composition. Griffith quickly turned his back on *Faust, Carmen* and such classical subjects. The first saloons, the first fighting scenes, the first really wicked men and unhappy girls of the cinema owed their existence to him. He seemed to desire to break away from theatrical methods of presentation, and by looking about him at the everyday world found settings and situations better adapted to the screen.

These experiments began to worry the Trust, which was against innovations of any kind. In 1908 their bolder members had tried to steal the enemy's thunder with a *Life of Moses*, a long "art" film after the Italian model, with milling crowds, a bearded prophet, papier-mâché scenery, burnt sacrifices and a plump golden calf. This was issued in parts, as a serial, but met with a lukewarm reception. The Trust fell back on its usual recipes.

The Independents were all for experiment. Under the direction of William W. Hodkinson they organized a chain of halls through which they could release their films. They gradually accustomed their public to longer films and better ones. Subtitles had already replaced the commentators who yelled out explanatory comments on the action. The nickelodeons were giving way to more comfortable, better-ventilated and more expensive theaters. An organ, or if that was not possible, a piano, provided music. There were chairs instead of benches.

The Independents were winning ground and the Trust was compelled to make longer films. This was the heyday of the Western film, through which the entire world became familiar with Mexican pants, automatics and cowboy hats. Since 1906 Selig, at odds with Edison, had concentrated on making adventure films for which he hired cowboys, Indians and a circus collection of wild animals. His heroes were equipped with both revolvers and lassos, but to make them more likable they were also appointed always to rescue young and pretty girls from untold dangers. Broncho Billy, who prudently used another and more experienced rider to double for him in the hard-riding scenes, was the idol of that time. Films of this kind were far from elaborate at first, for Selig had many worries besides film production. But when peace was signed with Edison, Selig was free to develop this genre. Between 1910 and 1914 his output was immense. He engaged a cowboy from Oklahoma called Tom Mix. Through innumerable films, Mix offered the combined attractions of the rodeo, the cinema and an auto-da-fé. Across the wide pampas, through carefully impenetrable jungles, Mix raced his magnificent horse, flirting with death, riding at the head of bands of Sioux Indians, escaping at the last moment from hideous tortures at the hands of his enemies. Before becoming a film actor had not Mix actually led the life of a cowboy, captured dozens of bandits and swum countless rivers? The magazines said so. Greatly upset, Broncho Billy retorted by forming a new company to produce Westerns in Colorado, and took particular pains that everything in these new films should be absolutely authentic— save his own equestrian performances. These characteristically American films, so purely local and autochthonous, provided audiences in Europe with an enjoyable contrast to the product of their own countries and the stock characters and situations of the European movie dramas.

The prestige of the Italian films was still very great. In 1913 Griffith, still employed by the Trust, undertook a new kind of production, *Judith of Bethulia*, which proved much more to the public liking than *The Life of Moses* but was not a financial success because the Trust's system of distribution was so poorly organized. Griffith at this time left Biograph and joined the Independents.

The Italians were to introduce to the Americans a formula

which was to prove very popular. George Kleine, who had produced *The Life of Moses* five years before, was so much impressed by *Quo Vadis* when he saw it in Europe that he bought it for the United States. Back in New York he rented the Astor Theatre and presented *Quo Vadis* there in April 1913 with as much ceremony as though it were a play. Its success was immense: the Astor had full houses until the end of the year, and twenty-eight chains of cinemas also presented the film first-run throughout the United States and Canada. This gambit rang the death knell of the Trust. Their system of short films and daily changes of programs was condemned out of hand when a second superfilm followed from Europe to reinforce rival methods and start the American film off on a new cycle.

In 1912 Adolph Zukor decided to go in exclusively for the production of big films. He began by purchasing from Mercanton, for the unheard-of sum of eighteen thousand dollars, the rights of Sarah Bernhardt's *Queen Elizabeth*. Advertised and presented in lavish style, the film netted him sixty thousand dollars. Intoxicated with success, he announced that he would thenceforward produce a film a week. He bought up the best plays, hired Edwin S. Porter of *Great Train Robbery* fame, and a troupe of actors to work under the title of Famous Players. At the end of 1912 the first of these Famous Players films appeared —*The Prisoner of Zenda*. A few weeks later Zukor signed up Mary Pickford.

At the same time Jesse Lasky (earlier and rather disastrously the producer of a *Folies Bergères* in New York) went into partnership with his brother-in-law Goldfish and a young man called Cecil B. DeMille, and arrived in Hollywood with about twenty-five thousand dollars and some big ideas. The Jesse L. Lasky Feature Play Company had decided to start off boldly by filming a stage hit of the day, *The Squaw Man*. Five thousand dollars went to Dustin Farnum as star, five thousand for the film rights, and the rest was spent on production. The firm did not have enough money to establish itself in Los Angeles, but had to be content with a barn in a miserable little district on the outskirts where no respectable producer would have been found dead.

This dismal place was called Hollywood. But *The Squaw Man* was a hit. A few weeks later Lasky's capital had doubled and his firm was famous.

Both Zukor and Lasky were up against the problem of distribution. The Trust, which provided programs to the majority of cinemas, refused to change their procedure to make place for films produced by its rivals and offered singly. Zukor approached Hodkinson, owner of a circuit in the West which had already assured an outlet for the numerous films produced by the Independents. He proposed forming a joint renting agency to distribute the films of all the important Independents and thus put up real competition to the Trust. Hodkinson agreed, worked out a system and a few months later a formidable combination of the Independents, including Hodkinson, Zukor, Lasky and DeMille, was formed under the name of Paramount and undertook to distribute feature films issued weekly or biweekly.

The birth of Paramount brought the adventurous era of the American film to a close. The American film so far had developed quite independently. Despite the success of pictures such as *Quo Vadis*, the industry, overoccupied with its own internal struggles, had drawn almost exclusively on material ready to hand, on its own national mythology. In Europe, American films at that time were esteemed far below those of France and Italy. It was only later * that, thanks to the war, its peculiar fauna was so triumphantly to invade the neat European gardens and there couple with other monsters already spawned by the French and the Italians to produce the numerous and weird denizens of the make-believe world of the cinema. Cowboys and clowns were to rub shoulders with erring society women and doughty bankers in a grotesque dance at which we still gaze with admiring delight.

Publicity, posters, magazines and sundry journalism were to aid this growing industry, which was to furnish the world with such plenteous pipe dreams. It is impossible to understand the cinema without taking into account these concomitants—the fan magazines, the cock-and-bull stories hatched by journalists, the

* See H. L. Mencken's *The American Language*, Alfred A. Knopf, New York, 1937, footnote p. 37, for confirmation of this.

whole output of gush and nonsense which two hundred different nations were to devour. It was a work of genius to make a whole world film-conscious, to make it impossible for us to open a newspaper or gaze up a street without having thrust at us the image of women all curls and smiles, of men like centaurs, eternally mounted and armed with rope, without reading yet another anecdote, still another personal interview, yet another fairy tale about the handsome heroes and lovely women of the screen.

People acquired the habit of going to the movies every week to follow the absorbing adventures of these godlike beings. Often the story was familiar in advance, for the daily newspapers had begun to publish these tales of bloodshed and kidnaping, revenge and betrayal. The Chicago *Tribune*, first to denounce the immorality of the films, had also been one of the first to print film serial stories. From 1913 on, readers could thus follow *The Adventures of Kathlyn* in their newspaper as well as on the screen.

SERIALS

Many a primitive film drama, many a movie adapted from novels and especially from those of Dumas and of Balzac, as well as the little films turned out by Pathé, had prepared a way for the posterity of *The Great Train Robbery* and its cousin *The Story of a Crime*. In September 1908, Eclair began to issue a series of *Nick Carter* films, about which was written: "Detective stories are perfectly suited to the cinema. With their brisk and simple plots, an absence of complex psychology, their logical development of events, their rapid jumps, their crimes, waylayings, kidnapings, and chases they are fundamentally cinematographic."

A new fashion had thus been launched, and from that time on audiences were able to follow the same hero and heroine week by week through vicissitudes of every description. Further *Nick Carter* series, one about *Morgan the Pirate*, a *Nat Pinkerton* from Eclair and even series of historical episodes such as *The Dragonnades under Louis XIV* taught the public the habit of regular moviegoing. They wanted to follow the adventures of the char-

acters. It was an important step in winning over a permanent
audience. The climax was to be reached by the films based on
the popular novels of Marcel Allain and Emile Souvestre, under
the general title of *Fantomas*—material ideally suited for filming.
The serial attained feature length with *Fantomas:* one episode,
"Fantomas the Pseudo-Magistrate", was even five reels long. A big
publicity campaign, three times more posters than usual and
twenty illustrations in *Le Cinéma* paved the way. With this film,
the battle between the short-endians and the long-endians was
finally concluded with a Lilliputian victory for the latter.

Fantomas made Louis Feuillade really famous. The future
director of *Judex* had truly discovered a new type of film, long
before *The Exploits of Elaine* came from New York.* Earlier,
he had directed Léonce Perret for Gaumont, and all sorts of films
with wild animals and cowboys, as well as a series with a child
actor called Bébé—*Bébé and the Landlord, Bébé Cures Father,
Bébé's Masterpiece, Bébé's Discovery. Fantomas*, with its mysterious bandit, its disguises, its houses bristling with trap doors
and contrivances, its kidnapings and rescues, its scaling of rooftops and, in short, its whole marvelous and reckless improbability, crowned him with glory.

To offset the *Fantomas* films produced by Gaumont, Pathé
now issued an equally ambitious *Rocambole*, based, however, on
material considerably less to the public taste than the books of
Allain and Souvestre. But the principles and the length of the
longer film had been established: *The Exploits of Rocambole* was
four and a half reels long, and was followed by many others.
People were urged to see Rocambole drag a man into a cellar,
to view the victim's struggles to save himself from drowning and

* The sequence was actually as follows: in 1912 the Edison Co. issued
What Happened to Mary, a series of episodes each complete in itself, not
"to be continued" and therefore not a true serial. The episodes also ran
concurrently in a magazine. The first episode of *Fantomas* was released in
France in May and in America in July 1913. The first real serial film
made in America was *The Adventures of Kathlyn*, beginning December
1913, both on the screen and in the Chicago *Tribune. Dolly of the Dailies,
Lucille Love, The Perils of Pauline*, and *The Million Dollar Mystery* all came
before *The Exploits of Elaine*, but perhaps were not shown in France until
later.

"the amazing adventures of Rocambole in the watery deeps." Big scenes were always advertised in this fashion—a method borrowed from America. Train smashes and bridge wrecks all had their own particular devotees who wanted to know what to look out for.

Films in the American manner and those like Gaboriau's *Monsieur Lecoq* were creating a new and permanent mythology. In *Fantomas versus Fantomas*, just as in *Rocambole*, a childish morality was borrowed from melodrama, the characters from detective novels, the extravagant plots from blood-and-thunder stories. There is no mistaking these films, any more than the posters that advertised them. In *The Youth of Rocambole* one watches the rapid development of "this Night-Prowler, this Bird of Prey, this Spirit of Evil, the perfect prototype of the cynical adventurer and the 'beau joueur.'" Thick with thieves in automobiles, supercrooks, kidnaped women, mocking laughter and benignant police inspectors, here was a universe, to create which Balzac seems to have collaborated with Conan Doyle. In this imaginary world the *femme fatale* is queen and love rules all. We see it not only in *Judex* and *The Exploits of Elaine* later, but again, after the coming of talkies, in many of Marlene Dietrich's pictures. This dream world was invented, nevertheless, in the French and American films along with the early serials.

REALISM

To find out how all these films were made, one need only consult the film periodicals of the time, in which the problems of the directors are freely discussed. Capellani when questioned about methods of production replied:

The great problem is *time*. While the theater disposes of all the time in the world, we can only use the actors for a couple of hours in the mornings, since the rest of their day is taken up by the theater. Thus in two hours we have to take two or three scenes, each of them often twice over. What is more, the film is compelled to be absolutely accurate. The public insists on it. Not only the representation of characters but the settings too must be scrupulously correct. Real antique furniture was used for *Mary Tudor*. Zola's *Germinal* was made in a mine. The *Assassination of the Duc d'Enghein* was taken at Vincennes. In the *Chevalier of Maison Rouge* the door which one sees close behind Marie Antoinette as she enters prison was one which actually stood in the Temple prison at the time of her incarceration, since removed to Vincennes where it was filmed. All the costumes are copied from costumes of the period.

Capellani goes on to say that in one instance alone the cinema was condemned to inaccuracy—as regards color. Red and pink photograph black, he says, blue and violet appear whitish. It is impossible to use white linen or china. If the characters wear yellow or green they seem indistinct. The best material to use is some neutral-colored stuff touched up with blacks and grays to bring out the values. New clothes must not be worn because they take the light badly. Tights must not be worn in scenes after the antique. Tablecloths, napkins, curtains and draperies must be gray. The patterns on china ought to be red or green. Genuine paintings must not be used because on the screen they look like oilcloth, so engravings or chromolithographs must be substituted.

In spite of the use of trick photography, many acrobatic feats were demanded which necessitated the actors' being absolutely fit all the time. M. Sablon has recalled in an interview his experiences while playing in *L'Or qui Brule*, about the burning of a fishing vessel with a solitary sailor on board, who has to jump into the sea with all his clothing on fire.

"When the film was in production," Sablon relates, "it was obvious that nobody seemed particularly keen to undergo so rapid a transition from hot to cold as first setting oneself on fire and then plunging into an icy sea (it was December) promised to provide. I offered to take this dangerous role. They prepared the boat by pouring 100 liters of petrol, 50 liters of tar into it and filling the hold with straw. A fuse connected the various parts of the boat. I wore an oilskin suit weighing 12 kilos and over it I had them wind strips of sacking. They poured gasoline over me and at a given signal the fuse was touched off. Enormous flames shot up all over this storehouse of inflammables. Fire and smoke suffocated me as I ran along the boat, a living torch. Unable to bear it any longer, I finally jumped overboard. The water was below zero and the sea very rough. Numb with cold I attempted vainly to swim. The boat appointed to rescue me had great difficulty in hoving to and it was a full quarter of an hour —which seemed to me an eternity—before they managed to haul me aboard. It was none too soon. Hampered by my heavy clothing and paralyzed with cold I was about to go under. The following day the boat was again made ready and I started all over again. The entire population of Volendam (for the action took place in Holland) was watching from the shore. Women in little pointed bonnets wept, men with wide braces buttoned on with silver dollars shook their heads ominously. Fishermen prophesied my certain death. Despite their prognostications I burned for the second time without serious injury; but I shall never forget making that film."

There were exploits even more daring. The audiences liked sensational scenes whether they were faked or not. In *A Flight for Life* a woman appears on the top of a flaming tower—impossible for her to escape! At that moment an airplane appears and begins to circle round, closer and closer to her. The airman throws her a rope, she grasps it and is drawn up into the machine. This was said to have been really done, in a Paris suburb.

Another scene of the kind was the high spot of *Through the Clouds*, made in London. A young girl, desperately clinging to the guide rope of a balloon, is on the point of letting go. At the fatal moment, a rescuer lassoes her round the waist. This was photographed from a second balloon. And in one American film, the actor, after consuming a hearty meal, inserts himself into a rocket ten feet long and a yard wide. A charge of gunpowder hurls him into another world, but, at the end of the parabola of its flight, the rocket opens, a parachute with a parachutist emerges and calmly returns to earth, the actor having apparently suffered nothing worse than a little giddiness which might very well be attributable to the big lunch he had eaten.

One is hardly surprised, therefore, to read in the "for sale and wanted" columns of a film periodical of the period a request of this nature: "An American firm wishes to purchase three old warships, to use in a naval battle." In 1913 one company bought two railroad locomotives to stage a train smash. Tickets were sold to onlookers and thousands paid fifty cents to see it. Unhappily, through some miscalculation the boilers burst: seven people were killed and about thirty injured.

There were actors who specialized in accidents. In England there was Lieutenant Daring, a past master of catastrophe for whom neither parachute descents, high dives, rope climbing nor hairbreadth escapes had any terrors, until one fine day he was miserably killed by a clumsy "villain" who accidentally hurled him down a precipice. The actress Gene Gauntier was not merely attacked by Bedouins in the heart of the Sahara, almost buried alive in the quicksands of Florida, laid out by a kick from a horse, hurled into the air by an exploding ammunition dump, but was finally trapped in one of those extraordinary movie fires and only escaped from the burning house by tearing a hole through the roof with her bare hands.

But actors of all sorts were exposed to danger. André Deed, known as Gribouille, was swimming to safety with two companions pursued by a pack of police dogs at a convenient distance behind them. One of the actresses with him was seized with acute cramp, gave a scream and sank. André Deed dived after her and brought her up but unfortunately found that this unrehearsed incident had wasted a lot of time and that the pursuing animals were now on top of them, so that Deed was under the necessity of holding up the lady and fighting off the dogs (who of course did not know that they had arrived too precipitately) until help arrived. In one detective film Servas had two ribs smashed. In another costume drama Valbert had half an ear sliced off by a rapier. An actor had the nerves of one hand severed. During a rehearsal of Richepin's *The Snare* one scene called for Mistinguette to be knocked on the head with a hammer. The hammer had been padded with cotton, but either insufficiently, or the actor who wielded it overdid his part: Mistinguette was knocked senseless.

Films were becoming costly. Each extra got five dollars a day. Three hundred costumes had to be hired for *Mary Tudor*, seven hundred for *Fatherland*, at a total cost of $4,000. Settings were expensive. For *The Pied Piper of Hamelin* the Edison Company built a whole medieval town. The building of Rome alone for *Nero and Agrippina* cost $6,000. For Kalem's *From the Manger to the Cross*, in which episodes of the life of Christ were re-enacted in Egypt and in Palestine, forty-two actors were sent out to the Orient for several months. The film cost more than $120,000 and unfortunately appeared just after the Pope had condemned religious films.

Realism was extended even to the selection of actors. The crowds in Red Indian films, so popular in 1913–14, were said to be entirely composed of Ogolobos headed by their chieftain, Red Beaver. Prince Quirilio Behanzin, grandson of the famous king, was in great demand to play royal princes. Other good-natured persons offered their services free, as when Mutual wanted to make a film of high society and asked a millionaire to lend them his Fifth Avenue residence. He consented. On the appointed day, the cameramen found themselves photographing not merely his gorgeous drawing room but a whole party of his guests as well, among them some of the most glittering members of the Four Hundred, and Paderewski, too. They played their parts admirably, and the film, at least in New York, was a triumph.

At the same time actors were already earning fabulous salaries as well as international fame. Everybody in France knew the American stars, Mary Fuller and J. Warren Kerrigan, as well as the Italian stars, Francesca Bertini and Lydia Borelli. Cissie Loftus was earning $2,000 a week in America. Prince, André Deed and Max Linder earned over $20,000 a month. Cécile Sorel earned $160 a day from Pathé, Réjane and Bartet $200 each and Sarah Bernhardt as much as $360 a day plus a percentage. Asta Nielsen signed a contract which guaranteed her $80,000 a year. Muratore and Lina Cavalieri made *Manon Lescaut* in Chicago and earned in salary and percentages all of $200,000. A cinema conservatory was opened in Palermo, and there was talk of starting a cinema course at the Paris Conservatoire.

It was not America but France that first gave us the most precious legacy of the prewar days—the film comedy. On seeing again many of the prewar comedies it is impossible not to feel sad. They are often crude and the humor rudimentary, as is to be expected, but they induce regret for what has since befallen a genre which in those days was really *genuine* film comedy, capable of taking trick photography and all the other cinematic devices in its stride. Méliès, a profoundly simple and good-humored man, was the first to understand it. But other forgotten directors, between 1905 and 1914, also attempted authentic film comedies and sometimes succeeded. Actually, much that has brought new inspiration to the cinema has been merely an inheritance from these early days. What were the settings of *Caligari*, which so amazed everyone by their nonrealism, in comparison with those of Méliès, inevitably brought to mind by Robert Wiene's Hoffmanesque transcription? René Clair's greatest merit is that he realized the necessity of studying not only the American comedies, especially those of Chaplin, but also the French comedies of 1905.

The seeds of René Clair's *Paris qui Dort* were already present in a simple little film called *Onésime Horloger*, one of a series widely circulated before the war and recently revived. The actor in it was relatively unimportant, a mere buffoon in the tradition of the circus and cheap music halls. But the subject is one entirely to the taste of those early days when the movies pretended to be no more than a childish amusement. It is the story of a young man who is to inherit a fortune from an uncle in twenty years' time. To shorten the period of waiting, he tampers with the controls of an electric clock and so arranges it that whole days shall elapse in a few minutes. Life is consequently speeded up. By means of one of the simplest cinematic devices—the contrary of the one used by René Clair in *Paris qui Dort*, which arrested both time and movement—a joyous sequence of nonsensical and amusing conceits was contrived. A house is being built: bricklayers and upholsterers are imbued with extraordinary celerity, in the twinkling of an eye the house is up and finished, and being equipped with furniture, draperies and engravings in the taste of the day. A marriage also takes place at top speed. The happy couple have hardly had time to exchange the nuptial kiss and are still in all their bridal finery when their first child arrives and proceeds to shoot up (still in swaddling clothes and a little bonnet) into a fine lad six feet high. "The joys of family life are always the best," says a subtitle. This example—one among thousands—indicates how the basic feeling for comedy, despite its exaggerations and faults, was at that time as truly original and cinematic as any of the films of Méliès, of René Clair or the Marx Brothers.

Naturally not all the early attempts at comedy were as praiseworthy. There were hundreds of crude farces and, in particular, many with a military tinge. Some of the comedians specialized in this sort of thing, notably one Rigobert, who created the character of a stupid recruit who never learns to salute properly, ruins his uniform the first time he goes out and leads a miserable existence of fatigues and of trouble with his sergeant.

Moreover, the Film d'Art was to wreak untold havoc in this division of film fare. As opposed to the spontaneous "low" comedies, the Film d'Art attempted to produce "refined" comedies, to which we owe so many subsequent film adaptations. In 1914 it was considered a triumph when Léon Benière's *Papillon dit Lyonnais le Juste* was filmed with Polin as Papillon. Briefly, these translations from the stage had no other merit than to help develop film acting; they deflected the film comedy proper from its path.

Very different from those pale theatrical ghosts of films were the pictures of a few comedians of no great talent, perhaps, who confined themselves to genuinely cinematic material. We have already cited Onésime and Rigobert, but there was also Léonce, who, under this title, gained popularity and fame long before he became known as Léonce Perret. He had made his first films in Germany for a branch of Gaumont—*The Golden Lily, The Good Judge, The Boatman's Sweetheart, The Little Grenadier*—

all half a reel long. Back in Paris in 1908 he made (according to his own estimate) two or three hundred more films. About 1910 he invented a comic character which was sustained through the enormously popular Léonce series, neither very good films nor particularly witty. But people laughed a lot at them and the film journals wrote, "Is there a man alive who does not know the big grinning face of this podgy fellow?" This is a long cry from the gravity with which they wrote later of Léonce Perret of *Koenigsmark* fame, when he had become a director with semiofficial standing.

The comedian Dranem appeared in *Dranem's Shoes* for Zecca. When he saw himself on the screen he remarked: "I never imagined I could look such a fool."

Besides Dranem, there were series of films with Polycarpe, with Zigoteau and Calmo, with Boucot, who appeared in *Gavroche*, and André Deed, formerly an actor at the Théâtre du Châtelet, who made two famous series for Pathé, the Boireau and the Gribouille series. Nor must we forget the little fellow they called Bout-de-Zan who was at once the envy and admiration of our childhood—at three and a half years of age he was one of the most celebrated of actors. An *enfant terrible*, he terrorized his parents and his nurse. In *Bout-de-Zan as a Vaudeville Author*, for instance, we see him writing a love letter for his nurse, but he maliciously appoints a rendezvous for 8 A. M. instead of 8 P. M. The nurse is out when her handsome fireman-lover arrives at the appointed hour. The evil child tells him to hide in the coal cellar and, of course, along comes a coal merchant and dumps a load of small coal all over him. The plot develops in the most farfetched manner, which the uncritical filmgoers of that time thought perfectly splendid, fancying they were watching a second Déjazet.*

It was also a series of comedies which made Rigadin's fame. Through countless shorts, the actor Prince as Rigadin, with his caperings and his lugubrious clown's face and upturned nose, played the helpless Pierrot forever at odds with fate, with men,

* A famous actress who made her debut at the age of five in 1800. She died in 1875.

women and inanimate objects. Always hopelessly in love, he was the forerunner of all the film comedians like Max Linder, Fatty Arbuckle, Buster Keaton, Harold Lloyd and even the master, Charlie Chaplin. But the time was not yet ripe for a Charlie Chaplin; Rigadin never tried to move his audiences to tears, only to laughter, and always with the familiar stock in trade of the circus buffoon. He was an actor from the Variétés, a Conservatoire medalist of 1896, who had been engaged first to play in a film comedy from a scenario by Max and Alex Fischer, *The Two Burglars*. He scored such a hit that he was asked to act in several more pieces—*A Ridiculous Legacy*, *Thy Neighbor's Petticoat*, *The Clown and The Pasha* (with Mistinguette). Then his director, Georges Monca (who was later to present Maurice Chevalier, as a schoolboy, some time before he appeared with Mistinguette in *The Reversing Waltz*), christened him Rigadin, under which name he appeared in one film per week from 1910 to 1920.

Nothing came amiss to him, neither vaudeville nor the trick film (in *Rigadin and His Sons* he played the father and both of the two sons as well) nor parody. As *Napoleon-Rigadin* he strolled abroad in imperial array, forcing the astounded soldiery to present arms as he passed. In *Rigadin, Victim of Love* he received a letter bidding him to a rendezvous; of course the letter was intended for somebody else. In *Rigadin and the Ants* he visits the country, tries to photograph a pretty girl whom he meets out walking, but sits down unknowingly on an anthill. Driven almost insane, he tears off his coat, then his vest, then his pants. Two elderly ladies, seeing him attired only in a shirt, scream bloody murder and summon the police. He is arrested. Fortunately, it proves that the young girl is a lawyer, member of the great Maître Ciceron's firm. She undertakes his defense and he is acquitted—one of the rare occasions in which all ends well for Rigadin. Admittedly his comedies are not very polished, but they gradually taught the director how to tell a story, how to simplify the action. Out of the worst depths of vaudeville and farce they gradually developed a comic style which was pictorial. It is possible to see the origins of genuine film comedy in *Rigadin Seeks*

Election, Rigadin as President, Rigadin as Foster-Father, especially in the last-named. The comedian receives a hamper. In it he finds a baby. He tries to return it to the post office, without success—much like Chaplin in *The Kid.*

Occasionally an accident provided unexpected comedy. In *Rigadin and the Obstinate Lodger,* Georges Monca had already photographed all the scenes in the drawing room when Rigadin fell ill. Upon his return to work a fortnight later he had lost twenty pounds. When the film finally appeared, the audiences laughed uproariously to see Rigadin always so plump when he was in the drawing room and so thin in the other rooms; the film was a riot.

Rigadin was world-famous. They called him Whiffles in England, Moritz in Germany, Salustiano in Spain, Tartufini in Italy and Prenz in the Slavonic countries. Imitators both in France and abroad added to his renown. One of them was almost as well-known as himself; whereas Rigadin had a turned-up nose, the other had a long flat nose like an oyster-knife. This was Marcel Levesque. He had appeared on the stage in *Le Petit Café, Le Million, Triplepatte* and other plays, and refused at first to act for the films. In 1910, however, he agreed to appear in *The Arrest of the Duchesse de Berry,* under Paul Gavault for the Film d'Art. Impressed by Prince's success, he shortly afterwards went to suggest some ideas for comedies to Léonce Perret. He played in chase films like *The Station Hotel* and under Louis Feuillade in *The Sleep-Walker, The Illustrious Boaster, Pingouin the Impostor, Spring Is Here,* etc. Bout-de-Zan, Marcel Levesque and Prince were the bright stars of the prewar comedy. The cinema owes much to them. They taught America a great deal. But their luster was to be dimmed by a more celebrated actor, Max Linder, who was Chaplin's teacher.

MAX LINDER

Max Linder, medalist of the Bordeaux Conservatoire, formerly an actor at the Ambigu, had just been signed up by the Variétés,

where he appeared in *Miquette and Her Mother* and *The King*,
when he met Pathé, who invited him to make films. This was in
1905. His first film was *The Collegian's First Outing*, followed by
An Unexpected Meeting and *A Skater's Debut*. The last-named
was a bitter memory for him. "This film cost me much more
than I earned by it," he said. "I tore my pants, I smashed my top
hat for which I had paid $5, and I lost a pair of gold cuff links."
This did not deter him, however, from appearing later in another skating film, *Boxing Match on Skates,* which in 1912 ran
in the Paris cinemas for many weeks.

Under different directors, but especially with Louis Gasnier,
the future director of *The Exploits of Elaine,* Max worked for
Pathé for five years. He then asked for a salary of $30,000 a year
with a three-months contract, and before long was earning even
more than that. Pathé built up his reputation by careful publicity: "We understand that the gilded shackles which bind Max
Linder have attained the value of a million francs a year. . . .
One million! The imagination boggles at such a figure!"

He was the most famous of them all, this rather prim and elegant actor whom audiences regarded as such an "aristocratic"
comedian, and who had something of André Brûlé, of Victor
Boucher and of Adolphe Menjou about him. His films, generally
a reel long, were usually colored. They were the epitome of
comedy as it was then understood. Trick effects, comic situations, chases and falls are measured out skillfully in them; and if
most of the humor is superficial one cannot but be impressed by
the restraint and obliqueness of Linder's acting, especially in contrast to the frenzied style of his contemporaries. He suggests
laughter rather than provokes it. In his best films this merry-
andrew in a formal suit, who might have been a mere buffoon,
seems to prophesy Chaplin's performance and even, in pure comedy, almost to equal him.

He made a great many films—less perhaps than Rigadin but
still many: *A Rustic Idyll,* which introduced the theme made famous by Chaplin in *Sunnyside, Max the Pedicurist, Max Earns a
Decoration, Max's Holidays, Max Collects Shoes, Never Kiss the
Maid, Max Takes Quinine, Max's Marriage. Max's Marriage* opens

with a subtitle: "Max is getting married, unknown to his uncle." Then one sees Max shutting his wife up in a trunk so as not to be parted from her while he pays a visit to this uncle. In *Max at the Inauguration*, we see him take the place of a piece of official sculpture, calmly listening to the roll of drums and trumpets, the playing of the "Marseillaise" and the speeches. It is almost identical with the beginning of *City Lights*. Just as in vaudeville, the plot is built around gags. But, unlike vaudeville, all the gags here are visual instead of verbal. That is why Max Linder was the real creator of screen comedy.

In *Max Takes Quinine* the title is only a pretext. Max is ill and swallows so much quinine that he becomes drunk. He picks a quarrel first with a police commissioner, then an ambassador, then a general, each of whom challenges him to a duel. He hands the visiting cards they thrust upon him to the policemen who are trying to arrest him for drunkenness, and they obediently get him into the homes of the commissioner, the ambassador and the general—actually, into the arms of the general's wife. Finally Max is thrown out of the window and falls at the feet of the three policemen, who immediately come to attention. This skit is handled so skillfully, the comic gestures are so expressive that it is amusing even today. The final salute of the police and one or two other incidents confirm the belief that it was Linder who really discovered the indirect and visual language of the screen. There is a moment when Max, entangled in a tablecloth, sees a policeman coming and for one brief moment flourishes the cloth at him like a toreador before a bull. It is only a tiny thing, but Chaplin alone has done anything better. The same lightninglike effects occur in the films of both men. Everybody sees the point and the laughter is instantaneous. *A Dog's Life, The Immigrant, The Gold Rush, The Pawnshop* were later to reveal this same power of suggestion through symbolical gestures.

After the war Max Linder, who had been to America, suffered much from comparison with Chaplin. He said: "Chaplin has been good enough to tell me that it was my films which led him to make films. He called me his teacher, but I have been glad enough myself to take lessons from him." But it was Max who was the

initiator. No film library would be complete without a number
of pictures by this comedian who was popular for so many years
but now seems sadly forgotten. At the period under review he
had as yet made only short films and it is perhaps in these that
he was at his best, for he could not always sustain the pace
through a feature-length picture. The nicety of his acting, the
malicious irony of his gestures and his expressions make his performances even today seem models of finish. We shall meet him
again later, in the fullness of his second flowering, in *Be My
Wife*, *Seven Years' Bad Luck* and *The King of the Circus*. At the
time we speak of, he and Méliès were the two really original
workers in the film.

AMERICAN COMEDIES

In comparison with Linder, the American comedies at first
seemed very poor. It was America, however, that, instructed by
France's example, was to discover and develop the elements of
film comedy as first outlined by Linder, Prince and others. It is
true that chase films had been made in France, for one of the
very earliest pictures, *The Pumpkin Race*, was of this type. But
this purely vulgar element, child of the circus parade, developed
into something of real importance in the hands of the creator of
American comedy, Mack Sennett.

He had been discovered by Vitagraph,* where he rapidly rose
in importance. But it was as producer of the Keystone comedies
for Kessel that he was to invent his characteristic brief pieces,
filled with chases, falls and various diversions. He introduced the
"bathing girls," those charming young ladies in undress who always appeared a whole troupe at a time (like the girls in Méliès'
films), who so pleasingly kicked up their pretty legs and brought,
for no very good reason, a dash of operetta into all their scenes.

Sennett's comedies were always burlesques or else parodies of
detective dramas, like those Sherlock Holmes absurdities he made
with Fred Mace. His most important contributions lay in the

* It was Biograph, not Vitagraph, where Sennett learned his métier, first
as an actor and then as director. He went thence straight to Keystone.

realms of visual humor. In the circus you can make people happy by kicking up a lot of noise. On the screen, sights must replace sounds and so, in place of noisy thwackings, Sennett substituted the pie, so admirably suited to be spread over the human face. He not only introduced the pie to the screen: he must be said to have abused it.

In these lively comedies that seemed to be making fun even of themselves, what most delighted audiences was the atmosphere of unreality and nonsense in which the characters moved. The heroine carried off by masked bandits, the chase in automobiles, airplanes or trains are constant factors. These admirable short comedies embroider simple themes with unflagging inventiveness and the use of every device known to cinematography. Men take leaps of a hundred yards, jump over trains, impale themselves on the top of masts. The automobile chases especially, making use as they did of rapid-motion photography, began to take on a grotesque quality which has delighted us since in many a Harold Lloyd or Buster Keaton picture. Part of the fun consisted in the fact that these films were a parody of the automobile chases—grimly serious, of course—in so many screen dramas of the day. Then fresh conceits were introduced every few minutes to tickle the audience and save the film from its own naïveté. A traveler's hat blows off when he looks out a window. He runs madly through the train and just manages to grab it as it flies past the last coach. A torpedo aimed at a motorboat sends it hurtling forward at double speed, so that it wins a race. A sailor suspends his hammock from the door of a railway carriage, where, swinging in the breeze, it mows down telegraph poles as though they were ninepins. The action inevitably winds up with a mad race, motorcycles swoop down waterfalls, cars rush down rapids and a sort of fine critical sense as well as good humor blends the whole into an endless delight.

Sennett first organized those groups of specialists who in America have developed film making into an art as precise as clockwork. Theirs is the task of thinking up incidents which, when artfully introduced into a plot, will set people laughing—it may be at something as simple as a mere kick shrewdly delivered, a pie thrown, a chair which collapses or a crook pursued by his victim. It is up to these men to think up ideas: they are gagmen.

Along with Sennett and Keystone some of his collaborators must be mentioned. These were people whom he discovered and developed, for he was an incomparable teacher. They were Mack Swain, Fred Mace, Mabel Normand and Roscoe Arbuckle, better known as Fatty. There were also Al St. John, called Picratt in France, and Ben Turpin. Gloria Swanson was one of his pupils. Most important of all, there was Chaplin.

THE COMING OF CHAPLIN

Charles Spencer Chaplin was born in the spring of 1889 in a London suburb. He was the son of a singer and a dancer, Charles and Hannah Chaplin. His father died. His mother was of Jewish extraction. When she found no work dancing she took in sewing and taught her sons, Charles and Sydney, to sew, too. At ten years of age Charles made his first appearance in the music halls, doing a clog dance. He became an actor and played Billy, the office boy, in *Sherlock Holmes.*

He learned the rudiments of his art in London with Karno's pantomime troupe, who faithfully preserved the ancient traditions of circus and pantomime and gave their own versions of old favorites like *The Drunkard's Return, The Bicycle Thief, The Boxing Lesson, The Clumsy Juggler.* Charlie was seventeen when he joined them: they were to be his university. He stayed with them for five years, and traveled to America with them more than once. There are traces of this influence in many of his films, one of which, *One A. M.,* is constructed around the theme of a pantomime produced by Fred Karno in which actors represented the various props, furniture, carpets, etc.

But it was from his mother, so Chaplin says himself, that he acquired his all-important gift for observation.

I often wonder [he has said] * if I should ever have made a success in pantomime if it had not been for my mother. She was the

* Quoted from Louis Delluc's *Charlie Chaplin,* John Lane, London, 1922, pp. 56-57.

most astounding mimic I ever saw. She would stay at the window for hours, gazing at the street and reproducing with her hands, eyes and expression all that was going on down there, and never stopped. It was in watching and observing her that I learned, not only to translate emotions with my hands and features, but also to study mankind. Her power of observation had something wonderful about it. One morning she saw Bill Smith come down into the street. "There's Bill Smith," she said. "He's dragging his feet and his boots aren't cleaned. He seems angry. I'll bet he's had a row with his wife, and come away without breakfast. He must have, because he's going into the baker's for a roll." And sure enough, in the course of the day, I would discover that Bill Smith *had* had a row with his wife. This way of observing people was the most valuable thing my mother could teach me, for it is by this method that I have got to know the things that people find funny.

In 1913 Chaplin made his first film. Kessel had seen the little Englishman in a Broadway music hall. Chaplin was reluctant to leave the stage, despite an offer of $150 a week. Sennett (still producing Keystone comedies for Kessel) talked him around, and Charlie made *The Kid Auto Races*. His name was not mentioned in the billing, or indeed until the time of *Tillie's Punctured Romance*, which was anything but his first film though one of his longest for years to come. He gained popularity almost immediately, though he did not immediately adopt the costume which was to be so peculiarly his. He had seen men in Whitechapel in clothes like that, with bowler and cane. As for the overlarge trousers, it is said that he borrowed them one day from Fatty Arbuckle and then stuck to them. At first Charlie wore a forked beard and a considerable mustache. The beard soon vanished, but right up to the war his mustache remained fairly bushy.

He made about forty films with Keystone: *Making a Living, Dough and Dynamite, Caught in the Cabaret, Musical Tramps (His Musical Career)*—one of the best, an uninterrupted flow of comicalities—*The Kid Auto Races, By the Sea, Caught in the Rain (Between Showers), The Star Boarder, His Prehistoric Past, The Property Man*, etc., etc., often with Mabel Normand. They are pure farce, in which the poor wretch is the butt of misfortune, just like the traditional clown. He was a sort of delicately articulated puppet in a disorderly world.

The public liked him, so much so that Essanay, Keystone's rival, decided to tempt him away. They offered him $1,250 a week, and he began to work for them in *His New Job*. A new Charlie was gradually to emerge, although the little figure in the large pants had already been established while he was with Keystone. He was still simply a clown, a little more skillful than the others, a little funnier, with that touch of humility so artfully introduced which was to be his greatest quality. Intelligent members of the industry began to realize just what his merits were. It was not until during the war that Europe went mad over him, yet by 1914 he had already become an actor of importance and had realized his own gifts and his own potentialities. A farseeing individual might have predicted the important role he was to play in comedy but not, certainly, that he would be for so many years the one all-round genius of the screen.

THE THIRD INDUSTRY OF THE WORLD

In 1914 it was estimated by the Italian paper *La Tribuna* that the film industry represented a capital investment of twelve billions of francs and had thus risen to third rank in importance in international trade, next to wheat and coal. In France alone the cinemas took in sixteen million francs at the box office, and the Paris cinemas nine million.

It was the films we have just considered that the prewar public liked. The cinema was no longer, as it had been at first, confined to uneducated or humble audiences. Celebrities of the various arts, famous scientists when interviewed as to their opinion of the cinema, already displayed a sound interest in it, if not positive enthusiasm. When the Sultan of Morocco visited Paris he was taken to a film studio and left with the ubiquitous Mme. Robinne a written testimonial of his enjoyment.

People were already wondering if the cinema would kill the theater. "I confess," said Courteline * in an interview, "that I like

* French satirical writer, 1860–1929.

the films enormously. I do not see that they can or ever will endanger the theater. Good plays will always have an audience and bad plays will always make money."

The popular novelist Léon Sazie repeated arguments already familiar: "The cinema will be the salvation of the theater. It has already abolished in its own halls both *ouvreuses* and tipping, its seats are comfortable and there are no intervals." And he went on to insist that the theater had been dead for a long time and would be revitalized by the influence of the cinema.

Henri Bergson said, rather noncommittally, in 1914: "Nothing lacks interest for the philosopher. I went to the cinema years ago and have seen films from the start. Obviously this invention suggests many new ideas to us philosophers. . . . Above all, the films will be a priceless document for our successors, whereas we ourselves undoubtedly entertain the most erroneous ideas about what the past was really like." He then continued in well-chosen words to speak of the usefulness of the cinema as a means whereby actors could study themselves, and compared its good offices in this direction with the revelations that photography had provided for painters.

This was a general opinion. The success of actors like Wague and Séverin-Mars had also made people suspect that film acting was essentially nearer to pantomime than to theater. On October 18, 1912 Colette, then a music-hall actress still known as Colette Willy, told a newspaperman: "There is no question that the best films, all the really good films, are those in which the scenarist and the actors have conceived and interpreted everything according to the rules of pantomime and by its means alone." This opinion was undoubtedly correct at the time and even today remains partly true.

To such an extent, then, writers, actors and journalists really concerned themselves about the cinema. It was not generally considered that it was an art. Few suspected that it was, above all, a new language able to express both human life and nature in a way of its own and unlike that of literature or the stage. But people realized that it was curiously appealing.

One fact, hitherto overlooked, is of considerable importance.

The advance-guard writers and painters of the day who had already half-seriously and half-jokingly gone wild over *Fantomas*, so beloved of Guillaume Apollinaire, were profoundly interested in this new form of expression which mankind had discovered. In June 1914 Marinetti, the high priest of futurism, began work on a futurist film in collaboration with Valentine de Saint-Point. The settings and the costumes were all to be designed on futurist lines and to introduce the spectator to a quite imaginary world, the world of painters and musicians, a world like that of *Caligari* in years to come. The outbreak of war prevented its being made, but Marinetti's rough outline undoubtedly constituted the first attempt at an advance-guard film anywhere in the world.

The cinema had earned respect. As early as 1911 there was a demand for the creation of a film library, which we still lack.* It was little realized, however, that almost the only films of real merit produced between 1908 and that time were the comedies, and particularly those of Max Linder and Mack Sennett. People then chiefly admired the film dramas, which flattered the public with their bombastic poses, famous actors and third-rate literary flavor. No need to condemn them further. They were nearer to the theater (and what a theater!) than to the screen. Their incredible plots, the absurd gestures of the actors (of even the greatest of them, even Sarah) incite us to nothing but laughter. Yet here and there appears an isolated shot, perilously near to the worst kind of picture postcard, yet displaying an effort to prove that the film is primarily a visual art. Gradually the pictorial compositions, the landscapes and the details of the settings (as for instance in that overpraised final shot of *Cabiria*) become as significant as the actors. Let us forget the actual results, and remember only the good intentions. There was hope in them for the future.

The film makers were searching to discover the rules of a new syntax. It is difficult to set an exact date, but whether it was in

---

* The Museum of Modern Art Film Library, established in New York in 1935, preserves motion pictures of all types and all periods in its archives and makes them available for study throughout American educational institutions. The Cinémathèque Française in Paris, founded in 1936, the Reichsfilmkammer in Berlin, N.I.S. in Moscow also have extensive film archives.

the struggles of the Film d'Art or in Griffith's pictures, the
cinema began to develop from the moment when someone photographed a spray of flowers shedding their petals against an au-
tumnal landscape to indicate the waning of passion, or suggested
young love with shots of vernal blossom. These simple artifices,
these absurd associations of ideas, this imagery already worn
threadbare by poetry and fiction, were nevertheless prime novelties in the history of an art destined for so long to derive its
inspiration from symbolism and ideographs. Through pantomime
on the one hand and symbolism on the other, the art of the film
developed during the prewar years.

PART THREE

The Cinema During the World War

1914–1918

THE outbreak of war in 1914 almost put an end to the history of the film [in France—*Ed.*]. Most of the actors were called to the colors. Audiences momentarily needed no distractions, the studios were commandeered and it seemed as if movies were the one thing which the army did not want. Overnight, the French film lost its pre-eminence. In Germany likewise the industry, struggling feebly against the competition of its Scandinavian neighbors, seemed doomed to expire. For four years, virtually no films were made in France and those made in Germany were not shown outside the national frontiers. The supremacy passed to the neutral countries—to Italy first, then to Sweden and finally to the United States. Outstanding events were the appearance of an Italian film, *Cabiria*, of a brilliant American film, *The Cheat*, and the rise of Chaplin's popularity. Meanwhile, despite a few feeble efforts, France really passed out of the picture though it is true she gathered together some quite extraordinary newsreels in her military archives.

NEWSREELS

During the war, despite initial difficulties and some opposition, it was soon realized—largely through the activities of M. Prévost of Pathé—how important films might be as a record of events. A film unit was established in most of the army divisions, and cameramen, often with extreme courage, ventured everywhere on the field of battle in the most dangerous spots and even into submarines and airplanes. Newsreels became of the first importance to distributors both in France and abroad. Eclair-Journal, Ciné-Gazette and the Agence Générale Cinématographique issued innumerable scenes of actual warfare, of the transportation of supplies to the Front, of the arrival of the British Expeditionary Army, of the burning of Louvain and the retreat of the Belgian Army. These violent and artless scenes were greatly liked by the public and were widely shown until censorship stepped in to curtail the activities of the cameramen. Even then they continued to grind away as best they could on all of the fronts. Today there are thousands of miles of war film stored away in the military archives which few people have ever seen.

Now and then the authorities permit someone to exhume a fragment of this material to insert in a movie or, as has happened recently, to make into a film montage with added sound track—usually consisting of nauseating commentary in the worst of taste. The pictures themselves, covered with "rain" and yellow with age, nevertheless retain a singularly moving quality and lead us to anticipate the time when some future poet of the screen will delve into this living record and recompose a visual symphony of the past out of what other men photographed twenty years ago.

As they exist now, these war records represent a sort of snapshot of life. Some among them are accidentally beautiful, such as one film of inundated Flanders with troops on the march splashing through the mud—a scene of earth and water which looks, in its contrasting blacks and whites, like a Goya. There are shots of groups of refugees drearily making their way along the soaking roads, with bird cages slung under their carts and an aged crone perched on a bale of straw. One of the most stirring of them shows the parade-ground in front of the Invalides where the high old-fashioned taxis are assembled, packed with soldiers, ready to set off pell-mell in the great drive for the Marne.

The scenes of actual fighting are confusing and all look much alike. The best of them date from 1918, and show a wide panorama of the Front dotted with tiny men advancing, widely spaced out, under machine-gun fire. The most valuable things these war records do is to preserve small precise detailed shots of a wounded man on a stretcher, a corner of a trench, little Poincaré like a truck driver in his black pants and peaked cap, the fidgety Crown Prince, the Czar hearing Mass with the Czarina at his side in a feathered hat, and Clemenceau—the only civilian who escapes looking ridiculous—with his enormous mustaches, his balaclava helmet and a fierce gleam in his gray eye. Then there are the aerial fights, the sailing of the *Lusitania*, Fonck looking like a mere schoolboy and Guynemer as thin as a rail, the Germans in retreat, the troops marching into Strasbourg, the Victory Parades in all the capitals. Here are the Americans, slain by the thousands the first time they went into battle, the turbaned Indians and that strange white war of the Italians in white uniforms amid the Alpine snows. There must be much else also hidden away in the archives, awaiting the hand of a master editor. The little that we have seen, usually issued upon the occasion of the death of some distinguished figure like Albert of Belgium, Alexander of Serbia or Clemenceau, or in one of the clumsy war-record films, remains of abiding interest. In these artless reels, born of accident and catastrophe, is some of the finest material of all the war years.

1. The Italian Film

IN OTHER countries film production continued as before. For the first months of the war Italy was not a participant, and when she did come in, her position was such that she could easily continue to turn out those movie spectacles so popular at the time.

Each big producing firm in Italy had its own company of actors under annual contract. Actors like Emilio Ghione (who was a director as well as an actor, and has written a brief essay on the Italian film), actresses like Maria Jacobini, Gianna Terribili-Gonzales of the unforgettable name, and the pre-eminent star Francesca Bertini, directors like Gabriellino d'Annunzio, Negroni, Righelli and Guazzoni all made up a picturesque and lively group. There were also Augusto Genina and Carmine Gallone, who were later to direct some fairly good films in France. Ghione's films, such as *The Masked Amazon* and particularly the series called *Za-la-Mort*, as well as those of Negroni and of Pasquali (*Gipsy Love, Between Men and Beasts*, etc.), all exhibited the same emphatic style, the same rather touching naïveté, the same overabundance of gestures and declamatory motions. The worst faults of the American film were already apparent here, and on an even larger scale. Film stars in Turin and Rome were far more pretentious and exigent than they have ever been in Hollywood.

Francesca Bertini, Hesperia and Pina Menicelli all created tremendous scenes with their producers and their directors, threatened to stop work unless they were given immense contracts,
came late or not at all to rehearsals and engaged in bitter feuds
with one another. Francesca Bertini insisted on making a *Camille*
because Hesperia had just made one. Each of these ladies was
backed by a lawyer, Bertini by Barattolo and Hesperia by Mecheri, both of them millionaires who engaged in a mutual contest
of "bigger and better" films and financial coups, to the lasting
injury of the Italian film. Actors too, in emulation of the actresses, all became extremely temperamental, insisted on being
given contracts and thought up fresh ways of being difficult.
Febo Mari, while making *Attila*, refused to wear a beard, whereupon Alberto Capozzi, appearing in *St. Paul*, declared that he
saw no reason why he should sport so ridiculous an appendage
and insisted on being clean-shaven too. This war of the beards
was typical.

Incidents of the kind did not prevent the Italian films from
being very successful. By the time people had got used to the
idea of the war, the Italians realized that the war itself could be
exploited. They produced *The Honor of Dying for the Fatherland* and *The Fighting Blood of Old England*. As Maciste was
popular, they turned out *Maciste the Bersaglieri*, *Maciste the
Alpinist*, and dragged the huge furniture-mover through every
conceivable heroic situation. A big war film, *The Survivor*, was
given its première in France in the presence of the Italian ambassador. "The public hailed the representative of our gallant Ally
with unheard-of enthusiasm and applauded the adventures of the
valiant soldier to the echo." The scenario of the film was written by Giannino Antona Traversi, the ambassador's brother-in-
law.

Italy was making three different kinds of film—war films, of
which *The Survivor* was an example, spectacles of ancient times
like *Cabiria* and the production that followed it which, naturally,
was *Salammbô*, and sentimental films. Two of the best-liked of
the third type were *Wedded in Death* with Lina Cavalieri and
Lucien Moratori, and *The Royal Tiger*, which introduced a new

star, Pina Menicelli. This was one of those dramas of modern
life inspired by Henry Bataille, full of fine new "modern" furniture, adultery, veils, bouquets and sofas. This tragic piece had a
Slavic setting and concerned a mysterious Russian princess. The
public loved it; indeed, people at that time were not very critical. When a film appeared rather freely modifying *Othello* no
one objected, but when the firm Ambrosio made a *Julius Caesar*
in which Brutus appeared as Caesar's son there were some ad-
verse comments and the Italians were only forgiven because they
had managed their crowd scenes so well: the crossing of the
Rubicon was considered marvelous. Otherwise, the Italians were
extremely popular and everybody went indifferently to see *Quo
Vadis*, which was always being revived, or Lydia Borelli in some
drama like *The Moth, The Wedding March* or *The Daughter of
Jorio* (after d'Annunzio and regarded as the very last word in
art), in *The Ship* (from an original by d'Annunzio), in *Carmen*
or even in *Crime and Punishment*. None of these, however, was
as successful as *Cabiria*, which people continued to talk about for
years, long after it had been supplanted at the Vaudeville by
Christus, which ran for two hundred and fifty nights. This was
the most complete and for many years the best of the religious
films. In some parts of the world, especially in the Orient, this
same *Christus* is revived every Easter: crowds weep and groan
while watching the Crucifixion, women faint and children go
into trances. This is perhaps the strangest fate that has ever befallen a film, to become thus, despite its falsities and its taint of
commercialism, an object of piety and a cause of spiritual exaltation.

The Italians had conquered the film market. A few French
producers protested feebly, but otherwise everyone bowed down
before the "quality" of the Italian films. Thanks to their alliance
with Pathé they had a peculiarly favorable position enjoyed by
no other importations, for it was not until towards the end of
the war that similar facilities were granted to the Americans. Yet
they, too, were already on their way to winning a world monopoly, and were gradually establishing themselves on European
screens.

2. The American Film[*]

THE INDUSTRY

PARAMOUNT had won its supremacy at a most favorable moment. The war had paralyzed all but the Italian and the American producers. The American firms soon established distributing centers in Paris which assured an outlet for their films, despite the protests of the French producers. Actually, opposition to American films did not reach serious proportions until 1919, and during the two preceding years the Americans, with the valuable help of M. Jacques Haik, had entrenched themselves firmly.

In the United States the native films were prospering greatly. The Italian films had attracted a whole new audience of former theatergoers, who were willing to pay good prices to see films which were well presented and well advertised. The day of the nickelodeon was over, and the luxurious temples now being raised to the seventh art made it possible to charge much higher prices of admission. It was estimated that Paramount could make a net profit of thirty-five thousand dollars on an average film, putting out one film a week.

Paramount was turning out every kind of movie — films copied from the Italian spectacles, films like the French *films d'art*, films based on stage plays, short comedies, travel films both in black and white and in color, music-hall turns and war films—it made them all. American films now began to vie with French films in expressing their hatred of German barbarism and their enthusiasm for the preservation of civilization. It is even said that similar films of theirs served in Germany to bolster up hatred of France, the hereditary enemy, and enthusiasm for the preservation of German civilization.

Meanwhile the American film was developing rapidly, but largely outside of Paramount, just as earlier it had developed out-

[*] This section, like the earlier ones (pp. 59–68, 82–86) is largely based on Hampton's *History of the Movies (q.v.)*.

General Sherman's march to the sea from The Birth of a Nation (*1915*).

Pearl White in a characteristic episode from a serial film.

William S. Hart and Bessie Love in The Aryan, *directed by Thomas H. Ince (1916).*

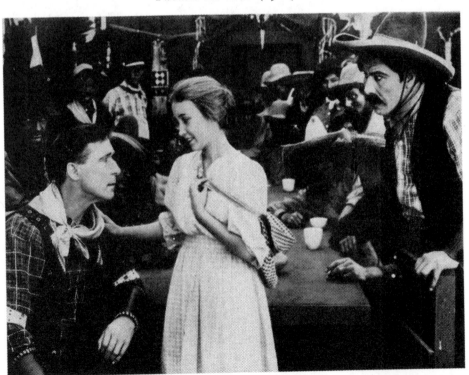

side of the General Film. Progress was due largely to the work of D. W. Griffith, whose most famous picture, *The Birth of a Nation*, set out on the road to wealth and glory in 1915.

The Birth of a Nation encountered considerable difficulties at the onset. Its story was based on a well-known novel concerning the Civil War. This subject, ever dear to Americans, offered real scope to a man who had already realized what could be done with cowboys and Indians, and learnt much from the Italian spectacles; but it would clearly be a costly undertaking. Griffith, who proposed spending a hundred thousand dollars on the film, was stubbornly opposed in his scheme by Mutual, for whom he was now directing. He ran here and there, applied to various bankers and after every kind of difficulty formed a new company called Epoch with one of his friends, Harry Aitken. His own master at last, Griffith was now able to put into execution ideas he had long dreamed of and some of which he had already experimented with successfully. He had broken away utterly from theatrical influences, under which films were produced as a succession of short scenes played in front of a stationary camera. He borrowed from Méliès, or rediscovered for himself, various devices for smoother continuity. He utilized these eagerly, not in order to create an effect, but rather in order to discover a new technique, and to interpret the material in a new and original manner. At the same time he used the camera—as Méliès had never done—as a mobile instrument, moving it about in order to register the most effective aspect of the action. A photographic skill,* still rudimentary but daringly original, gave Griffith's work an expressiveness unlike anything hitherto seen. In addition, Griffith was largely a maker of melodramas of the good old school, and he discovered how to cut his films so as to give the maximum stress to the vicissitudes out of which these thrilling affairs were built up.

These technical elements were not the only reasons for his success. The subject he had chosen also served him well, and certain poor or trivial elements only served to heighten by con-

* Griffith's cameraman for many long years was G. W. Bitzer, who deserves a place in the movie hall of fame.

trast what was meritorious in it. *The Birth of a Nation* showed the era of reconstruction in the South in a somewhat romantic light. The Ku Klux Klan played a glorious and active role, while the Negroes appeared principally as deep-dyed villains indulging in acts of terrorism. Was this deliberate? It had an immediate result. The first showings of the film were the occasion for angry brawls. Feeling ran higher and higher until in Boston a riot broke out during which the crowds and the police fought for twenty-four hours. The resultant publicity was extremely useful. Everybody in America wanted to see the film which had caused a riot. This first big "political" film made Griffith famous, and also revealed the immense potentialities of the medium.

TRIANGLE CORPORATION

The success of Griffith and Aitken gave rise to great ambitions. Financiers, dazzled by the sums earned in a few weeks by Griffith's associates,* were now willing to entrust vast sums to him. Everyone wanted to make another *Birth of a Nation*, provoke more riots and draw correspondingly big profits. Griffith formed an alliance with the two most successful directors of the day, Mack Sennett and Thomas Ince and, with Aitken, formed the Triangle Corporation. Griffith, who had always taken especial pains in selecting his actors, was yet unable to avoid the European errors which had been responsible for the Films d'Art. The new firm immediately set about trying to sign up America's most famous actors. Into this company came Douglas Fairbanks and William S. Hart, but even more important were Mack Sennett and Charlie Chaplin.

The public was all prepared to bless Triangle's efforts, for in the United States the same thing was happening that had happened in France in 1908. A part of that public which is regarded as the élite had condescended to interest itself in the new art. Now these people, as usual, believed that good films could only be made by employing well-known and popular actors and em-

* *The Birth of a Nation* cost approximately $85,000 and grossed upwards of $15,000,000.

ploying them in productions which would be costly and in which, therefore, only the most elevated sentiments could be expressed. A special cinema was rented for these people, the Knickerbocker Theatre in New York, in which they paid theater prices and warmly applauded the new films.

The common ordinary public, however, which cared nothing for art and tragic emotions and great gestures, proved unenthusiastic. As they also were less polite and much less prejudiced by tradition than the French public, they simply declared that the "great actors" acted very badly. In any case, an actor who is a celebrity in New York may very well be unknown in Alabama. So it turned out that the large public very quickly learned to avoid these elegant actors and to keep away from Triangle's films. The firm was so well financed that it would have been able to continue awhile but that it was hoist with its own petard. Many film stars were already earning big salaries. In order to sign up the famous stage actors it had been deemed wise to offer them even larger sums. The film people quickly realized that they were better "box office" at worse pay than these stage grandees. They demanded increases, and Triangle was under the necessity of paying two sets of actors at top prices, one set engaged on long contract and no good at all, the other very good indeed but continually demanding more money. Exhibitors refused to pay the high rentals demanded, and it was not long before Triangle passed out of existence.

THE ROMANTIC LIFE OF MRS. PICKFORD

Triangle had done much to enhance salaries and to create the star system. Every actor now wanted to earn more than his coworkers. The more popular they realized they were, the bolder their demands. It was Mrs. Pickford who set the example. Not for nothing had this little woman trailed for so many years from theater to theater, under circumstances anything but comfortable, in the wake of Thespis' chariot. She knew exactly what an engagement meant and how to make the most of it. Her bonnet and her gentle expression were a mere mask for her exceptional ability and her admirable grasp of affairs. As soon as she foresaw her daughter's success, she also foresaw what use it could be put to. Mary's early successes nowise caused Mrs. Pickford to lose her head, and one is torn between admiration of the stubbornness with which she could argue a point and the rapidity with which she came to the point of view that a salary of $1,000 a week is a mere pittance.

Mrs. Pickford's ambitions were rivaled by those of Charlie Chaplin. He had signed up in 1914 at $150 a week. A little later he joined Essanay at $1,250 and at the end of the year announced that he was free to consider offers. Both Chaplin and his brother Sydney were good businessmen, determined to profit by the situation. They hopped on a train and put the width of a continent between themselves and Los Angeles. They were followed hotfoot by the producers. When they finally traced Chaplin to his hiding place, he was in the bathtub and negotiations had to be conducted through the half-open door. Every now and then, brother Sydney passed back and forth with fresh proposals. After some argument, Chaplin agreed to accept a contract of $10,000 a week. The contract was not actually signed, however, and this oversight enabled a rival firm to make another bid. Hardly had Chaplin agreed to accept $10,000 a week when he signed up elsewhere at the same figure plus a bonus of $150,000. So it was that Chaplin joined Mutual.

The redoubtable Mrs. Pickford was still full of fight. She had already obtained $7,000 a week for Mary when she learnt about Chaplin's new contract. All through 1915 she conducted a warfare of threats, stratagems and ruses to regain the lost ground. She was victorious in the end, and "little Mary" was made happy with $10,000 a week and a substantial percentage.

These events were the despair of the various producers, who foresaw demands from all their players for ever larger and larger salaries. The system of distribution commonly practiced at that time did not really permit of such an outlay. The directors of Paramount, and especially Hodkinson, refused to change their methods. This obstinacy shortly proved a godsend to Adolph Zukor. By means of a series of complex and highly ingenious maneuvers he succeeded in getting Hodkinson out of Paramount, and then gained possession of Triangle by offering Aitken, in the midst of his difficulties, some favorable distribution contracts in order to get control of Mary Pickford. So, one fine day, the third industry of the world passed under the control of a patient Jewish furrier.

ZUKOR AND HIS WORRIES

Zukor planned to found his dictatorship on a new principle of distribution, that of exclusive rights. He had noticed how dearly the American public loved the stars, and decided that if he signed them all up and rented their films exclusively to his own customers then he could control the market. The passion of the public for the film stars was such that a movie theater which could show none of them might as well close. This was the weapon Zukor employed against theater owners who refused to sign up at his own terms for the films he was producing. At the same time he raised film rentals, which of course made the theater owners furious. The most powerful of them banded together and formed a sort of co-operative association, First National, and with the help of Zukor's competitors established a hold in several cities. By 1918 Zukor's position was seriously challenged. This fight between the two groups incited the stars to make even bigger demands: Chaplin left Mutual to accept "more than a million dollars a year." Mary Pickford, the keystone of Zukor's power and his trump card with exhibitors, was also seriously tempted to leave him. At the expiration of her contract she demanded remuneration in salary and percentages which would have netted her between $1,200,000 and $2,000,000 a year. If Zukor had agreed, he would have been compelled to increase his rentals beyond a point which the exhibitors would tolerate; yet if he refused her, his competitors would profit thereby.

It was a new idea which finally decided Zukor. The directors and the scenario writers and, to some extent, the whole technical staff of the studios had begun to feel that too much importance was being attached to the stars and not enough to the films.

Those who had studied Griffith claimed that his pictures had been successful because of their conception and execution, not on account of the actors. Was not *The Birth of a Nation* a prime example of a film without stars? This was the attitude to adopt for the future: it would lighten the financial burden, and the films as a result would be more original, better made and at least as attractive to the public.

This attitude was adopted most notably by a director associated with Jesse Lasky, Cecil B. DeMille. At the end of 1918 he suggested an experiment to Zukor. He proposed making two films without any well-known actors in them, *Old Wives for New* and another version of *The Squaw Man*. The two films, distributed under exactly the same conditions as those of Mary Pickford, proved to be exactly as profitable as hers. DeMille was convinced thereby that the time had come gradually to give up featuring well-known stars, whose increasing demands were bound sooner or later to ruin the producers who continued to employ them.

It was the opposite of Zukor's previous system; he did not accept the idea readily. Finally he half-adopted it, by putting DeMille in charge of one part of Paramount, with instructions to experiment boldly with films minus stars, while he himself continued to operate the rest of the concern as before. Mary Pickford and her mother thereupon passed over to First National.

D. W. GRIFFITH

The man whom these events had brought into prominence, especially after the success of *The Birth of a Nation*, was David Wark Griffith. It was through that film, then with *Intolerance* and above all with *Broken Blossoms*, that this thirty-five-year-old man attained his real development. Without positive genius, and entirely lacking in a sense of proportion, Griffith was the real father of the American film, at once its Cimabue and its Dumas *fils*. Through any number of films besides those mentioned—*The Great Love, The Greatest Thing in Life, Hearts of the World,*

A Romance of Happy Valley, True-Heart Susie—he labored to give the American film what it most needed: truth to life and lyricism.

His most ambitious effort was *Intolerance*, which Eisenstein admired so much and which really forms a link between the Italian spectacles like *Cabiria* and the films of Fritz Lang and Abel Gance.* The immense spectacles so beloved by first-nighters, applied to a humanitarian sermon at once childish and tumefied, combined to make this film into something strange and monstrous, as disordered and primary as *La Roue* or *Metropolis*, handling crowds † as brilliantly as they and, amid oceans of bad taste, overwhelming us with lightninglike moments of extreme brilliance. The film was based on a single theme repeated and developed through various stages of human history. Four parallel stories are related—a Babylonian one, the Life of Christ, the Massacre of St. Bartholomew and a working-class tragedy of today. The film was eighty reels long; Griffith finally cut it down to twelve reels.

The Babylonian spectacles far surpassed the sumptuous carnival of *Cabiria*, but Griffith's contribution was not confined to mere scale. Where the Italians had gone wrong, he seems to have thought, was in approaching the cinema as though it were an outpost of the stage. Griffith broke completely with the stage. The pomps and splendors of his picture, the crowds and great buildings were not in actual material very different from those of the Italian films, but they were designed purely for the screen, absolutely indifferent to the traditions, limitations and necessities imposed by the theater. Griffith had done over again what the Italians had done before him, but more freely, without being constrained by the memory of wings and apron stages, of up stage or exits, and he had avoided the temptation to wind up with a great triumphal ensemble. His crowds looked natural and their movements normal. His may not, in fact, have been any less arti-

* It is difficult to see any real resemblance between the work of Griffith and that of Lang, though he has much in common with Gance. The real successor to *Intolerance* was *Potemkin*.

† *Intolerance* proves on re-examination to be wholly unlike *Metropolis* in every respect.

ficial than the Italian manner but it provided a totally new kind of spectacle and it pleased people. Griffith was regarded as a keen observer because he was not imitating the style of the Scala in Milan, because his actors turned their backs to the camera, because they did not extend their arms, palms outward, in the conventional manner. He had instinctively hit upon a number of devices for achieving a much freer style and everyone was grateful to him. For years he was regarded as having discovered what a film should really be. What he had actually done was to free the screen from those theatrical traditions of which he knew nothing.* It was a great deal to have done and in 1916 was probably the most essential contribution any man could have made.

Other of his films showed clearly which were those characteristic tendencies that were to add to his fame, especially *A Romance of Happy Valley* and *True-Heart Susie*, in which we saw a timid and lovely girl, the unforgettable Lillian Gish. The film was about a poor village heroine in love with a young man. She sells her cows so that he may be educated. She suffers horribly, she does everything in her power to save the honor of her rival and, eventually, a happy ending leaves her married to the young man. It is only a thin-spun romance, but the gentle Lillian was wonderful in it, with her hat put on all wrong; and the details were wonderful too, such as the garden and the lamp out of which Griffith drew simple poetry in the manner of the English poets. Later on he was to utilize similar details to achieve his greatest successes.

CECIL B. DEMILLE

Griffith was not the only one who attempted to beat new paths for the cinema through the intimate drama. Another came to share his fame when Cecil B. DeMille made *The Cheat* in 1915. When this film first appeared in France in the middle of the war, audiences were entranced and producers thunderstruck. It seemed to make everything that had preceded it quite meaningless. In

* Griffith came to the films from the stage. He unquestionably rejected the theatrical manner by choice and not from ignorance.

it Fanny Ward and Sessue Hayakawa displayed a new, restrained, oddly eloquent and indirect style of acting absolutely unlike anything to be seen on the stage at that time. A few people criticized the plot, which was a ridiculous affair, but they were soon howled down. It really was a preposterous story: a man had stolen a hundred thousand dollars—money raised for charity. His wife promises to become the mistress of a Japanese if he will give her that same sum, and then refuses to fulfill the bargain when by chance she obtains the needed amount otherwise. The Oriental, furious, brands her on the shoulder. The husband is brought to trial for having attempted to kill the Japanese. The wife bares her branded shoulder in court and wins the husband's acquittal. Hayakawa is lynched.

What saved the film (it would probably not bear revival) was its fundamentally cinematic style, the simplicity of the acting, the luxuriousness of the settings and, above all, the impassive mask of Hayakawa. Delluc, who cared little for masterpieces ("Lord preserve us from masterpieces," he wrote), nevertheless recognized the virtues of this film. "*The Cheat*," he said, "has the merit of being a complete thing in itself. There is no touch of genius. . . . *The Cheat* is *La Tosca* of the cinema."

Thanks to this film, DeMille won a position to which his fundamental showiness hardly seems to entitle him. He was addicted to melodrama, violence and facile effects—all of them sure fire with the public. By the end of the war he had made many films—*Carmen, Temptation, Maria Rosa* and a *Joan of Arc* in which the handling of crowds and the feeling of spaciousness were remarkable for that time. Delluc especially admired the entrance into Rheims. Then there were *The Little American*, with Mary Pickford (a protest against German atrocities), *The Supreme Redemption*, and a whole series on marriage and home life, based on D. W. Griffith and blending a strong dose of puritanism with the morality of the French theater. These were, *We Can't Have Everything, For Better or Worse, Don't Change Your Husband, Why Change Your Wife, Male and Female*. He also made several pictures about renunciation and sacrifice with Hayakawa, but neither actor nor director ever recaptured the effects of *The*

Cheat. That film, odd though it may seem now, had given the cinema a sense of proportion.

THOMAS INCE

Along with Cecil B. DeMille and Griffith we must make place for another of the early directors who best understood the virtues of the American film—Thomas H. Ince. Occasionally he made psychological dramas like *Those Who Pay,* but his real successes were *Civilization* (a spectacular production in the manner of *The Birth of a Nation*), *The Aryan* and *Blue Blazes Rawden*—and all those films which featured the big strapping fellow with the rugged countenance, William S. Hart, best known in France as "Rio Jim."

Tom Mix and Broncho Billy had accustomed audiences to cowboy-adventure films. Bill Hart, with his hatchet profile, his finished and flexible acting, was to create a new type. *The Redressor of Wrongs, The Sheriff, Wolves of the Rail,* and, later, *The Caravan, The Avenger, Branding Broadway, His Last Errand,* which he made for Paramount under Lambert Hillyer's direction, all constitute one long screen epic which pleased the discriminating as well as the masses. Omitting his last films, in which the actor seemed merely to be repeating himself, let us rather consider those he made for Ince, in which this severe yet impassioned figure gave an entirely new turn to the romantic story of the bad man who does good deeds.

A pupil of Griffith,* Ince understood what cinematography really was, and the lyricism and the sweeping movement of his films from *Punishment* and *Civilization* to *The Wolf Inn* and *Blue Blazes Rawden* raised them far above the level of the Tom Mix and Broncho Billy films. *The Aryan* is Ince's most famous film. It is the story of a man who has become a bandit after being betrayed by a woman and who carries this woman off into the desert with a band of his rough companions. One day a little

---

* Ince was hardly a pupil of Griffith: he made only one Biograph picture, *His New Lid* (1910), then became a director for Imp, then for Kessel. There was no association with Griffith until Triangle days, though no doubt Ince may have been influenced by the other man's work. It should be noted that he was regarded as the best cutter and editor in the business.

group of pioneers on the verge of perishing from hunger and thirst comes by. A young girl begs him to give them water "to save her people." With a sudden flash of comprehension, he agrees to save the party and then, realizing that there can be no real happiness for him, rides off alone into the desert. Obviously, the infiltration of oversimple morality somewhat mars this film as a whole, but it is compensated for by the spaciousness, the sense of horizons and skies, the romantic and genuine spirit of adventure which it embodies. It is easy to see what a real inspiration such a film must have brought to the nascent art and why both Colette and Louis Delluc so much admired *The Evil Star*, *Punishment* and *Illusion*, in which brute energy is pitted against fate. The actual plot is never the important thing in these films, but the outdoors itself, the prairie, a wild horse, a bare gray wall against which anything might take place. Thanks to the acting of Bill Hart and to Bessie Love, the exquisite little girl with the round head, as well as to Ince's skillful handling of detail, these striking films with the grim equestrian hero were something more than mere entertainment.

By the end of the war Ince was more famous than Griffith. Delluc compared him to Rodin, to Debussy and Dumas, even to Aeschylus. "He is the first," he wrote, "to synthesize the confused but brilliant impulses of this art as it emerges from the matrix." His films brought something that re-evoked the childhood memories of Fenimore Cooper and of serial stories in *Je Sais Tout* which still lingered in the imagination of those who saw *Big Brother* for the first time. Writing of *Carmen of the Klondike* in 1919, Jean Cocteau said: "The plot is nothing extraordinary but this film contains a little masterpiece: the fight between the two men in the night under a torrential downpour of rain by the light of arc lamps. In the center of a half-blinded, rain-drenched and horrified crowd the two figures circle round in the mud. To follow them, the camera draws back, moves nearer, rises higher: we see them with the eye of the camera itself. Raincoats glisten, shirts are ripped apart, the naked bodies slippery with blood take on a sort of phosphorescence. Two mad creatures are at grips, trying to kill each other. They look as though they were made of metal. Are they kingfishers or seals or men from the moon, or Jacob with the angel? Is it not some Buddha, this great naked figure which falls to its knees and dies there like a thousand little fishes in a lake of mercury?" Cocteau concludes: "M. Ince may be proud of himself, for a spectacle such as this seems in recollection to equal the world's greatest literature." It would be difficult to suggest more perfectly the plastic beauty of Ince's large and lively compositions. They provided a new, heroic style for the times. Throughout 1915 and 1916 his activity was prodigious. He had already made *The Battle of Gettysburg, Typhoon, The Wrath of the Gods, The Italian, Portraits of Souls.* In those two years he made *Civilization, The Aryan, The Coward, Tempestuous Love, Punishment, Illusion, Those Who Pay, Carmen of the Klondike.* After the breakup of Triangle, Ince became a supervisor and yet still found time to make *Blue Blazes Rawden, In the Shadow of Happiness, Respect the Woman* and *The Last Frontier.* He died in 1924 at the age of forty-four, in the prime of life but having for some years ceased to produce films of any great interest.

Thanks to him the films discovered several basic truths, above all the fact that in a dramatic film the actors are only a part of the mise en scène and that inanimate objects, trees, roads and winds, can here once more assume their ancient and proper role. The cowboy's horse and his dog are characters as important as himself and, as Louis Delluc observed, the pail out of which Hart drinks, the dice he throws on the counter, the card he lays down, are all significant. One must not overlook these dream symbols, nor the stone jug full of whisky, nor the heavy silver belt, nor the huge revolvers, nor the leather cuffs studded with copper on Hart's wrists.

"There is something more [wrote Delluc in 1923]. I think that Rio Jim is the first real figure established by the cinema; he is its first genuine type and his life the first really cinematic theme, already a classic—the adventures of an adventurer in search of fortune in Nevada or the Rocky Mountains, who holds up the mail coach, robs the mails, interrupts the dance, burns the rancher's house and marries the sheriff's daughter. It is already a rigidly established theme, so much so that we shall shortly find it tedious.

Nevertheless, it is the cleanest-cut and the most attractive theme that has yet been evolved." Delluc goes on to sum up what one finds in these heroic films, in which Louise Glaum seemed to him a new Clytemnestra and Bessie Love another Electra, for the future of the film will lie, he thinks, in celebrating a "simplified humanity." "Bare gray plains, mountains as steep and as luminous as the screen itself, horses and men in all their brute strength, the tremendous intensity of a life so simple that it has all the room in the world for beauty and harmony and contrast, and lends an incomparable spark of humanity to the simple sentiments like love and duty and revenge which spring from it."

Thomas Ince and William S. Hart have the honor of having given the cinema its first lyrics of the open air, those crude Iliads so well suited to the taste of young people with their intense love of life. Moreover, Ince was infinitely superior * either to Griffith or to Cecil B. DeMille.

THE FRENCH IN AMERICA

There were others who contested with them in the race for success. As early as 1914 a few French directors—fascinated by the legendary land of rich uncles and dollars—had crossed the Atlantic, or were sent over by firms like Gaumont and Pathé. During the war these men succeeded in winning important positions for themselves.

Maurice Tourneur, who was afterwards criticized for not having promptly joined up with the French Army, was one of these. He was a good, sound workman and little more, whose reputation has much diminished. He directed serials like *The White Circle* and several quite adequate pictures such as *The Isle of Lost Ships*, a first *Treasure Island* and *The Last of the Mohicans*. All of them were skillful enough but entirely without originality.

As for Léonce Perret, he made propaganda films (*Lest We Forget*) and modern tragedies (*A Modern Salome*) about which no more need be said. He arrived in America with a considerable repu-

* That Ince was superior to Griffith is an opinion with which few may agree, but his reputation in Europe is greater than in America.

tation, though less than that of Capellani, who also crossed the
ocean about 1915 and did his best work in the States. It was neither
The House of Mirth nor *Social Hypocrites* which brought Capellani fame, but a whole series of films in which he directed the famous actress and dancer Alla Nazimova. Star and director gained
fame together, and it is difficult to know to which of them we
owe the pleasure that we derived from *The Red Lantern, Eye for
an Eye* and especially *Out of the Fog*, made in 1919. Nazimova,
with her little face and enormous eyes, with her burning aestheticism, was, like Asta Nielsen, one of the most intelligent actresses
on the screen for many years. She managed to inject into rather
elementary stories the sort of fire and seductiveness Garbo so often
supplies. It must be admitted that Capellani did not neglect, at
least in *Out of the Fog*, to utilize his utmost ingenuity. The story
is ordinary enough but some exquisite moments make up for this
—Nazimova at the deathbed, Nazimova under the lamplight, Nazimova kissing her own reflection in the mirror and, best of all,
the ghostly little figure of Nazimova in the water. A lighthouse
in the night, the shade of a dead girl against the watery background
of the ocean compensate for the conventional characters and the
pathetic plot. Nazimova was never so lovely, nor for that matter
did Capellani ever do better.

Others who went abroad met with varying success. Henri d'Abbadie d'Arrast worked with Chaplin and so did Count Jean de
Limur, but not until after the war. The most successful of the
emigrating Frenchmen was Louis Gasnier.

SERIALS

New dreams far less simple and much more vulgar than those
evoked by "Rio Jim" were being provided for young people. The
war years were, above all, the era of serial films. After the success
of the French episodic pictures and especially of Feuillade's *Fantomas*, the Americans saw a fortune to be made by this formula.* To
this end they hired a man who knew Feuillade and his methods
extremely well—Louis Gasnier, who had been Linder's director.

* See note on page 69.

Thus it was that the spirit of *Fantomas* was unleashed on the American public, became naturalized and a little later, on the rebound, engendered *Judex* in France. Twenty serials now appeared on the screen, all of them with Pearl White—*The Exploits of Elaine, The Laughing Mask, The Queen Is Bored, By Force or Trickery.* Then came *The Red Circle* and *The Sacred Tiger* with Ruth Roland, *Ravengar* with Léon Bary, *The Master of Mystery* with Houdini, *The Idol of the Circus* with Eddie Polo, and many another. Audiences, because they wanted to find out what happened next, increasingly acquired the habit of regular weekly filmgoing.

Gasnier was the author of the most famous of the serials, *The Exploits of Elaine* and *Ravengar*. It was these films that taught the world to revel in new terrors, familiarized it both with the custom of killing men by means of mysterious rays and with the man with the red kerchief ever emerging from the shadows, and accustomed it to sympathizing with Pearl White, trapped in an enormous cast-iron pipe in which the water is gradually rising and from which she certainly will not be rescued by the detective until next week's episode. There were fights amid raging torrents, on the top of church steeples, up and down luxurious houses and along the exotic American highways with their early Ford cars. These films scored a hit all over the world.

In France *The Exploits of Elaine*, adapted by Pierre Decourcelle as *Les Mystères de New-York*, was published in *Le Matin*, beginning in October 1915, to the accompaniment of an immense amount of publicity. Each week fresh news about it was given out, there was a Clutching Hand Club, and it was rumored that Taylor Dodge would pay five thousand dollars to the first person to solve the mystery. Barefaced imitations of the film tried to cash in on its success. There were parodies of it, like *The Moving Foot* and *The Mysteries of a York Ham*. Their only result was to increase the fame of the original. Because of the success of *Les Mystères*, a sequel now appeared: "The Man with the Red Kerchief unmasked by Clarel is no longer a menace. But the great French detective does not remain idle. Next he pits himself against a formidable gang of Chinese who plan to seize the immense wealth of the Clutching Hand. At the same time, this man who loves

France even more dearly than the woman of his choice, sees her menaced by an ignoble enemy and determines to consecrate all his efforts and all his scientific skill to his country. We shall see how he plans to present to her a marvelous invention which will be of untold service to the French armies, but it is not without serious risks that he will carry out this patriotic scheme." Thus a dash of patriotism was added to the customary excitements. Ordinary adventures seeming tame to them, the Americans also crammed their serials with the most extraordinary catastrophes: trains crashed into raging rivers, automobiles ran into one another head on, and the cinema became a happy hunting ground for acrobats and athletes.

TOM MIX AND DOUGLAS FAIRBANKS

There were actors well able to profit by this fashion. Tom Mix and his celebrated horse continued to offer stiff competition to William S. Hart in America, and outshone him in Europe. He had made a fortune for Selig, and in 1915 Aubert took over the distribution of a long list of his films on the Continent. He represented a less complex version of the romantic tradition than did Hart, and it was much appreciated by the public. Tom Mix and the buffalo as well as the many *Nat Pinkerton* films were just the stuff for children.

It was at this time that there appeared a robust and smiling figure who was long to be one of the cinema's greater glories. This was Douglas Fairbanks, who came from the theater, where he had already appeared in 1912 as a likable sort of adventurer who leapt off balconies and sprang over walls. His play had scored a hit in Chicago. He discovered the cinema with *The Birth of a Nation*, and went to see Griffith.* After his first film, *The Lamb*, he was urged to appear in Mack Sennett comedies, but instead he made *Double Trouble* and a number of pictures based on scenarios by

---

* It was Kessel and Baumann who got Fairbanks to join Triangle and sent him to Los Angeles. Griffith advised Fairbanks to go into Keystone comedies. Eventually a unit consisting of John Emerson, Anita Loos and the actor were "packed off together . . . to work out their own destiny."

Anita Loos *—*The Half Breed, The Americano* and so on. It was about 1916 that he completely established the character of a harum-scarum sort of chap who will fight his way along any route that leads eventually to a pretty girl: he made *Flirting with Fate, The Good Bad Man, The Habit of Happiness, Reggie Mixes In*. His biggest success came in 1916, when he made *American Aristocracy*, playing the part of a Southerner of good family [who collects butterflies, becomes acquainted with some snobbish Easterners and gets involved in all sorts of melodramatic adventures— Ed.]. A lot of airplane work was entailed and even acrobatics on a hydroplane. In the last two years of the war he made a number of pictures for the Douglas Fairbanks Corporation—*Wild and Wooly, He Comes Up Smiling, The Man from Painted Post, Reaching for the Moon* and—most important—*A Modern Musketeer*. Dumas had always appealed to him, and Ince had just made a version of *The Three Musketeers*.

His Picture in the Papers, The Matrimaniac, The Americano, In Again, Out Again and others made the world conscious of his dashing good humor and perpetually gay animation. There was little depth or humanity in his characterization, but plenty of animal spirits well adapted to American tastes, which, however, in the long run are apt to pall. His essential quality was his grace and physical fitness: it was a pleasure to see a man so obviously full of the joy of life. It may be that this is hardly sufficient to entitle him to the name of a great artist, but Fairbanks, even before he had made his most famous pictures, already in *A Modern Musketeer* had fully developed his very likable characterization and had done everything in his power to make people realize that the film's most essential quality lies first and foremost in movement.

THE COMEDIANS

Fairbanks made people smile because he was always smiling himself. Real comedians very seldom smile, and this truth is amply

---

* And, almost equally important, with subtitles by Anita Loos which made wisecracking a familiar language and also made subtitles shorter.

verified when one comes to consider those American comedians, both famous and relatively obscure, who first appeared in American films during the war.

Mack Sennett had discovered a goodly number of these comedians and was employing them in his amazing and crazy farces, packed full of chases and falls. The best-known of them all was Mabel Normand, whom he starred in a delightful comedy, *Mickey*, a preposterous but witty satire on high society, and one of the first really important American comedies. Another actor as nimble as a cat, who peered out innocently from behind glasses and a small mustache, was frequently seen hurling himself with serene optimism into the most disconcerting of adventures. He was known as Lonesome Luke in America, but the French called him "Lui." His tortoise-shell glasses made him famous. Later on he got rid of the mustache and the nickname and became Harold Lloyd from 1917 on, when he was making burlesque comedies with Bebe Daniels—*Luke Joins the Navy, Luke's Fatal Flivver, Fireman Save My Child, Lonesome Luke in Tin-Can Alley*, etc. He threw a great deal of zest into these early exercises. Another prentice hand was a little fellow with a frozen face who was to become Buster Keaton. He acted with Fatty Arbuckle at that time.

The portly Arbuckle was the most important of them all. He appeared in a whole series of buffooneries with Mabel Normand —*Mabel in the Park, Mabel at the Party, Miss Fatty on Vacation, Fatty the Airman, Fatty Makes a Conquest*. He brought to the screen the never-failing absurdity of a very fat man but, as with many others of his poundage, there was a certain delicate wit in his enormous body. In *The Butcher Boy* he had terrific difficulties with some spaghetti, just as Chaplin was to have later. In *The Garage, The Bell Boy, Good Night Nurse* he sustained a certain impassive calm and a surprising agility throughout a whole series of misfortunes. There are really excellent things now and then, such as the scene in the rain when Fatty tries unavailingly to light a cigarette and persuades a one-man orchestra who happens along to play the national anthem, thus compelling all the passers-by— even the policeman who is about to arrest him—to stand at attention bareheaded in the downpour. In *The Sheriff Out West* one sees him arrive, proud as Punch of his new appointment, riding a little donkey into a Western town. On the outskirts he passes a cemetery, with hundreds of tombstones stretching as far as the eye can see. "Oh, that's the cemetery for sheriffs," somebody tells him. A little further along he comes to a big building at every window of which a weeping woman is seated: it is the home for the widows of sheriffs. Fatty is petrified with terror.

It was absurd and often macabre inventions like these that were the salvation of his films. At times he carried them, amusingly enough, to the length of parody, as in *A Reckless Romeo*, where, when a rival lies in wait for him behind a dark curtain, he fires a dozen shots into him without interrupting for a single instant the long kiss he is placing on the lips of his girl. The man had a lot of talent.

Along with him were many others, almost forgotten now, whom it is difficult to realize were once regarded as the peers of Chaplin, Keaton and Lloyd—Al St. John (known in France as Picratt), Clyde Cook (Dudule), Larry Semon (Zigoto), cross-eyed Ben Turpin with the big mustache, who was forever involved in the most ridiculous fixes and eventually developed a sort of delightfully insane style, Hank Mann (Bilboquet), Harry Pollard (Beaucitron), and Sydney Chaplin, Charlie's brother and often his screen companion, as in *Shoulder Arms*. Those who make us laugh but do not know how to change their original recipe are quickly forgotten, though unjustly so. We must remember that the comical inventions and gags with which the old films of Ben Turpin, Larry Semon and others were filled are far from being themselves forgotten. They have all been carefully preserved and catalogued, and we see them reappear in contemporary pictures, enlivening the works of Lloyd and even of Chaplin. There is no gag without an ancestor, and just as the circus is founded in tradition, so the film comedy (possibly the most absolutely successful department in the whole art of the screen) has its traditions too, recorded on celluloid or listed for the use of gagmen.

CHARLIE CHAPLIN

But all the comedians, however gifted, grew dim in comparison to a new star, Charlie Chaplin. Both in Europe and in America he rapidly earned an unprecedented degree of popularity and fame.

Western Import and its representative, M. Jacques Haik, launched the Keystone comedies with Mabel, Fatty and Charlie in Europe in 1915; other comedies of theirs not distributed by this house were suppressed. In a very few months Chaplin had replaced Linder as king of comedy, and cinemas had to book *A Night at the Show* weeks ahead. Western Import was even compelled to place photographs of Mabel and Charlie on sale so as to make their appearance widely familiar and to discourage imitators. For there were imitators galore. The firm of Bonaz had brought over the films of Billie Ritchie, who wore the same mustache, the same pants, the same hat as Chaplin's, and carefully copied his movements. He shared Chaplin's success for several months. There were other doubles, not to mention Lloyd, who also sported the little mustache. There was a Jack and, after the war, even a Charley; then this Charley and Billie Ritchie went to law, accusing each other of plagiarism. Both of them lost. All of this merely added to the fabulous prestige of Chaplin.

Naturally enough, so great a success as his was bound to annoy some of the producers. In 1916 there was quite a lot of feeling against American importations in the film world. *Le Cinéma* published an article signed by Jean Yvel which violently attacked Chaplin. His *Tillie's Punctured Romance* had just appeared, an insane comedy with Marie Dressler and Mabel Normand. "His art, if we may call it so without profaning the word, is more simian than human. . . . Charlot is not a comedian, he is a twopenny-ha'penny jumping jack." After calling on the sacred names of la belle France and of education, this writer concluded: "What a far cry is this from the artistry displayed by Prince in the Rigadin films!"

And though not in his sense, it *was* a far cry from Rigadin. Chaplin's first films for Essanay, with whom he worked during 1915,

were infinitely more developed than the rather clumsy clowning
of the Keystone films like *Mabel's Busy Day* or *Between Showers.*
There were fifteen or more that he made for Essanay: *His New
Job, A Night Out, The Champion, The Tramp, The Woman,
Shanghaied, The Jitney Elopement, A Night at the Show, Work,
By the Sea, The Bank, In the Park, Police, Carmen.*

Some of these are still mere clowning, like *A Night at the Show,*
which is simply a series of mishaps. Yet his technique here is already more developed; it is well-nigh faultless, and if some of the
comic effects miss fire, they are never Chaplin's. As these are all
short films, the plots are extremely simple—Charlie gets the best of
some given situation. He is a boxer, with a horseshoe concealed in
his glove, or he is forced to turn sailor much against his wish and
reveals all the horrors of being forced into a job for which one has
no vocation. Edna Purviance was now his partner, and Ben Turpin
also appears. Among these early Chaplins are two which suggest
future possibilities and hitherto unsuspected traits—*The Woman*
and *Carmen.*

The Woman is a rather disturbing piece of broad comedy in
which Charlie disguises himself as a woman and cuts off his mustache, in order to circumvent the opposition of his sweetheart's
uncle. Of course the uncle at once begins to flirt with the supposed
girl; and there is something about Chaplin's face when one sees
it clean-shaven which is unexpected and utterly unfamiliar. One
catches a glimpse of one aspect of the man about which volumes
could be written, an almost equivocal and feminine quality born
of humiliation, which can be detected in later films. That is why
The Woman is so important, as a sort of curiosity.* Otherwise, it
is still a prentice piece with few first-rate inventions in it, but ex-
hibiting a curious sureness of touch at least as impressive as the
slightly dubious quality of some of the humor and some of the
incidents.

As for *Carmen,* one might dismiss this parody entirely were it
not that the comedian's gift for pantomime is revealed here (something not of the cinema, but much more ancient, which was to
blossom forth anew in *The Pilgrim*). Moreover, it contains one

---

* Chaplin had previously appeared as a woman in *Putting One Over* (1914).

extraordinary scene, the death of Don José, when, suddenly, Chaplin's expression becomes tragic, with a hint of bitterness, and extremely moving. From that time on, Chaplin wanted to make a dramatic film. Essanay would not consent, but the wish was an indication.

When he left Essanay, he contracted for twelve films to be made in twelve months for Mutual. They were produced in 1916 and 1917, and there is not a single one among them but contains at least one really remarkable scene. These are *The Floorwalker, The Fireman, The Vagabond, One A. M., The Pawnshop, The Rink, The Adventurer, The Count, Behind the Screen, The Cure, The Immigrant, Easy Street.* Some of them seem to be a development of the Keystone and Essanay comedies, like *The Rink,* based on a familiar theme dear to most of the movie comedians and previously utilized by Max Linder. Certain incidents in it are the vulgarest buffoonery, as when a whole cat is served on a dish to customers in the restaurant. But the chase on roller skates has a magnificent swing. As for *One A. M.,* this was a peculiar affair in more ways than one. Adapted from a vaudeville turn, it has no plot whatsoever. We see a man coming home after a spree, in evening dress and high hat (not a trace here of Chaplin's usual costume), struggling to open the front door, attempting vainly to pass a clock whose pendulum keeps getting in his way, wrestling with a decanter and glass on a revolving table which continually skids under his grasp and then—as a finale—wrestling with a bed which collapses on top of him, rises up when he tries to sit down on it and has every appearance of being animated by an evil spirit. There is nothing that he does here which Linder might not have done; the film throughout recalls Linder and the primitive films as a whole by its use of trick photography and the importance of the roles played by inanimate objects. There is really nothing invented‧ here at all, nothing original, and yet Chaplin's precision and restraint are such that one realizes how, out of this low farce and out of pantomime inherited from the circus, a really original screen technique and a new language are being evolved. The struggle with the bed predicts the struggle with the deck chair in *A Day's Pleasure* (1919) and the scene with the alarm clock in *The*

Pawnshop. Eventually Chaplin will cease to struggle with inanimate things, no longer match his wits with them but draw comedy out of himself alone.

He was already inventing comic plots, no doubt with the memory of Mack Sennett in mind. In *The Floorwalker*, Chaplin makes eyes at a wax mannequin, throws the various counters into utter confusion, drenches the bosses in water. A dreadful monster grabs him, drags him down: it is the escalator. This moving staircase and a lift are really the heroes of this film. As the department head is a thief who closely resembles Chaplin, there are long animated quarrels in which Charlie is accused of having robbed the safe, whereas actually he was rushing in pursuit of the thieves; this gave occasion for some fierce combats in the elevator and on the moving staircase. *The Fireman, The Adventurer* and *The Count* are brief affairs in which he deftly continues to develop his technique. At times the clowning is more subtle, as in *Behind the Screen*, a sort of parody on slapstick comedies. The little actor is full of bright ideas in this; he gives a shampoo to a bedside rug and combs and arranges its hair with exquisite care. He later appears carrying a dozen chairs over his shoulder, looking like a giant hedgehog, and mows down the various actors as he passes. This is decidedly low comedy, and only the talent of the principal performer makes it significant, but he is perfection itself. It is the same in *Easy Street*, in which we encounter the first of his satires on puritanism. Charlie enters a mission hall and falls in love with the preacher's daughter. A colossal gangster, so powerful that he can bend lampposts like straws, is the terror of the neighborhood, but Charlie manages to shove his head into one of the street lamps, turns on the gas and asphyxiates him. The gangster, a thoroughly reformed character, now starts going to church and Charlie marries the preacher's daughter. *Easy Street* is one of the gayest films of this period.

There are three of them which stand out: *The Pawnshop, The Immigrant* and *The Vagabond. The Pawnshop* is rather slow in movement and badly constructed, with a great deal of slapstick and a ladder with which Charlie has much trouble, but it contains one superb scene in which a poor wretch of a man brings in an alarm clock to pawn. Chaplin auscultates it with all the gravity of a doctor, opens it as if it were a can of food, uncoils the springs, which he eyes as if they were wriggling worms, then sprinkles them with an oilcan to "kill" them (for by now the spectator is convinced they are alive) and finally hands the whole mess back to its owner with a peremptory "It's absolutely worthless." His virtuosity here is stupendous, so exactly is every movement calculated to suggest another quite different movement, such as that of a doctor with a patient or somebody opening a can. This scene stands comparison with the best moments of *The Gold Rush*.

We are still in the realm of unadulterated comedy, however. In *The Immigrant* there is something more. Here we find Charlie in the steerage of a liner, on his way to seek his fortune in the land of liberty and dollars. It is a brief but charming piece, with few sustained sequences save that of the dinner he eats and cannot pay for, and the fits of terror which seize him when he sees six or seven husky waiters fall upon a customer who had not quite enough money to pay *his* bill. There is a tender and restrained love story which concludes one day in the magistrate's office. One interesting thing about it is the crowd, which now, for the first time in any of his films, takes on a certain importance: there are Jews in queer headgear, shabby, suspicious-looking characters, a whole ghetto swarms up on deck. In the midst of them all, Charlie smiles timidly and delicately begins his courtship. In the first scene we see him hiccoughing over a rail: he appears to be seasick, but no, he is really hauling in a big fish. At no time is either the comedy or the sentiment presented quite "straight," and it is one of the first films in which this subtlety appears. Some of the incidents are really startling, as, for instance, the glimpse of the Statue of Liberty immediately followed by the brutal examination of the immigrants. The injection of satire and of sentiment into this film gives it a curious perfection.

We personally like *The Vagabond* better, for here Charlie's own poetic quality is expressed for the first time and here he is unhappy in love. An enchanting atmosphere of rusticity is established in the opening scenes: Charlie sits down beside a dying campfire, then leaps up with the seat of his pants on fire. He turns farm hand, milks a cow by maneuvering its tail up and down like a pump handle, waters the trees scrupulously drop by drop and, with the air of a Knight of the Round Table, does battle with tree stumps. There is a wretched young girl for whom he plays music on his cheap fiddle, but she does not return his devotion: she is in love with the young artist who is painting a picture of her. There is a charming scene in which Chaplin, who longs to be an artist too, also tries to paint her portrait and only succeeds in producing a childish caricature. Finally the girl's long-lost mother turns up and bears her away to a life of riches and ease. At the very last moment the girl stops and comes back to fetch Charlie, but somehow this ending does not strike one as very probable.

By now the complete Chaplin had been evolved, completely equipped with comic resources and also with his own peculiarly appealing griefs and his quiet bitterness. Very few touches remained to be added.

In 1918 Chaplin joined First National, with whom he remained until 1922, making eight films. The two earliest, released before the end of the war, were *A Dog's Life* and *Shoulder Arms*. At the time it was issued *A Dog's Life* seemed Chaplin's most complete and most typical film. His technique, patiently perfected during the two years with Mutual, now blossomed out in this well-constructed and almost flawless piece. Charlie, the penniless tramp, has a dog. He discovers treasure and fights for it with some crooks. He falls in love. Hidden behind a curtain, he disposes of his enemies as they pass with a sharp tap on first one skull, then the next, from the little mallet of his Keystone days. Two substantial cronies are eating lunch. He knocks one of them unconscious and then, slipping his arms through the vest of his victim from behind, pantomimes some lively gestures to convince the other man that the unconscious (or dead) fellow is thoroughly alive: he raps on the table, pours out a drink and raises it to the victim's lips. This is an astonishingly brilliant bit of acting. At the conclusion of the film we see him in the country, with his pretty wife and several puppies, the proud owner of a small farm set in a vast field in which he is planting wheat by making holes with his fingers along the tops of the furrows.

Shoulder Arms, which appeared at the end of the war, is even better, and, indeed, one wonders whether Chaplin has ever done anything finer. Charlie is an awkward recruit; he has great difficulty in forming fours and standing in line because his feet always turn outwards. Then he is at the Front, in the trenches. Everybody else gets mail: Charlie gets none. Peeping over the shoulder of another soldier, he reads *his* letter and on his face are reflected a vicarious joy and dismay and amazement in turn. He opens bottles by holding them up over the parapet. He strikes a light by scratching a match on a passing bullet. When he is shooting at the Germans from his loophole, he chalks up every direct hit on a plank, as if he were playing billiards or trapshooting. But when one of the "dead" men returns his fire, he calmly rubs out the last chalk mark. There is an unconscious cruelty about this which is amazing. Now the wet weather comes and the dugout is flooded. A candle end stuck on a board floats by; a frog sits croaking on the big toe of a sleeping soldier. Charlie rearranges his blankets, sinks gently under water and manages to breathe peacefully through the small end of a phonograph trumpet. Next morning he is sent out to reconnoiter. We discover him in the heart of the woods disguised as a tree and quite "invisible." At this point events take an extraordinary turn—Charlie captures both the Kaiser and the Crown Prince, and wins the war. In the original version the Allies give him a big banquet, M. Poincaré makes a speech, Charlie rises to reply and the King of England creeps up and sneaks a button off his uniform as a souvenir. Censorship banned this ending and in some places did not permit even the capture of the Kaiser to be shown for a long time.

This simple but subtle film was unquestionably the boldest of any of the works inspired by the war. It by no means lacks either bitterness or cruelty, and the comical elements in it are transposed, by the most ingenious and rapid use of suggestion, from simple incidents into cosmic mirth. It is a film about the courage and the cowardice of Man, a puppet show of human beings which attains the level of high art.

After *Shoulder Arms*, or for that matter after *A Dog's Life* and *The Vagabond*, we can no longer speak of prentice work. Chaplin's resources are complete and the world of his invention is finally created.

This great artist, in order to appeal to all sorts and conditions of people, has turned himself into a marionette, a marionette who inhabits a world of somewhat different marionettes. He always begins by transporting us to a toy theater. The setting in which we discover him is roughly a middle-western town, with a sheriff who has a brass star in his coat, a minister with his collar worn behind-before and a yellow-haired maiden in distress. This city is never New York or Chicago, and though presumably an American town it is not noticeably Americanized. The period is hardly indicated.* This realm of cardboard and three-ply is inhabited by exquisitely unreal people. The crooks are fearsome wretches, visibly evil from the soles of their shoes to their hats. The good characters are so extraordinarily good that they might serve to illustrate a manual on piety, or on civic virtue. Friends invariably exhibit the faith-fulness of bulldogs, except when the pangs of hunger give them bad dreams for which they cannot possibly be blamed.

Into this little country which has no history there drops from the skies a tramp. He walks like an automaton. He extends an arm, then drops it as though a spring controlled it. There is no real flesh on his body, it has no more density than that of a puppet. His mobile head, his little mustache and curly hair, his bright eyes are those of a doll. Just watch him as he bumps into everything, gets caught in doors, runs and falls down, then vanishes. He raises his hat like a clockwork figure. When he does something clumsily one fancies that it is because the strings have not been properly manipu-lated. When he is adroit, his movements are still not those of a normal human being. There seems to be machinery, or something that dances, inside him. Notice the extraordinary use he makes of the *weight* of his body when he treats it as an object like any other simple object, especially in the scene of the rocking cabin in *The Gold Rush*, where he uses it as a solid mass that blindly obeys the forces of gravity. When he dances with a girl in some barroom

---

* His setting actually is partly Cockney in character, and the period is somewhere between Dickens and 1915.

does he not seem to be mounted on a pivot, and to be revolving in an automatic waltz?

All Chaplin's short early films are about the adventures of a marionette. Then, gradually, he evolved an individual comic style based on the conflict between this little figure and a world ruled by somewhat analogous but radically different laws. Chaplin gets into trouble because he imitates the habits and the customs of real human beings, but he imitates without understanding them. He is a hero who dismays other heroes, a benefactor who profoundly shocks other benefactors. In its detail, his comedy arises most frequently from an extraordinary application of familiar gestures and reactions—he sows wheat as a child makes mud pies, opens a clock as a person opens a can, sucks the nails in the soles of his shoes as if they were chicken bones and swallows bootlaces as though they were spaghetti. In every case he has imitated, with the most scrupulous attention to detail, the behavior proper to quite a different set of circumstances. All this developed from an extraordinary power of observation and from profound reflection, as he himself has said. Amid the events of ordinary everyday life he seeks hidden comic elements. It was in a store that he realized how a moving staircase could be made use of and while watching a fire that he conceived *The Fireman*. He knows precisely why his acting arouses sympathy or pity. "It was lucky," he says, "that I was a small man." He realizes too that it is not enough for a marionette to make us laugh, but that the creature must also have a soul of its own.

"One or two custard pies are funny, but when laughter depends on nothing but custard pies then a film soon becomes boring. . . . A knowledge of human nature is the basis for any real success." *Shoulder Arms*, one of the few genuine masterpieces of the screen, proves how right he is: the future can do nothing but confirm his statement.

It was through Chaplin that the American film won its place in the sun, and Chaplin who continued to be its salvation, despite all the various financial maneuvers and all the bad films. The four war years, during which it was undergoing its real formation, produced that humble and joyous little figure who is the only universal hero of our times.

3. The French Film

CONFRONTED first with the war and then with the competition of the Italian and the American films, what happened to the French film industry during those four years? In August 1914 production practically came to a standstill. Little by little the various firms reorganized themselves, and American firms either opened branches in France or made arrangements for French distributors to handle their output. Various changes were made on the producing side and by 1915 the industry was once more functioning almost normally. But it had undergone considerable changes. Western Import had opened a big branch in Paris managed by Jacques Haik. Keystone was distributing all its comedies, notably those of Mabel Normand, in France through Aubert. Eclair never entirely ceased production but had kept going with war newsreels, on which it now continued to concentrate. The Film d'Art had passed into the control of Nalpas: he had reorganized its personnel but kept its character. Other firms, less well managed or less stable, had entirely disappeared, the one among them most to be regretted being, of course, that of Méliès.

The making of war newsreels led naturally to the production of patriotic films. In 1915 Film National brought out an ambitious picture based on Victor Margueritte's patriotic novel, *Frontiers of the Heart.* "Extolling as it does the national sentiment of France," so the producers advertised, "this film has been so adapted as to fit perfectly with the following patriotic airs: The Sambre-et-Meuse Regiment, The Bugle Call, The Marseillaise, The Call to the Colors and The Charge." The same firm announced *A Sacred Love,* "showing on the screen the most poignant conflict of emotions that could rend the heart of a young Frenchman today." They also produced *The Burgomaster's Daughter* and *The House at the*

Ferry, not to mention *The Independence of Belgium from 1830 to 1914*, a piece which was highly edifying as well as historical.

This was right at the beginning. Before long, they realized that films about the war displeased more people than they pleased. What was needed was either adventure or love stories, as a relief from all the fighting and killing which filled the daily newspapers. People wanted to forget—which was the reason why the American films were so popular at that time. The industry now adopted as its device "films for relaxation," and it became as patriotic to make people laugh at Rigadin as it had been, earlier, to make them cry over the misfortunes of soldiers and their mothers. The film trade papers of the period are positively indecent on this topic.

Nevertheless, some war films continued to be made right up to the time of the Armistice, though in fewer numbers, even after 1917 when the government asked the film industry to throw its weight behind the effort to create "moral support" behind the lines. Gaumont brought out some patriotic comedies in an effort to kill two birds with one stone, and Léonce Perret, who has a good many other crimes on his conscience, now added that of having made *Léonce Loves the Belgians*. This was actually sent over to America as propaganda, to induce the Americans to show and to produce big patriotic films there also. Little Bout-de-Zan was made to appear in *Bout-de-Zan the Patriot*. *L'Intransigeant* might protest against these histrionic mummeries of the war, censorship might exhibit unusual severity towards overpatriotic films: they still continued to circulate in the provinces "to keep up morale behind the lines"—films like *The Avenging Poilu, Sweethearts of 1914, The Angelus of Victory* and *Christmas in Wartime*, from an original scenario by Félicien Champsaur featuring Léon Bernard of the Comédie Française.

Abel Gance, still working for the Film d'Art, also made a picture in this vein, *Paddy's Heroism:* a title that speaks for itself. In a number of other films the exaltation of patriotism was spiced with the excitement that a little espionage lends, as in *Kit, The Boche's Daughter*, and *The Minister's Daughter*. The most successful of these was Gaumont's *Marraines de France* and Arthur Bernède's big film *The Heart of a Frenchwoman*.

Meanwhile, try as they might, the French producers could not prevent the influx of foreign pictures or prevent them from scoring a tremendous success, for they were all the more popular because the American producers and their films paid little attention to the war. So, gradually, the Frenchmen fell back on their old evil ways and without a single trace of originality once more began turning out absurd and sentimental films acted by the Comédie Française.

In 1915, as we have already seen, *The Cheat* had arrived from America like a bolt from heaven. Everybody rushed to imitate it. A Japanese actress called Tsuri Aoki was hired and featured in a film about the earthquake, *The Wrath of the Gods*, in which she played her role, according to the producers, "with all the more conviction because she had actually lost many relatives and friends in the catastrophe." It is not everybody who would find such an experience inspiring.

Others, without actually tapping Japanese resources, fancied that the "treasures" of French literary drama would suitably provide material to enable them to compete with the producers of *The Cheat*. Towards the close of 1916 Aubert, who had just finished *L'Aiglon*, presented Jane Marnac in a drama designed to put the Hayakawa opus quite in the shade, *The Faltering Heart*. Altogether the influence of *The Cheat* cannot be said to have been beneficial: it simply bolstered up the influence of the *films d'art* and thus encouraged the dismal practice of filming current plays. Louis Delluc observed that *The Cheat* encouraged producers to model themselves even more closely than before on M. Bernstein and, at the same time, to deck out their films with artistic lighting effects. The French lacked both ideas and enterprise and only made *The Faltering Heart* because that sort of melodrama was the fashion. They also made many realistic dramas; and Mistinguette's biggest successes, *Fleur de Paris* and *Chignon d'Or*, date from 1915.

There were renewed efforts to catch the public taste by employing celebrated actors. This was a mistake, for, as someone said, "Duse is Duse and the cinema is not of her time." In *The Return of Ulysses* Mounet-Sully and Mme. Bartet had previously missed fire.

Sarah Bernhardt had fainted away when she saw herself in *Camille*. This, however, had not prevented her from continuing to act for the screen, and Delluc even imagined a picture based on the *Iliad* in which he thought she might do well. But for the time being he wrote, in an admirable sentence, "When one sees her in *Mothers of France* or in Tristan Bernard's *Jeanne Doré* one cannot but feel that this superb companion of Racine is not really at home in the shadowy, uncertain world of the screen." No more was Suzanne Després in Germaine Dulac's *Enemy Mothers* nor Réjane in *Alsace* nor many another, yet this was the way in which the producers thought to make attractive pictures. As the films they made failed to appeal to the public, they looked elsewhere—to realistic drama and then, above all, to material in the nature of *Fantomas* and of the enormously successful American serials like *The Exploits of Elaine* and *The Laughing Mask*. While the realistic drama appealed to the critical because it was comparatively well mounted, the other drew the crowds by catering to their taste for excitement.

The Exploits of Elaine had a huge progeny. After *The Vampires*, which was issued not in weekly episodes but at much longer intervals, there was *The Mysterious Mr. X*. Undeterred by mockery or criticism the producers, backed by the big newspapers, expected great things from these. *Le Matin* had published the serial story of *The Exploits*; *Le Journal* serialized a novel of Maurice LeBlanc's in 1916—*The Red Circle*. There was a great deal of insistence on the fact that *The Exploits* was really not an original film at all, that it was no better than *Fantomas* and that Pierre Decourcelle could easily whip out stuff just as good. Hurriedly, Decourcelle's *Two Little Kids* was filmed and Pouctal also made *Chantecoq*, which even quite intelligent people liked. *Ultus* and *The Return of Ultus* were in much the same style as *Rocambole*. Finally the whole trend culminated in the "masterpiece" of all French detective films, which completely obliterated the memory of the Man with the Red Handkerchief from New York and drew in the crowds by thousands—the famous *Judex* serial.

It first appeared in 1917, and Louis Feuillade directed it. Today there are innumerable people alive who can still conjure up pleas-

Douglas Fairbanks in American Aristocracy *(1916)*.

Gloria Swanson in Male and Female, *directed by Cecil B. DeMille* *(1919)*. (T. HUFF COLLECTION)

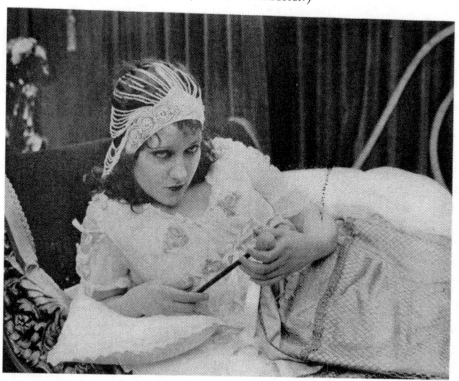

Mary Pickford in Pollyanna *(1920).*
Barney Oldfield's Race for a Life, *a Mack Sennett comedy with*
Mabel Normand (c. 1913).

urably the image of the Empire desk at which René Cresté sat
and pondered his problems—Cresté, that handsome fellow equipped
with all the stock in trade of melodrama, including the broad-
brimmed hat and that magnificent black cape which he flung about
his shoulders with such a noble gesture. In fact Cresté's cape *was*
Judex. The rest of it was unimportant; for all its kidnaped heroines,
its crooks, fights on precipices, fearful risks, last-minute rescues
could have been found just as well in *The Exploits of Elaine* or,
better still, in *Fantomas*. In all that endless history of wrongs
righted nothing really mattered but Cresté's cape. Because of this
cape and Cresté's good looks and charming smile every schoolboy
in France at the end of the war dreamed of being like Judex. This
film really succeeded where *The Exploits* had failed, where *Ro-*
cambole and *Fantomas* had succeeded, thanks to the novels on
which they were based rather than to the films themselves—it
evolved a new character, at once symbolical and stereotyped, and
stamped a new name on the public mind. There is no *name* that
one specially remembers in *The Exploits*. Justin Clarel the detective never really became popular, whereas one remembers Judex
just as one remembers (though a little less clearly) Tom Mix and
Bill Hart. Louis Feuillade's films—absurd and grotesque as they
were, and much as they disgusted all those who were interested
in the development of the film as an art—really gave birth to a new
stock figure which persisted for many years, that of the Redressor
of Wrongs, who, under the name of Judex, now entered the crude
mythology born of the cinema.

This was the most important of the French productions at that
time. Feuillade later directed *The Two Boys*, *Vendémiaire*, *Bar-*
rabas, *Vindicta* and *Lucette;* he died in 1924 while working on
The Stigmata, without ever having recaptured his earlier success.
It was *Judex* and *Judex' New Mission* which enabled the French
to stem the tide of the foreign film invasion, against which nothing could wholly prevail despite the marked xenophobia of the
period. There was no use reviving or remaking old films; there
was no use crying out, "Support French films," or trying to pretend with a straight face that the American films (before 1917)
were really "German importations in disguise." The trend of pub-

lic taste was unmistakable, and when cinemas announced Griffith's *The Avenging Conscience* they referred to him as the "famous David Griffith," an adjective which speaks volumes. Had it not been for the immense success of *Judex* the foreign conquest would have been complete, in the realm of the dramatic as well as the comic films. Mabel and Fatty and Charlie eclipsed everything else, despite the valiant efforts that were made to offer them competition. Max Linder, the best of the French comedians, made few pictures during this period: there were only *The Little Café* directed by Raymond Bernard, *Max Médecin Malgré Lui*, *Max Between Two Fires* (a parody on *The Clutching Hand*) and two films which he made while in the United States, *Max in America* and *Max and His Taxi*. The last of these, in which Max appeared with a bunch of cheerful drunks, is full of funny things (the horse harnessed the wrong way round, the taxi which refuses to budge) and even of charming things (the dance of the telegraph wires) which indicate how completely Linder was master of his own technique at that time, and how sure was his touch.

Rigadin, of course, remained. For a time, during the first two years of the war, he had no competitor, and now that censorship had called a halt to the production of lugubriously patriotic films "in order to spare people's feelings," distraction was to be provided. Actually, since the theaters were closed, the war had done the cinema a good turn, far from injuring it, and had given it a permanent hold in the absence of its honorable rival. At the beginning of 1915, when Pierre Mille went to a cinema for the first time since the outbreak of war, he complained that he could find nothing but Rigadin—*Rigadin's Deception*, *Rigadin's Happy Home*, *Rigadin This* and *Rigadin That*. He came to the conclusion that "people's feelings" could not really have been very sensitive.

There was another man whose work stood out among the French output of that time, one for whom despite all his faults the *cinéastes* have always had a tender spot—Abel Gance, who began to blossom forth during the war. The films that he made were, admittedly, both incredible and involved. He made them because he had to earn a living—films like *The Ten O'Clock Rid-*

dle, and *Barberousse,* which came out serially. He himself believes that there was some merit in *The Zone of Death* and *The Right to Live,* and he liked his *Mater Dolorosa,* featuring Gémier, well enough to remake it as a talkie. It is a gloomy affair in which we are supposed to get very much concerned at the supposition that a doctor may not save the life of his child in order to punish the mother, who, he thinks, has been unfaithful to him. The whole thing was composed of a medley of shots so grotesque as to be almost magnificent. In *The Zone of Death* and *The Tenth Symphony,* Gance was busily acquiring the Victor Hugo-like style which was to become his chosen method of self-expression. In order to understand Gance's later work it is essential to remember these earlier films, crawling with sentiment, full of melodramatic situations, dense with unconvincing gestures, floods of tears and symbolism, combining the worst elements of the penny novelette and the serial story, of Hugo, Zola and Romain Rolland. Louis Delluc, who was always favorably disposed towards him, wrote after seeing *The Zone of Death,* "Bravo, Gance! and be sure to stick to the heroic manner." After seeing *The Tenth Symphony,* however, he recognized what was Gance's greatest vice, an utter inability to be simple, and added (not without a tinge of admiration), "He is another d'Annunzio."

Jacques de Baroncelli also made his appearance now and directed *The King of the Sea* and *The Return to the Land,* both workmanlike pictures in which he expressed nature after his own fashion, which is to say in the facile manner of a designer of picture postcards. Germaine Dulac also made several films—*Enemy Mothers* with Suzanne Desprès, *The Mysterious Géo, The Tempest of Life, Souls of Madmen, The Happiness of Others* with Eve Francis—and while thus learning her job also tried to inject a little psychology into what she was making. Louis Mercanton of *Queen Elizabeth* fame made *The Torrent* with Signorelli, *A Tale of Love and Adventure* with Sacha Guitry and *Bouclette,* all of them well-enough-made films that people complained were too well made. The scenarios for *Bouclette* and *The Torrent* were by Marcel L'Herbier, whom we shall meet again later.

The main essentials of the postwar film, when Baroncelli and

Léonce Perret were to dominate the scene, were thus all ready prepared. Actually the sum total of the French wartime film is rather a sorry one. There was neither development nor originality to be found; only the old Film d'Art on the one hand and the serials on the other. In between these there occurred no genuine contribution to the art of the film, now stemming rather from Chaplin and Ince and Griffith in America. There was in France only a film industry and the desire to exploit popular taste. The war was doubtless to blame, but so were the producers, and the writers who lacked courage, and the absolute lack of any standards, and the prevailing bad taste. The prophetic words of Louis Delluc might appropriately be repeated here, for though they were written in 1919 they remain true to this day: "I should like to believe that we shall eventually make good films. It would be very surprising, for the cinema is not in our blood. There are few nations which nurture all of the arts, and France, which has so much to pride herself on in poetry and the drama, in painting and the dance yet has no feeling, no understanding and no love for music. I prophesy—we shall see in the future if I am right—that France has no more aptitude for the cinema than for music."

4. The German Film and the Danish Film

AT THE outbreak of war the firm of Nordisk of Copenhagen still dominated the German market absolutely. Then, at first, the Germans did exactly the same as the French—they sat back and waited. When the fighting settled down along more or less permanently established lines of trenches, a number of new firms were launched in the hope of making a lot of money. Sentimental and heroic films about nurses and soldiers were turned out by the score, but with the Iron Cross playing the part that the *Légion d'honneur* played in France. Nordisk, with a shrewd grasp of the situation, also began producing pictures about the defense of one's country and so forth, for the German market, and as this firm was by far the most powerful and best equipped, it quickly obliterated or absorbed all its competitors. The Union, one of the most important firms, eventually gave up the ghost, and by 1917 the only firms of any importance that remained were Nordisk and Decla-Bioscop.

These two houses, knowing exactly how successful the American serial films had become, made up their minds to do without imported movies just as they managed under the blockade to do without so many other things. Germany began to provide her own home-made serials and detective films, in which Mia May did duty for Pearl White, and all the other actors were carefully chosen so as to correspond to their American prototypes.

Since the Allies were producing patriotic films intended for exportation to neutral countries, like *Marraines de Guerre*, so Germany in 1917 founded B.U.F.A., which began by producing instructional films for the army, establishing five hundred cinemas on the Western Front and three hundred on the Eastern Front. It was at this moment that Krupp and the big banks chose to recognize the power of the motion picture: they formed a company known as Ufa with a capital of twenty-five million marks, and within almost no time this new firm, which flourished amazingly, had absorbed B.U.F.A., curtailed the success of Nordisk and—thanks to the munition makers—became one of Europe's most powerful industrial forces. At the Armistice there were only two companies of any importance left in Germany, Ufa and Bioscop.

In the interval, the German film developed quite independently in isolation. No foreign films were shown. The former favorites vanished, all save Henny Porten, Lotte Neumann and the exceptionally gifted Asta Nielsen. New figures came into prominence —Werner Krauss, Emil Jannings, Paul Wegener and Pola Negri. Wegener directed as well as acted; so did Richard Oswald, Eichberg and Lubitsch. Eichberg earned much praise for his *Let There Be Light* and *Ferdinand Lassalle;* Wegener for his romantic and Hoffmannesque *Student of Prague*, in which the German preoccupation with the macabre and fondness for occultism mixed with science are already evident. They were also evident in Nordisk's *Homunculus*. As for Jannings, he made his screen debut in a Lubitsch film in 1915, then appeared in a version of Daudet's *Fromont Jr. and Risler Sr.*, directed by Robert Wiene in 1916. Next he was seen in Arthur Robison's terrifying *A Night of Horror* and in Lubitsch's *Marriage of Louise Rohrbach* (1917).

These films enjoyed an immense success. Cinemas, many of them quite luxurious, sprang up all over Germany. Max Reinhardt was paid four hundred thousand marks for making a single film. Actors earned as much as one hundred and fifty thousand marks. By the end of 1918, in spite of war, famine and threatening revolution, a profound feeling for the film had been deeply implanted in Germany and already there was an originality about the German product which was to develop very fruitfully.

The Danes, whether in their German productions or in those made actually in Denmark, can be distinguished only with difficulty from the Germans. Their neutrality at first stood them in good stead. To compete with America, now gradually cornering the European market, Nordisk made more than three hundred films in the first years of the war—films adapted from novels or from plays and a quantity of short comedies featuring the Danish comedians Stribolt, Alstrup and Buch. A newly formed Danish company also brought Benjamin Christensen to the fore; he had made his first film, *The Mysterious X*, in 1913. But little by little, Nordisk, faced with ever increasing competition, lost its preeminence and the Danish film on which such high hopes had been founded was finally defeated in the battle for the European market. Christensen went to Sweden and made his best film, *Witchcraft*, there. By the time the war was over Ufa had killed the Danish film.

5. *The Swedish Film*

During the war the Swedish film, safely removed from the hostilities, really got under way. Each year Victor Sjöström, who was to become the foremost of Swedish directors, made four or five films in which he also acted. In 1914 it was *One Among Them*, *Judge Not*, *The Traitor's Money*, *Vultures of the Sea*. In 1916 it was *Therese*, *Dödskyssen* and—most noteworthy of them—*Terje Vigen*, after Ibsen's *Brand*. All of them revealed a photographic sense quite exceptional at that date, a strong national flavor and, at the same time, a markedly literary content, all of which indicated the direction in which Sjöström was to develop in the near future. He was much superior to Stiller, who in the same year directed *Prima Ballerina*, featuring Lars Hanson and the young Jenny Hasselqvist, shortly to become the great Swedish star.

Here as elsewhere in Europe the new American films had come as a revelation. Stiller was profoundly affected by them, dreamed of conquering the world himself and made a film about the movies which was nevertheless still a refined stage comedy, entitled *Thomas Graal's Best Film*, in which Sjöström acted. He also made *Their First-Born*. Sjöström, who had fundamentally a much better understanding of the medium, now made *The Outlaw and His Wife* (*Berg Ejvind och hans hustru*), one of his finest films, in 1917. This merits detailed consideration.

It is no longer possible today to look at *The Outlaw and His Wife* with the same eyes with which people looked upon it in 1917, or just after the war when it came to France. Its greatest weakness is in the acting: Sjöström was far from being as talented an actor as he was a director, and the rest of the cast, even more than he, overdo their facial contortions so that one is uncomfortably conscious of eyeballs, of sardonic laughter, set grimaces and all sorts of melodramatic excesses, though the tempo of the acting is slow and entirely unlike the fireworks and frenzies fashionable in film acting at that date. For this reason alone *The Outlaw and His Wife* constituted a marked step forward. But, as frequently happened in the Swedish film, Sjöström also fell down over the more dramatic incidents, and when they occur there is a lack of harmony in this film adapted from a play much admired in Scandinavian countries. That explains why audiences who now see this film, twenty years after it was made, regard the second half in a quite different light from the first half. In the first we see a man, recently escaped from prison, who comes to work on a big farm. He earns the love of the woman who owns it. When she finds out the truth about him [as he is about to be rearrested—Ed.] she follows him into hiding in the mountains. There [where they live as outlaws—Ed.] everything gradually goes wrong—an old friend joins them and falls in love with the woman, they are tracked down and finally perish of cold in the winter snows. This is almost pure melodrama, though the last scene but one is well handled and even quite moving: the man and woman recall the happy past and then begin to reproach each other, as they crouch in their miserable hut—"It was all your fault." "It was not, it was all your doing." But the earlier scenes, in spite of some faulty acting, are really admirable. Not until the Soviet films were we to meet again with such beautiful pictorial imagery, such an unfaltering sense of rhythm, so fine a feeling for composition. Sjöström works on a large canvas, in which a love for light and for the half-tones is evident. He throws a golden haze like a nimbus around the outlines of his figures, and lingers lovingly over simple objects, a hand or some other familiar but significant detail. The opening of the film is masterly: we gradually discern through the grayness some indistinct shapes moving, a milling about of vaguely animal forms and, as the screen grows lighter, there emerges out of the darkness, half-guessed at first and then distinct, a flock of sheep. Sjöström uses this device again several times in the film, slowly drawing his composition out of the shadows as if, like some demiurge, he were creating it from nothing. It is a device which Pudovkin was to employ, notably in *Storm Over Asia.*

To these film makers of the North everything in the life about them had cinematographic value—the early-morning rising of the servants, their meals, the arrival of the head steward. Sjöström only occasionally betrays his love of the national folklore and of the national landscape. Usually he emphasizes neither, but with remarkable skill uses the landscapes to provide a vivid background for his simple plot. Now and then some exotic detail catches one's attention, as when the outlaw cooks his food by plunging it into the boiling water of a geyser—for the setting, like the play of Johann Sigurjonsson which it follows, is Icelandic. Yet even these details blend naturally, at least in the early part of the film, into this rich and unified work; the cinema was learning how to tell a story.

At its best, this film of Sjöström's remains both moving and beautiful. In 1917 it was of an extraordinary freshness. Here was a man really interested in what he was doing, loving the film as though it were one of the noble arts and realizing that it is, above all, the child of light. To him it seemed to have far more kinship with painting and music than with the theater and with elocution. Admitted that the acting and the slow pace are open to criticism; but there are other essentially important qualities in the film—a love of the visible world, a need for simplicity both in the action and in the characters, and the realization that the medium is more akin to poetry than to the other literary forms and, in poetry, to familiar national epics. Sweden produced its first great film in *The Outlaw and His Wife;* it was an important event in the history of the cinema and perhaps the most important one since 1895, because here for the first time a film *consciously* invaded the domain of art.

In the same year Victor Sjöström directed *The Girl from the Marsh Croft,* from a story of Selma Lagerlöf's, and from this time on Miss Lagerlöf exercised a profound influence on the Swedish film. The work of this woman of genius, which curiously blends ardent puritanism with a passionate love of nature and the echoes of old sagas, juxtaposing the figure of Jesus Christ with witches and gnomes, is most typical of the Nordic writers. Towards the end of the war, Sjöström also produced films adapted from the two first parts of her *Jerusalem—Ingemar's Sons* and *Karin, Ingemar's Daughter.* Mauritz Stiller also made *Song of the Red Flower,* and it was to Selma Lagerlöf that the Swedish film owed much of its charm and its grandeur, its wide landscapes, its special morality, its emphasis on cold and winter and the elements. Nothing of this had previously been captured on the screen. There had been dramas and farces and a number of relatively successful condensations of novels or, as with Méliès, some exquisite fantasy, but never before had one seen daily life pictured in a poetic light, or the little everyday incidents, the whole life of a people, employed to stir our emotions and to interest us as no verbal description of the same material could possibly do. Through Sjöström and Stiller, each in his different way, the film was discovered to be an art primarily of *atmosphere.* In the next years, which were to witness the apogee of the Swedish film, the classical standards of the silent film were, slowly and painfully, to be formulated, and it would be impossible to exaggerate the radical importance of the part which Sweden played in formulating this aesthetic.

6. The Russian Film

IT IS not generally realized that these years spelt prosperity for the Russian film industry. Though Germany had cut them off from communication with the Allied countries, the Russian people nevertheless wanted to see films, and the firms Khanzhonkov and Yermoliev therefore provided them in large quantities. During this period Ivan Ilitch Mosjoukine, an actor-director who was afterwards to become famous, first came to the fore. Born in 1889, he had won success in the modern theater both at home and abroad, particularly in *L'Aiglon* and in *Kean*. He played the Devil in Starevich's *Christmas Eve*, adapted from Gogol, then appeared in *The Terrible Vengeance*, also by Gogol, and in Pushkin's *Ruslan and Ludmilla*. Next he played in *A Tomboy*, *The Chrysanthemums*, *Do You Remember*, *The Slums of St. Petersburg* and several Tolstoy pieces—*War and Peace* and *The Kreutzer Sonata*. He passed into the hands of Protazanov, one of the most productive of directors, and made seventy films with him, into which all the romanticism of crime and the underworld was packed, all the succedaneum of Stendhal and Dostoevski—Raskolnikov even became a sort of hero of the criminal world. Rimsky directed *The Darker the Night the Brighter the Stars*, about two lovers, one of whom was blind and the other disfigured. Meyerhold directed a *Dorian Gray* and Starevich a "medieval tale" called *Jola*, also *Stella Maris*. Aestheticism and the Apocalypse were the principal ingredients.

Between 1917 and 1919 Volkov and Protazanov made their reputation with somber dramas—Protazanov with *The Queen of Spades* and Volkov with *Father Sergei*. The latter, who had discovered the lovely, mysterious Natalie Lissenko in 1917 in *Behind the Screen*, now evolved *Danse Macabre* about an orchestra leader who goes mad while conducting Saint-Saëns' symphonic poem.

Mosjoukine and Protazanov collaborated in *The Prosecuting Attorney*, an exciting affair in which an attorney falls in love with a spy, while his *Satan Triumphs* celebrated the picturesque qualities of sinister streets and poor hovels. Meanwhile, Tourjanski had made Maupassant's *Yvette* with Natalie Kovanko, Kuprin's *Twilight*, *The Pearl Fishers* and *Mary Magdalen*.

When the Revolution dawned, Yermoliev was anxious not to lose all of his money. Mosjoukine agreed to act in a propaganda film, directed by Protazanov, called *Andrei Kozhoukov*, about a revolutionary shot by the Czarists. In spite of some fine "panic" scenes this film was considered too tame. Yermoliev moved his studio to the Crimea and ultimately left Russia altogether, taking along with him the last of the Czarist films, *An Agonizing Adventure*, which he completed in Paris. Tourjanski, who had shown signs of realizing what the Russian film was to become in his *Balgospoden* (based on popular ballads) and a film of the outdoors, *Mirages of the Swamp*, which reconstructed in the Crimea the scenery of *The Broken Dream*, now with the firm of Biofilm followed in Yermoliev's footsteps and emigrated. One period of the Russian film thus came to a close. The films of that period were to be of considerable use to the Soviet directors, who, cut off completely from the rest of Europe and its films, had little else to study during their apprenticeship but these gloomy, romantic films made during the war.

Conclusion

IN FACT, a whole period was drawing to a close everywhere. In France, it is true, there had been no very noticeable change; they had simply continued to exploit the prewar themes in a feeble way. But Sweden had begun making significant films, America had equipped herself to conquer the world and Chaplin had made his appearance. In the years to follow the art of the film was to develop rapidly, and we were to see also for the first time the rise of different schools of cinematography and of rival aesthetic creeds. It was really the end of an epoch, an epoch during which the film had established itself as a part of everyday life and the public had acquired the habit of seeking a weekly opiate in the movie theaters. This fact had been widely observed; M. Doumic in 1918 wrote in the *Revue des Deux Mondes:* "So prevalent an influence merits attention. May we not have entered upon the Age of Cinematography?"

What had actually been achieved? Apart from the films of Chaplin and of Ince and Sjöström's *The Outlaw and His Wife,* the rest is mere history—all the serials and *Judex,* DeMille with *The Cheat,* and Griffith.* Yet just as literature in its beginnings started with the epic, and created supernaturally heroic figures like Achilles and Hector, Roland and Charlemagne or Beowulf, so had the infant cinema stamped itself on the imagination of the public by creating *types.* Later on it was to lose sight of this primitive function, which corresponds to a public need, but, in film after film, certain actors had stamped themselves on the public imagination so that their names had become proverbial. The comedians like Keaton, Lloyd and Fields were to perpetuate this tradition, which is of course typically that of Chaplin, but during the war it was not the comedians alone who obeyed it. There were Rigadin and Chaplin, but there were also Judex and Bill Hart and Tom Mix. By means of the simplest conventions, these figures adapted themselves to a medium which has usually found psychological subtleties beyond its capacity. With one or two accessories and a smile, a cape or a gun, these types were established, easily recognizable by the audiences who thrilled in response to their adventures. By 1919 the cinema had already created a mythology and a collection of gods.

It had also created its own special universe, which has changed very little since that time. A few years later, Elmer Rice perfectly described this universe in a book † which is rather long-drawn-out and a trifle heavy-handed but full of legitimate malice. He describes the strange creatures which populate this world. "These workers," he tells us, "are almost invariably young and beautiful

* I cannot follow the authors here. Griffith's *Birth of a Nation* and *Intolerance,* for example, are much more than mere history.
† *A Voyage to Purilia,* Cosmopolitan Press, New York, 1930, pp. 83–85.

girls, as yet untouched by the ravages of industrialism and usually destined to escape from the industrial world, at an early age, by contracting a marriage with a young and handsome man of wealth. (Nor was I ever able to discover the exact nature of their occupation, for I found them always absorbed in the disentanglement of some emotional difficulty which seemed to occupy all their time and attention.) . . . Actually the country is without political institutions. In consequence the fortunate land is free from all those complex and perplexing problems of government and politics with which humans are only too familiar. Occasionally one does meet an administrative officer; but these 'Governors,' as they are called, have no other duty than the consideration of pleas for mercy, in behalf of prisoners who have been condemned to death."

In describing the various inhabitants of this strange world Elmer Rice has omitted only the *femme fatale*. If we add her name to that of the police inspector, the cowboy and the strong, silent man and glean from his book the code of behavior practiced there, we shall have the whole geography of this world clearly before our eyes. This land of the cinema is one in which taxi drivers never give any change, where trains are never seen except when rounding a curve, where no boat sails without encountering a storm, and ships' orchestras always play the national anthem during a shipwreck, where on every street we always see one society woman in an automobile and one working girl carrying a hatbox, where hotels have no lavatories and a person can regain his lost memory by being given a shrewd blow on the head. Such was the world of the silent films; most of its customs and other peculiarities can still be detected in the world of the talkies. This universe had already taken form by the end of the war: the coming years were to add little to our knowledge of it.

PART FOUR

The Emergence of an Art

1919–1923

1. The French Film

IN THE creative period that followed the Armistice—a period which may arbitrarily be regarded as lasting until the end of 1923—the French film played an important part. Much that was produced during those years left a great deal to be desired, but it was at this time that, through the influence of several directors, critics and writers, the intellectuals began to take a keen interest in the cinema. The Swedish films first, and then the German films, gave rise to new theories and new concepts. Many of them were erroneous or exaggerated, yet it was thanks to the various enthusiasms and experiments of those four years that cinematography as a whole managed to extricate itself from the rut into which it seemed to be slipping.

TRADITIONAL ELEMENTS

Films made for the masses continued, of course, to be ground out, featuring ladies from the Comédie Française and full of unscrupulous crooks and intrepid police inspectors in the *Judex* tradition. Things like that do not disappear in five minutes. Gradually public taste developed; audiences learned to appreciate better-constructed films and more ingenious plots. It is difficult to realize that men like Baroncelli, L'Herbier, Raymond Bernard, Poirier and Tourjanski were once in the advance guard; nevertheless these honest workmen were among those who contributed to the development of the art, and it was during this period that they did their best and their most daring work. They educated the public, taught it to *see* and to use its imagination—not as Delluc and Sjöström did but with comparable results. From an historical point of view it would

147

be wrong entirely to overlook them. All of them worked amidst hostile businessmen, who were determined at all costs to keep the cinema down to the lowest and most unintelligent level. The Société des Ciné-romans was still active, Louis Feuillade continued to produce for it, and it was too much to expect the old type of films to disappear all at once.

Antoine continued to keep in suspense those admirers who believed in him, and made a rather pleasant adaptation of *Mlle. de la Seiglière,* in which some landscape shots with animals, a farm as pretty as a picture and some bounding deer were much admired. Unfortunately he remained fundamentally a man of the theater, so that when he directed a film of Zola's *Earth* he mustered up the whole Comédie Française—Bovy, Alexandre, Hervé and the rest —for his cast and also considerably tamed down that brutal story.

Louis Nalpas, who had come into the picture during the war as manager of the Film d'Art, had the good sense to take Louis Delluc under his wing. His *Sultane de l'Amour* was well liked. In this Arabian Nights' tale the loves of an Arab prince and the Sultana Daoulah occupied a great deal of footage, and Marcel Levesque played a very unusual role in it. It was all pretty obvious, even the shots of the shimmering waters of the pool into which Nas'r was eventually to plunge, but people found it quite pleasing, just as they did later his *Tristan and Isolde,* made in the Italian manner.

Films of this kind enjoyed all the more success because during the war there had been so little originality. But the large public, of course, in no way interested in aesthetic problems, much preferred *L'Agonie des Aigles* which Dominique-Bernard Deschamps directed in 1921, featuring Gaby Morlay and a great deal of sentimentality about ex-soldiers. They liked even better Diamant-Berger's *Three Musketeers* (1921), one of the biggest postwar successes. Aimé Simon-Girard lent the figure of d'Artagnan a great deal of presence, and all the furniture was reputed to be authentic. The cowboy films had taught the French directors how to put movement into their work, and as Fairbanks' *Three Musketeers* had been denied exhibition everybody thoroughly enjoyed this jolly but rather theatrical and mock-heroic picture with its echoes

of the Théâtre de l'Ambigu and its melodramatic effects. As Plan-
chet, Armand Bernard started on his deplorable career. This film,
like the films of Antoine and of Mercanton, was really though
not very obviously the offspring of the good old Film d'Art.

Other directors, able enough and quick to seize upon the discoveries of their more truly creative rivals, also kept the same tradition alive. Léonce Perret now refused to go on playing drunks:
he had grown ambitious, and when at the end of 1923 he directed
Koenigsmark with Huguette Duflos, it was regarded as a national
triumph. The actress bore not the slightest resemblance to Pierre
Benoît's heroine, but scenes such as the hunt, the fire or the lake
in the early morning provided considerable stimulation for all who
regarded themselves as responsive to beauty. Undeniably in films
like *Koenigsmark* the commercial film did give evidence of real
progress and better taste. So did *The Battle*, with Sessue Hayakawa, in which the Japanese actor again gave one of his masterly
and inscrutable performances, while the naval engagement was
directed with considerable skill.

At the close of 1924 a film came along to eclipse the fame of
either the *Three Musketeers*, *The Battle* or *Koenigsmark*, and
brought into prominence a quite able director, Henry Roussel,
who had previously made *Odette Maréchal's Mistake* and *Open
Countenances and Secret Souls*. It also brought into prominence
an exceptional artist who had won fame in the music halls—Raquel
Meller. This film, *Violettes Impériales*, told a charming story of a
little flower girl befriended by Eugénie de Montijo against a Second Empire background: even the more critical people found it
enchanting. The meeting between Napoleon and Eugénie in the
sunny Madrid Square in 1850, the charming groups *à la* Winter-
halter with the Empress surrounded by her ladies in waiting were
really quite ravishing. As for the lovely pale Spanish heroine, as
Jean Tedesco said, "Raquel Meller is the high point of the film
. . . she is more than that, she is one of the wonders of the world."
She afterwards played in various mediocre films, and then went
back again to dance and sing in Spain and comes our way but
seldom, pale as ever, huskier of voice and more beautiful than
before.

In May 1924 the one man died who had perhaps done more than anybody in France to create a proper understanding of the motion picture–Louis Delluc. Shortly afterwards a strange film by Julien Duvivier and Lepage appeared, *A Machine for Recreating Life*, a film about the motion picture which included a considerable quantity of old movies, from *Lunch Hour at the Lumière Factory* to *Brasier Ardent* and even *Caligari*. One month later Chaplin's *A Woman of Paris* opened in Paris. The period during which the film as an art was being developed had come to an end.

EXPERIMENTS

Who were the men that nurtured the growth of this youthful art? Which were the important films made in France? First there was a Loïe Fuller film, based on a story by Elizabeth, Queen of Rumania, *Le Lys de la Vie*. Superficially it was just a modern fairy tale, with a Prince Charming setting out in search of the flower of happiness. But this film, which featured a dancer and made use of the technique of the dance, opened a whole new world to the motion picture. It made use of slow motion, in which the dancers looked like budding flowers, it made use of shadow shows and of negative in place of positive. In the Land of Fear the Princess is pursued by bodiless hands against a sheer black background. Loïe Fuller discovered all the romanticism of the German film that flowered in *Caligari* and *Destiny* in this picture, which was the first film to be conceived and carried out as a visual composition.

In the same year, 1920, Jules Romains published his scenario *Donogoo*,* never as yet filmed. This already famous writer now elected to think in terms of cinematography and to make use of certain technical film devices–almost to invent them–such as the use of a series of extremely brief shots to indicate simultaneity.

---

* *Donogoo-Tonka ou les Miracles de la Science. Conte cinématographique*, Gallimard, Paris, 1920. *Donogoo* was filmed in Germany in 1936 by Schunzel, with both German and French versions.

Mack Sennett had played with the idea,* Jules Romains gave it its letters of introduction into society, Delluc and Gance actually used it. *Donogoo* is only a book, but it helped enormously to make the motion picture aware of itself and its potentialities, and the author of *Men of Good Will* must be given some credit for this. But still *Donogoo* was only a book and *Le Lys de la Vie* only a fantasy. Who made the true films?

MARCEL L'HERBIER

One of the first films to attract the attention of the intellectuals after the Armistice was *Rose France* by Marcel L'Herbier, who had been Mercanton's scenarist during the war. Before being converted to the films, he had been an aesthete-author and published some Wildean volumes like *Le Jardin des Jeux Secrets*. *Rose France* had a gloomy and ridiculous story about a young American millionaire extremely jealous of the girl he loves because she loved only "la belle France," which did not prevent him, however, from giving 100,000 francs towards the rehabilitation of the devastated areas after the war. The film is also full of the worst kind of overacting, gush and patriotism, but notwithstanding its faults there was something of real interest here, even in spite of certain moments in very questionable taste, as when, between two scenes verging on the torrid, there comes an enormous close-up of the mutilated hand of an ex-soldier holding a rose. This was violently criticized, and rightly so, but its daring and indecency indicated the liberties that the film was about to take, though possibly Marcel L'Herbier did not do so very much to assist this. His *Carnival of Truth*, the following year, was admired by a few. It was nothing more than a melodrama tricked out with millionaires and blackmail, a revolver and a masked ball. There was a certain boldness of technique about it, but L'Herbier has always been

---

* The authors seem deliberately to overlook the fact that Griffith's *Intolerance* had introduced rapid cutting as, for instance, in a scene near the climax when successive shots measure, in feet, as follows: 1, 3, 2, 2, 2, 1, 2, 2, 2, 1½, 2, 2½, 2, 4, ½.

handicapped by his rather feeble romanticism and his undistinguished plots. *L'Homme du Large*, made in 1920, also based on a Balzac novel, was infinitely better, for here his adaptation was extraordinarily skillful and smooth. The simplicity and the loveliness of the landscapes—despite an overemphasis on the picturesque elements of Brittany (like the famous "pardon" scene)—make it possible to see this production again, even today, with considerable pleasure, though it is perhaps a trifle too smooth and too clever. At the time it helped the French to realize, as Antoine and the Swedes had also done, how important natural settings can be.

Don Juan and Faust, in 1922, was rather different. This was an original story, not an adaptation, though it evinced a strong literary flavor with its tale about an encounter between Faust and Don Juan. Here too some major faults prevented one's wholehearted admiration, but L'Herbier in his clumsy way definitely established the fact that no subject is taboo to the film, not even symbolism and not even thought itself. He reiterated the same thing in another fashion in the sketchy *Prometheus Is a Banker*. This was really the "message" of most of his films at that time.

One of them, however, is of considerably more merit, better even than *L'Homme du Large*: that is, *Eldorado*, produced in 1921. It made a considerable hit. What remains of interest about it is not the romantic tale of the dancer Sibylla, who sacrifices herself for her child, but the technical audacity of the piece, the newly fashionable use of soft focus and the many compositions modeled on Ribera, Velasquez or Goya. In *Eldorado*, with its picturesque Andalusian settings, the film became a plastic art, and not just photographically, either: when Sibylla wanders distraught near the walls of the Alhambra, they become distorted and dim. Besides these technical experiments the face of Eve Francis and the passionate note on which the action is sustained lend a romantic appeal to this film, which is one of the few really successful pieces made during this boldly experimental but fumbling period.

Eventually L'Herbier returned to his literary preoccupations. Towards the end of 1923 he completed *L'Inhumaine*, based on a scenario by MacOrlan, with special music by Darius Milhaud, and sets designed by Fernand Léger, Mallet-Stevens and Caval-canti, all more or less cubist. Eve Francis, with her tragic expression, tried vainly to inject some life into this abstract and false work, one of the biggest of all the intellectual failures of the screen. It was L'Herbier's last experiment: he was compelled for the future to apply what he had learned to commercial films made for the masses.*

JACQUES DE BARONCELLI

Jacques de Baroncelli, whose work was much more uneven than that of L'Herbier, also tried to hit the balance between commerce and art. One must admit that commerce won, as always in such cases, but for a little while after the war he played a role of some importance, for he brought with him, along with the stock in trade of the ordinary film, some excellent qualities. He directed many films, including detective pictures like *The Secret of Lone Star.* He made a quite good one out of Henry Bernstein's *The Squall,* which Delluc did not really admire but considered as competent as *The Cheat.* Actually it was a good deal less absurd, but it was not the sort of thing in which Baron-celli excelled. What he really liked was to make adaptations of famous books in which a landscape could figure and picturesque settings could lend their glamour to the emotional sufferings of the characters. He did this sort of thing very well. In 1919 he had made *Ramuntcho,* which caused something of a controversy about adaptations in general. Though Pathé had insisted on numerous cuts before distributing the film, it made a hit; the general public responded to the director's sensitive handling of landscape and atmosphere as though he had been a painter, and the picture caused a certain amount of talk about "the impressionism of the French film." But Baroncelli was quite without

* This is only one opinion. There is considerable support for the view that *Eldorado* is pretentious nonsense and that L'Herbier's *Late Matthew Pascal* (1925) with Mosjoukine and Lois Moran is a film of abiding interest—unquestionably a better piece than *Eldorado.*

originality, and in none of his films does the background play
a really vital role as it does in the Swedish and the Soviet films:
it always looks like a nice picture postcard. Yet, at the time,
what he did was important.

Balzac's *Le Père Goriot*, Chérau's *Champi-Tortu* and Zola's
Le Rêve were his next efforts to attempt the rather thankless
task of translating literature to the screen—the visual expression
is almost always so much less rich than the written work. His
talents were not fully employed until he tried to catch the loveliness of Bruges on the screen, in a plot he had made up himself
about a bell ringer's daughter, *The Midnight Carillon*, a really
quite respectable effort. But his two best films were to follow
when, after making *The Unknown Woman* in 1923, he directed
Nène and *Pêcheurs d'Islande*.

As for the first of these, he published a revealing letter to
Ernest Pérochon, the author of the novel on which it was based,
explaining that he had changed the heroine from a sturdy peasant
into a sickly girl because she was unhappy and on the screen
physical appearance must correspond to character. (Elmer Rice
has some delightful comments on this in his *Voyage to Purilia*.)
Despite her delicate constitution Nène did not commit suicide
in the film as she had in the book, because, Baroncelli explained
very seriously, people did not like drowned women. Pérochon
took these explanations as best he could, though sadly, and nobody seemed to see the humor of such a correspondence, so
eloquent of the cinema's hatred for nuances. It tells us much
about Baroncelli.

There were some handsome landscapes in *Nène*, but it was
in *Pêcheurs d'Islande* that Baroncelli came into his own. Grace-
ful Sandra Milowanoff as Gaud, the cloudy skies, the young
woman walking in the cemetery of the drowned sailors with its
crosses that mark no graves, the sense of the sea and of death
which it evoked all combined to lend this film a quite remarkable sureness and power. Able though he was, Baroncelli lacked
many requisites: he lacked real talent, he was never able to rise
above a sort of proficiency born of experience, or to do more
than create rather hackneyed or sentimental imitations of literary

works rendered even more hackneyed or sentimental by the conventions of the motion picture (as his letter to Pérochon shows). Later on Baroncelli, like Poirier and Léonce Perret, was to catch the public favor without really making many concessions, since he had little to sacrifice. Yet when one recalls his *Pêcheurs d'Islande* it somehow seems a pity, but there it is: compromise is always perilous.

FROM LÉON POIRIER TO RAYMOND BERNARD

It was on the score of landscape scenes that Léon Poirier, too, was later to make claim to artistry, though he had started out with a mixed variety of productions, a few of which were rather ambitious. In 1920 Edmond Fleg had brought him the scenario of *Le Penseur,* a rather oversimple affair which, however, gained considerable notice because, as in some of L'Herbier's and Delluc's films, it attempted to express ideas. Its hero, obsessed by the thought of Rodin's sculpture, which provided a theme for the whole film, discovered how to read people's thoughts. This gave rise to a host of superimposed images—revelers turned into parrots and jazz players into skeletons. The picture was accepted as "a film of ideas," and it actually was an attempt to delineate thoughts, though greatly abusing the fashionable device of superimposed pictures. Poirier afterwards gave up such experiments. His *Jocelyn* and his *Geneviève,* faithfully modeled on Lamartine, proved that he had an excellent sense of the past and a great deal of taste. People were delighted with their period costumes and with their landscape shots, which seemed to flood the screen with air. For their period they were two quite successful attempts at making intelligent films. In 1924 Poirier scored a success with *La Brière,* Alphonse de Chateaubriant's novel, in which he did justice to both the desolate atmosphere of *La Brière* and Austin's wild adventure, getting into it much more than Baroncelli could ever have managed to do, since he was dealing not with charm but with a character of some weight, alternately friendly and hostile, which he succeeded in delineating with considerable sureness and skill. In the French postwar school of landscape films this picture of Léon Poirier's entitles him to a distinct place. There were high hopes for him and also for Raymond Bernard, who had directed Max Linder in *Le Petit Café* during the war, and now in 1920 attempted a psychological comedy based on a story by his famous father Tristan Bernard, *The Secret of Rosette Lambert*. Today not even Mallet-Stevens' settings can prevent this "subtle" comedy from boring one. It was Raymond Bernard who also in 1924 essayed the historical spectacle, *The Miracle of the Wolves*.

Fairbanks had recently made costume films popular, but history as reconstructed by the French is very different from history reconstructed in the gay American manner. To Raymond Bernard's credit must be reckoned his scrupulous care, some handsome scenes such as that of the medieval Mystery play, and a good deal of skill in narrating a thin plot taken from an unworthy novel. The taking of the city (filmed in Carcassonne) was as well done as the famous miracle in which hungry wolves were seen to crouch down piously in front of a young girl praying. Charles Dullin gave an excellent portrayal of Louis XI, radiant with youth and love of France, so unlike the stereotyped portrait. *The Miracle of the Wolves*, which one can still look at today with some pleasure and which has become quite a famous film, has nothing in it of the fire, the wildness of Abel Gance's best work. Everything about it is well managed, it is never ridiculous and there are no serious faults in it, but there is also no great virtue in it either: it is one of those *genteel* films.

Léon Poirier, Raymond Bernard and Baroncelli were really literary men. There were others at this period who tried, somewhat timidly, to inject a little intelligence into the motion picture. Especially must we note the work of one of the few women directors, Mme. Germaine Dulac. She made a great many films and has disowned most of them, for she turned her hand to almost every kind of material—not only a *Belle Dame Sans Merci* but also a serial called *Gossette*. She was apparently only really interested in one film, *The Smiling Madame Beudet*, from a play by André Obey and Denys Amiel, filmed in collaboration with Obey. This was a psychological drama, for Denys Amiel and Jean-Jacques Bernard had made a reputation by sponsoring a new style, giving particular stress to words and gestures apparently of no great importance. This play, an example of the new "école du silence," and modeled on *Madame Bovary*, seemed an intimate drama that demanded to be filmed. Germaine Dulac proved in it, with extraordinary skill and subtlety, that the motion picture as it became more refined could exactly reduplicate the effects of certain stage plays. She did not prove that it can express psychological subtleties.

LOUIS DELLUC

Yet there were many people who thought that she had done so, among them Louis Delluc—the most important figure in the French film world at that time.

Delluc was an extraordinary fellow—novelist, reporter and journalist. His reviews of films, frequently quite crazy, are alive with wit and sense and are extraordinarily prophetic. Passionately interested in the cinema, he made few films, though he wrote several scenarios which other people made into films pretty much as he had intended them to be. Germaine Dulac collaborated with him on *La Fête Espagnol*. He introduced to the screen Claudel's attractive interpreter, Mme. Eve Francis. Through his articles, his conversation, the example that he set and his undoubted talent he did more than any other man in France to develop an art of the film. But for him we should hardly have learned to appreciate the motion picture.

The films that he directed can only be considered in relation to the time when they were made. *La Fête Espagnole*, one of the best, seems today a rambling affair: the heroine, Soledad, is loved by two men, who urge her to choose between them. She says she will accept whichever one "comes back alone." They fight, and kill each other, as Soledad goes off with a stranger. In this slow-moving and short film, which displays the lingering influence both of Mérimée and of Louÿs, there is a certain admirable warmth and passion, as well as an individual style.

In most documentary films we are shown everything, nothing

is omitted; but when Delluc and Mme. Dulac want to include a bullfight they show us one small sunny corner of the arena with one or two cruel faces, and yet contrive to suggest all the atmosphere of Spain. Such conciseness is pure cinema. Also in this film Delluc, quite exceptionally, came nearer to the ballet than to psychological drama.

Afterwards Delluc threw himself into innumerable experiments, not all of which were successful, though all of them were useful. Like L'Herbier and Poirier and the Swedes, he was in love with superimposed images and with all those tricks that free the film from the laws of the visible world; nowadays they seem rather clumsy to us. In *Fumée Noire*, a sort of detective story, the film opens with a conversation between a husband and wife, after their mysterious Uncle Patrick has just turned up. They are saying, jokingly, "How do you know that I have never killed anyone?" "And how do you know that you were the first man in my life?" The uncle dies, the husband and wife lose their heads and each begins to suspect the other. It was not a very good film, though it made liberal use of those things that delight amateurs of the cinema—foreshortened shots, "mental impressions" photographed from above, settings in strongly contrasted blacks and whites, and superimposed images, all very much in Delluc's own style, as were also an excessive interest in psychological behavior and an exaggerated habit of showing what people were thinking by means of oversimplified images. The commercial films were later to abuse this use of superimposed images to indicate what characters were imagining.

In *Silence* we see a man waiting for a woman. When at last she arrives, he has killed himself, for while waiting he fancied that he saw his dead wife, whom he had killed because he believed her unfaithful, come back to protest her innocence. The wife was played with a great deal of feeling by Eve Francis, and Delluc attempted to tell her story by a liberal use of superimposed images to convey both what the husband was remembering and what he was imagining. It was of course a mistaken method but one which did much to extend film technique and usefully render it more supple. So did *Le Tonnerre* and *Le Chemin d'Ernoa*.

La Femme de Nulle Part, made in 1922, contrasted the fate of a woman who had sacrificed everything for love and that of another woman who had resisted temptation and remained in her husband's home. The first woman has nothing left but memories. It was a really daring experiment, this purely psychological story, and some of the shots at the opening, the child's balloon floating into the screen, have a purely cinematic quality. When the camera shoots down on the staircase where the heroine stands as she recalls the past, it catches the sensation of her own giddiness. At the end, when Eve Francis in her flowing dress walks along the deserted road through a wide bare landscape, there is something moving about it even today. So uncompromising a treatment as he used—and a basic approach which is radically wrong—are rather disturbing, and one asks oneself whether the film by relying only on imagery and a succession of shots can really bring a character to life. The conclusion is that it cannot. That is what makes Delluc's films, intelligent and arresting though they be, seem old-fashioned and faded.

However, he also made *Fièvre*, his best film and perhaps a really great film. It is too slow and too insistent, but it brought to the screen for the first time that atmosphere of low haunts and brief encounters which was so popular after the war. In a sailors' bar in Marseilles a group of extraordinarily individual and convincing characters are gathered—the woman Patience, the little clerk, the man with the gray hat. Then sailors arrive from some distant port, laden with curios. There is a brawl, someone is killed, the police appear and a little Oriental girl finally manages to creep up to a flower she has been gazing at enviously—only to discover that it is artificial. A cloud of disillusionment seems to hang over this picture, from which Jean Epstein of *Cœur Fidèle* and Cavalcanti of *En Rade* were to learn so much. It contained any number of devices which were afterwards to be worked to death but were absolutely new then.

Before he died in 1924, Delluc had finished *L'Inondation*, based on a Provençal novel by André Corthis. Eve Francis was admirable in it as a badly-dressed and bewildered country woman. It was not the shots of the flood nor the plot that were important; it was the attention given to the expression on people's faces, and to the carefully convincing grouping and composition. The realism of Antoine, the poetic realism of the Swedes had taught Delluc a great deal. Had he lived he would perhaps have helped the French film to produce the rustic dramas and folk films that it lacks and which it is so well adapted to create. In *L'Inondation* with its shadowy interiors, its sharp and lifelike exteriors (which were only used as settings, since Delluc cared more about men than about things) one cannot escape this feeling. Had he been able to put more vitality into his films, had he loved the world more, he could have done it.

In any event, even if we regard him quite unjustly as merely a theoretician, as one who dreamed of films rather than made them, Louis Delluc is still the most interesting of all the artists born of this new art in France before René Clair. His *Fête Espagnole* and *Fièvre* remain memorable, and in everything that he did, not only in his books, there is the same intelligence, the same restless fire, the same feeling for people and for things. Had he come ten years later Delluc would have found a more developed instrument to his hand and an easier task. As it was he had perforce to become a pioneer, always an ungrateful if honorable role. Certainly no one in France before him had set out deliberately to reveal the beauty that is in a human face, the beauty that is in the world about us. No one before had made films like these, expressive of the pathos of failure and the illusory nature of life, and quite ironical. It was this atmosphere of disenchantment which really lent a certain unity to his otherwise loosely constructed works, that sought to express the diverse elements of our world. To documentary films and dramatic adaptations alike such utter disenchantment can lend something both subtle and profound. All existence is painful, all life a failure, so *La Femme de Nulle Part* and *Fièvre* suggest: all the flowers we long to pluck prove to be artificial. Louis Delluc was one of the first French directors to stamp his work with his own personality and with a sort of pessimistic poetry.

Among the directors in whom the highest hopes reposed, who seemed best fitted to carry out Delluc's theories and realize his ambitions, was Jean Epstein. He, too, came from the world of literature, a rather pretentious world. He is a bad writer, and his recent essays are hardly better than his *Lyroscopie*. Delluc and René Clair seem to have been the only two film men with any literary ability.

He began in collaboration with Jean Benoit-Lévy with a film about Pasteur, made at the time of the centenary. His real debut was *The Red Inn*, from one of Balzac's stories. It was not a particularly adroit affair, burdened with period costumes and wigs as it was, but two scenes earned him favorable notice—the card scene and that of the execution. In the same year, 1923, he also made *Cœur Fidèle*, which many people found delightful, though, as it was badly constructed, it annoyed all those who regarded *Koenigsmark* as a masterpiece. It was nevertheless a work of merit, probably made under the influence of *Fièvre*. The sequence of the country fair, where the mobility of the camera made it seem actually to participate in the general movement, raised the film far above the ordinary level, and its ordinary everyday characters, its rather squalid atmosphere, evoked a sort of popular poetry such as René Clair was later so delightfully to express. But Clair transforms everything into fantasy whereas Epstein is addicted to realism, his peculiar *forte*. His special merit arises from an accumulation of details, an emphasis on truthfulness to life and a considerable technical ability. *Cœur Fidèle* established prostitutes and pimps and low haunts in the postwar cinema imagery, which Carco had first introduced and MacOrlan had improved upon. The film which at the time seemed so daring today seems very simple, though in a manner which reminds one of *A Girl in Every Port* and *Lonesome*.

Towards the end of 1923 Jean Epstein also directed *La Belle Nivernaise*, after Alphonse Daudet, and so entered the ranks of the French landscapists. Everyone knows this story of the child who had been adopted by boatmen, then found by her wealthy relations, who is unhappy at school and only regains happiness when she escapes to freedom and her beloved boat "La Belle Nivernaise." It is a charming story, charmingly handled by Epstein, with its beautiful riverside settings and that rather melancholy feeling for nature which afterwards was to become one of his most appealing qualities. The film was not as important in his development as *Cœur Fidèle*, but it was skillful and moving.

There was much to be expected of the young man who had made these two pictures, and there seemed little likelihood of his relapsing into the commercial slickness of a Baroncelli. His honest craftsmanship, his sensitive approach to the object and his frank acceptance of facts would doubtless preserve him from such a course. Epstein was in fact apparently to create a world of his own, a rather harsh world but swept by clean breezes. Alas, in the years to come he often gave the lie to such predictions: it was a crime to be reckoned against the cinema that it made so gifted a man into what he now is. Yet we must not forget Epstein's early contribution.

JACQUES FEYDER

At about this time an honest workman also made his entry into the field with no great flourish of trumpets. This was Jacques Feyder. In 1921 he was given the job of adapting *L'Atlantide* from the famous novel of Pierre Benoît (who, incidentally, received a mere 6,000 francs for the rights). The monumental Napierkowska was engaged to represent Antinéa, whose body was that of a young girl. Everyone thought her ridiculous but the film had a sort of vigor, though no wit whatsoever. In much the same style he also directed Raquel Meller in *Carmen*, but nobody would have dreamed of ranking him above Léonce Perret had he not in 1923 made *Crainquebille* with Féraudy.

This film is still of interest today. In it Feyder employed the device of the dream which has been such a stand-by to other directors—Dr. Mathieu has a sort of nightmare in which he sees the judges flying about like great birds, and the police court as a sea of eyeballs staring at the bewildered Crainquebille. When the testimony was being given, the screen showed a colossal policeman with a tiny witness for the defense. All this was done with great technical ingenuity, which Feyder was seldom to make use of in the future and which somewhat obscured his real gifts, for what gave *Crainquebille* its abiding merit was that here for the first time there was an attempt to bare the mysteries of a human soul. From Anatole France's mocking tale Feyder had made a patient, almost heavy film in which he tried to express a psychological truth. He is one of the few who later developed fairly complex characters on the screen and by purely pictorial means gave life to a pessimistic but accurate study of human nature. In *Crainquebille* it was realized with some surprise that the director of *L'Atlantide* without in any way sacrificing his skill had evinced definite originality, and an originality which sprang from within.

ABEL GANCE

Unquestionably the most famous of all the directors of this period, the one in whose hands the future of the French film was thought to lie, was Abel Gance.

Immediately after the war, already famous by reason of his preposterous *Tenth Symphony* and *Mater Dolorosa*, he made his first "superfilm," *J'Accuse* (1919). He had been planning it for quite some time, as he had too *The End of the World*. His notebook, so we are told, contained lines such as: "Transfiguration of a brute into a good and kindly man through war sufferings." "The birth of religious sentiment in a writer who believed in nothing at all." "How hymns like the Marseillaise are created."

It was in such a mood that he evolved his "modern tragedy" in which Séverin-Mars and Romuald Joubé took part and Blaise Cendrars too, as Gance's assistant. *J'Accuse* is really a horribly melodramatic affair about a woman who is raped by German soldiers and has a child. The husband suspects that it is the child of his best friend, who is, in fact, in love with the woman. All the characters shortly find themselves at the Front, in search of a heroic death. People were staggered by this medley of humanitarian and patriotic ideas. As for its artistic merits, Louis Delluc much preferred the equally absurd *Zone of Death*, which seemed less stilted and more original because it had some lyrical quality. In *J'Accuse* he saw nothing but some well-composed pictures, too well composed, and compared it also to *The Cheat*.

J'Accuse today would seem supremely ridiculous. The cuts which were made in it merely emphasized the clumsier and coarser elements in the film. Also, it should be realized that Gance had used color in several places. In the opening sequence there was a huge close-up of an enormous red *Légion d'honneur*. In the following scene, a soldier with an enormous vermilion wound in his left breast cries out as he dies: "Never thought they'd slap a *Légion d'honneur* on me!" This use of color was a device not at all characteristic of Gance.

After *J'Accuse* this same man nevertheless evolved an extraordinarily suggestive, vivid and striking cinematographic vocabulary such as he used in *La Roue*, which he began to work on in 1919 first in Nice, then in the Col de Voza and the Bossons glacier, finishing it by 1921. It was so long that it cost two and a half million francs and could only be shown in a curtailed version. Like Griffith's *Intolerance* and von Stroheim's *Greed* it is one of the monstrosities of the cinema, but an extraordinarily important monstrosity.

The story is unbelievably complicated. An engine driver finds a little girl in the wreckage of a train smash that has killed her parents. He adopts her and falls in love with her, as does also his son, but he marries her off to an engineer. There are accidents and catastrophes galore, the engine driver goes blind, his son and the engineer are killed, leaving the modern Oedipus and his Antigone together. This gloomy tale, redolent of Zola and his *La Bête Humaine*, of Hugo and a dozen other romantic writers, would have been laughed off the screen had not everything else been effaced by its technical mastery and a very genuine and even nobly poetic quality which this technique served to express.

The early part of the film vividly re-creates the mechanical world of steel and smoke and steam and tracks. No one had realized before how amazingly the film can express the modern world or to what extent a new type of pantheism can endow inanimate things with soul, with a life of their own. It was because he did this and not because of the plot he developed that Gance's work had real worth. Signals and wheels, pistons and manometers seemed to *live*. The camera with a hitherto unknown flexibility, with almost startling ubiquity hovers over all of them, revealing them in unfamiliar guises and aspects, lending them an epic quality. Inevitably at times Gance goes wrong: the engine expiring amid a bank of flowers is almost comic. Yet virtually throughout the film the moment he turns from human beings to the mechanical world he sweeps us irresistibly along with him.

What is more, *La Roue* was the first work of any real scope to be composed according to an exact rhythmical pattern. "The film," Gance had said, "is the poetry of light." He regarded the rhythm of a film as being akin to that of Latin verse, with its long and short feet; and *La Roue* was actually based on a careful metrical pattern, with blank film punctuating the end of scenes and sequences. In imitation of *Donogoo*, Gance made use of rapid cutting to give an impression of simultaneous happenings and discovered how to achieve an accelerated tempo by means of shorter and shorter shots to give the feeling of flight, of giddy descent and of inevitable catastrophe. The most stirring moments of *La Roue* are those which this brilliant and unhesitating technical ability emphasizes.

After *La Roue* it was clear what Gance was to become. His disorderly but undeniable talent was to be irresistibly applied to a rather vague ideology, to pathos and to improbabilities. He would contrive to redeem everything by his very great gifts, by that inventiveness and vigor which were to make of him one of the most unequal but one of the most powerful of film men and, in fact, a sort of Hugo of the screen.

MAX LINDER

While French directors were busying themselves usefully with experiments, the most famous French film actor was making most of his films abroad, and they had little or no relationship to what was happening in France. Max Linder continued being Max Linder, and the only influence to which he was subject was really a sort of boomerang, for he was now undoubtedly influenced by Chaplin. Before his tragic death this most charming of prewar actors, the original king of mirth, had appeared to good purpose in several feature films which are positively astonishing to see again today because one so keenly regrets having forgotten them in the meantime.

He made *Be My Wife* (excellent fooling full of gaiety and of invention), *The Three Must-get-theres* and *Seven Years' Bad Luck.* Back in Europe he made *Help!* with Abel Gance (a fantasy with some almost tragic episodes) and then went to Austria to make his last picture, *The King of the Circus. The Three Must-get-theres* was a rather coarse parody of no great importance, though it was amusing to see the three musketeers springing out of bed when they are needed during the night and sliding down a pole like firemen to land plunk on the backs of their steeds. *The King of the Circus* was much better. All the first part is devoted to the quarrel between Count Max, a confirmed roisterer, and his uncle. One morning after a night's heavy drinking, Max is discovered asleep in bed in the window of a big furniture store, while a delighted crowd gathers to see him. The latter half, in which Max, in love with a circus rider, becomes an animal trainer, is less attractive, though Chaplin had not forgotten it when he made *The Circus.* The troubles which Max has with the lion, though often fairly obvious, are extremely funny.

Linder's best film was unquestionably *Seven Years' Bad Luck.* The opening is excellent: Max's servant has broken his master's mirror, and in order to conceal the fact he makes one of the other servants stand behind the empty frame and imitate everything that Max does. It is an old music-hall turn which the Marx

Brothers have also used, but there is something really delightful about the way in which the consequences of the situation are developed and the whole thing is carried off so airily. When Max finds out what is really happening he naturally tries to give his double a shrewd kick, but in the meantime a new glass has been put in the frame and he breaks it. The rest is rather dragged out, though there are two amazingly funny incidents—Max distributing free railroad tickets, and the journey he takes while disguised as a Negro.

What did this first-rate actor lack that prevented him from going further? Broadly, he lacked imagination and also, in order to become the equal of Chaplin (whom he closely resembled and so many of whose comedy devices he previously had sketched out), he lacked the skill to mingle a deeper emotion with laughter. The character that he most commonly played was that of a reveler or man about town, whereas the character that Chaplin plays is a tramp. There is a vast difference here: the poor tramp with his humility and his resignation gets knocked about both by men and by things generally, whereas the reveler takes his misfortunes lightly and so we take them lightly too. He is a purely comic figure out of vaudeville, and he has little opportunity to touch our emotions. But limited though his comedy may have been, Linder's films were nevertheless of very great importance. But for them we should never have come to love Keaton or Lloyd or even Chaplin: he taught them an immense amount. He possessed an infinite share of wit. The only real French comedian disappeared when he died.

In the next years the French directors were to complete their experiments. Actually they tended to conclude them with compromises of a more or less regrettable nature. Nevertheless, for three or four years the French film had given birth to much that was new and original. It is all the more regrettable that it has since lost that distinction.

2. *The Russian Film*

WHEN the Russian Revolution had been successfully concluded, the Russian studios were bankrupt and virtually useless. Actors and directors fled first to the Crimea, then to Germany or, more of them, to France. Everything had to be reorganized, a task which was not completed until 1925. Up to that time the real Russian films—though few recognize it today—were those made by the Czarist *émigrés* in Paris, where they continued the work that they had started during the war and with the same personnel, with Protazanov and Volkov and, even more important, with Mosjoukine. Their work was strange and chaotic, sometimes overclever, and destined to die out or to become denationalized in exile, but it produced some attractive films immediately after the war. Meanwhile in the U.S.S.R. other men on the track of new cinematic laws and theories were laying the groundwork for Eisenstein and Pudovkin's future success. Here it is well to consider how it was that this nation, cut in half by the turn of events, nevertheless contrived to express on the screen the unity of the Russian genius.

THE ÉMIGRÉS

It was at Montreuil, first with Yermoliev and then with Albatross, that the Russian exiles tried to preserve both their customs and their ideas about films. It would be foolish to consider them as a branch of the French film, since their producers, directors and actors and even at times their financial backing were Russian. Rather were they a branch of old Russia planted in new soil. Of course, as the genuinely Russian firms disappeared the group was broken up, actors took engagements elsewhere, either in France or abroad, and directors likewise. But for a few years this bit of Russia-in-France preserved its entity. Naturally the ideas of French directors influenced these people; in fact it might almost be said that their chief ambition seemed to be (and they were extremely able folk) to imitate and almost to popularize the boldest of French experimental production. They disguised what they were doing, however, with a romantic, or perhaps exotic, flavor which recalled the more famous of the films which had emanated from the old Russia.

Without much question, the most distinguished of the exiles was Ivan Mosjoukine, who enjoyed international fame for a few years. He had played in any number of films under Volkov and Protazanov and was to direct again, as he had formerly done in *The Prosecuting Attorney*. He made *A Child of the Carnival* and played in Robert Boudrioz's *Tempests* and Volkov's *House of Mystery*, then later in Epstein's *The Lion of the Mongols*, *The Late Matthew Pascal*, under L'Herbier, in Tourjanski's *Michael Strogoff*, in *Casanova* and in *Le Rouge et le Noir*. His films were shown in America, whither he departed in 1926. No matter who his director might be, he himself was the person who actually inspired and controlled the films he played in. His most characteristic films were *Kean* and *Shadows that Pass*, both by Volkov, and *Le Brasier Ardent*, for which he wrote the scenario and which he also directed.

His acting was somewhat theatrical, and his favorite expression, like that of Sessue Hayakawa, was one of impassiveness or, ironically, one of stupidity. He had, however, a wide variety of gestures and attitudes and he loved to play multiple roles. In one of his earliest pictures, *The Parliamentarian*, he played two parts, while *Le Brasier Ardent* showed him in a variety of guises. In Volkov's *House of Mystery* his characterization proceeded by a series of explosions separated by long intervals of imperturbable calm. This was not a bad film, it was rather exciting and quite well constructed, and included a brilliant scene of convicts escaping from prison. *Casanova*, on the other hand, with all its scenery and Venetian splendor was only a star-vehicle without much real action. As for *Le Rouge et le Noir*, poor Stendhal's book had been changed into an adventure story with much galloping through woods, revolutionary risings, duels, orgies and fights in taverns. Mosjoukine always loved adventure, like Douglas Fairbanks, and in *Casanova* he did battle with twelve enemies at once in the best tradition of Lagardère. In all his best films one finds the same rather wearisome skill, the same passion for surmounting difficulties, for technical tricks. *Shadows that Pass*, a burlesque with sentimental additions in which he attempted to reveal a new aspect of himself, somewhat reminds one of Keaton and of Chaplin but also of Sacha Guitry. As for *Kean*, this was pure romanticism: Volkov and Mosjoukine between them had made of Alexandre Dumas' play a skillful and rather sober affair in which the actor could give free vent to his passion for the theater and for make-up. Two high spots are famous: the death of Kean (almost pure melodrama) and the sailor's jig in the Coal Hole—an amazing scene in which the dance, led by Mosjoukine and Koline (who played the part of the stage prompter), develops into a mad rout. The camera caught it first in longshot, then just the heads of the dancers thrown back in abandon, the joined hands, the lively legs. Every known resource was used here, and for the sake of this bit of bravura *Kean* is worthy of being remembered.

Le Brasier Ardent, 1923, seems entirely composed of bravura. Here a whole series of experiments was drawn upon, those of Epstein and Delluc, those of Loïe Fuller and of Wiene and even of the old Russian films. (Volkov had made *Satan Laughs*, an earlier version of *Le Brasier Ardent*.) It was a really remarkable picture, little understood at the time but full of good things. Not wholly unlike James Cruze's *Beggar on Horseback*, it starts off with a nightmare in which out of a confused background a man materializes, calmly, now as a beggar, now as a bishop or a fashionable dancer. When the victim of this nightmare wakes she tells herself that it all came from the various disguises adopted by the detective X in the novel she had been reading before she fell asleep. But there is a burglary in her home, and her husband goes to consult this same detective X. The two characters now find themselves in situations which correspond to those of the nightmare, and Natalie Lissenko remembers, each time, the dream symbol (beggar, dancer or bishop) which corresponds to her present feelings.

The slickness of this device might have made the film seem

childish had it not been enlivened with imagination. For instance, the heroine while thinking about her past life is looking at some negatives of old photos and they come to life, but as negatives, with the blacks and whites transposed. Some quite lovely shots, like those of the lights of an automobile passing through a little town hidden in darkness, a goodly number of amusing incidents, like those of the extraordinary detectives' club, made *Le Brasier Ardent* very popular both with the general public and with those interested in the resources of cinematography. Slow motion, rapid motion, soft focus, negative in place of positive and rapid cutting were all utilized in this delightful tale of detectives and sentimental intrigue against a background of Paris and its underworld.

The faults of *Kean* and *Le Brasier Ardent* are self-evident: they lie in excessive cleverness and an abuse of technical devices. But merits such as they contain are not so common that we can afford to dismiss the films, faults or no faults. A somewhat mechanical fantasy of this sort has its value and belongs properly with fertile inventiveness. It is a great pity that Mosjoukine soon abandoned such experiments for films of a more popular order in which he was little more than a talented actor. The other Russian directors, though less ambitious, had already set him an example. Tourjanski made sumptuous films like *The Arabian Nights Tales, The Masked Woman* or adaptations from de Maupassant (*That Pig Morin, The Ordonnance*) and finally scored a real hit with *Prince Charming* and its lavish settings. There was nothing original about any of them, they were simply capably made. Every now and then the exiles, with considerable melancholy, remembered that they were Russians: Strizhinski made a *Taras Bulba* for Yermoliev in 1923. At other times they attempted to pay tribute to the country of their adoption, as when Protazanov filmed Bourget's *Sense of Death*. Delluc reproached him with never having abandoned the theatrical traditions of the prewar Russian film, which he compared rather unfairly to the Italian film. The really interesting thing about this film was a young actor who appeared in it. In *Le Crapouillot* M. René Kerdyk wrote that this actor "in the part of the young engineer revealed himself as the Dehelly of the seventh art, or, rather, as an eighth art all of himself." We were to learn more of this man, but not as an actor. His name was René Clair.

Protazanov * also bid fair to escape Delluc's criticism in a rather meritorious piece, *The Shadow of Sin.* In this simple little film about two cousins who fall in love with the same woman there were some attractive outdoor scenes, especially one of a grape harvest. Nature was here taking a part in a Russian *émigré's* film as it was to do in so many Soviet pictures. The most interesting of the exiles, with the exception of Mosjoukine, was one whose work lay outside the usual channels. He had collaborated with Protazanov in *Towards the Light* and *For a Night of Love,* but from 1921 he began to work by himself and rediscovered in a new series of fairy tales the spirit of Méliès himself. This man, Ladislas Starevich, holds a quite individual place in the cinema, something akin to that of Disney.

As he had done previously in Russia, he consecrated all his talents to the making of marionette films. *The Marriage of Babylas, The Scarecrow, The Frogs Who Wanted a King, The Little Nightingale, In the Spider's Web, The Queen of the Butterflies* created an unforgettable and delicious world. Occasionally some human figure, a little girl perhaps, appeared among the flying fish, the animals that talk, the swollen frog, the extraordinary vegetation. (In *The Little Street Singer* it was Starevich's daughter, Nina Star.) The pleasure these films afford comes from the charm of these terrestrial or submarine landscapes, from their ballets of beasts and vegetables. A frog made out of cloth or paper climbs up a ladder to the top of a toadstool to harangue the crowd. The movements of his lips, the trembling of the leaves and the branches is clearly visible. In *The Town Rat and the Country Rat*, mice perform a complicated dance during the banquet. Elsewhere demons play cards for souls. Their solidity gives the marionette film a delightful consistency which makes it superior as a materialization of dreams to the animated cartoon. It brings the genuine world of childhood before us, a world of dolls' houses and mechanical toys in which we can imagine get-

* He returned to the U.S.S.R. in 1925 as a director for Mezhrabpom.

ting into a toy train or winning an automobile race in a kiddie-car.

Starevich was the most eminent of the Russian exiles. His diminutive creations, worked by invisible strings, photographed frame by frame, are truly original; it would be impossible to imitate them. But the other directors also made their contribution. Though they were finally absorbed into the commercial film they nevertheless helped at first to develop the film as art.*

THE BEGINNINGS OF THE SOVIET FILM †

During this time the Russians of the U.S.S.R. were discovering the political and visual capacity of the motion picture, set-

* Though the authors properly recognize the film as a profoundly *popular* art (see p. 14), there are passages here which suggest that they are sometimes misled into confusing would-be "artistic," or highbrow films with examples of genuine cinematic art, which are invariably *popular* in nature, and not, of course, "artistic." Chaplin and Disney and Eisenstein made commercial and popular films for the general public, not "artistic" ones, but theirs is the art of the film.

Avant-garde or experimental films are important because they often hit upon devices which are then incorporated into the commercial films and thus make their contribution to the art of the motion picture.

† This brief section is scrappy and confused, like so much that has been written about the early Soviet film, largely an unknown quantity to other than Russian critics. The only exact account of this period by a non-Russian writer seems to be that of Mr. Jay Leyda in his history of the Soviet film now in preparation. This will undoubtedly be of real service to the student. Meanwhile, it may be helpful to tabulate the main events, and Mr. Leyda has kindly done so.

1918—First newsreel experience of Vertov.
    The first Soviet production group, the Petrograd Kino-Committee, begins work with Lunacharski's scenario *Congestion.*
1919—Nationalization of the cinema industry.
1920—Kuleshov makes a film at the front, *Red Front.*
1922—*Polikushka,* a film by Sanin in collaboration with the actor Moskvin, of the Moscow Art Theatre.
1923—*Little Red Devils,* a popular adventure film made in Georgia by the Goskinprom.
    First issues of Vertov's regular newsreel experiments, *Goskino-Calendar* and *Kino-Truth.*
1924—First professional film by Kuleshov and his workshop, *The Adventures of Mr. West in the Land of the Bolsheviks.*
    Protazanov returns from France and makes *Aelita.*

ting forth upon the extraordinary, almost monumental adventure of the Soviet film, out of which were to evolve eventually five or six real masterpieces.

As we have already seen, many directors had emigrated in 1918. The Russian people, always addicted to spectacles and entertainment, adored the movies; but as there were none to be had, the cinemas had to be closed. Lenin, however, had grasped the enormous importance of the infant industry. "Of all the arts," he said, "the most important for us in my opinion is the film." Gradually the studios were reorganized, raw stock was purchased from abroad and new theories of production outlined under the influence of a young madman called Dziga Vertov.

The first films, however, still bore the stamp of theatrical realism and, when they began to find their way abroad, gave little evidence of propaganda content. This first period of the Soviet film lasted until 1925. Neither French nor American films exerted any influence upon them. Possibly some of their directors may have seen some of the more important foreign films not generally seen by the public, but it is worth noting that Russia was the only country in the world where Chaplin was quite unknown. For that matter Eisenstein is not interested in Chaplin: we have heard him say so. The only influences to which the Soviet films were subject were the German films, their own prerevolutionary films and that of the Russian theater.*

It was from the theater that the Soviet film learned so brilliantly to handle crowds. The Ukrainian director Dovzhenko,

---

Kozintsev and Trauberg and their FEX group enter films with the fantastic *Adventures of an Octoberite.*

1925—Eisenstein's first film, *Strike.*
January 9th, an historical reconstruction by Viskovski.
Potemkin, by Eisenstein.
1926—*Bed and Sofa,* made by Room at Sovkino.
Mother, made by Pudovkin at Mezhrabpom-Russ.

As will be seen from the above, the authors have jumbled the two periods 1919-1923 and 1923-1926 and their comments here are consequently somewhat meaningless.
* Chaplin was not unknown. American films were closely studied and had enormous influence; Eisenstein would deny that he "is not interested in Chaplin."

director of *Earth*, was to write later, "There is no reason to avoid the use of players who are not professional actors. One must remember that every man can play himself on the screen at least once." This was the attitude that impelled them * to make films that employed no regular actors at all. "In the big proletarian films," writes Eisenstein, "like *Old and New* and *Ten Days that Shook the World*, the big crowd scenes were almost entirely played by workers who appeared in these scenes by their own choice and for no payment. When in *Ten Days* we filmed the attack on the Winter Palace two or three thousand workers came every day or every night with bands and offered to take part in the scenes we needed. The shooting in the street was entirely played by volunteers: nearly all of them were men who in 1917 had taken part in the same action to much grimmer purpose." He adds, "If an actor in order to play the part of an old man needs a day or two to prepare himself to enact the role and to rehearse it, an old man has had sixty years in which to perfect his characterization. . . . One should choose from a crowd those faces, expressions and types that one needs and which correspond to the ideas one has preconceived, and discover among these living human beings the characteristic types which are shaping movie imagination. We must plunge into life itself." But it was the Russian theater which had taught him this.†

Even the early Soviet films had something of this nature in them. They were closely related to the theater both by the exaggerated gestures of the actors and even more by their plots, but they were struggling towards a quite independent expression. The films of Kozintsev and Trauberg, of Eggert, Tarich's *Czar Ivan* are highly dramatic and produced with great care but still far from the desired goal. Sanin's *Polikushka* and Zheliabuzhski's *Postmaster* were already more expressive. The great actor Moskvin, from Stanislavsky's theater, played the principal role in both films and emphasized their theatrical nature, but an extreme interest in visual details, the care given to lighting effects already

---

* Two or three directors only.

† It is not the Russian theater but Eisenstein's own work in the Russian theater which had taught him this.

lent them a genuinely cinematic quality. It was Kuleshov who was the first to react violently against the theatrical influence and to attempt to draw the essentially cinematic quality out of his material. He was not always successful, though his theories were heeded respectfully and to many he seemed a veritable leader and prophet. He used and abused close-ups, forcefully emphasized details and stylized the acting in his pictures. Despite the faults there are portions of *By the Law* and *The Death Ray* which are as important in the development of the Soviet film as some of Griffith's and Ince's films were important in the development of the American film.

In these first productions some new themes were developed. In *Polikushka*, from a story of Tolstoy's, Moskvin played the part of a poverty-stricken peasant crushed by social conditions. In *Czar Ivan* and *The Demon of the Steppes*,* though they recalled earlier historical films, there was already evident a special interest in crowds. The latter especially, by Leon Scheffer, avoiding both experiments and subtleties, gave people a hint of what the really important Russian films (often suppressed by censorship abroad) were to be or were indeed already becoming.

Some of the producers went astray, as did Abram Room, whose *Bed and Sofa* was shown abroad. It was a film about the early revolutionary period with its housing difficulties, and it indicated roughly a new sexual morality. The heroine hesitating between the two men, and the general psychological mix-up seemed laughable to the French, who regarded it as nothing but a vaudeville sketch tricked out in Russian dress. There was something in this point of view. *Bed and Sofa* is clever, a sad and well-photographed film which, despite its moral, is still a psychological comedy and therefore not really cinematic.† The Russians were not often to fall into similar errors—at least not until the coming of talkies, but that is all the more reason for commenting upon this film. It was interesting in any event as a document on the new morality born of new social conditions,

---

* Produced later, in 1926.

† *Bed and Sofa* was not made until 1926, and it seems not to have been understood in France.

and its oversimplicity does not exclude a certain picturesque quality.

Other productions of this formative period also have their importance, such as *The Decembrists* of Ivanovski and *Black Sunday* of Viskovski. Here are genuinely revolutionary films that contain scenes of an intensity that predicts Eisenstein and Pudovkin. As yet, however, there is not a great difference between them and the films of the exiles; and the art of the early Soviet films derives similarly from theories of stage production and from the same masters, Stanislavsky and Gordon Craig.* The two branches of the Russian film, divided geographically by the rest of Europe, were in a sense united. One was shortly to expire and the other to forge ahead towards the discovery of true cinematography, but its roots were nevertheless the same and are to be traced back to the chaotic Russian films of wartime.

3. *The Scandinavian Film*

IN THE first years after the war the Scandinavian film and the Swedish film in particular attained such importance that there were many who believed that the northern countries had become the chosen land of the motion picture. No month passed, in 1920 and 1921, but there appeared in Paris some new film by Sjöström or Stiller, in all of which the beauties of the landscape and the nobility of their simple plots constantly expressed a love of nature and a heroic attitude to life. The influence of Selma Lagerlöf, most of whose books were filmed during this period, continued to be extremely strong for several years. Thanks to this talented woman, both purity of heart and devotion to duty took on new meaning, and, whether under her inspiration or not, men like Sjöström, Stiller, Hedqvist, Brunius and Petschler for an all

* The suggestion that Craig influenced the Russian films or that they derived from theatrical influences at all is manifestly absurd, though it has been put forward by other writers in equal ignorance of the facts.

too short period set before our eyes a sort of solemn and spiritual beauty such as the screen was seldom to give us again.

Victor Sjöström, who was much admired as an actor, despite his faults, because he was good-looking and virile, and as a director was the peer of the very greatest, absolutely dominated this entire period. In 1919 he made *The Duke's Testament* and *The Monastery of Sendomir*, in 1920 *The Stroke of Midnight* and a character study, *Masterman*, in 1921 *Love's Crucible* and in 1922 *The Burned House*, after Pierre Frondaie, and *The Hell Ship*, from an original story by Hjalmar Bergman. He had also made in *Karin, Ingemar's Daughter* a sequel to *The Sons of Ingemar*, from Selma Lagerlöf's *Jerusalem*. Leaving aside *The Burned House*, which was an error, and *The Monastery of Sendomir*, a sensitive transcription of a highly dramatic Austrian novel by Grillparzer, Sjöström hardly ever abandoned the Swedish scene. It is Sweden and its snows, Sweden and its springtime which we find again and again in all these very different, unequal films, all of which breathe the same inspiration and the same faith in the potentialities of the motion picture.

At times, as in *The Monastery of Sendomir*, he essayed, clumsily but energetically, to express the drama of thought and feeling and to give external expression to inner conflicts. *Masterman* was rather similar. More often he flooded his sober plots with a sort of radiance, with a sort of nostalgia and all that atmosphere for which the Scandinavians have created an untranslatable word —*Stemming. Love's Crucible* tells a tale of olden days, of an unhappily married woman who is planning to poison her husband when he dies suddenly. She is accused of murder and condemned to prove her innocence by the trial by fire. Sjöström's characteristic pantheism makes the fire itself, the forked and creeping flame, the most important character in the film, just as in other Swedish films water plays the chief role. In *The Hell Ship* the story evokes the same supernatural quality which distinguishes Sjöström's most famous film, *The Stroke of Midnight*, based on a fa-

The Covered Wagon, *directed by James Cruze* (*1923*).
Séverin-Mars in La Roue, *directed by Abel Gance* (*1922*).

Greta Garbo in the Swedish film, The Story of Gosta Berling, *directed by Mauritz Stiller (1923–4).*

mous novel by Selma Lagerlöf about Salvationists. This story of the redemption of David Holm, a drunkard beloved by a pious young girl, was not properly understood in the Latin countries, and many of the Salvationist scenes were cut out, such as the one in which the young girl persuades David Holm's wife to take him back, thus bringing tragedy to them and their children. There was more fatalism and more intelligence in the piece than the cinemas could accept readily. What drew both the general public and the highbrows to the film, and made it one of the most famous of all films, as famous as *The Gold Rush* and *Caligari* and *Potemkin*, were the scenes in which David meets his old boon companion George, who had died on New Year's Eve, and so becomes driver of the ghostly cart that comes to collect the souls of sinners. This supernatural figure, who was the focal point of the human story of Selma Lagerlöf, also dominated the film to such a point as to obscure its other qualities.

The Stroke of Midnight seems rather old-fashioned to us today, partly because of its somewhat excessive moralizing and partly too because technically it was at the time so very important and so new. It seemed literally dazzling then: now it seems almost obvious. It was the first time that the supernatural world had been brought to the screen with anything like so much talent, but Sjöström, like Delluc, had tried to express the supernatural and make thought tangible by means of the rather tedious use of double exposure. Later on it was to be realized that this method of showing one rather dim image over another fairly distinct image, in order to convey a hidden thought or spiritual truth, is an extremely material and physical device, and an erroneous one. The moment it is translated into the perceptible the invisible is invisible no longer but just a clever photographic trick.

Nevertheless, some of the scenes in *The Stroke of Midnight* are of remarkable brilliance and rare emotional power. Also, the director of *The Outlaw and His Wife* possesses a marked ability to visualize and to compose, and he loves nature with intense passion. Therefore, in the "vision" scenes, one enjoys most the wide empty road on which, as in a dream, the strange equipage of the death driver suddenly looms through the fog and the rain.

The road, the sea, the cemetery carry us to the realms of poetry and of piety as powerfully as when the film was made. And at the same time the grave bearing of the participants makes us realize that the film can really at times attain artistic perfection by the truths it reveals through the human face and the human body.

In 1923 Sjöström left Sweden to go to America, became Seastrom and carried away with him the greatest glories of the Swedish film. With him went much of the hope for the industry and the art of his country.

MAURITZ STILLER

If the man who made *The Outlaw and His Wife* and *The Stroke of Midnight* is the greatest of Swedish directors, he nevertheless shared his glory with his erstwhile companion Mauritz Stiller. Less forceful and less literary than Sjöström, more of an aesthete, he was also an artist who more than once merited the closest attention by his original and striking works. It was in 1919 that he made his masterpiece, *The Treasure of Arne*, after Selma Lagerlöf. The following year he made *The Vengeance of Jacob Vindas*, in 1920 *Across the Rapids* and *Erotikon*, in 1921 *The Emigrants* and *Gunnar Hedes Saga* and in 1923 *The Story of Gosta Berling*.

Erotikon, though pleasing enough, was not particularly original and resembles the slick work which Cecil B. DeMille was doing at about the same time. *The Emigrants* was also subject to various international influences. But in his other films Mauritz Stiller, like Sjöström, extolled Sweden, its history and its national customs.

He was never to surpass *The Treasure of Arne*, which, like *The Outlaw and His Wife*, was a period piece. The Swedes have never regarded their past history as something dead and gone: they have always treated it as part of an undying legend, realizing to the full that the essential elements in it were drama and atmosphere and the snowy landscapes whence all its romance stemmed. Arne's house, the sailing ship frozen in the ice, the inn

—a host of carefully and beautifully composed pictures—gave to
The Treasure of Arne the charm of a Breughel. Today we care
little for the dissolves, the masks, the superimposed images which
were the instruments by means of which the Swedes emphasized
their skill. What compels our attention is the composition: fairs
and meals and groups of sailors, the natural backgrounds and
the unforgettable funeral procession at the end of the film, with
its ranks of black and gray figures bearing a heavy coffin shoulder-
high across the snow. What strikes us most is the sincerity of
these faces: the pastor's aged wife, the woman who keeps the
inn, the ship's captain, the fisherman's wife and pretty Mary
Johnsson. Here Stiller at least equals or, perhaps, surpasses Sjöström, who was always rather too much the actor, too sensitive
to theatrical beauty. Stiller composed his films like a painter, not
like a dramatist, and it is this which makes his films so attractive.

Gunnar Hedes Saga, though it was not particularly successful, was nearly as good as *The Treasure of Arne*. It is the story
of a big house, whose master goes insane while he is driving a
great herd of reindeer into the mountains. The scattering of the
animals as they run free, then suddenly pause in alarm, their delicately trembling nostrils raised to a branch or a tree or snuffing
the air, the light play of their hooves as they move, now swiftly,
now leisurely, over the boulders of the narrow path provide one
of the loveliest pictures ever incorporated in a film.

Stiller determined to attempt the filming of Selma Lagerlöf's
finest book, *The Story of Gosta Berling*—a task before which
other directors had quailed. It was his last Swedish film. The
original version lasted for four hours, but in France only an ab-
breviated version was shown, and even this lasted two hours,
though a still more condensed version was widely circulated,
lasting only an hour, abominably badly cut and almost incomprehensible. It made it almost impossible to judge what the original
version was like.

Yet all the faults and all the virtues of the Swedish film as a
whole could be detected in this production, which was, in fact,
a sort of swan song. Selma Lagerlöf's novel, so richly poetic and
so complicated, was probably one of the most difficult of all

novels to reduce to the simple action which the screen requires. The film does succeed in telling the story of the clergyman Berling, torn between conflicting loves, but it seems a rather ordinary story. The strange existence led by a wealthy middle-aged woman, known as the Mistress of Ekeby, in the great house where she has taken in a horde of merry and drunken ex-officers, the whole atmosphere of wild parties and banquets, the mysterious romantic quality of the book are seldom if ever expressed. We get only glimpses of the story, compressed and curiously threadbare when compared to the strident, sonorous music of the original. Here are only a few weak echoes; not even the magical power of nature is suggested. Its violence becomes absurd because the actors are not convincing with their melodramatic gestures; it is difficult to stifle one's laughter while watching the scene in which the Mistress of Ekeby is cursed by her mother. The whole picture is too literal a transcript, and it makes the radical error of translating the original text picture by picture and scene by scene instead of re-creating it afresh.* This was a common fault of the Swedish films.

Stiller, nevertheless, displayed considerable skill in this film. When the Mistress of Ekeby resolves to burn down her house to cleanse it and lift her mother's curse from the place, it is really of no great importance that the fire is too apparently a conflagration of fireworks: it is still an impressive spectacle. The scene in which the wolves pursue Gosta Berling in his sledge against the great snowy background captures moments of sheer beauty. And in fact Stiller does at times succeed, by his artistic discretion and by the strange atmosphere which he creates, in catching the essence of Selma Lagerlöf.

The finest thing about the film is, once more, its choice of types, the faces of its people. The Mistress of Ekeby and her old mother, particularly, are peculiarly convincing with their curiously *real* expressions, their time-worn faces; there is an incomparable touch here. The finest, the most striking scene in the film

---

* The film by no means follows the original faithfully: there are some quite radical changes, as well as many omissions.

is the one in which the Mistress of Ekeby seeks out her mother, the mother who had cursed her long years ago. She arrives and silently begs for forgiveness. The two women, one at either side of a great press, now begin slowly and without exchanging a word to turn it, walking round and round like two beasts of burden, or two slaves at the treadmill. It is a superb scene.

The Story of Gosta Berling is not a great film, but it is one which may be seen over again with pleasure, and is quite lovely at moments. One can see how much it must have meant at the time it was produced. The youthful face of Greta Garbo, already at the age of seventeen having a tragic, almost hieratic quality, the restrained acting of Lars Hanson, and the almost inconspicuous, painterlike style of Stiller make this unequal and disturbing work (it could hardly have been otherwise) one of the curiosities of the motion picture. Like Pabst's *Don Quixote*, it is important because of some of its parts, which are admirable, and it helps to define the limits proper to the film on one hand and literature on the other.

OTHER DIRECTORS

Sjöström and Stiller were not the only men to celebrate the Swedish legends. In 1919 John Brunius made his appearance. He was to maintain the prestige of the Swedish film after the two really creative directors had departed. He directed *Puss in Boots*, then a delightfully poetic version of Björnson's *Fairy of Solbakken*, then *Thora von Deken* before, the following, he started upon a whole succession of historical pictures with *The Gay Knight*. Next came *The Burning Mill* and a few others. In 1923 he began work on *Charles XII* and also directed a really excellent piece, *Johan Ulfstjerna*, about the struggle of the Finns against the Russians. It was made in Helsingfors, with the collaboration of the population of Helsingfors, and six cameras at a time (an extraordinary number for that date) photographed the rioting, which was extremely cleverly handled. Cleverness was usually the dominant trait of Brunius, but occasionally his workmanlike qualities, with the help of some native spirit, lent more than mere competence to such dazzling and dramatic films as *The Burning Mill.*

Besides Brunius, mention must also be made of Ivan Hedqvist, an actor of great ability who became a director and made the delightful *Dunungen*, adapted from Selma Lagerlöf in 1919. It was only a photographed play, about a girl who preferred a frail graybeard to a young scamp, but it was so skillfully adapted that one forgot its theatrical origins. Later Hedqvist was to make *Pilgrimage to Kevlaar*, filled with poetry and mysticism and the equal of Stiller's best. He derived inspiration from Heine, whose poetry provided him with the subtitles for his handsome historical scenes, full of life and vitality.

Then the director Petschler made a second version of *Men of Varmland*, with its lively feeling for landscapes and folklore, and the Danish director Benjamin Christensen evoked the rugged fourteenth century in *Witchcraft Through the Ages.* Even rather mediocre pictures like Rune Carlsten's *When Love Rules*, and the films of Gustav Edgren, still maintained a certain literary refinement, an atmosphere and nicety which it is hard to find elsewhere.

Unhappily, after the departure of Sjöström and Stiller the various producing firms and even Svenska fell into financial difficulties. Though the older films had been so successful and new directors were coming to the fore, the industry began to go downhill. Renewed efforts were made to capture the foreign markets, but the concessions to international taste that were made only resulted in robbing the films of their peculiar national character. In the other Scandinavian countries it was much the same. The tale of their glory was lamentably brief.

THE FINNISH FILM

The Finnish film is in reality only an offshoot of the Swedish film and was much influenced by it. Finnish culture in any case has its roots in Sweden and Swedish is spoken in the best society.

Stiller was of Finnish origin. There is a strong tie between the two countries.

Films had been produced in Finland since 1908, but no industry was really organized there until about 1919. They began, inevitably, by filming plays: those of the great Finnish writer Kivi —*The Betrothal, The Country Bootmakers*—and in 1921 *Anna Lisa* from a play by Minna Canth closely modeled on Tolstoy's *The Power of Darkness* and considered very daring because its heroine was a girl-mother who killed her child. Afterwards they continued adapting plays but also drew on national inspiration after the Swedish pattern, celebrating the life of their raftmen (*The Raftman's Wife*), their smugglers (*The Fisherman of Stormskar*). Compared to the silliness of the current French and American love stories, these were admirable subjects to develop, which makes us regret all the more that the Scandinavian films did not succeed in establishing a world supremacy.

THE DANISH FILM

By comparison with the Swedish film, the Danish film was of little importance during the years that the artistic conception of the film was being formulated. The check that Nordisk met with in Germany towards the end of the war, when Ufa was founded, led to its losing the world market. For the future its output was to be workmanlike but undistinguished. Asta Nielsen was to work henceforth in Germany, and her favorite director, Urban Gad, followed her there.

There were, however, two quite gifted directors, Sandberg and Carl Dreyer, who began their careers in their native country with the reorganized firm of Nordisk. Sandberg attempted to transfer to the screen the novels of Dickens, a rich fund of cinematographic material which has never been fully exploited. He made *Our Mutual Friend, Great Expectations, David Copperfield, Little Dorrit*. They were faithful adaptations enacted by leading stage players, such as Paul Reumert, but they contributed nothing new to the art of the film. The best Danish film was probably *Four*

Devils, made in 1921, an undeniably pleasing and technically brilliant film about a worn-out acrobat dying of love for a fair lady but containing some extraordinary trapeze scenes, almost as striking as those in *Variety*.

Meanwhile, Dreyer was learning his job. This honest man and conscientious artist began by imitating the Americans. Griffith's *Intolerance* had greatly impressed him. He directed *Leaves from Satan's Book*, then went to Sweden, where he directed *The Fourth Marriage of Dame Margaret*, but returned home to direct a comedy, *Once Upon a Time*, for which he dug up from somewhere an eighty-year-old actor who was magnificent in the role of the king. Here one already divines the stamp of the man: the human countenance is all in all to him, he already knows what use can be made of the most formidable of stage celebrities, whether it be the venerable Peter Jernsdorff, or Silvain, or Falconetti. He is already studying the human marionette and learning how to make it obey him.

The Fourth Marriage was an allegory. A poor wretch of a man has applied for the vacant ministry, but among his many duties he is also obliged to marry the former clergyman's widow, who is over eighty and has already buried three husbands. He goes through with it, although he is in love with a charming girl. The film is amusing and lively. In the end the old lady has the sense to die and so the man of God can marry his beloved. It was an unusual subject for Dreyer but he carried it off admirably by a careful attention to detail, by making it convincing because he believed that the legendary past is just as living as the present.

Finally the Danes succeeded in breaking into the foreign market with comedies. As was customary, the names of the actors were denationalized and Schenstrom and Madsen were known in France as Doublepatte and Patachon. They were an earlier incarnation of Laurel and Hardy: their facility and their coarse good humor earned them wide popularity. They made a fortune for their firm, Palladium, and for their director, Lan Lauritzen; but it was a matter of business rather than art.

Throughout the four or five years when their films were at their zenith, the northern countries like Germany had made the world realize that the art of the motion picture is really an art. It had drawn its subject matter from national sources, thus giving an example which the Russians were to follow. Rather too much history, too many picturesque costumes and too much literature gave their films, admittedly, an over romantic air. But a real effort to express thought and feeling led the Scandinavians at the same time also into overstressing technical devices which occasionally prove wearisome, and into an excess of morality which is prone to become disagreeable.

For all that, in *The Outlaw and His Wife*, in *The Stroke of Midnight*, *The Treasure of Arne*, *Gunnar Hedes Saga* and *The Burning Mill* they showed us how to attain a poetical quality which even today is still captivating. Snowy wastes and simple hearts were brought together in these skillful features in a manner both astounding and deeply moving. No one before them had shown us nature itself, and natural backgrounds, as part of man's very existence; * there was something here very different from the films of the French landscape school like Baroncelli's or Léon Poirier's. Though the Swedish film was to decline, its teaching would not be lost. Its influence was to be detected in many a film to come, even inadequate ones, and we shall always remember, rather wistfully, that Sweden was the country that first revealed the visual and emotional beauties of the screen.

4. The German Film

WHEN the last gun had boomed over No Man's Land Germany was to remain familiar with the noise of machine guns and hand grenades for some time to come, even for years. The German film was born of war and revolution. Fortunately, there are some industries and some forms of human activity which can proceed heedless of riots and disorders; among them are banking and munition making. The German film, luckily, was in the hands of

* Except the Wild Western film, which undoubtedly influenced the Swedes.

the bankers and the munition makers: Krupp and Hugo Stinnes were in no danger and were not likely to abandon it. Ufa could go ahead calmly, under this double patronage. Of course, the foreign market seemed rigidly closed. The cinema proprietors of Paris had solemnly decided to ban German films from their screens for at least ten years. The English had followed suit. Yet as soon as it became known that the Germans were producing films of considerable interest, people wanted to see them. Since it is always possible to adapt one's nobler sentiments to one's interests, various distributors began to offer certain films of no known country of origin. They were German. Others handled some very peculiar Danish films. They also were German. The ban became ridiculous. Journalists took the matter up. *Caligari* was shown by private societies or clubs, as *Potemkin* was to be shown later. In the end, the patriotic resolves were thrown overboard, though some distributors continued until 1925 to disguise the German films they handled as Scandinavian. Krupp had scored a peaceful victory.

Modern literary and dramatic movements were also to assist the development of the German film. Germany is a country where new theories quickly penetrate to the general public, a country in which the commercial film was strongly influenced by the advance guard, entirely unlike what happened in France. During the war the theories of Reinhardt and of Gordon Craig about scenery had completely revolutionized the theater, and were followed by those of Georg Kaiser and Leopold Jessner. They stressed the importance of scenery, as playing a role at least as important as that of any character in a play, and needing to be designed by an artist, not simply to imitate the banal appearance of everyday life. It was to such theories that we owe the expressionist films of the German postwar period and, more particularly, *Caligari*. But first the influence of Krupp was to produce films of another type.

HISTORY AND PROPAGANDA

The first films through which Germany sought expression after the war gave evidence of none of the spirit of Weimar. They were strenuously nationalistic works of propaganda. Readily influenced by the Italian films, whose prestige had not yet declined, a number of directors turned to historical subjects, as a pretext for lavish spectacles, but carefully livened them up with a controversial air. They chose their subject matter from abroad in order to throw a disobliging light on the past of their recent enemies, the Allied nations. Ernst Lubitsch directed *Madame Dubarry (Passion)* against France, *Anne Boleyn (Deception)* against England and Dmitri Buchovetski made *Danton (All for a Woman)*. Jannings, who won renown for his Danton and his Henry VIII, Conrad Veidt and Werner Krauss as Robespierre and Marat, and Pola Negri all attained prominence. A rather childish kind of sexuality gave color to these films, in which history is regarded as a supreme fantasy. Ernst Lubitsch was to add a *Loves of Pharaoh*, a good match for *Cabiria* and having considerable decorative qualities; Buchovetski made *Peter the Great* and a slightly ridiculous *Othello*, in which slender Lya de Putti and Jannings at his hammiest gave a performance which might conceivably have pleased the provincial playhouses.

Sometimes the propaganda misfired, as when von Czerepy made *Fredericus Rex*, in which his hero was so ponderously characterized, in which there was such a complete lack of any sense of either what is ridiculous or what is distasteful that they were able to present the film in Brussels as an anti-German production. It was quite a success.

As history was not enough, some of the directors turned to satire. One of Lubitsch's first attempts was *The Oyster Princess*, a rather vulgar satire directed against Americans, in which audiences were shown a profiteer exposing his posterior, a secretary vomiting, a father playing Peeping Tom on his daughter. We see here how much real taste Lubitsch, the future director of *The Love Parade*, always had. The only interesting thing about the film was its settings and the handling of the dancing crowds. These were anything but naturalistic in tendency and showed clearly the influence of the new theories of stage production.

EXPRESSIONIST FILMS

All of this was not really of prime importance. What gave the German film its importance during the early postwar years was the productions in which new theories were blended with the old Hoffmannesque predilection of the Germans for the macabre. To begin with, stories about madness were admirably suited to expressionist films, for the distortions and unrealistic nature of the settings made sense in such cases and the whole thing could be carried out logically in that manner. The Germans fell into the habit of using somber stories, full of ghosts and vampires and haunted castles. Robert Wiene's *Caligari* is the best example of this tradition, but there were others—C.-H. Martin's *From Morn till Midnight*, Wegener's *Golem*, Fritz Lang's *Dr. Mabuse*, Wiene's *Genuine*, H. Kobe's *Torgus* and Murnau's *Nosferatu* continued for some time to follow the vogue for nightmares. Through these films the Germans found expression for that profound romanticism, that fascination with cruelty and fear and horror, that marrying of sex with death which were to intoxicate so many of her sons after the war.

Not all of these are equally good. Murnau's *Nosferatu*, with its haunted castle, its doors that suddenly open, its gusts of wind and its monster, is as absurd as a melancholy novel of the eighteen-hundreds. In *Genuine* Robert Wiene related the story of a painter in love with one of his canvases, a picture of the bloodthirsty priestess Genuine. It is a very somber affair, though entertaining enough, with cubist settings which seldom sustain their interest. Yet there are fine things in it, such as the scene, as extraordinary as anything in Poe, in which a little black-clad man with white gaiters climbs up a long steep staircase. The characters seemed to blend into the settings as though camouflaged and then from time to time stood out against them boldly in an extraordinary fashion.

Destiny, by Fritz Lang, was far superior to these and revealed the talents of a really able director. A young girl seeks out Death to get her sweetheart back from him. Filled with pity for her, Death shows her three lighted candles, each representing a single life span. We see her with her sweetheart in Morocco, in Venice, in China. The young man is killed in each of these lives and each time he dies one candle flickers out. At the end of the film the girl chooses to die too.

The opening sequence (Death's arrival at the inn) is admirable. Later the film tends to become a series of big spectacles, though many interesting effects are obtained with real skill, as when somebody makes the Chinese Emperor a present of a real army of tiny soldiers, an effect obtained by double exposure on two different scales. The heavenwards-reaching staircase of *Genuine* was used again, and at the end we were shown Death transporting the two lovers to the top of a bare mountain. There were probably all sorts of fundamental errors about it, but in spite of them the film had a curious power to stir the imagination.

The sum total of Paul Leni's *Waxworks*, of Arthur Robison's *Warning Shadows*, of *Torgus*, *The Golem*, *Genuine* and *The House of the Dead*, with all their necrophagous lords and their monstrous beings, really merited Canudo's opinion that they were cousins-german to *Fantomas*. Yet at times, by the sheer horror of certain details and striking pictures of sea monsters and carnivorous plants, a director would far outdo *Fantomas* and threaten us with an inimical and ravenous creation that was not without a certain beauty. We may pass over the use of fabulous and terrifying scientific contrivances in *Dr. Mabuse*, which fell to the level of the penny dreadfuls.

The film that endures best is *Caligari*—not that it is either particularly powerful or very frightening. The story concerns a victim of the mysterious Dr. Caligari, who compels the sleepwalker Cesare to carry off his sweetheart. At the end we realize that the protagonist is a madman, the doctor an estimable character. The madman's hallucinations are admirably rendered not only by the story itself and the actors (Conrad Veidt gave one of his finest performances as Cesare) but also by the settings.

These painted backcloths are stage rather than film settings; they make no attempt to look real. The little town perched on a knoll is frankly a painted city, not a geographical reality. Wiene had no intention of deceiving us. He simply carried us right back to Méliès' conception of film décor, which is probably the only sensible style for use in fairy tales and fantasies. But by 1919 Méliès had been utterly forgotten, and the steep paths along which Conrad Veidt, clothed all in black, dragged Lil Dagover and her white draperies, the nightmarelike country fair, the shadows daubed in roughly with paint, even the badness of the painting itself, which was no more than a crude, violent daubing, created an extraordinarily sharp and lasting impression. *Caligari* seems to mark one of the extreme limits of cinematography, a point where it merges with painting itself, so that it seems necessary to daub the faces of the characters themselves, to slap on eyebrows with a brush so that they may harmonize with the settings, so that one regrets that they possess either density or weight and that they cannot be as free and as one-dimensional as the characters in animated cartoons.

Actually *Caligari* was leading the films into a blind alley, for it restricted them to a subject matter of madness and nightmare. This did not prevent others from following its lead, though in vain. The influence which this intelligent and interesting film exercised was therefore less extensive than has sometimes been thought, but it had stressed, as no other film did, the importance of settings. The German film was never to lose sight of this.

LITERATURE

Following upon the success of the fantastic films, the Germans proceeded to satisfy their poetic souls by turning to adaptations of famous literary works. There were some of these which kept alive the traditions of the very earliest of postwar films, that is to say of the Italian films, yet even in these the settings were very much more important, as in *Helen of Troy* or Manfred Noa's *Nathan the Wise*. The films of Richard Oswald, *Carlos and Elisabeth, Marguerite and Faust* were adequate and no more; so was Felner's *Merchant of Venice*. We had to wait for Fritz Lang's *Siegfried*, which appeared in 1923, to go beyond the Italian models and wed expressionism to literature.

It was all a question of propaganda, even then: Germany wanted to make profoundly national films, to bring to the screen the old Germanic legends. Fritz Lang, assisted by his wife Thea von Harbou, whose influence was so often detrimental to him, based the film not on Wagner but on the ancient sagas. *The Death of Siegfried* and *Kriemhild's Revenge* both have the appearance at times of some Gargantuan opera. Both of them were entirely studio-made, and it is of course possible to discern that the lowering castles are made of pasteboard,* but the misty meadows, the forest, the rocky plains, the pool were all also fabricated with the same scrupulous care; these compositions are beautiful enough to be genuinely impressive. Here more than at any other time Lang gave expression to his love for *pictures*. The beauty of much of *The Nibelungen* is a static beauty. At other times Lang seems as addicted to grandiloquence and gesturing as Abel Gance. It is for this reason that one finds these two films irritating as a whole, though they achieve at moments (the forest, the castle, the hunt, the little spring where Siegfried drinks) a genuinely epic quality. After seeing *Destiny* and *Siegfried* one had great hopes of Fritz Lang.

The Nibelungen, however, constituted a period composition in which the freest expression could be given to new theories of décor. At the same period the German taste for what was abnormal or morbid also inclined them to another sort of literature. There are few writers who so stamped themselves on the film at that time as Dostoevski. Robert Wiene made *Raskolnikoff* as a handsome Caligaresque nightmare, Froelich and Buchovetski made *The Brothers Karamazov*, and others followed their lead. It would have been difficult to film such books without falling down somewhere: the very abundance of Dostoevski, his romantic quality, the sudden psychological changes are fundamen-

* They were not pasteboard, but plaster.

tally opposed to the art of the motion picture. Yet it was through adapting his works that Germany attained an "inner truth" which was to remain her permanent possession.

It was much the same in the case of other films, with *Phantom*, which Murnau adapted from Hauptmann, and *The Ascension of Hannele Mattern*, adapted from the same writer's work. Asta Nielsen's former director, Urban Gad, came to Germany with his star. She, however, did not appear exclusively under his direction: one of her most discussed pictures was her *Hamlet*, directed by Svend Gade. Erwin Gepard had written the scenario for her, basing the action not on Shakespeare but on the old Nordic legends. In this liking for the barbarian past he resembled Fritz Lang; and Asta Nielsen in male attire, overintellectual and overliterary in her interpretation, tried to register a concept of which the motion picture is hardly capable.

GENUINE CONTRIBUTIONS

Besides literary adaptations and the fantastic there were other territories to explore. Lubitsch had attempted to explore them in *The Oyster Princess*, Leopold Jessner in *Backstairs*. The ablest postwar directors in Germany had learnt much from *Caligari* while tempering the arbitrary and undeviating quality of this very important and uncompromising work. At the same time, perhaps by adapting Hauptmann to the screen, they also rediscovered the realms of the Théâtre Libre. Passionately fond of objects, they were to make of each object a little still life, bathed in light and shade, with the result that before long German photography and lighting became paramount. As they got further away from *Caligari* they ended up by trying to express the humblest and obscurest of everyday life on the screen, wringing out of it the fantastic elements which it, too, contains, as Dostoevski had shown them.

It is not to be wondered at, therefore, that the most extraordinary and the most expressive of German films of that time were made by the very men who had ventured into the realms of fantasy and of literary transcriptions. Murnau made *The Earth Burns*, one of his best pictures, and an intensely dramatic one, in which pictorial qualities are subordinated to psychological conflict; he had apparently abandoned those experiments into fantasy with which *Nosferatu* was full.

In one of the most famous films of the period, *Shattered*, Lupu Pick in 1921 used absolutely no subtitles whatsoever, making a point of telling his story in pictures alone. Nowadays this same story of a trackwalker's daughter who is seduced by a company engineer seems a little tiresome and somewhat ridiculous; it smells of the Théâtre Libre. But at the time it revealed a simplicity such as had never before been seen, and some of its scenes seemed unbelievably beautiful, as for instance the one in which the trackwalker walks along the tracks in the darkness with his lantern, which serves for a leitmotif for the whole film, as a symbol of the monotony of everyday life. And then Karl Grune in *The Street*—which is no more than a little story of a petty robbery that ends in a murder, and in which the chief character is really the street itself—introduced into the German film the poverty, the pitiful sexuality and the poetry of the house of ill fame. We shall find this theme again later, with its shady characters, all the meanness of man and woman, and a whole debased and weary humanity, but all transformed by an amazing skill in lighting.

The German film was not merely fantastic or morbid. There is something in common between *Caligari, Siegfried, Shattered* and *The Street:* it is a common root in painting. For no other nation has the film been a plastic art as it has in Germany. At times too deliberately pictorial, too static but always full of lovely and brilliantly composed scenes (whether it be an ordinary kitchen or the wide vistas of an epic), their films constantly remind us that their directors were artists. Murnau, Wiene, Karl Grune are painters; Fritz Lang is a painter and an architect too. From this time on nothing was to come amiss to the Germans—psychological dramas, epic, mystery, fantasy, romance, naturalism, or fairy story. They were to attempt all these, and attack them as painters. It was as though the Rhenish artists, the early lovers of chiaroscuro, had been reincarnated in these businessmen who wanted to give Germany a new art, and who succeeded in doing so for a few years.

5. *The Italian Film*

THE Italian film went gradually downhill from the time of the war until 1923. After the Armistice there had seemed, however, considerable hopes for its commercial development. The lawyer Mecheri had just gained control of the Itala Films with its enormous resources and hordes of actors. A combine had been effected under the management of Mecheri's rival Barattolo, the Italian Cinema Union, which gradually bought up all the remaining studios and actors. Actually this was the beginning of the end.

At first by sacrificing everything for prestige, Barattolo gradually brought the Union to the verge of ruin. Then the actors and directors, under the strange dictatorship of this businessman, lost interest and pride in their work and worked simply to make money. The Union also invented the horrible system of block booking which other firms all over the world were to imitate, beginning with Paramount and Pathé-Natan. It is familiar enough now: films were grouped into lots of ten and were supposed to consist of three featuring stars and seven second-class productions. The whole block was rented for 100,000 lira a district, exclusively. Often a man who found one good film to nine duds was lucky, but it was impossible to obtain that one without also taking the others. It was this system which ruined the Union and endangered the foreign firms which adopted it—if it ruined them, it served them right.

To fight the Union another firm was organized, the F.E.R.T. This firm gave a great deal of liberty to its directors, but one can hardly say that they used it to much purpose: Ghione's films (*The Golden Quadrant, The Blue Countess*) were about the same as those of Righelli (*The Rose Queen, Scarlet Love*) or those of

Genina (*The Two Crucifixes*). All of them were in the Italian melodramatic tradition, as their titles indicate. It was with two bursts of fireworks that the Italian film was to expire, two bursts of fireworks which really repeated the earlier success of *Cabiria*.

The director Caramba made a superfilm which screamed aloud that it was a masterpiece: *The Borgias*. It would be idle to imagine that either historical accuracy or imagination were to be found in it, though of course Caramba omitted none of the disputes among the cardinals, the baseness of Alexander VI, of Lucretia and of Cesare Borgia, none of the incest or crime. One sequence, however, appeared sufficiently well handled and dramatic to be regarded as quite striking at the time. Enrico Ghione has described it: "The cardinals are in full conclave, each one seated in a huge chair under a baldachin bearing his family coat of arms: they are whispering to each other, or lost in thought, or dreaming. Borgia is fighting to get his own way, promising important posts to one, threatening another, bribing a third. He leaves no stone unturned. On the various faces fear, or greed or envy is written as Borgia gradually gains ground. One pallid cardinal, hunched in his chair, alone keeps aloof, watching Borgia's actions with bitterness. As the other cardinals finally drop their votes, most of them venal and some of them given at pistol point, into the ballot box, this white-faced man who is Prince Della Rovere, rises to his feet quivering with rage and shouts 'Rome! Rome! What infamy will be heaped upon you!' "

Despite the faults and absurdities of Caramba, there is a glimpse here of what the Italian films might have been. Had they been able to submit to the laws of the medium, they might, out of the violence and the turbulence of the passions, have created films of a somewhat theatrical order but sufficiently transmuted into visual imagery to possess the power to move us. The scene of the conclave in *The Borgias* remains to indicate what might have been.

The film raised hopes in Caramba and in the Italian film. The firm of F.E.R.T. hastily went into production again, made Enrico Ghione produce another Za-la-Mort series and even attempted to translate Dante to the screen in Caramba's *Vision of Beauty*. The

U.C.I. was put quite in the shade; the firm consequently made an heroic effort and launched into a *Quo Vadis*.

This film had been made twice before by the then famous Enrico Guazzoni, first in 1912, when it had counterbalanced the success of *Cabiria* and again a few years later during the war. This time U.C.I. wanted to surpass all previous efforts. The direction was entrusted to the German Jacobi, under the supervision of Arturo Ambrosio (who had previously perpetrated a *Theodora*) and with the collaboration of Gabriellino d'Annunzio. Naturally these three men did not get on with each other. Each of them was blessed with bad taste of marked degree but of varying kinds, and each of them brought a quite different conception to the making of this production in the manner of Sardou, a manner which has always been that of the Italian film. There were also several untoward incidents and a few accidents: a lion ate up one of the extras, which considerably dampened the ardor of the other actors. When the film finally appeared it was a great disappointment: it seemed less excellent than its predecessors. But in the role of Nero an actor already famous won fresh laurels: it was Jannings.

The failure of *Quo Vadis* hastened the ruin of U.C.I. Then F.E.R.T. was also feeling the American competition. Internal unrest in Italy was serious. The Fascist victory did little to mend matters for the film industry: Mussolini had other things to worry about at that time, and was not to interest himself in the cinema until some years later. Enrico Ghione tried to reorganize the financial end of the industry but was unable to do so. He made one more film, *Our Country*. Augusto Genina presented Carmen Boni in *The Last Lord*, which scored quite a hit in Germany. Carmine Gallone took Garibaldi for his hero in *A Wild Ride*. The end had come. After three or four more years of sporadic efforts the Italian film virtually expired with *The Last Days of Pompeii*.

This film, in the familiar tradition of *Cabiria* and *Quo Vadis*, was given much publicity. An enormous number of actors were engaged and a few reels were shot. Then Amleto Palermi ran off to Austria with the negative to sell the unfinished film. In Vienna he found a buyer, who, however, insisted on the cast being changed. Palermi agreed, then went on to Berlin, where prospective distributors suggested a few more changes. On his return to Rome the actors who had been got rid of demanded huge compensation. Several million lira had already been spent. Palermi gave up and asked Carmine Gallone to finish the picture. It was the most costly of all Italian productions and, need one add, one of the worst.

In any case it was only a hang-over, for in reality the Italian film industry was in its death throes—the industry, not the art of the film. It was not until the Fascist reconstruction was really under way that any interesting films were to appear—not, in other words, until the talkies came in. From its very beginnings until 1923 the Italian film was really a monstrosity. In it one sees as through a magnifying glass all the worst faults that endangered the course of the European and the American film alike and even endanger it yet. Its chosen domain lay in the garbling of literary works, in submitting to the pernicious influence of Sardou, d'Annunzio and Sienkiewicz, and an extravagant habit of re-creating the past, and especially the history of antiquity. As faults, these were not peculiar to Italy, though there they were indulged to a degree almost phenomenal. They were to reappear elsewhere, in that masterpiece of all the productions in the Italian manner, namely, the American-made *Ben Hur*.

6. *The American Film*

THE END of the war coincided with a crisis in the American film industry. Most of the companies had undergone radical changes during 1918. Towards the end of that year the influenza epidemic swept the country; many of the cinemas closed, and it was difficult to get anyone to rent a film. At the same moment, public taste underwent a violent change. Overnight everyone suddenly sickened of the patriotic war pictures which had been turned out wholesale: miles of film had to be scrapped, other pictures taken out of production. There was a general shift from the heroic virtues of wartime to the light fare more suited to a victorious mood —comedies and love stories were in demand now. For many of the film people it was the end of a beautiful dream. The population of Hollywood diminished noticeably in a few weeks. It looked as if ruin stared the industry in the face.

A remedy was found almost as quickly as the crisis had arisen. The early months of 1919 saw the crowds streaming back into the movie theaters in almost greater numbers than before. A host of young people—youths who fancied themselves as comedians and girls who imagined they resembled Mary Pickford—bore down on Hollywood. It was necessary to establish a special agency to deal with (and send back home) the unwise fortune-seekers who arrived there penniless. The studios were snowed under in an avalanche of scenarios which it took weeks to examine, classify, discover useless and finally return to the various firemen, plumbers, bank clerks and dressmakers who had submitted them. More ingenious souls decided they could grow rich by bringing suit for plagiarism against the wealthier companies; for in order to secure tranquillity the firm so accused would, though innocent, sometimes make a settlement out of court. One individual more enterprising than the others went so far as to claim one hundred thousand dollars damages from Cecil B. DeMille, on the grounds of having "lent" him the scenario of *The Ten Commandments*. Ever since then, the studios have kept proof of having returned unopened all unsolicited scenarios submitted to them.

The growing interest in the cinema was not manifested by these gratuitous contributions alone. A large public, enriched by the war and growing even more prosperous during peacetime, now poured into places of entertainment; they were willing to pay good prices for seats and no theater could be too luxurious. It was a gold mine, and although the producers competed strenuously with one another, there was scope for them all.

Movie directors now began to rival the stars in importance. New York was still the financial center of the industry. A director in his Los Angeles studio could assume the role of dictator, since the quarterly visits of his particular magnate did not really do much to limit his power. As more and more money was being spent on publicity, the directors realized that they would do well to use some of it on their own account and make themselves famous, to compete with the growing renown of the stars. Actually by no means all of them succeeded, though George Loane Tucker earned a considerable degree of celebrity through his religious film *The Miracle Man*, which the Christian Scientists helped to make successful. But only two directors attained real prominence, and these, as before, were Griffith and Cecil B. DeMille.

D. W. GRIFFITH

Even more than *The Birth of a Nation* or *Intolerance*, it was *Broken Blossoms* which definitely earned for Griffith his peculiar eminence. When the film came out in 1919 everyone was overwhelmed. Its story was a rather improbable affair as full of uplift as a piece by Dumas *fils*, but in the land of puritanism such usually makes a hit. It concerned a delicate girl, the child of a coarse bully, who in her innocent way loves a young Chinaman. (Since the time of *The Cheat*, Orientals had enjoyed a vogue.) When the father discovered this shocking association, he killed his daughter.

It was not, however, the subject matter which caused this film to be regarded as a masterpiece so much as certain scenes in it which were carried off with really tremendous skill, with such sureness of touch and such serenity that one might have fancied Griffith had the theater's three centuries of experience behind him, not a mere twenty years of cinema. These were the scenes with Lillian Gish cringing before the whip, the flight of the crooks dragging the girl with them along the riverbank through the fog, the poor little heroine shut up in a closet, flinging herself desperately this way and that and then turning round and round, and the bully making melodramatic gestures on his deathbed. All of these were strangely convincing, and directed with an attention to detail which occasionally attained real style; they made it possible to accept this Grand Guignolesque story about a martyred maiden, to which Lillian Gish's sensitive face and haggard eyes lent so much charm and conviction. It was this loving care for detail and a certain romantic quality that gave *Broken Blossoms* its importance: but for it, *A Woman of Paris* might never have been made.

It was not, however, a great success at the box office, and Griffith, who had almost been ruined by *Intolerance* (he finished paying the bills in 1923), was forced to seek material more popular than this sensitive and complex story. He made *Orphans of the Storm*, against a rather crude late-eighteenth-century Paris setting, and *The White Rose*, which was a frankly commercial venture. But he also made *The Love Flower*, *One Exciting Night* (a sort of murder mystery, perhaps intended as a parody), *America*, which recalled *The Birth of a Nation* and, better still, *Way Down East* and *Dream Street*.

In *Way Down East* the heroine was, once more, the timid and delicate Lillian, eternally condemned to suffering. Its climax was the great storm and the breakup of the ice, with the heroine swept away on a floe while her sweetheart struggles against the elements to save her. The most important thing, however, about this film based on a popular melodrama was the natural backgrounds into which the action so agreeably blended, so that in a sense they played the same role that an orchestra plays in an opera, heightening the situations without overwhelming them. This is Griffith's great charm, even if time has somewhat faded this touching tale of a forsaken girl-mother, complete with baptism of dying baby and ice floes *à la Uncle Tom's Cabin*.

Dream Street was more complex; its naïve theme recalls *Intolerance*. Really an attempt at symbolism, sometimes clumsy and sometimes moving, it had a curiously rhythmical quality; short sequences are opposed to long sequences with astonishing boldness. Unfortunately, the masked violinist symbolizes evil, and the crowd which surrounds him symbolizes suffering humanity. One might have been moved by this story of two brothers who listen alternately to the voice of good and to that of evil but for an overdose of moralizing which spoils so much of Griffith's work. Technically remarkable, it also evinces a certain tender and romantic love of humanity. But it is terribly argumentative and elementary. One can never quite overlook this, and the years to come were merely to confirm the decline of this remarkable man who created the American film. But for him, it is probable that we might not yet know how to tell a story in pictures. His conventional melodramas served to create a style, to create that sort of cinematic eloquence which still affects us today in so many films. All honor to him!

CECIL B. DEMILLE

The efforts of Griffith (not to mention those of Ince) represented an attempt to lay down the canons of film art. With Cecil B. DeMille we encounter a man with other preoccupations, more nearly related to commerce than to art. In this figure, who for five or six years enjoyed fame as great as that of the most illustrious stars, can be detected the origins of much that was to orientate the cinema towards a brilliant mediocrity. He discovered and adapted formulas which were so successful commercially that they discouraged research by independent workers. All the familiar clichés owe their origin to him—sex appeal, wild parties, highfalutin sentiments, gorgeous heroines and the whole world of luxurious sport and fashion. He shares with the Italian film producers the responsibility of having been the spiritual ally of the financiers.

The discovery which was most peculiarly DeMille's was that of sex appeal. The "vamp" had appeared on the screen as early as 1912, but she had been displayed only dramatically and diabolically as a temptress, and appeared only in somber dramas that ended in the ruin of the poor man who had allowed himself to be led astray. DeMille realized that vamping offered a much more fruitful field than did such discreet glimpses into the hinterland of sin. The public liked an appearance of gilded luxury to mitigate the tale of sinfulness, and henceforward we were to meet with heroines dangerous enough to be alarming but still fundamentally decent enough so that all might end well. The addition of a generous share of make-believe could calm troubled consciences without disguising the sensual flavor which, if sufficiently respectably presented, might be agreeable to many people. As the action invariably took place in high society, where, as is well known, really

first-class seductions and sentiments of admirable fitness can both
be discovered with ease, the remoteness of the subject and the elegance of the manners succeeded in reassuring everybody at once.

So it was that Park Avenue came to the screen. To Babbitt, enriched in the stock market and timidly concupiscent when confronted by vistas of extreme luxury, the cinema now supplied a
complete series of documentary films about high society. Dazzling
women, each of them gifted with extraordinary and discreetly per-
verse charm, now took shape on the screen against a background
of the most elevating stories. It was DeMille who taught Babbitt
how to kiss a countess' hand, how to peel a peach, use finger bowls
and keep his hands out of his pockets. Cinema attitudes, cinema
drawing rooms, cinema society women, cinema sentiments, cinema
adulteries and forgivenesses were established. Under the gifted, the
twenty-times-creative hand of DeMille, a whole world of conventions and stupidities, destined to flourish brilliantly in the future, now took shape on the screen. Purilia, the city of the movies,
was molded into shape.

DeMille, shrewd man that he was, also took thought for Babbitt's wives and daughters. Every night the cinemas revealed the
innermost secrets of the Rue de la Paix to millions of women in
three-dollar dresses. Sex appeal and high society were unimagina-
ble unless accompanied by elegance in the grand manner of the
best French or American dressmakers. The star wore thirty dresses
and twelve wraps in each film. Shoemakers established representatives in Hollywood, famous hairdressers set up shop there. The
cinema became a catalogue of fashions. Thus the movies were
stamped with DeMille's mark, and, in a sense, withdrew from the
realm of art for several years. Only the comedies, which the glories
he dispensed had not been able to affect, kept the film on the right
track.

As for the director of *The Cheat*, among his studies of smart
society, after *Forbidden Fruit, Something to Think About, Why
Change Your Wife*, he made at least one agreeable comedy, *Male
and Female*, after Barrie's *The Admirable Crichton*, but it was not
often that he was to fall into the error of demonstrating good taste.
Before long *The Ten Commandments*, reported to have cost

$1,000,000 and having as its principal attraction the Israelites cross-ing the Red Sea, proved that the Italians had met their master and that it was possible to graft a sermon onto a spectacle.

HOLLYWOOD SCANDALS

It would be a mistake to suppose that DeMille provided a new source of inspiration without encountering any resistance. In spite of his prudence and the concessions he made to morality, his in-vention of sex appeal quickly alarmed the puritans. DeMille him-self would have been careful to appease everybody, but no one is master of the fashions he launches. The success of sex appeal was soon realized by a number of fly-by-night producers who were prepared to utilize his discoveries without discretion. It is readily imagined what his ingenious ideas became in their hands. And since their efforts did not seem wholly to displease the pub-lic, there were bigger firms ready to accuse of timidity those who insisted overmuch on the limits to which good taste and decency could go.

Clergymen shuddered, women's clubs became exercised. A little skill would perhaps have appeased these signs of dissatisfaction had Hollywood not at that same moment attracted a regrettable sort of attention to its own private life.

First, the newspapers were somewhat severe about the divorce of Mary Pickford, who had now married Douglas Fairbanks. Peo-ple were the more severe towards the beautiful but inconstant girl because they had admired her so much. But Mary Pickford was so charming and everybody liked Douglas Fairbanks so much that all would readily have been forgiven. Unfortunately, an ugly inci-dent now occurred to upset everything. This was the death of one of the companions of Roscoe Arbuckle at a party in San Fran-cisco. It has never been clear what really happened. Arbuckle was acquitted of the charge of murder over and again, but that sudden death and, still more, the circumstances which accompanied it threw a strange light on the film people.

The excitement caused by this affair had hardly died down when a director named William Desmond Taylor was found murdered in his bungalow. It looked as though jealousy had been the cause of the crime. Taylor's private life was investigated: he had had affairs of a more or less serious nature with various actresses. The murderer was not discovered. This mysterious event caused a stir throughout the whole country: every newspaper sent a special correspondent to Los Angeles. The most exaggerated stories, the wildest rumors circulated. Taylor's murder sold more newspapers than the entry of the United States into the war had done. Naturally enough, while the hunt for the unknown murderer was on, accounts of Hollywood scandals continued to multiply. Everything and anything was published. As eagerly as it had followed the rise of the film celebrities to fame, so the public now eagerly drank in stories to their discredit. The fabulous sums of money that the stars earned were recalled. So it was for Babylonian orgies, drink, drugs and the most horrible excesses that those magnificent salaries were spent! Hollywood came to be regarded as a subdivision of hell. A crusade was started against the film people.

The clergy increased their activities, the women's clubs demanded government intervention and the creation of a national censorship. A powerful wave of propaganda was launched against the industry. The topic became one of prime importance. Scandal sheets reaped a fortune. The scandals were rendered more acute by the fact that Los Angeles, besides being the film center, was also an oil town and had thus attracted all sorts and conditions of people. To evade the strict Californian law, which regards everyone unable to prove a regular means of livelihood as a vagabond, most of this floating population from the oil fields had enrolled themselves as film extras. Reporters did not inquire too closely, and eagerly announced that a ravishing film actress had been arrested after a night's orgy or that she had been mixed up in a shooting affray, and so credited to the genuine film people the misdeeds of women as to whose profession there was no possible doubt.

THE DICTATORSHIP OF VIRTUE

The situation soon became so serious that a dictator seemed necessary: Will H. Hays, postmaster-general in President Harding's cabinet, was engaged to restore virtue to Hollywood. Actors who had compromised themselves seriously were abandoned to their fate: Wallace Reid died in a sanitorium. For the other unhappy idols in Los Angeles there now dawned a sort of White Terror— a reign of virtue without hope and without compromise. A ruthless organization controlled every gesture, every look (this was long before the merits of the grapefruit had been discovered, or young lives began to be sacrificed to beauty through diets stricter than those imposed on the aged and dying). Hays acquired an army of assistants who were ordered to establish a model of good conduct such as would have suited the strictest convent of nuns. Suddenly the film world became as strait-laced as an old maid's home. Divorce was prohibited—temporarily. Famous actresses acquired homey backgrounds and entertained the parson in the evening. In every film residence was to be found a pious and docile young couple whose life held no mystery, unless it were the childlessness with which heaven had afflicted them. The extra players also paid the price. The most gloomy stories were spread abroad, emphasizing the sufferings of newcomers, the horrors of unemployment, the bitterness of the fight to obtain work. Pretty girls in Detroit and Cincinnati began to think that it was easier to find gold in the Klondike than to get a job as lady's maid in Los Angeles.

Meanwhile, those who disregarded these warnings were dealt with firmly. A central bureau received all applicants. The Czar's police would have seemed gentle compared to its officials. First they wore down the patience of the candidates by continually demanding their birth certificates and baptismal certificates, next they took them before sociologists, a group of which experts held permanent sittings. Some astonishing tests had been invented to reveal the slightest inclination towards violence, drunkenness or love. An applicant, before he was eligible to play a small part, was subjected to as many tests as a knight of old. And so, after a time, this Hollywood registry office had the satisfaction of having provided the films with a few thousand unemployed as healthy as policemen, pure as boy scouts and sober as Quakers.

There remained only the regulation of production. A sort of gentlemen's agreement was promulgated, which all the producers agreed to observe. This formidable document was composed of interdictions. Here are the essentials of this screen Code of Morality:

Sex

The sanctity of the institution of marriage and the home shall be upheld. Pictures shall not infer that low forms of sex relationship are the accepted or common thing.
1. Adultery, sometimes necessary plot material, must not be explicitly treated or justified, or presented attractively.
2. Scenes of passion should not be introduced when not essential to the plot. In general, passion should so be treated that these scenes do not stimulate the lower and baser element.
3. Seduction or rape.
    (a) They should never be more than suggested, and only when essential for the plot, and even then never shown by explicit method.
    (b) They are never the proper subject for comedy.
4. Sex perversion or any inference of it is forbidden.
5. White slavery shall not be treated.
6. Miscegenation is forbidden.
7. Sex hygiene and venereal diseases are not subjects for motion pictures.
8. Scenes of actual childbirth, in fact or in silhouette, are never to be presented.
9. Children's sex organs are never to be exposed.

Vulgarity

The treatment of low, disgusting, unpleasant, though not necessarily evil subjects, should be subject always to the dictates of good taste and regard for the sensibilities of the audience.

Obscenity

Obscenity in word, gesture, reference, song, joke or by suggestion, is forbidden.

Dances

Dances which emphasize indecent movements are to be regarded as obscene.

Profanity

Pointed profanity or vulgar expressions, however used, are forbidden.

Costume

1. Complete nudity is never permitted. This includes nudity in fact or in silhouette, or any lecherous or licentious notice thereof by other characters in the picture.
2. Dancing costumes intended to permit undue exposure or indecent movements in the dance are forbidden.

Religion

1. No film or episode may throw ridicule on any religious faith.
2. Ministers of religion, in their character as such, should not be used as comic characters or as villains.
3. Ceremonies of any definite religion should be carefully and respectfully handled.

National Feelings

1. The use of the Flag shall be consistently respectful.
2. The history, institutions, prominent people and citizenry of other nations shall be represented fairly.

Now the films were considered to be safe again. In actual fact, for a few months the specialists in sadism and sex appeal kept more or less quiet. Nevertheless, as anyone could have foretold, the Code of Morality merely helped to strengthen puritan hypocrisy, to make the films shy about certain serious subjects and, as far as public morality was concerned, to prevent absolutely nothing.

NEWCOMERS

Despite the crisis and despite the new restrictions, a few newcomers were hewing out a path for themselves in the film world whilst other eminent figures of the war period were doing little but rest on their laurels, like Thomas Ince, who was to die in 1924. Capellani returned to France, and Nazimova, who needed another

director, found him in the person of her husband, Charles Bryant.
Under his direction she made some mediocre films—a *Salome* after
Wilde with settings that looked like the cheapest kind of art pictures sold by the big stores, and an agitated and feverish *Doll's
House. Camille* was little better; the work of this woman, too overintellectual to adapt such works suitably to the screen, is not without its similarity to that of Asta Nielsen. Hers was a great failure
and one regrets it, for few actresses possessed more reserves of
feeling hidden under an artificial aestheticism, or more real intelligence.

Among newcomers one of the most successful was Charles Ray.
He had made his debut in 1913 in *The Coward* under the direction
of Thomas Ince and played the shy young lover with considerable
subtlety. *The Coward* and *The Clodhopper* put him in the first
rank; then followed *The Old Swimmin' Hole* and *The Girl I
Loved*, both of them fresh and touching pictures. Today Charles
Ray is almost forgotten. In 1922 his discreet style was often compared to Chaplin's, and people found more humanity and more
poetry in his films than in those of Griffith. His delicacy was perhaps too thin-drawn to endure.

James Cruze now also rose to fame. This man who had directed
*Less than Kin, Alias Mike Moran, Valley of the Giants, The Lot-
tery Man* and *The Roaring Road* was just another director when
he made *The Covered Wagon*, which was immediately likened to
the older Western films, to the Bill Hart pictures and *The Aryan.
The Covered Wagon* lacked the merit of Ince's films and today
seems rather dull and superficial, but this story of a land rush in
1848 appealed to the Americans as being a sort of national epic,
and indeed the scene of the wagons crossing the river is particularly fine. The success of *The Covered Wagon* endured so long
that Chaplin took account of it and produced *The Gold Rush* as
a comic or human counterpart. Before that, Cruze had made a
rather good film about prohibition, *One Glorious Day;* later he
made a comedy, *Ruggles of Red Gap*, to be remade later with the
actor Laughton, and also a satire on the movies called *Hollywood*.
But [in Europe—*Ed.*] his most famous film is *A Beggar on Horseback*.

Edna Purviance and Adolphe Menjou in A Woman of Paris, *directed by Charles Chaplin (1923).* (T. HUFF COLLECTION)

Zasu Pitts in Greed, *directed by Erich von Stroheim* (1924).

Emil Jannings and Lya de Putti in the German film Variety, *directed by E. A. Dupont* (1925).

A Beggar on Horseback was one of the few American films to have been influenced by the experiments being carried out at that time in France and in Germany. It is a nightmare story, staged in great and extremely solid detail. A poor composer wants to marry a girl and, in wedded bliss, devote himself to music. The dream suggests to him all the worry and trouble that lie in store for him. Despite all the double exposures and huge sets and grotesque characters in the film, Cruze only succeeded in creating an extremely childish effect. The true path of the American film did not lie in this direction.*

Flaherty was to provide it with an excellent model in 1922 with his *Nanook*, but unhappily he had few disciples. This story of the life of an Eskimo, attached to his icy surroundings like a peasant to his fields, has an abiding and natural charm. The hunt, the snow, the harpoon, the howling of the hungry dogs furnished some exquisite pictures; the struggle with the elements, dogs and men huddled inside an igloo lighted only by a square of transparent ice, the bargaining with the fur traders are subjects that we shall meet with again. But, that first time, the resignation of the hero to his circumstances, and that perfect combination of documentary film and cinematic fiction seemed irresistibly bewitching. The Americans seem little concerned with the poetry of nature: among them only Flaherty and Van Dyke come to mind,† but the work of these two men is of real originality and power.

DOUGLAS FAIRBANKS

In 1919 "the big four," Griffith, Chaplin, Mary Pickford and Fairbanks, agreed to form United Artists through which, as soon as their outstanding contracts permitted, they would release their own productions. The dashing young Fairbanks, who was to marry Mary Pickford the following year and form with her the typical screen couple, was now reaching the apogee of his fame.

* In Europe Cruze was given credit for all the novelty and fantasy of this film, from lack of knowledge that it was really a transcription of the play by Kaufman and Connelly and of the producer's and designer's ideas for the play.
† Why omit Schoedsack and Cooper?

That year, he appeared in *His Majesty the American* and the following year made two films under the direction of the excellent Victor Fleming, *When the Clouds Roll By*, a trick film which occasionally reminds one of *A Beggar on Horseback*, and *The Mollycoddle*. Later he appeared in *The Nut* and a version of *The Three Musketeers* in which he was superb. Directed by Fred Niblo, it confined itself to the episode of the [Queen's diamond—*Ed.*] studs, which included some furious horseback riding. But in the interests of decency d'Artagnan was in love with the niece of M. Bonancieux, not with his wife. This was in 1921 and the censors were alert. The film is a monument, as usual, to Douglas' good nature, fitness and agility. He was to put the best of himself and his formula into a film of adventure and acrobatics which remains famous, *The Mark of Zorro*, also directed by Fred Niblo. It was in its way a masterpiece.

Douglas now resolved that the public might tire of such a monotonous character as he played, and that he must do something fresh. Cecil B. DeMille had shown the way. Without ceasing to be the robust and chivalrous acrobat with the Fairbanks grin, he now played his adventures against imposing settings, preferably historical. He made *Robin Hood*, in which the story is garbled so lightheartedly that it would be absurd to take anybody to task about it. A new fairyland opened before him: he had won Mary Pickford's love, a great deal of fame and any number of dollars.

COMEDIANS

Most of the comedians who had made their debut during the war were now developing their style. Fatty Arbuckle, it is true, was to disappear from the screen for the most regrettable of reasons, scandal. But there remained, even if we omit Larry Semon and Ben Turpin, two men of decided importance—Buster Keaton and Harold Lloyd.

At first, Buster Keaton appeared in a number of short comedies (*Neighbors, The High Sign, One Week*) in which he already opposed to destiny an impassive face and exceptional agility. Then for First National he appeared in ten pictures—including *The*

Electric House, The Frozen North, Balloonatics and *Cops*—which were all full of the craziest invention and bore resemblances to many of the prewar comedies. For example, in one of these Buster plays several parts at once, applauds himself on the stage and displays a startling ubiquity. These were short films such as were always shown before the feature: not until 1923 did Buster appear in a film of greater length, *The Three Ages*, but his prentice work was already done and the years to come were to give him his true place.

Meantime, good-natured Harold Lloyd had developed his charming and facile talent. He was featured in a great many films, *Never Weaken, High and Dizzy, Haunted Spooks* and then *A Sailor Made Man, The Freshman* and *Safety Last*. In all of them he confronts the worst catastrophes with an air at once silly and cheerful. Admittedly there is little logic in his gratuitous humor, which often seems a trifle forced, but in *Safety Last* he takes such pleasure in his strange acrobatics up and down a building that one cannot resist his rather obvious comedy devices, some of which are derived from Fairbanks, some from Chaplin, others from Linder and the older comedies: applause comes wholeheartedly. The later films in particular, longer and better made, form a kind of comic allegory on luck, for Harold Lloyd, despite appearances to the contrary, is always lucky and seems protected against misfortune by some titular deity. That is what makes the public like him. However, he too was to be surpassed by Chaplin.

CHARLIE CHAPLIN

At the end of the war, by reason of *Shoulder Arms* in particular, Charlie Chaplin had definitely won an outstanding place in the world cinema. He was thenceforth to cease turning films out rapidly as he had done in the days of Keystone and Mutual, though his films were fairly numerous as long as he remained with First National, which he joined in 1918. It can even be said that after *Shoulder Arms* Chaplin began to learn his craft all over again, though in a manner different from that of *His New Job* or *One A. M.* The success of *Shoulder Arms* gave him food for thought.

Now he attempted, patiently and artfully, to realize his real ambition, which was to be something more than a funny man. He tried to extend his repertory, launch out into romance and even into drama. Some of the films which appeared between 1919 and 1923 are far from possessing the exquisite unity of *The Tramp*. They lack a center of gravity, they are cumbrous with effort and with faults. That is what makes them interesting and what enables one to date from these years a renewal-from-within in the art of Chaplin.

In 1919 he produced *Sunnyside* and *A Day's Pleasure*, in 1920 *The Kid*, in 1921 *The Idle Class* and in 1922 both *Pay Day* and one of his real masterpieces, *The Pilgrim*. Finally in 1923, after completing his contract with First National, he released through United Artists not his best but his most important picture, *A Woman of Paris*.

Sunnyside, which began the new series, is an exquisite thing, packed with amazing details. Charlie in the country drives his cows dreamily to pasture, loses them, tries to find them and carelessly prods a stout lady. In the morning at the farm where he is a servant they waken him brutally; he taps on the floor with his shoes without getting out of bed to make them think he is up. When he prepares dinner, he milks the cow directly into the cup, and puts the hen into the frying pan so that she may lay a fried egg. The whole thing is poetical and enchanting: the imaginary village, the lanes, the ladies going to church, the Sabbath day sanctified to the Lord. Out in the fields, Charlie has a dream: nymphs dance with him. It is a slightly heavy, slightly sentimental dream —there is nothing very ethereal about these healthy American nymphs. Nevertheless, this is probably exactly the way in which Charlie imagined them, and here the chromolithograph comes to life. We prefer, however, his assiduous courting of a pretty girl: he tries to ape the elegant young men who own cuffs, spats and canes which contain concealed cigarette lighters, but his spats are old woolen socks all frayed out and he has only a candle to put in his walking stick with which to light his two-cent cigar. Rarely have bitterness and grace been compounded with as much subtlety as in this film, at once so nonchalant and so precise, which resumes the themes of *The Tramp* and of *A Dog's Life* but uses them here to extol the pastoral virtues.

A Day's Pleasure, in which Charlie is married and the father of a family, is merely a comedy—it reminds one of the older films. On the deck of a boat Charlie struggles with a chair, as he fought with his bed in *One A. M.* It is a remarkable exercise of virtuosity but no more, and so is the automobile ride.

With *The Kid* Chaplin attempted something new. It is a strange and deceptive film, which has aged greatly and reveals certain of Chaplin's incurable faults, which, however, have their own charm. It begins in the worst melodramatic style with a woman abandoning her baby. All this is laid on very thick: Chaplin has seldom ventured so far into bad taste. It is as though, in his joy at finally abandoning pure comedy, he had lost his equilibrium. Fortunately, at this point, Charlie himself appears and takes the baby under his wing.

The child's part was, of course, played by Jackie Coogan, who was perfection itself with his chubby face and the great cap that came down over his ears. In 1919 Charlie had noticed a child throwing banana peels under the feet of the passers-by. He called out to him:

"Hey, kid, would you like to work in the movies?"

The child answered, coldly: "I might consider it."

"Take me to your father," said Chaplin.

"I am five years old," replied the boy. "I can manage my own affairs."

That is the way, so they say,* in which Jackie Coogan was engaged.

The Kid was made without any scenario or script: Chaplin often works like that, and the lack of unity in some of his long films is probably due to this method of improvisation, though it is also true that, since 1920, he has formed the habit of inserting into his pictures episodes which bear little relation to the main plot.

The Kid remains one of the most uneven films that he has made. Some of its details are perfection—as, for instance, when Charlie becomes a glazier, the kid throws stones at people's windows

* The story seems to be apocryphal.

and breaks them; then Charlie comes along and mends them. This causes complications with the policeman who has discovered the trick. Later on the kid is ill, Charlie fights with the authorities to keep him, and finally hides him in the flophouse to which he goes for the sake of warmth. The flophouse episode is one of the most touching that Charlie has ever composed. One day the child's mother, now a wealthy woman, offers a reward to the person who will restore him to her. Tempted by the five thousand dollars, the owner of the flophouse takes the child to her.

Charlie is unhappy. He dreams, as he dreamed in *Sunnyside*. He is transported to a strange and ridiculous world where angels rock him and even policemen have wings. This famous episode, like the one in *Sunnyside* and the vision in *The Gold Rush*, is not wholly successful. Chaplin's imagination develops best in the everyday world of reality, from the meal which a tramp eats or the life of a small town: he is less adept with the imaginary world. Even if we attribute the clumsiness of his visionary scenes to his own naïveté of character, we are still entitled to find them rather heavy. In any event, he is recalled abruptly, as here, when the kid, now rich, comes back to lead him off with his mother towards a life of ease. This is obviously the artificial happy ending of a romance that began in the manner of *Camille*. Yet for all its violent changes of mood, its heavy sentimentality, *The Kid* is a work of supreme importance. Here for the first time Charlie was wholly himself, with all his perturbation and sadness and an admixture of grotesque yet poetical social satire, somewhat in the manner of Griffith. Even if we think that Chaplin can do better than imitate Griffith, nevertheless the film remains unique and attractive.

With *The Idle Class* and *Pay Day* he seemed to be treading water, content to attempt comedy alone. In *The Idle Class* he played two parts, the elegant husband and the tramp who resembled him so closely. The tramp goes to a fancy-dress dance and persuades the lady, who thinks that it is her husband, to kiss him. Horrors! The husband is not disguised as a tramp but as a knight of the middle ages. He charges at Charlie, armor and all, but when he cannot raise his visor it is Charlie who comes to his rescue with hammer and can opener.

The end is excellent, in a different key. The wife's father, having somewhat maltreated the tramp during the dance, now repents and goes to shake Charlie's hand. Charlie slyly gives him a hearty kick in the pants and runs. It is one of the rare instances in which Charlie revenges himself. It is not the only time he feels like doing it, for volumes could be written about a certain toughness in Charlie and the suppressed resentment which often lends a strangely human note to his misfortune: he is less resigned than we sometimes imagine.

As for *Pay Day*, here his touch is extraordinarily sure: there is not one scrap of waste footage in it. As most of the action takes place at night, it is an unusually picturesque comedy which (like *The Gold Rush*) indicates how circumstances can dictate an interest in pictorial elements, in composition and in lighting, which were usually far from Chaplin's mind. Here we see Charlie going home late one Saturday night, his cautious arrival in stocking feet and the angry awakening of his wife—an old and often-exploited subject. The best thing in it is Charlie's climb into the overloaded trolley car: newcomers gradually push him towards the rear door, he hangs on by a fat man's suspenders but is finally thrust out. It was in this film that he hit upon one of his most touching and most significant gestures: he fears that his foreman will punish him for being late for work, and conceals behind his back a flower which he intends to offer him. Wonderful symbol, both funny and enchanting, worth more than all the sermonizing in the scenes which open *The Kid* or in the films of Griffith. Such discretion is the sign of great art.

The same restraint distinguishes *The Pilgrim*. It is a delightful picture, more pantomime than film, and reminds us that Charlie was born into the circus. When he is mistaken for the new parson and taken to church to preach a sermon, he enacts the story of David and Goliath with his hands, whirling about and gesticulating threateningly. That bit of bravura is the masterpiece of a man more mimic than screen actor. There is also the opening sequence in which Charlie as an escaped convict picks out at random the name of a station from a depot placard, and happens to light on Sing Sing. When he finds something more attractive, he grips the railings for a second with the gesture of a prisoner clutching the bars of his cell. On arriving at the town he has selected, he holds out his hands to the sheriff who awaits him, as he would hold them out to be handcuffed. It is incidents of this kind which give the film its perfection (as well as the simple, straightforward plot), as when Charlie tries to save the girl he loves from one of his former convict friends, and the little gesture of farewell he makes at the garden gate when he is arrested. Infinitely preferable, these, to the horrible child that covers the bowler hat with whipped cream, though it is true that Chaplin does not particularly stress this. The end is famous: at the Mexican frontier, the sheriff sends Charlie to pick flowers, then gallops away. Charlie has not realized that they want to give him a chance to escape; he runs after the horse and offers up his bouquet with the expression of a faithful dog. The sheriff has to send him on his way with a kick. Beaming with joy Charlie now runs off, but a bandit with a blunderbuss springs up from behind a Mexican rock. Charlie hurls himself back into the United States. Up pops a second bandit, no less terrifying. The film ends with Charlie loping away, one foot in the States and one in Mexico, astride the frontier.

Just as in *Shoulder Arms* and *Sunnyside*, in *The Pilgrim* Chaplin achieved a nearly perfect combination of humor and tenderness. Unfortunately, the puritans disapproved. At that time the Chaplin divorce case was on. The most unpleasant rumors about him were in circulation, and now he had dared to ridicule the clergy. He had done it before, what is more, in *Easy Street*. The puritans, extremely active in the United States, especially since the Hollywood scandals, tried to make of the situation one similar to that which their spiritual ancestors had made out of Molière's *Tartuffe*. It only just missed being successful and putting a total stop to Chaplin's freedom.

Happily, at United Artists he was now his own master, and in 1923 he produced *A Woman of Paris*. The comedian does not appear in this film, though Chaplin once crosses the screen in it briefly, as a porter. Did he want to prove that he too was capable of writing a story and directing a big film without appearing in it, like Griffith and DeMille? Was he afraid to abandon the character of the tramp to which he was thenceforth condemned? Impossible to say. The important thing is that in this rather naïve society drama we can readily recognize the author of *Shoulder Arms.*

A Woman of Paris, whatever its admirers may say, has worn badly, and this could have been predicted at the time. The reason is simple: it is the same which made *The Cheat,* with a far more absurd plot, also wear badly. Everything related to the horrible stuff which Augier and Dumas *fils* brought into fashion in the theater inevitably ages rapidly. Sentimental dramas and dramas about high finance alike, they all quickly become covered with thick dust and it is practically impossible to see a ten-year-old play of the "contemporary drama" without boredom. In copying the theater the films were terribly mistaken, not only because there is no connection between these two arts, but because the films imitated a bad and abominable theater, doomed in advance: that is to say, the French commercial theater which developed from the horrible theater of the nineteenth century.

However, *A Woman of Paris,* if it borrowed some of the faults of this regrettable style, also oddly surpasses its model. But for the intimate film plays of Griffith and DeMille, Chaplin would hardly have thought of making this remarkable if melancholy picture, yet it is far ahead of both Griffith and DeMille in its concept of life. The story is simple, although somewhat facile, and reminds one both of *Camille* and of the less admirable parts of *The Kid.* It concerns two young people whose parents forbid them to marry. They decide to elope, but through a tragic mishap the young girl awaits her fiancé at the station in vain. Thinking herself abandoned, she goes away, and we find her next as the mistress of a rich, middle-aged man, Pierre Revel. Later she meets her fiancé again, he commits suicide and she goes back to Revel.

"I treated that subject," Chaplin said, "in the simplest possible manner," and he mentioned with satisfaction the two details which seem to have struck the public most and which were most characteristic of his economical style. "First, the fact that I indicated the arrival and departure of a train without showing the train, then the gap of a year in the woman's life which was neither indicated nor explained."

The first scene is famous. It shows the lights from the train passing across Edna Purviance's face. The emotional response which the scene aroused (it was the first time that such an indirect method had been attempted) was actually the result of necessity: American trains are unlike French trains and *A Woman of Paris* takes place in France. As there were no coaches of the proper kind at his disposal, Chaplin had the idea of showing only the reflections from the coach windows and, afterwards, realized the effectiveness of his ingenuity. No matter how it occurred, it is highly significant, as is also the silence maintained as to the heroine's life from the time of her desertion until we meet her again. The details were unimportant: one imagines pretty well what her life must have been. What was important about it was the wearing down of her resistance, the adjustment she was compelled to make to life and the gradual disintegration of her pride. Until this time, films had never before shown characters who are neither good nor evil but who are doomed to unhappiness and unable even to give expression to their finer feelings. Pierre Revel, as Menjou interpreted him, is one of the most exceptional characters portrayed on the screen. He is a skeptical but not a wicked man who knows exactly what to expect of life. Possibly he loved Marie Saint-Clair. It is probable. But with a scrupulous tact, to which Menjou's performance lent real conviction, he never betrays it. Few scenes have been as real or as cruel as the one, so quietly played, in which the woman returns to this man,* after the young fiancé's suicide.

Things like this enable us to accept the characterization of the fiancé and other somewhat old-fashioned elements in the film. Chaplin's film is an indictment against humanity rather than a problem play or an indictment against society—and even so it is a passionless statement rather than an indictment. Here it is easy to recognize the work of the man who made the comedies, for what he had previously suggested through farce he here states clearly. His tramp cannot love, cannot even move without creating ca-

* It seems, from this, that the ending of the film as shown abroad was unlike the one we saw. The heroine, far from returning to Revel, devoted herself to good works.

tastrophes. *A Woman of Paris* shows us that it is the same with all men.

The film was important. Henceforth, it was impossible to look upon Chaplin as simply an entertainer, or as a more or less imaginative clown. All that he had been attempting in his latest films blossomed here in this simple story, the melodramatic ingredients of which we can overlook in order to admire its profound humanity. But at the same time, following as it did upon four years of experimentation in the Swedish, the German and the Russian films, its very simplicity of technique was rather disconcerting. Here were no difforming lenses, no double exposures—just a straightforward narrative. The aesthetes decried it, but soon it was realized that *A Woman of Paris* contained a valuable lesson. The efforts of the technicians had resulted in smoother rhythms and in a better use of the camera, but technical efforts should not be obvious: in work of real excellence they are imperceptibly incorporated. And so, despite its faults, which arise from a mistaken attitude towards the theater and the novel but not from a mistaken attitude towards the film, *A Woman of Paris* provided just that lesson, which is that of classicism.

Through the whole First National series which led up to *A Woman of Paris*, Chaplin had concentrated on something more than pure comedy. He had not abandoned his own particular style, especially the use of reflex actions, but he had attempted in addition to express his personal lyricism. He had taken refuge in a dream world of a rather coarse and naïve kind; he had moved nearer towards drama of a simple sort, in order to create the tragicomedy of frustration, which is his favorite theme. He substitutes for the American scene his own small towns still filled with a breeze from near-by forests. It would be a mistake to regard him as a rebel against modern society. There *is* rebellion in him, which sometimes leads him to fall into artistic errors and makes him seem imperfect and human—for it would be wrong to think that Charlie is always good. When he meets someone smaller or weaker than himself he may very well perk up and take his revenge—but almost invariably a most innocent revenge—on fate. Neither is he brave:

in the presence of large and husky men he assumes a timid and caressing air. This is what is worth more than all the speeches in the world, the parsimony and bitterness of the existence with which he has endowed the character he plays, and also the less transposed and less poetical characters in *A Woman of Paris*. After this film and after *Shoulder Arms* Chaplin became the poet of men's humiliated adjustment to their misery, which is to say to life itself.

Summary

To CONCLUDE briefly, it was in America, in Sweden, and in France between 1918 and 1924 that the film as we know it and love it really took shape. America offered few models except the brilliant work of Chaplin. Elsewhere the film had begun to be regarded as an "original" art. This was something new.

No matter what false starts were made during these all-important years, there was a real effort to create a genuine style and a new language. Attempts had been made before the war in the realms of comedy and of fantasy. After the war, the discoveries made in comedy were neglected, and experiments were made along other directions. People everywhere became interested in the new art. Special cinemas were established, particularly in Paris, at the Ursulines and more notably at the Vieux Colombier, where Jean Tedesco succeeded Jacques Copeau and tried to establish a repertory cinema. Intelligent magazines managed to find a public, such as *Cinéa-Ciné pour Tous*. Writers like Canudo, Louis Delluc, Galtier-Boissière and Moussinac tried to teach the French that the films exist. As early as 1919 *Le Crapouillot* began publishing extremely interesting special numbers devoted to the cinema. The film had entered the common domain of the arts.

PART FIVE

The Classic Era of the Silent Film

1923-1929

By 1924 the film had created its own form of expression. With the range of its technique extended by the French (who are too frequently overlooked), the Germans, the Russian *émigrés* and the Swedes, it was to experience a few too short years of relative tranquillity during which little was to be invented but much interesting work was to be done. From now on its possibilities and its future were clear.

Méliès had discovered virtually the whole of its primitive alphabet. As early as 1908 Griffith had perfected the use of the close-up, the mobility of the camera was an established fact, and in 1915 soft focus was used for the cradle-rocking figure which links the several themes of *Intolerance*. The public no longer grew angry, under the impression that it was being given bad photography, when soft-focus pictures appeared, as in *Jocelyn* and in *Eldorado*. In a Bryant Washburn film of 1919 a minute person was seen moving about at the bottom of an immense door—perhaps the first purposeful use of scale contrast. Douglas Fairbanks' *When the Clouds Roll By* used difforming lenses at the same time as the Swedish films and, of course, double exposure was all the rage. Finally, Jules Romains suggested the use of rapid cutting,* which was to be used by Charles Ray in *The Girl I Loved* and by Abel Gance in *La Roue*. Once all these devices had been assimilated and *A Woman of Paris* had given a lesson in simplicity, it remained only to proceed and furnish examples of a serious and complex art.

1. The French Film

The French film during the subsequent years has been much criticized and nearly always with justice. France and America alone had produced films continuously since the invention of cinematography. France and America alone had consumed large numbers of films and made fortunes temporarily for the film industry.

* See note on page 151.

But the French industry was so badly organized that in the end everything was subordinated to catering to the lowest and most ridiculous public taste; then came loss of money and finally the dollar triumphed. Little by little the French firms fell under American control. Eclair practically disappeared, Gaumont was absorbed and the basis of the French industry, the old firm of Pathé, was bought by the Natan brothers, Rumanians who had established a small firm in France before the war. It might be said truly that the history of the commercial cinema in France between 1920 and 1925 is the history of Pathé-Natan. It is not a pleasing history. This powerful and well-organized firm hardly produced one good film and always favored the greatest nonsense, the most outworn ideas, alternating the vulgarest vaudeville with the stupidest sort of historical rubbish.

The efforts of certain independent journals, and of cinema proprietors like Jean Tedesco (Le Vieux Colombier), Tallier and Myrga (Les Ursulines), Jean Mauclères (Studio 28) and others, only influenced a small public. Fortunately, that public was to increase in time. The daily press, at first printing no film criticism, gradually became interested in the medium: it would be ungracious to overlook the excellent fight which Canudo first, then Jean Prévost and next Alexandre Arnoux put up in *Nouvelles Littéraires;* Léon Moussinac in *Le Crapouillot* and *L'Humanité;* Jean Fayard in *Candide;* Pierre Bost in *Les Annales;* François Vinneuil in *L'Action Française.* Thanks to these men it became possible to discredit the purely commercial cinema in at least some minds and to discredit, at the same time, those impudent film criticisms which were nothing more nor less than publicity and which appeared in so many newspapers simply as an adjunct to paid advertising.

It would be unfair to dismiss all films along with those purely commercial examples of which no more need be said. The productions of Léonce Perret, of Diamant-Berger, André Hugon, Marco de Gastyne, Ravel and the rest are unimportant and so are numbers of other competent enough pictures. We can dismiss the second *Les Misérables* and Maurice Tourneur's *Equipage,* which was so warmly praised. Of far more importance were the independent efforts made by the courageous group of young men who followed in the footsteps of Louis Delluc and his school.

UNFULFILLED PROMISE

The saddest thing during the coming years was to see certain directors abandon their first efforts and begin working for money alone. Such is too often the case. It might have been foreseen in the case of a man like Baroncelli, though he was still to make some distinctive and competent pictures, or in the case of Raymond Bernard, who had a passion for enormous sets. But the future of others was less predictable.

About Marcel L'Herbier there is little to be said. After *Eldorado*, he wavered between commercialism and the emptiest aestheticism. *L'Inhumaine* was cold and abstract, a sort of desiccated *Caligari*. By contrast, *Le Vertige*, after Charles Méré, *Feu Mathieu Pascal*, after Pirandello, *Le Diable au Cœur*, after Lucie Delarue-Mardrus, are simply commercial films of practically no interest.* *L'Argent*, L'Herbier's next, extracted from a novel of Zola's brought up to date, was rather better. The scenes at the Bourse, the aviator's departure, the excitement as Paris awaits news of the raid, the party which the banker Saccard gives are all good. In the presence of so much regrettably misused skill we can only look back mournfully to the time when L'Herbier made *Eldorado*.

Jean Epstein has also come in for severe criticism, often justly, though he frequently by a sudden about-face gives the impression that his career is far from ended and that we can still count on him. *Le Lion des Mongols* with Mosjoukine can be dismissed as disarmingly tame, so can the episodic *Robert Macaire*, and the extremely boring *Sa Tête*, wherein Epstein filmed a gloomy murder story in which an innocent man is accused. He attempted here to create a low-toned and stark film like the one which Germany gave us in *Variety*. He unfortunately only succeeded in being profoundly boring. A little earlier, he had not greatly amused us

* In the editor's opinion, *The Late Matthew Pascal* was a film of considerable and abiding interest.

either when trying to acclimatize Caligarism in France with his *Fall of the House of Usher*, based on the famous Poe tale but also partly on Poe's *The Oval Portrait*. It is, in spite of the genuine mystery of a few scenes and the romantic trees and sinister water, a weak and dull picture.

As for *L'Affiche*, this was a brief and somewhat pretentious melodrama. A young woman who goes for a trip to the Marne with her sweetheart is afterwards abandoned with a child. The child wins in a beauty contest, a poster of him is made and then he dies. The mother sees everywhere the poster which reminds her of her little one, tears it down and is arrested. In the usual cinema tradition she later meets her seducer again, marries him and lives happily ever after. Unfortunately the beautiful landscapes at the beginning do not outweigh the mediocrity of the whole. In *Six et Demi Onze* at least the opening was technically ingenious, with its story of a man, in love with an actress, who, while developing a roll of film, discovers that the mistress of his brother had caused the latter's death. This carried one back to the time of *Le Brasier Ardent* and other highbrow films. At more or less the same period *La Glace à Trois Faces* vulgarized a clever novel by Paul Morand: here a man, seen by three different women, appears under three different aspects. The screen is probably incapable, despite all appearances, of translating such simple subtleties for, alas, it does not suggest them, it shows them.

Thus between commerce and literature it seemed that Jean Epstein had slowly been submerged and had lost all of the charm that in the past had given us *Cœur Fidèle* and *La Belle Nivernaise*. Suddenly, however, he came into his own again and there resulted a film of great merit, *Finis Terrae*.

It must be admitted right away that *Finis Terrae* is rather boring and fails to hold one's interest. A documentary film in fictional form is a difficult thing to attempt if one wants to achieve something out of the ordinary, and this story of a fisherman who develops a septic finger in a lonely part of the world where there is no doctor may be touching but it does not always manage to grip our attention. Despite this and despite an overemphasis on the picturesque, in no other French film have sea and wind and salt been so well interpreted. The little tumble-down village, the weather-beaten fishermen soaked to their skins, the nets set out to dry, the rocky roads that lead to the church are presented conscientiously with a precision which compels admiration. *Finis Terrae* is not perfect and, but for the Swedes, might never have been made, but it is a film almost alone of its kind in France, for it expresses what the French usually only admit when it has been seasoned with romance—nature undiluted, in all its primitive harshness, with all its dirt and its odors. That is the real merit of a film which is sometimes clumsy and ponderous but which enabled us not to despair too much of Jean Epstein's future.

Léon Poirier, who omitted no bid for the public's favor, worked nevertheless very conscientiously. A film like *Finis Terrae* might, at a pinch, have been his. Nevertheless, after *La Brière* he was to abandon the virtually untouched subject of the French countryside to make *Amours Exotiques* and a quite skillful picture of the Citröen expedition to Central Africa, *La Croisière Noire*. There followed his most important film, *Verdun, Visions d'Histoire*.

It is a war film and avoids none of the faults of that species. The symbolism, the conventional characters, the bombast always so unseemly in such a subject make it well-nigh unbearable. It is really the sort of thing which the average Frenchman would imagine, with the addition of a clever admixture of pacifism and of heroism, of Deroulède and of Erich Remarque, in which the dual cries of "We'll get them" and "Never again" seem to echo alternately. Virtually the same thing happens every time the French venture on that magnificent but dangerous subject.

There is, nevertheless, in Léon Poirier an undeniable talent, a sort of heavy and intense probity and so much conscientious care for detail that his scenes of fighting and of shellfire seem not to have been enacted but to have been taken actually on the battlefield itself. Also Poirier had the excellent idea of borrowing from the military archives some real war films: Joffre, Foch, Pétain, the Kaiser appear in their own persons. Commandant Driant, who was killed at Caures Wood, is shown only as a silhouette and a uniform; his face never appears. Most of the actors were old soldiers, ex-servicemen who had put on their uniforms again, so that in spite of its faults *Verdun** at its best moments became a sort of documentary film, an unadorned transcription of reality. It is one of the few French films which remind one of the Russians.

ABEL GANCE

Another man, superior to Poirier, who attained his maximum fame about 1926, also attempted to remind us of the Russians; this was Abel Gance, celebrated director of *La Roue*. For years he had been working on a film about *Napoleon* which was to have included the Emperor's whole career, from Brienne to St. Helena; but as time, money and a sense of proportion were all lacking he got no further than the Italian campaign, and disposed of his scenario on St. Helena to Lupu Pick. As it stands, his film is impressive and sums up better than any other the disorderly genius of its maker. It contains no new technical inventions (save one) to compare to those of *La Roue*, the forceful but jerky style of which he merely repeats. His camera is again extravagantly mobile: Gance did not hesitate to attach it to the chest of a singer in order to record a scene of a theater audience responding to the exact rhythm of "La Marseillaise." He even attached it to the tail of a runaway horse. In the admirable scene with which the film opens (it is probably the best thing Gance has ever done), the snowball fight at Brienne where young Bonaparte's genius for tactics is revealed, the camera positively takes part in the battle—it is struck by missiles, it runs away, stops, considers and escapes. It becomes the eye of the principal actor and is no longer a mere machine. The constantly quickening rhythm, a masterpiece of rapid cutting, shows the Corsican boy's face gradually lighting up with a smile through a succession of violent images composed with exquisite care. This is still, however, in the style of *La Roue*.

The one new invention in this immense *Napoleon* was the triple screen. Gance expected much from that device for breaking the

* *Verdun* bears some similarity to the British war-record films, *Mons, Ypres, The Somme*, etc. There seems to be a conspiracy of silence about these productions, which have considerable historical interest.

monotony of a single screen. Sometimes he used it simply to enlarge his image, as in the charges of the dragoons or for battle scenes or to show the vast panorama of the Armée d'Italie being harangued by its leader. Sometimes he used it as a triptych, as in the unforgettable episode of the descent into Italy, where the central screen showed the front ranks of superb, ragged soldiers with women hanging about their necks as they bawl, "Auprès de ma blonde," while the two side screens showed longshots of the great column of the army on the march through the fields. Never had the very incarnation of an epic been so magnificently transferred to the screen. Unfortunately that costly process had no future, and even *Napoleon* often had to be shown without the lateral screens.

There was sufficient power in that unequal and sometimes absurd film to interest one in its other qualities. It is true that Gance did not escape the dangers of his own lyricism. As in Hugo, that lyricism was often merely oratorical, and the form which this takes on the screen is inevitably double exposure, most literary of screen devices. A stormy session of the Convention (that famous scene) inevitably conjured up the image of a tempest, while a glance of Bonaparte necessitated also the image of a ruffled (rather than imperial) eagle, not to mention the interpolation of terrestrial globes, Josephine's face or the cast-off women who inevitably remind Gance of dead leaves.

Those perversions of history, this total lack of good sense, this Revolution so palpably created by ruffians and harpies, not one iota of whose picturesque hideousness is toned down, all shock one profoundly. However, there are times when Gance grants a respite. Violine's sentimental adventure, so incongruously incorporated into the main theme, is far from attractive, but this director of so many tumultuous melodramas at least had the skill to portray the Directorate and its waltzes with brilliance. There are details which are excellent—not the storm in which Bonaparte, admirably portrayed by the thin, feverish Dieudonné, uses a tricolored flag for the sail of his boat, but the siege of Toulon, where compositions as precise as chromolithographs show us the holes where the veterans stand up to their bellies in water, and the ride on the island,

and—best of all—Brienne, and Napoleon's arrival at the Armée d'Italie's camp, and the review of the troops, and the unrivaled descent into Italy.

Gance's handling of crowds and mob scenes is prodigious; he stamps the most volatile and monstrous expressions on all those unknown and nameless faces: everything becomes lawful before the passion and the power of the masses. Gance's style is at once learned and barbarous. The skill of his editing and the conscious beauty of the shots are a product of science, for Gance is one of the directors who best knows his craft. But he also believes in inspiration and is guided by creative fire, by a sort of revolutionary resurgence within himself. His camera, jostled this way and that by the extras in the mob scenes, drawn into the whirlpool of the riot, trampled underfoot by the crowd, rolling on the ground, seizes amid the confusion some admirable bits of reality to be cut into the sequence afterwards; these are to this director what moments of sudden inspiration are to a poet. This combination of disorder in the creation and of control in the composition provide astonishing results. Among many others let it suffice to mention the incident of the two thick and bloody hands that hoist up to the balcony where Bonaparte stands a stiffened rope from which a prisoner dangles, while the shadow of the spears and the glimmer of the torches flicker in turn across the future Emperor's face.

That creative chaos, at once so deliberate and so spontaneous, produced a sort of baroque masterpiece which is irritating and wearisome in its virtuosity, its constantly changing images, its total lack of critical judgment and even, perhaps, of intelligence; but it is the only French film wherein history does not appear stiff and lifeless like a waxwork show. With all its errors and omissions, this epic of Abel Gance's marks the height of his achievement. He had never before attained to such power, even in *La Roue;* he was never again to have such uncommon good fortune. This man who could work only with millions, this man without taste who suddenly displayed such exquisite inventive power, had at least succeeded once in producing a work which, though parts of it were still-born, contained scenes which are among the finest ever produced.

JACQUES FEYDER

The career of Jacques Feyder seems modest beside that of Abel Gance. He is no genius and does not pretend to be one. He works judiciously and conscientiously like a good workman, with ever-increasing concern for the "job well done." He assimilates the discoveries of others, and he also doubtless wishes to make money. His films are nearly all pleasing. It is only in the long run that one discovers the originality hidden under their rather rugged and simple exterior. In *L'Image*, from a story by Jules Romains, this originality is expressed by fairly obvious technical devices which recall *Crainquebille* and the school of Louis Delluc. Nevertheless it is a radical originality, with a feeling for truth and the things of the spirit; it even has a certain secret cruelty. This is clearly visible in two delightful pictures which somewhat resemble each other in their mischievous tenderness, their bittersweet sentimentality— *Gribiche* and *Visages d'Enfants*. Their slightly theatrical realism (always a fault with Feyder), their echoes of Alphonse Daudet have probably dated them. At that period Jackie Coogan, discovered in *The Kid*, was making a success in a number of films about children—*Circus Days*, *A Boy of Flanders*, *Long Live the King;* and André Hugon also filmed *Le Petit Chose*. But *Gribiche* and *Visages d'Enfants* are better. It is no cruel stepmother in the latter, but simply an indifferent one, who is the cause of the little boy's suicide. An overdose of sentimentality (as in the prayer to the mother's picture) distresses us, but little Jean Forest is serious and charming, the Valois villages in the snow and the funeral in the mountains have much simple beauty. Feyder often possesses the power to make us overlook the facile attractions of a clumsy plot and pleases us by dint of his truth-to-life, even if that truth is a little obvious and somewhat too theatrical.

"The most important thing in a film," Feyder once said, "is suggestion. If I had the time I could put Montesquieu's *Esprit des Lois* on the screen." In somewhat similar vein Eisenstein was to speak later of filming Karl Marx's *Capital*.

After he had made *Carmen* with Raquel Meller, that same art

of suggestion served Feyder well when he made his silent masterpiece, *Thérèse Raquin*. He made it in Germany, and it is very
nearly a film in the German manner, with its wonderful lighting
and chiaroscuro. One would have thought it difficult to make a
film of Zola's long novel,* yet Feyder succeeded because he omitted everything that weighs down the book and preserved only the
theme of the couple's obsession with their guilt, after the crime.
Thérèse and Laurent are stripped of their peasant qualities, their
greed and their passion for money: they are simplified and become
symbols of sexuality, damned souls who are all too human. The
opening scene, so curiously reticent, of the heroine's bridal night
at the side of a groom who is not only an invalid but a spoiled child
as well, gives the whole key to the pitiable story and raises it to
a sort of poetry. No complication of plot is provided to sustain
one's interest, and yet it was impossible not to be profoundly impressed by the stifling atmosphere of a film which, much more
appropriately than Pabst's, might have been called *Secrets of the
Soul*.

After that powerful study of suffering, *Les Nouveaux Messieurs* seemed no more than a soothing comedy, though it alarmed
the censors. It was an agreeable and unpretentious film, though
rather slow, and as far removed from Robert de Flers' adaptation
of the drama that gave it birth as was the film *Chapeau de Paille*.
What adaptation can best mean is brilliantly shown in the scene
of the Chamber, as seen by a deputy who is making a speech there.
At first he sees only a Right and a Left, far apart, one cheering
him on, the other booing. As he continues to speak, gradually the
Center takes shape. In many other scenes too, such as that of the
inauguration of the workers' city, Feyder's visual humor furnished
some delightful effects. After *Les Nouveaux Messieurs* Feyder
was engaged to go to America. Not one French director had been
invited to go to the United States since the war, but Feyder's robust simplicity, and that cleverness of his which occasionally puts
one in mind of Bernstein, had predestined him for the perilous
journey. Within relatively few years he had become important

* The novel is not particularly long, certainly not in comparison with
L'Argent, etc.

enough to attract the public's attention and, even more difficult, that of the critics.

Feyder, like Léon Poirier and Marcel L'Herbier, had entered the field right after the war. When Louis Delluc and a few of the directors had blazed the trail, certain other young directors also appeared whose work gave considerable promise.

Jean Renoir, second son of the painter, had started off with *Catherine* and *La Fille de l'Eau*. These were fumbling efforts, but one fragment of the second, the girl's dream, attracted attention. It was enough at that time to make a director's reputation for him to have his hero, with head hung low and standing under a tree, declare his love to a mysterious and frail girl. Jean Renoir's wife, Catherine Hessling, now appeared with her lively silhouette, her enormous eyes, her childish and fairylike air. Unfortunately, Jean Renoir did not immediately realize where his gifts lay. He made a rather breathless *Nana* and some commercial films of no great worth, *Le Bled, Le Tournoi dans la Cité*, and only began to find himself in that uneven but exquisite picture *La Petite Marchande d'Allumettes*. This is one of the few successful cinema fairy tales, suffused with a light which seems to emanate from Andersen himself. Catherine Hessling in the snow, Catherine Hessling in toyland, Catherine at the feet of a kind policeman, Catherine carried off by a procession of Chinese shadow shapes furnishes many exquisite compositions which suggested that a new artist had been born to the screen. It was in other directions, however, that Jean Renoir found success. *La Petite Marchande d'Allumettes* remains his masterpiece,* somewhat slow and precious but perfectly enchanting.

As for Alberto Cavalcanti, his ultimate failure seems by far the most regrettable of anything in French film history. It is true that from the start his work was uneven. *Rien que les Heures* was the delight of the advance guard, so was *La P'tite Lilie*, woven around

* *La Petite Marchande* was one of those deliberately "artistic" films which deceive so many people; seen in the cold light of today it seems puerile.

a sentimental song and parodying prewar films, with Catherine Hessling in a slightly forced vein of comedy. *Le Train sans Yeux* from a novel of Delluc's was no more than a skillful imitation of American adventure films. Then Cavalcanti made *En Rade*.

En Rade, which was truly appreciated by very few, is one of the most deeply moving of French films. It reverts, certainly, to the atmosphere of *Fièvre* and of *Cœur Fidèle*—to a bar in a large port. It introduced the theme of escape, so dear to the postwar mind, and showed us how it appealed to simple souls. The story by Philippe Hériat, who also acts admirably in it as a madman, somewhat resembles the future *Marius* of Marcel Pagnol—the son of a washerwoman dreams of islands and longs to travel. His mother, out of jealousy, prevents him from running away with a little waitress in a sailors' bar. It is a simple tale endowed with a curious, feverish unrest by Catherine Hessling, while Natalie Lissenko as the mother played her role with admirable simplicity. I admit that the film has faults: the views of ports shot against the light are too like picture postcards and the faces in close-up are much too white. But there is a miraculous continuity of feeling, the story is told magnificently, and there are some unforgettable sunlit scenes, compositions of stones, of washing hanging out of windows to dry and the purest "poetry of escape." Nothing was forced, there was nothing literary about the young man's emotions. Coming after Delluc and Epstein, Cavalcanti unquestionably surpassed them in this hymn to the romance of distant lands. Since that time, caught in the toils of commerce, he has produced nothing. *La Jalousie du Barbouille*, a comment on a Molière farce in which a cuckold hatches gigantic eggs, was rather dull, though interesting as an adaptation. *Yvette*, after de Maupassant, was clever enough. But then came *Le Capitaine Fracasse* and the talkies of Marcelle Chantal. Director of a few picturesque films and of one near-masterpiece, he seems to have stopped short, though the fault was not entirely his.*

Among other less talented newcomers was Jean Grémillon, an able but undistinguished director, as *Tour au Large*, *Maldone* and *Les Gardiens de Phare* showed; Jean Benoit-Lévy and Marie Ep-

---

* Cavalcanti has since done excellent work in England.

stein are far superior to him. Among many films not without interest especial attention is due to their *Peau de Pêche*, a charming story about a child of the slums which occasionally predicts the freshness of *La Maternelle*. Peau de Pêche in the midst of a circle of attentive children on the Place du Tertre, with a straw hat tilted over one ear as he imitates Maurice Chevalier, has undeniable charm.

Other young directors conducted their experiments on different grounds, remote from the general public's interest.

THE ADVANCE GUARD

A special place must be reserved for those poets of the screen who attempted to translate into visual terms the beauties of music. Surrealism has preached the virtues of absolute freedom, but these poets of the screen are seldom surrealist because they are not free: they are logical; they are organizers. They translate certain fundamental concepts into images linked by the strong bands of analogy. The images recur or disappear following a rhythm such as Gance had introduced into *La Roue*, as exact as Latin scansion. These films which the advance guard bestowed on us so generously in the beautiful years of its youth cannot properly be regarded as having no subject matter; they have no narrative plot, but nearly all of them have a subject and are occasionally as effective as fantastic or nonsense poems, and as provocative of ideas.

One of the first attempts in this manner was Fernand Léger's *Ballet Mécanique*, so reminiscent of his paintings, in which various metal utensils are made into an intelligent if frigid composition. One scene goes beyond this intellectual exercise—the one in which a charwoman climbs a long flight of steps. It is repeated fifteen times and gives an impression of the labors of Sisyphus, of a mechanical and cruelly repetitious destiny.

After Léger, other directors attempted similar exercises: Henri Chomette made a charming *Jeux des Reflets et de la Vitesse*,* while Germaine Dulac experimented along other lines. She attempted to translate musical works, notably Chopin's *Arabesque, Disque 957*

---

* Better known as *Of What Are the Young Films Dreaming?*

and *Thème et Variations*, to the screen. She also filmed a surrealist scenario of Antonin Artaud's, *The Seashell and the Clergyman*. On the whole it would seem that Germaine Dulac has not entirely fulfilled her destiny; her role as critic has been more important than her role as creator. More than anyone else, by what she said and published she helped to establish certain wholesome ideas, fighting with the commercial people to insist on films without stories, fighting with the snobs for the rights of films with stories, and stressing the relationship between films and music.

Of all the directors of abstract films, undoubtedly the most important was Man Ray. Not all his experiments have equal value— *Le Retour à la Raison, Emak Bakia, L'Etoile de Mer, Le Mystère du Château du Dé*. The last-named shows some rather feeble scenes in juxtaposition with some beautiful landscape shots. *L'Etoile de Mer* is admirable. It is the only film in which surrealism becomes human. Even without understanding it, it is possible to be pleased by this poem of love and regret with its magnificently handled photography, its brilliant use of soft focus and of distortion. A woman seen through glass * takes on the appearance of a miraculous Renoir, the lovers walking together as seen through the same translucent veil are as easily understandable and as moving as the most romantic farewells in Lamartine. If surrealism has produced something of importance it is through the works of this American photographer.

A little later one fancied that it had produced something of importance in the Spaniard, Luis Bunuel's, *Le Chien Andalou*. The hand swarming with red ants, the eyeball slit by the razor blade, the bleeding calf on the piano have an abiding interest still in the same way as in *L'Age d'Or*, which followed it, and which was banned because it shocked morality. The films of Bunuel lack unity. They are made up of a succession of aggressive or startling photographs, many of which are beautiful, but the sexual sadism which dominates them is not enough to supply them with a satisfying rhythm. Without some interior unity, studies of this kind defeat themselves and lose interest.

In order to obtain that threatened unity, other young people

---

* Sheets of mica.

elected to interpret the documentary film, too little esteemed. André Sauvage's cold and subtle studies of Paris, of which *Paris-Port* especially was exceedingly clever, deserve mention. George Lacombe in the same vein was successful with *La Zone*, which displayed much feeling and skill. Lucie Derain and Jean Lods were also to interpret the beauty of Paris and Claude Lambert that of London. Jean Tedesco strove to interpret the picturesqueness of metallurgy; Marc Allegret returned from a journey with Gide with a quite clever *Voyage au Congo*. One must not forget, too, those admirable films of plant life taken in laboratories with rapid-motion photography which compress days of growth into the space of a few seconds and reveal in terrifying fashion the "intelligence" of nature. Colette has written of these miracles, of the "greedy yawning of the cotyledons from which bursts forth the darting serpent's head of the first bud," of the "formidable distension and explosion of the bud of a lily, parting its long flat mandibles to reveal a dark crawling of stamens in a greedy and masterful efflorescence."

The most original of these directors was the scientist Jean Painlevé, who specialized in documentary films of submarine beasts. His films of sea urchins, sea horses, plant-animals and carnivorous plants, magnified from one to ten thousand times, provide glimpses of startling beauty. No one could ever forget the courtship of those marine animals like chrysanthemums that caress each other with their petals, or the many tragic or romantic incidents, recorded sometimes in rapid and sometimes in slow motion, that make many of these films into monuments of subtle and terrifying pantheism which reveal the very soul of nature. These in their own way are undoubtedly the most perfect and the most imperishable creations of the screen, for it is difficult to imagine that they could ever seem old-fashioned.

During the last years of the silent film there were also the amateurs with their hired cameras who bore down on town and countryside alike trying to transmute into pictures their emotions and their ideas. Sometimes they made use of a little sentimental plot, but usually they were content to steal from the sunlight and from nature some pleasing compositions afterwards to be lovingly edited into a film. These pictures were shown in specialized theaters like L'Oeil de Paris, Studio 28, and the Agriculteurs. They gave hope for the motion picture—a hope of putting it within everyone's grasp and freeing it from the power of money.

Some of these amateurs were familiar with the film industry; they were assistants or journalists. The important thing was that they were free and concerned only with expressing their own imagination. Albert Guyot in *Mon Paris*, in *A quoi Revent les Becs de Gaz*, in *L'Eau qui Coule sous les Ponts* composed some charming pictures in which he featured his wife, Mireille Séverin of the childlike face. Michel Carne's *Nogent, Eldorado du Dimanche* was the best of these amateur films. Since money was lacking, all of them attempted to endow objects with life, because objects do not demand salary, and thus they made certain discoveries. A simple room in *L'Eau qui Coule*, a public dance in *Nogent*, a street in the early morning, a soldier asleep in the fields provided them with their subject matter. It was discovered that water provides an admirable subject and that nothing is more beautiful than an oar striking the surface of a lake, nor more lovely than the furrow a plow makes. The wine harvest, about which Georges Rouquier made a picture, the crops and the animals were discovered. They could not, it is true, provoke strong emotions, but these films attempted to express the poetry of simple, even ridiculous, things like picture postcards, hurdy-gurdies, lovers in a field, couples dancing, a little working girl all alone. Of such ingredients was *Nogent* composed, and despite poor photographic quality and an excessive use of odd or distorted images it displayed an exquisite freshness and naturalness. *L'Eau qui Coule sous les Ponts* with its splendid automobile ride and its rather forced sentimentality displayed more art but also more artifice.

No matter; all these films and those of Pierre Chenal and of Claude Autant-Lara had one thing in common—youth. Some of these young men attempted to introduce other elements: Jean Vigo, who died all too early, made a documentary film about Nice, romantic but full of magnificent cruelty, in which the absurdities of amorous elderly ladies, of gigolos and of the decadent bourgeoisie were fiercely stigmatized. For lack of money these films boldly attempted themes which the cinema as a whole has neglected. Nothing is more regrettable than the dearth of experiments of this kind since the advent of the talkies.

Finally, besides Man Ray, the names of a few Russian directors must be mentioned. Ladislas Starevich, that good old magician, remained apart, patiently constructing his miniature miracles with their unforgettable submarine adventures, fantastic animals, ambulant plants and a wonderful fairyland in which his exquisitely fashioned marionettes dwelt. Unfortunately he produces less and less and lives in retirement. There was also Eugene Deslav who composed *La Nuit Electrique* out of the illuminated signs of Paris at night, and made *La Marche des Machines* and *Parnasse*. There were also Dmitri Kirsanov's charming films, unequal but delicate—*L'Ironie du Destin, Menilmontant* (made with the most loving care), *Sables* and *Brumes d'Automne.*

The first dates from 1924. The actors were Nadia Sibirskaya and Kirsanov himself, and it had no subtitles. The plot was extremely simple—just the tale of a forsaken woman now growing old and of a man equally desperate and alone. They encounter one another on a park bench and find that happiness has passed them by. The rather obvious symbolism—the stream, the turning wheel —might seem displeasing today, but the film displayed great delicacy of feeling and a profound love for Paris as seen from the rooftops, for the streets, the busses and that whole urban life which it approached with an affection as great as that of René Clair. *Brumes d'Automne* is a sort of poem to Nadia Sibirskaya's face, around which images crystallize—the angle of a roof, chimneys, a pond, a fireplace, the woods of Seine-et-Oise. A woman recalls the past, and her memories are shown on the screen. She is burning old letters; there is rain outside, and puddles; leaves fall to the ground. This may be cheap Lamartine, but it is redeemed by the beauty and skill of the photography of the gray skies, the poplars mirrored in the water, the tops of aspens falling obliquely and dimly across the screen. In a muddy lane, puddles reflect the branches of trees and bits of tree trunks. Elsewhere there is a battered old willow, and more water, then more treetops and more puddles. A prodigious use of reflections and of miniatures makes one think of

Van Eyck's paintings: a whole extraordinary Lilliputian landscape appears in a puddle in the center of a sort of lunar landscape created by the close-up of a ditch.

Such effects have been all too rare in the cinema—such a new use of the camera would have been impossible but for the experiments made by the advance guard. We are indebted to it for these attempts to show us an epic aspect of everyday objects, bringing us closer to nature and interpreting it. Such interpretation is the whole art of the film. *Brumes d'Automne* proves it, as do the films most characteristic of any made in France—those of René Clair.

RENÉ CLAIR

No matter how effective and powerful are some of the French films, and notwithstanding the fact that Abel Gance's *Napoleon* is the most important of them, René Clair is unquestionably the most interesting of France's film personalities.

René Clair, whose real name is René Chomette, was born in Paris in 1898. He started out in journalism and literature in 1919, became interested in films, began haunting the studios and appeared as an extra in *Parisette*. It is interesting to learn that he played, too, in the Loïe Fuller *Le Lys de la Vie* and in some of Protazanov's films. The experiments of the American woman and the Russian *émigré* were not to be without their influence on him. Then he became Baroncelli's assistant.

In 1923, at the age of twenty-five, he produced his first film, *Paris qui Dort*, or *The Invisible Ray*. It was a fantastic and satirical affair which recalled the lively American serials and also the prewar comedies. But here comedy was transformed by imagination, as we see in the scenes of deserted Paris, which suddenly takes on a curiously impressive air, and by the unusual aspect assumed by the most commonplace objects. *Paris qui Dort*, a fairy tale of suspended animation, mingled irony with its fantasy.

The following year he made *Entr'acte*, with music by Erik Satie and a scenario by Picabia. It was a great *succès de scandale* and it miraculously preserves the whole spirit of a now vanished and delightfully crazy period, for this classic of absurdity was in its own way a real classic.

In appearance it is merely a sort of dream without a subject and without a plot, in which the most incongruous images freely succeed one another, linked only by haphazard and arbitrary associations. We see a head of hair, a handful of matches, some cylinders resembling cigarettes which suddenly turn into the Parthenon, spots floating about the Place de l'Opéra, a ballerina who bends and stretches and relaxes in a lazy rhythm, an egg on a jet of water in a shooting gallery, a pigeon-shooting target, a funeral oddly like a wedding with a hearse drawn by a camel which later rolls down a long incline as the film concludes with a frenzied chase. The images succeed one another without any apparent connection; each one simply gives birth to the next, yet amidst this seeming incoherence it is not difficult to follow the clues. The events are taking place in the mind of someone sleeping the sleep of exhaustion after an evening at the fair. The sequence of the opening pictures is jumbled, as though the dream were fumbling and not knowing where to begin. The matches, the scanty locks on someone's head seen from above, the row of cigarettes in their box, the Place de l'Opéra and the sheet of water are seen on a horizontal plane. The ballerina, who reappears persistently as though to mark a rhythm and give the dream its form, and the egg on the jet of water are both seen on a vertical plane. The two planes occasionally mingle, as for instance when the box of cigarettes slowly straightens up and becomes the colonnade of the Parthenon, or when we see the dancer from beneath like an enormous flower opening out horizontally. These associations serve to establish throughout the film an order which, mysterious though it is, is nevertheless subtly grasped by one's imagination; there is a recognizable progress in the succession of images and a sort of harmony. It is too elusive to describe, but to a spectator who lets himself go with the film that ingenious interlacing of impressions provides a soothing cadence.

Towards the middle of the film there is a break, or, rather, a definite orientation of the dream. The egg on the jet of water suggests the shooting gallery, the shooting gallery suggests death, death suggests the funeral, which now becomes the principal subject. The associations here are much less original but the style becomes quite different. While in a sense the first part of the film is static with its play on slow motion, the second part is full of movement. The burlesque funeral starts out slowly, gravely, then the pace quickens, the hearse slides down a slope, people run and from running turn into sprinters, the race goes faster and faster, its pace evokes all sorts of ideas connected with speed—a road flashing by, crossroads, brakes being put on, sharp curves, a bicycle race, roller coasters at a fair—and finally all ends with a crash, the people vanish one by one, even the conjurer, who makes himself vanish by touching himself with his wand. The whole burlesque race has an admirable technical precision and, thanks to its sure, almost mathematical, cutting, gives increasingly an impression of dizziness produced solely by the purely physical acceleration of speed. Here living characters take part in the action but only as extensions of objects, for they are only regarded as being objects themselves; the procession with the hearse becomes a measure in a dance in which they take part and mingle with the objects.

Entr'acte is a macabre poem without a story, set in an imaginary world. Something more than a farce, it is a succession of themes which are droll rather than comical. The whole sums up to a very special sort of burlesque: cold, calculated and completely detached. It can be called a work of imagination because of its freedom, its fantasy, its atmosphere of unreality and especially its rhythm. But it is the work of an exact mathematician, as though some Vaucanson with a passion for mystification had produced it: there is not a trace of emotion or of self-revelation, only the precise technique of an engineer, a strange practice of weighing every object coldly and judging what weight of comedy can be got out of it—much as in *Le Dernier Milliardaire*, later on.

All its amusing images are strongly characteristic of a period not without daring. The film has an astonishing unity—the only one of René Clair's save *Quatorze Juillet* to have such unity—

which is the basis of film construction as René Clair understood it. If the film is born of pantomime for Chaplin, of painting for the German school, of music or even of the novel (for no real director can the film ever be born of the theater), for René Clair, after *Entr'acte*, the film seems to spring from dance and the ballet.

The whole atmosphere of the Russian Ballet, not merely that of *Parade* and of the *Mariés de la Tour Eiffel*, must be remembered in connection with his films. Though his work had been known before the war, Diaghilev was now supreme. René Clair, coming into a world enraptured by the dance, worked at first for the Swedish Ballets. Though he was willing to make use of actors and actresses, it is probable that he still considered them merely as objects; this was something he learned from the Russians, and he manipulated the strings of the enchanting puppets in his compositions much as the machinery of the Strasbourg clock animates its famous figures. Though he was to enrich and modify his formula later, the principle remained that of the dance of the objects in *Entr'acte*, for which, later on, the music of Georges Auric and of the Groupe des Six was to provide a collaboration which might almost have been predicted from the start.

In the same year *Le Fantome du Moulin-Rouge*, a story of a soul which separates itself from its body, is at times a burlesque, and showed that Clair did not yet know how to tell a story and that his fantasy fitted in ill with a plot. There is no feeling in this film, except ridiculous feelings, and for this he was criticized; actually it should have been criticized for its dullness. However, in 1925 *Le Voyage Imaginaire* came along to console us. This, too, is a fairy tale, more danced than acted by Jean Borlin, with some wonderful exterior shots, mellow lighting, some wonderful glimpses of Paris and a character who, at the touch of a fairy's wand, becomes a small dog, as well as some amusing chases in the Mack Sennett manner. Especially in the waxworks museum in *Le Voyage Imaginaire* do we find both Vaucanson and the ballet again. The poor hero, condemned to death by the waxworks revolutionary tribunal, almost touches our hearts. In spite of appearances, *Le Voyage Imaginaire* is linked to *Entr'acte* by

Les Mariés de la Tour Eiffel. Between the objects of Picabia's poem and the half-real characters which were to come later, these wax figures with eyeballs painted on their eyelids and their jerky motions, their mechanical and macabre humor, form a distinct link. Soon now the lovers will be smiling at one another in the shade of cardboard trees, and the dance which sweeps them along will include both real people and puppets, so that one can no longer tell which is which. But was there ever to be more than intelligence in these gay little diversions? René Clair seemed to have much more affinity with the eighteenth century, so reasonable, so charming and so arid, than with the postwar period. This was evident later, too, at the time of *Le Dernier Milliardaire*.

La Proie du Vent of 1926 was a rather odd film in Clair's output: based on a novel by Pierre Vignal, *L'Aventure Amoureuse*, it combines many rather intricate plots not one of which is fully developed. Its only interest lies in a certain technical ability which reminds us of Kirsanov. When a character takes a walk we do not see him walking, we see instead what *he* sees during the walk. The image of a woman is reflected in a pool, a triangle of light disappears, a door closes and, at the beginning, there is a ride in an airplane with a good deal of pitching and motion. Later on, far too many nicely dressed people were to go for walks amid beautiful surroundings and too many strange adventures were to remind us of newspaper serials. But Clair never again attempted to adapt a novel or a play to the screen in that manner.

He returned to the ballet. Despite the plot and despite the style, so characteristic of that period, Clair's only novel, *Adams* * (which, by the way, is about the movies), already indicates this. It shows all the characters Adams had portrayed, circling about their creator until all ends in the colossal comedy of the finale where even religions are ridiculed. The idea was better than the execution, and the book is not to be compared with *The Italian Straw Hat*. In this the ballet motif appeared again, informed the entire picture and became the very center and reason

* Published much later in English as *Star Turn*, Chatto, London, 1936.

for its existence. The mischievous puppetmaster drew upon his property box for each character, giving a shirt front to one, a single glove to another, a paper cap to Paul Olivier, his uniform to the captain. At the end of the film there is a delightful measure during which these objects take back their independence and, in turn, the glove, the paper cap and the hat reappear and then disappear before our very eyes. The director was pulling his puppets apart. When our backs were turned he would hang them up on a nail, head downwards. None of the emotions are genuine; nothing is to be taken seriously.

Having chosen, of all things, that enormous chromolithograph which is Labiche's farce, René Clair set to work to bring it to life. Those mechanical gifts which served him in creating the burlesque machinery of *Entr'acte* were now applied to the situations of a farce. Each character is the occasion for a bit of delicate composition: he makes a father-in-law out of a shirt front, an angry expression and new boots which pinch; then he makes a female cousin out of a guimpe, eyeglasses, a velvet waist trimmed with passementerie, high boots, a meager chignon and the long face of Alice Tissot. The Hussar is costumed exactly as in one of those colored plates of soldiers which one can buy for ten centimes, or those photographs which adorn family photograph albums, with an exquisitely adjusted dolman, a waxed mustache turned up against his cheek like a tusk and a terribly fierce expression. A cuckold calls for pronounced obesity, bushy mustache, bovine head, bathing drawers and a mustard bath for his feet. Customs and manners are studied with the minute care of a watchmaker, and so are the settings. There is a typical Henri II dining room, a typical bedroom, a standard apartment for newlyweds in which not a vase, not a china figure, not one clock or candlestick, not one lamp or tidy or occasional table is missing: the whole thing is reconstituted with canny and ferocious joy—even the wallpaper is absolutely correct. Satisfied with having attained the maximum of conventionality and of absurdity in both his story and his settings, he only had to fit these meticulously fashioned cogs into one another.

Did farce really interest him? It is to be doubted. He preserved the essential structure because that was necessary, but every time he turns to the plot the interest lags. When it is forgotten, marvels burst forth. The exquisite and wicked care with which Clair composed his apartments, the celebrated quadrille which is the best moment in the film, prove once more that this too is only a ballet—the story of the lovers surprised by a horse which eats the lady's hat is transformed into the theatrical rodomontade of a provincial production of 1895. The dream in which Albert Préjean sees his furniture being moved out of his house by men in evening dress comes straight out of *Entr'acte*. This is once more a ballet of objects, of inanimate or of human objects, and the return of the various themes at the end indicates this, as if we have not already suspected it. With considerable wit, the director amused himself by giving the film the rapid, jerky rhythm of those prewar films which had only sixteen frames to the second. It is the only experiment of this kind that we know of. One is inevitably reminded of Stravinski, incorporating fairground tunes like "Elle avait une jambe de bois" into the fair in *Petrushka*, and can imagine what "La fille de Madame Angot" might become if Ravel took the notion to rewrite it. There can be no pleasure more intense or more exquisite—though *Le Chapeau de Paille* has bored many people—than that provided by this Ballet Russe of the French bourgeoisie.

It is unimportant that *The Italian Straw Hat* is episodic or that, in spite of the general movement which the extraordinary dynamism of the old farce imposes on it, the film is somewhat lacking in unity. What delights us is that each character, dressed in stylized costume a little "off" the period and "off" reality, is ready to enter the dance. There is nothing conventional about this ballet but the determination to provide poetry to a period which was most lacking in it. A ballet need not be danced by nymphs in Louis XIV costume; the bourgeoisie of the Third Republic has a right to this honor too, and *Le Million* will show that the grocer, the dairymaid, the janitress, the taxicab driver and the policeman can also join in. Isn't the best thing in *Le Dernier Milliardaire* its dances?

Stravinski's magician thoughtlessly gave life to creatures with feelings when he hurled Petrushka, the Moor and the ballerina into the vivid tumult of Carnival. Would this hardhearted Clair not eventually come to love his puppets and listen to their pitiful secrets? The intellectual ballet could not long satisfy the man who one day was to reveal himself as a subtle amateur of dainty sentimental adventures. For a while longer he amused himself with the play of objects. His poetic documentary film *La Tour*, "that big, iron girl," is a delicate marvel of editing; he succeeded in giving us the impression of something rich and whole out of a few scraps of iron; and the arrival of the elevator takes on a genuine emotional value. Nevertheless, here still we are dealing only with the inanimate. The most widely known Clair, the Clair who likes popular romances, only really came into existence with *Les Deux Timides*.

This short film, quickly made, with no pretensions whatever, has been insufficiently appreciated. It is a minor work, no doubt, but one in which even the faults are masterly. We must even congratulate it on being imperfect, on seeming here and there to hesitate a little—which proves that Clair's dominant gift of tact and proportion arises not from any lack of power but from a striving after perfection.

Les Deux Timides undeniably overdoes editorial and technical tricks, but the two courtroom scenes, whether they use reverse motion or still photography, are nevertheless remarkable. They remind us that in all of René Clair's work we must never forget either the theater scene from *The Italian Straw Hat*, or *Entr'acte*, or his love of technical tricks and quips, or his irony, for if the delightful closing pictures form a triptych it is because that year had seen the triple screen of Abel Gance's *Napoleon*, and Clair is not averse to parody.

Yet for all the irony and the parody, this Vaucanson listens to what his marionettes are saying. He has turned away from the fashions of 1895; a few period touches suffice now, though the rich troupe of minor characters continues to perform its ballet. In order to costume Pierre Batcheff, or to manipulate the strings that control the young man's aunt, he relies again on mischievousness and care for detail. The mischief dissolves in a gentle smile when his principal characters go out of doors. The most exquisite French landscapes, the loveliest villages ever seen appear in *Les Deux Timides*. (Julien Duvivier in *Poil de Carotte* was merely Clair's most gifted pupil.) Children, at play in the springtime sunlight, pin paper fish to the suitor's pants; the lawyer and the constable run along the hedges. A delightfully fresh breeze and light such as we have seen nowhere else diffuse this little film. Here are the two lovers, poor Pierre Batcheff and a young girl in a big hat, who walk timidly towards the sunlit bridge and the French hills. The faintest touch of irony underlines the innocent boldness of the girl and the timidity of the boy; Pierre Batcheff lays trembling hands on the girl's shoulders. A breath of fresh air fills the screen and seems suddenly to ventilate the whole auditorium.

No doubt someday Clair will follow up his experiment in *Les Deux Timides,* and this man whose choice of subjects has generally required studio settings will once more lead his reawakened marionettes through similar landscapes. Greater experience will have furnished him with greater magic, but we shall never forget that the first of René Clair's great love scenes and—with those in *A Nous la Liberté* and *Le Million*—the most beautiful, occurred in the rustic scenes of *Les Deux Timides.*

Henceforth his ballets have a motive and are no longer the sole aim or *raison d'être* of his films. The cook, the country cousin, the fat lady who so happily appears in all of Clair's pictures, the lawyer, the village constable now draw back a little so that we may see two children in the center of the circle, and catch the refrain of their songs, "Il court le furet" or "La belle qui voilà." We were soon to hear those songs in actual fact.

René Clair completes the considerably interesting make-up of the French film around 1930. With this imaginative and witty man, with the lyricism unleashed by Gance, with Feyder's care for detail and the evanescent poetry of *En Rade* there was no reason to despise the French output, even though too many farces and dramas regrettably recalled the era of the old Film d'Art. With the best of her directors and those of the advance guard, France had assembled an imposing array of talent at the time talkies were invented.

2. *The German Film*

DURING the creative years, Germany played an important part; she continued to do so during the period in which—once experimentation had resulted in a degree of stability—the cinema was to produce its finest works. The German contribution is difficult to assess, particularly after 1925, for this country turned out a number of films without any merit—light comedies which were very heavy and society dramas—exactly like similar films produced in France. These were made for purely commercial reasons, but a few of the men who had really contributed something now conscientiously continued their work with striking results, and, since at the time little was known of the Russian films and Sweden was producing hardly anything of interest, they appeared to be the most notable figures in the European field.

THE END OF CALIGARISM

The elements which had made the fame of the German product were nevertheless to vanish with the posterity of *Caligari*. Emaciated Conrad Veidt was still to appear in terrifying and Hoffmannesque films, one of which was, inevitably, a *Dr. Jekyll* made to rival John Barrymore's, in which Veidt's slender silhouette was extremely effective.* But the primary interest of these attempts to endow the screen with fantasy was dissipated amid the banality of their too obvious effects. Directors who had established a reputation along these lines now merely repeated themselves or sought fresh fields.

Robert Wiene was to try to terrify us once more in *The*

* *Der Januskopf*, directed by F. W. Murnau, shown in U.S.A. as *Love's Mockery*, was made in 1920.

Hands of Orlac, a story about a pianist on whom the hands of an assassin had been grafted. He did not succeed, and threw himself into more commercial productions—*Rosenkavalier* and *The Duchess of the Folies Bergères*—which were as sumptuous as they were insipid. Karl Grune momentarily abandoned the realistic drama so dear to him, in order to make *Two Brothers* with Conrad Veidt, in which the famous actor played dual roles. Henrik Galeen, author of the scenario for *Nosferatu*, relapsed into *Alraune* first and then into a romantic tale of a young man whose shadow had been stolen from him, *The Student of Prague*,* often childish but filled with nostalgic Viennese charm. This was Caligarism's swan song.

Mention must be made of the famous abstract films, so popular for a time among the intellectuals, created by Richter, Eggeling and Walter Ruttmann.† Marbles rolling along slopes, studies of forms and of rhythms were combined into visual symphonies in which the repetition of patterns in black and white attempted to create the same pleasing effect as the repetition of sounds in a musical composition. These strange productions were not without their uses, although their mathematical coldness lacked the emotional quality characteristic of French films of the period. Walter Ruttmann, however, was to liberate himself from formulas and produce a much freer work, *Berlin, the Symphony of a Big City*, which traces the life of Berlin from dawn to midnight in a series of well-chosen shots. Here the all-important factor was rhythm, though it was necessary to wait for the advent of the talkies before Ruttmann was able to work out his theories completely.

G. W. PABST

After Lupu Pick and Murnau, Germany was actually growing more concerned with putting realism onto the screen than in allying it to dream and fantasy. Here G. W. Pabst occupies a place in the front rank. Always an excellent craftsman and some-

* *The Student of Prague* preceded *Alraune*.
† The abstract films of Eggeling also belong to an earlier period.

times an artist of real merit, this man has the distinction of having produced, right from the start up to the present time, an output which forms a continuous whole, though not always of equal value, without making overmany concessions. His debut was a triumph: there are few German films more celebrated than *The Joyless Street.** In it Asta Nielsen, in her decline, with her regal beauty and magnificent acting, crossed the path of a young girl just starting on her career and newly come from Sweden—Greta Garbo. Pabst threw into contrast in this film the pleasures of the rich and the misfortunes of the poor in famine-ridden Vienna during the inflation. As often happens, the pleasures were rather ill represented, but the miseries inspired Pabst to tragic and violent overtones. It was in *The Joyless Street* that we first saw queues of poor people waiting under the livid lamplight in the icy streets. Who can forget the amazing face of Asta Nielsen,† frozen to marble stillness amid her feathers and her pearls when, as the prostitute, she determines to send her lover to the gallows; or the horrible procuress, or the disgusting butcher who rules over the entire street and gives meat only to whom he pleases? The most summary ideology did not entirely spoil this film, for though the story was overpathetic Pabst saved everything by his ability to put on the screen as vividly as any painter the lights drowned in fog, the leprous houses, slimy staircases, poor dwellings and a whole downtrodden humanity.

Later on Pabst attempted something different. In *Secrets of the Soul*, a study of sexual impotence, in *Pandora's Box*, about prostitution, in *Crisis*, in *The Love of Jeanne Ney* he tried to bring to the screen psychological truths far more complex than are usually admissible. Censorship slashed these films, with their rather puerile applications of Freudian theory, yet so undeniably honest. *The Diary of a Lost Girl* carried these experiments further. This drab Balzacian story of an old man kept a prisoner by his servant had power to move one, though all the false romanticism of Hugo's Fantine and Cosette were packed into it. Pabst

* He had previously made *The Treasure*, so it was hardly a debut.
† In the version shown in this country Asta Nielsen was unfortunately omitted.

was evidently unable to avoid falling into errors of this kind. This Freudian period came to an end with the silent films. Perhaps not all of it is worth remembering, but his work had considerable influence. From the time of *The Joyless Street* it placed the maker of these tormented and elementary films in the front rank of his contemporaries.

THE NEW REALISM

Thanks to him and to a few other men, a new realism established itself on the screen. It was the realism of a psychologist and also of a painter, in its care for the humble and significant details of life. This was what gave to certain adaptations from plays, in which the old Théâtre Libre lived on, a sort of melancholy and brutal poetry in which it had been singularly lacking —as in *The Weavers*, directed by Friedrich Zelnik, and *Mother and Child* by Carl Froelich. Instinctive revolt, a more or less declared socialism, the unrest of conquered Germany dreaming of revenge and shaken by revolution were expressed here with a humility and a materialism which were enormously attractive.

The Tragedy of the Street, directed by Bruno Rahn, revived the theme of *The Joyless Street* and Asta Nielsen was again admirable in it. Yet, in this heavy, mournful story of an aged woman attracted to a young boy, the romance of low life is in no way comparable to that of Delluc or of Epstein. It offers no glimmer of hope, no dream of escape, and if it attracts us in some obscure way it is through its very heaviness. Man is almost always crushed by fate in the films of this period. Expressionism, now forgotten, had served to show to what extent the background of man's life is important, particularly if that background is to destroy him. That explains why we see so many shots taken by the camera (which itself seems endowed with feeling and the power to suffer) of walls or windows or dirty kitchen sinks or shabby furniture; that is what explains, too, so much oppressive insistence on, so bitter an obsession with despair.

Lupu Pick in his all too rare films was often the victim of

theatrical realism, yet if *New Year's Eve* seemed to us a sort of revelation which could never again be equaled, it was just because it represented dramatic action which, however, remained human and even humdrum. A mother-in-law and daughter-in-law hate each other almost without realizing it, attempt to strangle each other, and the husband, insane with grief, kills himself. In this brief hour of film with only three characters and no subtitles, there is a continuous contrast between intimate scenes and scenes taken outside the home, such as that of the violent quarrel between the woman and the daughter-in-law which is followed by the scene of people coming out of a night club early on the morning of New Year's Day. It must be admitted that this film still displays a regrettable dependence on the theater, even to respecting the unnatural conventions of time and place. Yet even today its tension and its oppressive brevity are still striking. At the very end, when New Year's revelers invade the house, the spirit of bad taste enters with them and the realism turns into expressionism.

The other films of Lupu Pick (apart from *The Armored Vault*, which is a detective picture) again display the same gift for understatement and the same significant settings. That is why Pick was so successful in adapting *The Wild Duck*, in which the heavy and magnificent drama of Ibsen with its human degradation is expressed with real intensity, while *The Doomed Pinnace* and *Fiacre No. 3* also grip us with their deliberate and intelligent atmosphere in which every gesture is profoundly calculated to express the utmost possible.

Murnau, equally deliberate and quite as solid, went off at various tangents. He tried to bring *Tartuffe* up to date and to direct a *Faust* as impressive as the *Nibelungen*. What one remembers him for is *The Last Laugh*.

The plot is simple enough: it is the tale of a hotel porter, proud of his uniform, who one fine day, because he is growing old and because he has been drinking, is put in charge of the washrooms and considers himself the most degraded of men. Thanks in part to the powerful and eloquent acting of Jannings, Murnau expressed in this film all that disillusionment with life, the bitter sense of time's passing, in which one can see symbolically reflected the picture of Germany at that time. It was perhaps a rather dull film, its technical effects are very obvious and are even insisted upon, much in it had been borrowed from the work of others and it expresses a markedly Germanic concept of life. But its very heaviness served Murnau, as Jannings' faults also served him; and the scenes in the street where everybody admires the old man, and in the restaurant, not to mention that door to the washrooms which swings to and closes on the distress of the old porter, all became widely significant.

Other less ambitious films were nevertheless successful in their way—*Nju*, in which Paul Czinner, like Germaine Dulac in *La Souriante Madame Beudet*, told the story of a good-natured husband and a romantic wife. There was no striving after technical effects in that picture; it was apparently the most scrupulously realistic film; but it had an admirable cast (Jannings, Elisabeth Bergner and Veidt) who acted it with extraordinary sureness. One might have deduced from it, probably, that Czinner was later to make commercial films, but his affection for psychological truth and his skill would always remain.

The new realism was feverish, unhealthy, excessively precise, haunted by sensual obsessions and sometimes profoundly touching. Karl Grune's *Jealousy*, Carl Froelich's *The Tragedy*, Richard Oswald's *Feme* (once again the story of a prostitute's redemption), Joe May's *Homecoming*, and actors like Jannings and Krauss all thrust the image of a violent and unhappy world upon us. If at times we were permitted to escape from it, we were never allowed to forget the hidden symbolism, the ignominy and bitterness of man's fate. Pabst did not forget it when, for once, he abandoned the city streets to give us *The White Hell of Pitz Palu*, nor did his collaborator Arnold Fanck forget it in *Peaks of Destiny*. These two pictures, with their glaciers, mountain winds and innumerable scenes in a hut (one remembers best the amazing shots of the skiers bearing away at full speed the body which they had gone to find), were attractive; but so much fresh air was not customary in German films.

E. A. DUPONT

All that had gone before was to be summed up eventually in the greatest of German silent films, *Variety*. E. A. Dupont actually made only two first-rate films, *The Ancient Law* and this one. Like *Nju*, *The Ancient Law* was a film of no apparent boldness, a simple story simply told of a young Jew trying to break away from his race. The aesthetes pulled long faces at it, as they had done with *A Woman of Paris*, and failed to perceive that *The Ancient Law* was entirely the offspring of the Chaplin picture. But everybody was agreed about *Variety*.

The story by Felix Hollander is the most banal imaginable: a man is betrayed by another and kills him. But the action takes place among a troupe of acrobats, and this permits Dupont to include scenes of unexcelled virtuosity. Moreover, the agility of the camera when it wants to show us the theater audiences, as seen from the trapeze by the protagonists, like a carpet of living eyes, is paralleled by a similar but subtler agility when the director wishes to show the emotional reactions of his characters. This camera sees everything—the blinking of an eye, the quiver of an eyelash, the contraction of a hand, the least movement of a foot. It becomes merged with the actors, who no longer seem conscious of it, and steals in upon their very life, their most secret impulses and thoughts. Without ever resorting to the methods formerly sanctioned, the slightest nuances are expressed by the director.

Because of its very perfection it is difficult to discuss this film. In reality it introduced nothing new; all it did was to crystallize five or six years of experiments and maybe thirty years of film experience. But to many people it, more than any other, revealed the art of the film. The vulgar music-hall scenes attained a sort of beauty, thanks to the camera's magic. The vision when the husband imagines the catastrophe, the extraordinarily discreet murder of the lover, whom we do not actually see killed, and the back of Jannings are quite unforgettable. None of the actors in this film was ever again to display as much sobriety or such restraint—neither Lya de Putti nor Jannings. At the time *Variety* seemed a complete work of art. I do not know if it is effectually one, but we may apply to it what Delluc said of *The Cheat:* it is a thing whole in itself, and the most complete work that the screen has produced. For that reason one was somewhat shocked to learn of its being remade as a talkie, without Dupont or Jannings, just as *Way Down East* was remade without Lillian Gish.

Dupont did nothing particular after it and went off to America. Jannings continued to be interesting because he is a great actor with something of Harry Baur and of Lucien Guitry in him. In *Variety* he acted with a sort of meticulous brilliance; the amiable face of "The Boss," his expressive back, his hands, his awkward gestures—these he was never able to repeat. Elsewhere he was to be theatrical, exaggerated: in Lubitsch's *Patriot,* in *The Way of All Flesh* (a pretentious affair about a middle-aged man led astray by a vamp) and in his first talkie, *The Blue Angel.* As Boss Huller in *Variety* he touched perfection.

DIFFICULTIES

After *Variety,* which dates from 1925, Germany came to a halt for a while, and began exporting purely commercial films without any particular interest. Many actors and directors had gone to America. Lubitsch had been there some time, Murnau and Lupu Pick * followed, then Dupont and Jannings—the glory of the German studios. The situation was rapidly becoming serious.

The reasons for this were fairly simple. After the immense success of *Variety,* America was disturbed † and tried to acquire as many directors and actors as possible in order to ruin a rival industry. This method had worked with Sweden. At the same time a considerable number of foreigners had rapidly crept into the German studios and denationalized them; they obviously

---

* Paul Leni went to America, but Pick does not seem to have done so.

† It would be more accurate to say that America was anxious to acquire for her own productions the directors, actors and technicians who had combined so brilliantly to make the outstanding German films.

A scene from the most famous of films from the U.S.S.R., Potemkin, directed by S. M. Eisenstein (1925).

Charlie Chaplin in The Circus (*1928*).

cared for nothing but making money. The Russians had tried to establish an *émigré* school there as they had done in France, though these Russians were admirable people and, moreover, talented. But a host of other people of dubious nationality had also decided to entrench themselves—as they had done in France and in America—and succeeded in doing so. It was they who introduced the vogue for vamps, ingenues, "girls," and night clubs, and who were freest with the picturesque qualities of low life and of the Bavarian landscapes.

With the German output of this period one must include the films made by those directors who emigrated to America. These were not particularly good. Paul Leni found a means to combine Caligarism with the detective story in strange films which oscillate between parody and seriousness—*The Cat and the Canary* and *The Last Warning*. It was the only way of serving up horror to the Americans. The failure which one most regrets was that of Lupu Pick. He made a rather human *Napoleon at St. Helena* from Gance's scenario and then directed *The Four Vagabonds* (a sound film in German and French versions): not even his ability could produce much of interest. Murnau proved to be of solider stuff, and something of his old power was seen in *Sunrise*, from a Sudermann novel, despite a great deal too much storm, a vamp and a dose of Anglo-Saxon morality—in spite, too, of its obvious denationalization. His last film, *Tabu*, made in Polynesia with the customary harpoon fishing and the no less customary ritual dance, was hardly better than other films in the Polynesian manner. When they left home the German directors clearly lost their originality in trying to cater to an international audience.

The situation was so grave that it called for a dictator. This dictator was Erich Pommer, who had amalgamated the two firms, the old Decla-Bioscop and Ufa. It was he who permitted *Variety* to be made, who protected Pabst and Fritz Lang. Since a man must live, there is no doubt that he likewise permitted a number of stupid or hackneyed films to be made, but one must admit all that was produced of interest in Germany after 1925 was made under his control and would have been impossible but for him.*

After the departure of Murnau only two famous directors remained in Germany—Pabst and Fritz Lang. Czinner directed *Queen Louise*, Karl Grune made *Waterloo*, Arthur Robison made *Looping the Loop*, Richard Eichberg directed *Song*, a rather affecting piece in which the little Chinese girl, Anna May Wong, loved a miserable outcast. But it was in Lang that the entire hopes of the German film seemed to reside.

Following *The Nibelungen* he set to work on a story conceived by his wife, the redoubtable Frau Thea von Harbou: the result was *Metropolis*, with its echoes of Villiers de l'Isle Adam's novel, *L'Eve Future*, of *Intolerance* and of some of Abel Gance's experiments. At times the film is profoundly ridiculous: one can only smile at the manufacturing of a mysterious evil woman who closely resembles a pure young girl in this city of the future. All the tricks of the horror film are used, but to little effect, and the confused ideology of Lang, the contrast between the fortunate beings who live in the sunlight and the unfortunate ones who live in the darkness, are disconcertingly childish. There are about two reels of the film, however, which are worthy of being remembered.

Metropolis creates a new world, and the first twenty minutes are admirable. Just as Lang succeeded in making us believe in his cardboard cities in *Siegfried*, so he gave to his models of a city of the future an unbearable and terrifying vitality. It was inconceivable that these tall buildings, rising a hundred stories into skies traversed by airplanes and machines as yet unknown, were in fact small models no higher than a man. Certain details in the sharp contrasts were both useful and striking, as for instance the procession of workmen lined up and marching silently

---

* Pommer was hardly a "dictator"; as production supervisor he seems to have been particularly successful. Directors working under him achieved results they never obtained elsewhere. Pommer went to America in 1926, but returned to Berlin in 1927. He is now in England.

towards the elevators. This provided a perfect image of a mechanical and inhuman world. The flooding of the city at the end of *Metropolis* contained some beautiful things which permitted us to overlook the basic confusion of ideas and the impossible story, as well as all the false romanticism. Fundamentally *Metropolis* was the last gasp of expressionism, which it incorporated into a film not without beauty.

Subsequently Lang was to make *The Spy*, an extremely well-handled detective film which showed him to be one of the best craftsmen in the whole industry.

CZECH FILMS

At the end of the silent-film era, Germany was not alone in producing films, and one must associate with her output the films also being made from time to time under the German influence in neighboring countries. Particularly in Austria there were a small number of studios, more or less controlled by Ufa, which produced some extremely carefully made pictures. Ludwig Berger's success, *The Waltz Dream*, had launched a vogue for Viennese subjects. Austria contributed several examples to that passing fashion, which, naturally enough, did not assume real significance until after the coming of sound films.

The Czechs have always been admirable photographers, and it was therefore natural that they should be attracted to cinematography. They produced some interesting films in various styles, strongly influenced by what was being done in Germany. One of them, so labored that it was almost a caricature, by reason of its timid boldness (for it was what was then called a study of sexuality) earned a certain success abroad: this was Gustav Machaty's *Erotikon*. It was not really very good. The Czechs, however, also produced a sort of masterpiece that sums up the whole of the German film, besides profiting by the lessons of the Russians and the Swedes: *Such Is Life* was one of the last of the silent films and, more than any other among them, made us regret that charming and forceful medium.

The director, Carl Junghans, unknown before and forgotten

since, made it under the worst of financial conditions, barely escaping being sold out at every moment and with unpaid actors urging him to finish it quickly. It was admirable. Apparently, it is a simple realistic story about an old washerwoman's life and death. But from the very beginning the magnificent face of Vera Baranovskaya suggests that this parable of a workingwoman contains much more than the individual anecdote. The pictorial composition especially is incomparable: the kitchen full of steam, the courtyard and the fields are treated with that respect for the medium, that feeling for light and shadow which the German directors suggested but which none of them had rendered with so much effect. The washerwoman's party with its gay repast, the little boy who falls asleep, the cobbler who brings along his gramophone with its amplifier, create moments of rather amused but touching beauty which are perhaps unique. No doubt this film had faults and sometimes verged on melodrama, but these were redeemed by its prodigious truth to life. After the heroine's death, Junghaus gave us a funeral of extraordinary power with all the people stiff in their black clothes and a funeral repast which ended in song in the cemetery wine-shop. It seemed here as if the silent film (much as in America with *The Docks of New York*) was uttering its swan song. In that region of strict realism transposed into bitter and familiar poetry, the theater had always remained impotent, and literature itself falls short of the screen, which can attain to that plastic beauty by which a great painter transforms at will the humblest objects and the lowliest scenes.

With *Such Is Life*, the German film school had fulfilled its destiny of transmuting realism into poetry. To that the expressionist experiments had contributed as much as the realism and the love of psychological truths which the adaptations from Dostoevski and Pabst's films had brought into favor, or the efforts towards tragic simplicity made by Lupu Pick, Dupont and Murnau. The films of other countries contributed their magic during that period of the silent film's blossoming, but none were more human or bolder, even in their very faults, than those of Germany.

3. *The Scandinavian Film*

THE FILM IN SWEDEN

DURING the period which might be called the golden or classic age of the silent film, Sweden, which had contributed so much to its formation, no longer produced outstanding pictures. Sjöström had become Seastrom in America; Stiller was about to join him there. Svenska still made films and in 1924 actually produced twenty, among which *Life in the Country*, directed by Hedqvist, and Brunius' *Charles XII* had some merit, while Edgren's peasant picture, *The King of Trollebo*, was not without interest. Yet in imitations lacking vitality or in a colorless naturalism, the vein seemed exhausted. The actors, too, were leaving Sweden—Lars Hanson, Einar Hanson and Greta Garbo. Before leaving, Lars Hanson had played in a somewhat bizarre and rather characteristic film of Molander's, a sequel to Seastrom's unfinished *Jerusalem*. Conrad Veidt also acted in it. Despite certain real qualities, it seemed, however, that the Swedish film had made no progress since Sjöström and Stiller: it was the work of a talented pupil who finishes the picture of a master, and it lacked both originality and life.

Olaf Molander, brother of Gustaf, committed radical errors. He adapted a play of Strindberg's, *The Republic of Women*, and even made a *Camille*, turning again to the theatrical form from which the films had taken so much trouble to escape. There were mistakes and hesitations everywhere. Runeberg attempted in an unsuccessful *Gustavus Vasa* to revitalize the historical picture. Theodore Berthels essayed the life of the Vikings. Gustaf Molander also filmed Strindberg. Others undertook to give Sweden comedies. Everywhere what had contributed to the profound originality of the Swedish film was vanishing.

In America, Stiller did not feel at home, and neither his *Confessions of a Queen* nor *Hotel Imperial* had the merit of his native productions. Seastrom fared better. After his first American film,

Name the Man, he made *The Tower of Lies*, and also *He Who Gets Slapped*, in which he managed to recapture on the screen something of the charm of the original play by Andreyev. *The Scarlet Letter* and *The Wind*, both starring Lillian Gish, almost equaled his former work, the latter particularly, where the desert sand and the wind played so powerful a role that they seemed to be the real actors in a film which was undeniably impressive.

Mauritz Stiller died on returning from America in 1928. The same year the aged Magnusson left Svenska. In 1929 the first sound film appeared, then the first "hundred-per-cent Swedish talkie," which was, alas, *A Hole in the Wall*. For several years the history of this country, once so important, seemed to have come to a stop. Sweden, like Italy, will doubtless be born again, but her great period was that of the formative years.

NORWEGIAN FILMS

Production in Norway, quite unlike that of Sweden, had been left entirely to chance. At the end of the war the first real company, Christiana Film, had to start from the beginning. Amateurs had interested themselves in the film; there was no lack of good will, and the example of the Swedes inclined the Norwegians to draw upon national tradition, local color and the beauties of nature. They made *Growth of the Soil* from the Knut Hamsun book, and filmed the lives of sailors and fishermen, but these pictures were not shown outside Norway * and in the opinion of the critics it was better so. It was only in 1927 and 1929 with Walter Furst's *Trollälgen* and the Finnish Georges Scheevoigt's *Laila* that Norway succeeded in providing any such response as the Swedes had evoked.

THE DANISH FILM

It was during the classic years of the silent film that two directors in Denmark, Sandberg and Dreyer, came to the fore. The former, after having tried to imitate the Swedish films in *Heaven's*

* *Growth of the Soil* was shown in America.

Revenge (1922), which included some beautiful landscape shots, aspired to become international, engaged foreign actors, produced in Italy, and remade old films such as *Marriage Under the Terror* and *The Maharajah's Favorite*. He was a capable director. Despite his efforts to please the public, his firm declined and finally he left it. Most of the other firms had disappeared by 1929, and only Nordisk kept reorganizing itself. The Danish film was in a poor way.

Dreyer, nevertheless, had directed in 1925 a film which at the time seemed of unusual interest, and which was shown all over the world—*The Master of the House*. This well-knit and sad love story demanded too much of the medium, overestimating the film's power to express individual psychology. The eternal moralizing of the Nordic people also marred it, but the film was so reticent and so honest, the actors were so restrained (actors are always excellent under Dreyer), the director displayed so much taste in the settings, in the atmosphere, in the details of everyday life and, above all, displayed so much humanity in handling this tale of an unhappy marriage, that many filmgoers were enthusiastic about it. The influence of the Théâtre Libre, so great among all the Nordic peoples, was evident throughout *The Master of the House* in its excessive naturalism and an overregard for truthfulness. The beauty of the photography and a very considerable skill, however, saved this realistic study from the slight degree of tedium which might have been expected. While it was not a very great film, *The Master of the House* was a model of sober and well-measured craftsmanship and of profoundly human bitterness; its gravity, its consistent avoidance of the dramatic (so reminiscent of the work of Jacques Feyder) compelled respect. Later on Dreyer worked in Sweden, in Germany, in France. It was in France that he produced his masterpiece, *The Passion of Joan of Arc*, with a French cast. This curious film, composed almost entirely of faces in close-up in which everything is allowed to depend on the performance of the actors, is nevertheless a genuine film and a complete thing in itself. Under the severe direction of Dreyer, Silvain gave a prodigious performance, while Falconetti exhibited a restraint and power which she was never to attain again. Whether she portrayed a convincing Joan of Arc may be debated. Physically she did, in the scene in which she appears haggard and tormented before the executioners. But her mood throughout is one of suffering; there is nothing here of the optimism or of the insolence of the real Joan that Madame Pitoëff revealed in the trial scene. Here she is only a young, martyred saint and this arbitrary limitation of the character cannot be denied. Once it has been admitted, her performance provides some prodigious moments—the childish gesture by which Joan reminds her executioners that justice exists, her glance at a tuft of daisies trembling in the breeze, her expression as they crown her, like Jesus, with thorns and arm her with a mock scepter and, above everything else, the moment at the stake when she stoops to pick up the rope which has fallen and offers it with divine complaisance to the executioner.

This extraordinary film was extremely daring; it could probably not be repeated. It offers a fine contrast to Gance's *Napoleon*, as a spiritual epic opposed to a physical epic. No doubt it was a dead end, an oversimplification of drama, but it was one of those magnificent failures which provide much food for thought.

4. *The Russian Film*

AFTER the inevitable years of experimentation, Russia succeeded in organizing her industry and created in 1925 the big central organization of Sovkino. Two masterpieces had already been made, Eisenstein's *Potemkin* and Pudovkin's *Mother*.

THE SOVIET FILM

In his essay on the Soviet film in which he seems more interested in economic conditions than in films, Léon Moussinac explains clearly why production was quite quickly organized in Russia. Each year a scheme of film production is drawn up by

Sovkino in agreement with the commissariat of public instruction, deciding upon the number and character of educational and of entertainment films, and of documentaries, to be made. Films for peasants, films for children, educational films and "artistic" films (which, at least until recently, were also "social" films) are all considered separately. A scenario office seeks subjects drawn from literary works, from topical subjects or imaginary events. As the public likes historical films and the study of the Revolution is always to be encouraged, they select, Moussinac says, some well-known historical event and give it the treatment which a Marxist approach imposes. Each category of films is carefully studied; thus films for peasants are cut less rapidly, the acting is more theatrical and more emphatic, since the peasants are not yet completely educated visually.

Once the subject is chosen, the scenario itself is completed and submitted to the central committee for the control of repertory, which acts both as artistic direction and as political censorship. This committee then appoints the director, a soviet of collaborators is assembled and what is called the Group is formed, comprising the director, the assistants, the cameraman, the art director, the actors and an administrator who has absolute control over the budget assigned to the group. Work begins.

At first, production was carried on under rather difficult conditions. First the Revolution, then the Whites had destroyed the studios and the equipment. Cameras had to be bought from France, sunlight and spots from Germany. When Moussinac went to the U.S.S.R. in 1927 he says that there was only one ultra-rapid camera. The studios of Wufku, the great Ukrainian organization, had just been destroyed by earthquake. Gradually, however, things were organized and Sovkino, at the time talkies came in, owned large studios equipped with the latest apparatus.

When a film is finished, it is again submitted to the censorship of a committee, then to societies of Friends of the Cinema, to journalists and afterwards to the committee of control, which pronounces upon it. Under such conditions, it is evident that a film cannot well be other than orthodox. The societies of Friends of the Cinema are particularly powerful and have done much to popularize films in the rural districts. It is owing to their care that Russia has managed to create a Film Library such as the capitalist countries vainly await.* Five years after being produced, every film shown in Russia must be examined to determine if it is suitable for preservation or not: the Film Library of the Ukraine is preserving more than 2,500 films—which seems rather a lot.

Sovkino's powers were augmented in 1928: it became Soyuzkino, and has the exclusive right to distribute films in Russia proper. It distributed Eisenstein's films and Vertov's. Mezhrabpom also produces films (those of Pudovkin) but depends on Sovkino for their exploitation and even for raw materials. Otherwise, though subject to the Communist Party and severely controlled by the state, these organizations function exactly as in capitalist countries. In the Ukraine the monopoly belongs to Wufku of Kiev; in White Russia to the Belgoskino and so on. But it is Soyuzkino which has the monopoly of exportation and of importation throughout the U.S.S.R. In addition there exist schools for training technicians, actors and directors. In Leningrad at the Institute of the History of Arts there is a course on the theory of art in which the history and technique of the film are studied.

The organization of the Soviet film industry is obviously both complex and at the same time well unified. The State Cinema works for the state. It is not astonishing that the films produced are stamped with the purest spirit of propaganda. In our aged Occident, which no longer believes in itself, what we cannot understand is that such constraint is not felt as constraint, at least not in its initial impulse. Eisenstein may not be a member of the Party, but he knows that he is expressing his era and that this era is a revolutionary one. Even if he is hampered in a few details, he is profoundly in agreement with revolutionary demands and necessities. The whole organization of the Soviet film industry, alive and plastic, serves as the framework for a faith. The excessive amount of propaganda, the stupidity of certain themes, the low intellectual level and even the lies which shock us so

* See note on page 88.

much are all part of this faith. We can criticize it and condemn it, but it would be foolish to believe that so formal an organization can be purely mechanical, or that it has suppressed inspiration. Whether we like it or not, this inspiration exists.

THE IDEAS OF VERTOV

Apparently the man who has had the greatest influence on the Soviet film was neither Eisenstein nor Pudovkin, but Dziga Vertov, who as a very young man founded the Kino-Eye group in 1921. Kauffmann, Kopalin and Beliakov belonged to it and it assumed a place in the vanguard of production. Vertov's films— *October Without Lenin, A Sixth Part of the World, The Man with the Movie Camera* and *The Eleventh Year* with its striking scenes of the life of the miners of Donetz, have counted for less despite their qualities than the ideas of the man who made them.

Vertov was the first to declare war, with his whole soul, on all theatrical influences. He decided that the essential thing in the film, as its founders believed, is documentation, that is to say, the unrehearsed scene not composed with art but seized by the eye of the camera just as the human eye involuntarily seizes everything before it. Hence the name of Kino-Eye adopted by his group. Documentation constitutes the basic and unalterable material from which the artist then constructs his film by selection and arrangement.

The theories of Kino-Eye are obviously very important. The role of creation henceforth devolves on the editor: Walter Ruttmann, for example, is wholly an editor and, as a disciple of Kino-Eye, contents himself with arranging what the camera has selected —no more drama, no more history, nothing but the composition of given elements.

Carried to the extreme, this theory singularly limits the scope of the film; not one of the great Russian directors has adopted it entirely and each one "romances" his films, even those which seem to be simple documentations. Vertov, as Moussinac has admirably said, tends to substitute reality for the sentiment of reality.

In any case, every effort is concentrated on the editing, which is clearly the essential thing in a film. What did Vertov conceive it to be? He conceived it in an extraordinarily scientific manner, and here his teaching has been understood by everyone, even by Pudovkin, who is so remote from the theories of Kino-Eye, and quite close to certain theatrical elements. The footage of each sequence is rigorously determined in relation to the total length of the film. The unity of time thus acquires enormous value. Every film in the Vertov manner can be broken up into a sequence of figures indicating durations.

The trouble probably lies in the fact that the quality of the movement of film images does not readily permit the eye to grasp this inner construction apart from a few very simple formulas: The main theme (of which Vertov actually makes very little use) is rendered much more perceptible by repetition than through the abstract notion of duration. This is what causes the relative failure of Vertov's own work. His films sometimes constitute magnificent picture albums, but what they lack is precisely a perceptible rhythm and form. In *The Eleventh Year* there is the general theme of the economic effort of his country. But in *The Man with the Movie Camera*, the crux of his whole theory, it is the whole of life itself in all its forms that the cameraman is supposed to seize; it is not surprising if Vertov has failed with this vast subject. Nor is it surprising if the execution is sometimes unfaithful to the theory and if the director (an absurd title according to Vertov) sometimes trims up and "romances" what the visible world offers him.

The importance that the films, the ideas, the writing and the associates of Dziga Vertov had for the Russians can hardly be realized. It is partly due to him that the Russian film orientated itself towards a sort of poetic documentary, the style to which we owe *Potemkin, Earth, Old and New* and *Turksib*. He is responsible for the making of films without professional actors, for the use of unknown players or whole crowds, for roles being interpreted by anyone whose face was considered beautiful or picturesque. It is because of him that the learned and rigorous experiments of Eisenstein and of Pudovkin have prevailed everywhere. In France little has been seen of his films save *The Man with the Movie Camera* and *The Eleventh Year* and, as said before, his films have counted for less than his ideas.

THE MARTIAL REVOLUTION

Together with the fashion for historical films, the concern with propaganda, with documentation and the ideas of Vertov, we find a whole body of films which aim at providing a new people with heroes by relating the proletarian epic to them. For three or four years the events of 1917 and those which preceded and followed them were the chosen subject matter of the Russians; and it was this martial revolution which served as the subject for Eisenstein in his first period.

S. M. Eisenstein, leading director of his country, is one of the greatest artists in the world, and a man of incontestable genius. We have only to remember 1925 with its American love romances and cowboy films, or the tumultuous and baroque *Napoleon* of Abel Gance, to comprehend fully the emotion aroused by *Potemkin* and its strange example of violence and restraint. *Potemkin* is one of the masterpieces of the cinema, and in spite of the censor everyone or almost everyone has seen it, thanks to the film societies and Communist organizations. (Such a film could not well have been shown in the public theaters.) We shall be able to look at it for a long while yet before it seems old-fashioned.

The theme of *Potemkin* is simple: it tells of a mutiny on the cruiser *Potemkin*, in 1905, when the crew hoisted the red flag because the food was bad, and threw their officers into the sea, while the population of Odessa demonstrated their sympathy with the rebels. The film opens with a great foaming wave as it breaks —a symbol of the revolt. Only the first part of the picture has aged: the jerky, quick movements of the actors, the exaggerated characterizations of the officers seem artificial and lacking in that admirable sense of caricature, of satiric realism, which later was to render scenes in *Storm Over Asia* and *Thunder Over Mexico* so striking. Yet certain figures, those of the priest and of the doctor, already stand out clearly. The doctor inspects the inedible meat: the screen is filled with putrefaction, where worms swarm in a vast, gray, leprous expanse—a symbol readily grasped and shown with the audacity of a visionary. From that instant the revolt is a foregone conclusion and the rhythm of the film becomes clear, with its long periods of quiet. The actual revolt is again a little confused, but we are shown one magnificent moment when the discontented sailors, condemned to death and covered with a tarpaulin, are lined up before their comrades, who have been given orders to fire. The tarpaulin heaves, the condemned men cry, "Brothers! Brothers!" The sailors throw down their rifles. Here we see the very essence of Eisenstein's method, with its two phases of calm separated by frenzy and movement; the whole structure of brief and breathless images gradually forms itself into a great emotional whole.

What follows is admirable. The whole ship seems to vibrate with joy. Meanwhile a sailor has been killed, his body is carried to Odessa, and there, before this corpse, the revolutionary impulse is born and increases. Eisenstein selects a group, a single figure, an old woman, men with hard, silent faces, women to whom understanding suddenly comes, a vociferous suffragette, an inquisitive bourgeois. The theme swells gradually; suddenly the whole town is caught up by it and embarks with tears of joy in a fleet of small boats to take provisions, meat and live animals to the cruiser. For a time this crusade of joy fills the screen. Then the rhythm changes again; the militia enter the scene and fire on the crowd.

There are few scenes more famous in the whole history of the film. Down the great flight of steps in Odessa men and women flee; a crowd in confusion screams; a perambulator goes bumping by; pitiful groups hold out imploring hands. Slowly, mechanically, inexorably the soldiers advance towards them; the measured pace, the rigid line, this terrifying mechanism of misfortune interrupts the inorganic disorder of flight. Nothing can withstand this fatal advance, this regular march, this rectilinear flight of steps.

Later the tension eases; we await an attack on the cruiser. But the other sailors in the battleships will not shoot. The word "Brothers" again fills the screen as the *Potemkin* passes through the fleet with honors to take refuge in Rumania.

The unequaled concentration and conciseness of this picture, its amazingly dramatic moments all owe their power to the film alone. It is a reconstruction which attains the direct truthfulness of a documentary film, but it is also a document which becomes a work of art, created deliberately, in which propaganda itself disappears before the eternal humanity of the true story of a struggle between oppressors and oppressed. Pudovkin, thinking of *Potemkin*, was to write of Eisenstein, "One can neither describe his work nor represent it on the stage; one can only show it on the screen." A total absence of visible ideology, the care taken to show only facts and more facts, make this statement strictly true. Eisenstein himself was, moreover, to write these striking words: "It is a question of creating a series of images composed in such a way that it provokes an affective movement which in turn awakens a series of ideas. From image to sentiment, from sentiment to thesis . . . I think the film alone is capable of making this great synthesis, of giving back to the intellectual element its vital sources, both concrete and emotional."

This is what *Potemkin* so magnificently achieved. It might be added that Eisenstein's cameraman was Edward Tissé, who had learned his craft in Sweden and brought to the Eisenstein group a great deal of experience and experiment in photography and lighting. Dawn in Odessa in the fog was obtained by stretching a little muslin in front of the lens. As the Russians owned no studios as yet, almost all the film was taken in daylight without artificial illumination. The Russians themselves did not at first care very much for their masterpiece: it was the Germans who made its fame, and for a long time *Potemkin* was announced in the Moscow cinemas as "the great success in Berlin."

Neither *Strike* nor *October* attained the same force or conciseness. *October* contains some magnificent scenes of crowds and of panic; of men dragging cannons against the light, which prove that Eisenstein is always a master of imagery; of nocturnal bivouacs half-revealed by the gleam from a wood fire in a landscape

of iron under metal pillars and great cranes. But the brevity of
Potemkin had imposed an admirable contraction upon its maker,
where *October*, larger and more ambitious, loses itself in details
and seems confused. A subject so sprawling and formless was to
prove fatal to more than one Russian director. Also, Eisenstein
tells a story badly; he needs more exterior unity to maintain his
work at the same level.

From that time on, however, his technique was perfected. It
is said that he was converted to the cinema by Griffith's immense
Intolerance. This is possible, but in spite of his violence he was
to bring to the medium a discretion and good taste which were
always lacking in Griffith and the Americans. He was also to
contribute his collective lyricism, his love for crowds. No story
is needed to express this, or only a story so recent that it seems
to be the present time itself. He is at ease only when this present
time can reveal its emotional reality; then he grows enthusiastic
and with his cold head and warm heart sets to work to compose
a film.

Nothing is more curious than the contrast between the epic
fire of his films and the cold science of the man, his care for
craftsmanship, his love of detail, his taste for a beautiful composition. When he wishes to make us admire an immortal moment,
Pabst stops to become a painter. This devil of a Russian never
stops; he makes his pictures dance and drags them into the general movement, yet they are just as beautiful as those of Pabst.

He uses no actors, choosing his characters from the crowd,
seeming to aim at that rhythmical documentation of which Vertov dreams. He selects characteristic details, seldom presenting
a vast panorama in which all the tones are gray and contrast is
lost; thus he avoids the danger into which Gance often fell. But
he economizes raw stock no more than Gance does, shooting the
same scene many times over from different angles and by different methods. In this way he collaborates with fate and tames
the savage and independent Kino-Eye. Afterwards this madman
grows lucid, difficult and critical: he judges, eliminates, destroys,
cuts, edits his free images, measures their footage, shuts himself

up and from a heap of celluloid obtains a few vivid and perfect feet.

Thus Eisenstein: who taught him? He cannot be said to have had no masters, since he admired Griffith and perhaps Ince, too. When he comes to deal with more pacific themes he reminds us of the Swedes. But this is of little importance. No one else has focused on the world a camera so precise or so deliberate. No romantic (for he is a romantic) has been more severe with himself, no sensualist (for he is the greatest sensualist in films) has been more profoundly intelligent. Abstraction and sensuality are mingled in him, as in the greatest artists. He would have become an artist anywhere, in America or in Germany, but he found his climate and his time in Russia. Later he was to prove that even that was not necessary to him and that the artist, even a revolutionary artist, carries his own universe and his revolt within himself, even across the world.

THE REVOLUTION ROMANTICIZED: PUDOVKIN

Much as Eisenstein and Vertov might wish it, a film like *Potemkin*, resembling as it does a superior form of documentary film, could not establish a school. The habits of the public, capitalist and communist alike, which the early revolutionary directors had not dared to break, were still to be reckoned with. The public needs a story, a thread to hold its interest. Russia therefore began to imitate everyone else, and, after having discovered in *Potemkin* the true essence of the film for their purpose, quickly forgot it in order to tell us stories. The task of adapting the Revolution to the public's taste was given to Pudovkin.

Less downright, less absolute than Eisenstein and definitely less great, Pudovkin is nevertheless an extraordinary artist. He is closer to the theater than is his rival, less interested in the documentary film; even Dziga Vertov could not bring him to heel here. Pudovkin willingly uses professional actors like Vera Baranovskaya and Inkizhinov, though it is true they are great actors trained to the harshest realism, the most extreme naturalness.

They enable Pudovkin to concentrate on the inner nature of his characters, just as the studio enables him to control his settings and his lighting. Pudovkin composes, invents, where Eisenstein seems to submit himself to divine chance and to the inspiration of the famous Kino-Eye. Nevertheless, Vertov was not without influence on the director of *Mother* and *Storm Over Asia*. It was he who taught Pudovkin that rhythm can be contained in a mathematical statement; that every sequence of images can be expressed by a figure corresponding to a duration in seconds proportionate to the duration of the whole. Pudovkin, a man who composes his work with extreme care, a man of the theater and the study, was able to envisage in this concern with rhythm another way to dominate his medium, and as a consequence his films are always extraordinarily orchestrated and their construction is often emphasized by the use of a dominant theme or by the repetition of themes. In *The End of St. Petersburg* three conflicting themes are readily identified at the beginning, and are united finally with the triumph of the Revolution. We are far from documentary film here. Everything has been selected and ordered—the actors, the sentiments, the settings, the lighting and the marked rhythm. No one has given more importance than Pudovkin to the permanent and profound control of the artist over his work.

Unfortunately, his ideology is summary and, as it expresses itself through a story, seems still more summary than that of Eisenstein. Pudovkin willingly narrates plots which are heavily underlined and even improbable; he calls adventure, crime and sentiment to his aid. Melodrama comes second to Marx. The method is sometimes awkward, and unfortunately it was to give rise to a school: the martial revolution was now succeeded by a romanticized revolution which ended up by becoming rather tiresome.

But Pudovkin avoided all serious errors in *Mother*, his masterpiece, as well as in the best scenes of *The End of St. Petersburg* and of *Storm Over Asia*. Nevertheless he remains somewhat theatrical, in a manner which is not always of the best theater.

Mother is magnificent. Eisenstein has described Pudovkin's characteristic method: "In his films the spectator's attention is not concentrated on the development of the plot, but on the psychic change undergone by some individual under the influence of the social process. Pudovkin puts real living men in the center of his work. His films act directly through their emotional power." *Mother*, inspired by a famous novel by Gorky, is the best example of this. We see a poor woman leading a miserable life under the Czarist regime up to the time when class consciousness awakes in her. At the opening of the film she is beaten by her husband, stupefied, unhappy; at the end of the film she bears a flag at the head of a procession, her face radiant with faith. Vera Baranovskaya, one of the greatest artists in the world, interprets the mother's role with prodigious humanity. Thanks to her and to the meticulous art of Pudovkin, it is this humanity which strikes one, rather than any social propaganda. In *The End of St. Petersburg*, attacking the same subject as *October*, Pudovkin touches us more deeply than Eisenstein, by methods analogous to those in *Mother*. At the beginning of the film we see a downtrodden workman who understands nothing of his true destiny. The revolution of October is explained to us by that one central figure, by that one man who suffers and rejoices. A similar theme was to be used often by Soviet directors. In Pudovkin it was full of novelty, and the ardor with which he developed it was a guarantee against any trite or hackneyed element.

Mother and *The End of St. Petersburg* are simple; not so *Storm Over Asia*, in which nationalism and propaganda are curiously mingled. It is the story of a Mongolian who is thought to be a descendant of Genghis Khan, and drives the English invaders out of his country. The film swings between melodrama, symbolism, document and the simple adventure film—at times dangerously. Parts of it are extraordinarily beautiful, like the trenchant caricature of the General preparing for the ceremony (that Oriental ceremony in which Pudovkin perhaps gave way too much to his love of the picturesque) and, still better, the wonderful fair at the beginning of the film. Light seems to cling to the furs, the seething crowd is disposed on the screen in a series of vast compositions which loom up slowly from the darkness, in the manner so dear to the Swedes. We are immediately captivated by the very first shots, so softly and gently gray, which gradually bring us nearer by three removes to a hut lost in the immense plains. The revolt of Bair, whom the English merchant tries to cheat out of his furs, the riot in the market, are handled with a *brio* and an impetuosity that the best American films come short of. Throughout he lavishes the greatest care on faces, on facial contours molded by time and worn by grief and toil: those admirable human compositions to which the Russians are so responsive. The professional actor, Inkizhinov, is wholly worthy of these natural artists and no greater praise is possible. The rest of the adventure—the great symbolic tempest and Bair's ride in the wind which carries off the invaders and the dead leaves—verges on melodrama in the manner of Gance. What is memorable is the opening, the sovereign skill in interpreting folklore and ancient customs and a great love for peasant epics and the human face.

Most of the Russian directors have similar tastes, be it Room, Trauberg, Kozintsev, Protazanov, Tassin. All of them have followed in Pudovkin's footsteps in exalting the romanticized revolution. Now and then Pudovkin and his fellow workers go outside their beloved Russia and Mongolia and draw upon their imagination, as in Kozintsev's and Trauberg's film about the Paris Commune, *New Babylon*. Among modern subjects they are particularly attracted to the dramatic contrasts possible in the material of imperialism, where the roles of oppressed and oppressors are very clearly defined. One such film, *China Express*, directed by Leonid Trauberg's younger brother, Ilya, is one of the rare Soviet films to be permitted public showing in France.* Leonid Trauberg and Kozintsev enjoyed their first success with an adaptation of Gogol's *The Cloak*, afterwards making a modern drama, *The Devil's Wheel*, and a Russian historical film, *SVD*. As well as of his dramas, Protazanov filmed some of the most successful Soviet satires. So that at this period we find, produced by him, dramas such as

---

* Aside from this film and one or two others, the few Soviet films French audiences and critics have had the opportunity of seeing have been exclusively rural and pastoral—which accounts for the authors' curious conclusions about the Russian obsession with nature.

The Man from the Restaurant and *The Forty-First*, as well as comedy-satires—*Three Thieves, The Festival of St. Jorgen,* etc. Whether making tragedy or comedy, however, the Russian directors have always displayed a distinct taste for ethnic types and for realism. In *Strike*, Eisenstein cut into the scenes of the massacre a shot of an ox in the slaughterhouse, then an enormous close-up of the eye of the ox in its death agony. Room, in *The Bay of Death,* showed the bodies of some dead children and was so scrupulous as to procure some from the morgue.

As for *China Express*, this is a good example of the average propaganda film. Nothing is missing from its capitalist Punch-and-Judy show, neither the frigid proconsul nor the servile general, the ignoble tradesman nor the missionary enslaved by capitalism. When we see the Chinese herded like cattle in their third-class carriage we feel by contrast that Trauberg here is obeying a sentiment of fraternity which inspires him to better advantage. The fight in the train may not be well handled, for corridors are a bad place for a picturesque battle, and we are not really made to wish for the victory of the third-class passengers over those in the first class: the symbolism is a little too simple. But there is a savage impetuosity about the uprising, and the film has the collective spirit that infuses most Russian pictures.

The Russians actually concern themselves less with individuals than with masses of men, ask for no individual sentiments or expressions but demand of them, of all of them, only a sort of stupor or suffering or collective rage which is, in a sense, the soul of the whole herd. It chooses actors because of the deep kinship their faces reveal, and not for their individual features, seeing in them a sort of choir destined to intone a very simple and almost animal plaint. Men of whom we distinguish almost nothing, but whose mighty and multiple voice we hear, provide cadence and rhythm with their bodies as the entire group sways to the song of toil and of misery. If Soviet films attain depth and truth it is not in the conventional expression of their propaganda, or by inventing handsome young proletarian heroes, but by rediscovering the eternal tendencies of Russian "Asiatism" in its national expression. So in a film like *China Express*, since it is not one of the best, we can rightly enjoy those somber and beautiful pictures of human distress hymned in unison.

Other films continued the tradition inaugurated by the earliest Soviet period, such as *The Living Corpse*, directed by Ozep and acted by Pudovkin, and *The Yellow Pass*, also by Ozep, which represent curious attempts at drama rather in the German manner, and *The Sold Appetite* by Okhlopkov. This rather ingenious satire tells of a proletarian with an excellent digestion who sells his appetite to a gastralgic millionaire. Afterwards he suffers when the other man stuffs himself and writhes in agony on an empty stomach. The moral is easily divined. All of these films were harmless enough, but a little heavy-handed.

THE PACIFIC REVOLUTION

It is not to be wondered at that, from considering men as the members of a group almost as if they were animals, the Soviet film at one stage in its evolution should have come to take nature as its principal character. Here the Soviet effort, whatever its ideology and whatever its shortcomings, must overwhelm us Westerners with shame. Here too, of course, the primary aim was propaganda, and Eisenstein before making *Old and New* quite clearly said what he intended to do. He explained that the revolution would continue not only in warfare but in peace, too, and that in order to fight one does not need a flag and a gun. "After the emotions of the great revolutionary struggle," he wrote, "after the blaze of revolt there comes the daily life of the peasants and of the farmyard. . . . We must inspire our audiences with enthusiasm and passion for the daily humdrum work of the peasant, for the fertile bull, for the mechanical steam plow with the bony little horse harnessed in front." There is "emotion in a cream separator," he says, and concludes in his spirited fashion: "What emotion, after that, can one expect to derive from the *Chanson de Roland*? Why should the hearts of spectators beat when, amid the rolling thunder of Wagner's fanfare, the chalice of the Holy Grail lights up with the fires of its thousand diamonds? What can that Spanish vessel possibly mean to us?"

Without going into the merits of the Spanish vessel, let us retain only the positive side of Eisenstein's affirmation. It is certainly true that nature, that agricultural labor, are noble themes which literature has forgotten for two thousand years. It is not the novels of peasant life which carry on the tradition of Hesiod and of Virgil: they lack that mixture of precision and of poetry which constitute the true Georgic. Eisenstein and Dovzhenko are the true Virgils.

In the Russian films of the pacific Revolution, nature is no longer a setting, but a character. The backwardness of the Russians in agricultural development permitted them to find novelty and beauty in things that are taken for granted by Occidental men. The struggle with the soil, the need for water, the effort to plow a furrow provide a dramatic conflict with its own victories and defeats. In truth all that is needed is eyes to see it, and it is the disgrace of the Occidental cinema that it has not known how to see. The building of a bridge is dramatic, sea fishing is a drama, but Jean Epstein alone in France has attempted to show this. Pretty photographs such as we have been given are not enough, for the director has not evoked the ancient poetry within himself, he has not been the singer, the contemporary Hesiod, of man's struggle with the soil.

What worries us in Eisenstein's *Old and New* is the basic moralizing which lies at the roots of this "educational film." The many comparisons between men and animals, the disdain for any spiritual life, are also annoying, but the film contains a series of pictures which compose a great bucolic poem in which there are no actors, only peasants. The introduction of machinery to the countryside ends by becoming a stirring episode in the human struggle. The film has its bad taste, as for instance when the peasant dreams and a monumental dream cow fills the heavens, yet with the sensual precision of this unique art it also shows us the fields and the clouds. There are some admirable compositions—the procession, the masterly scene when the communal bull goes to mate with the gently trembling heifer, the rugged faces of the peasants round the separator, the ignorance, the dirt, and suddenly triumph as the cream begins to form. Here all the elementary teaching is left behind; we are left with a song, an epic about tractors and the beauty of the modern world.

In Turin's *Turksib* the subject is the building of the Turkestan-Siberian railroad through a poor and waterless region. Everyone is waiting for water; the spectator himself begins to wait for it too, just like the men in the dried-up villages, just as the director himself waits for it. The earth is dead; then dirty trickles spring into existence, increase and form a stream to appease the drought. This story of irrigation, which might have been so ordinary, becomes a poem about water and suffering and joy. Continuing the lesson of Vertov, documentation has become lyrical.

Finally, in the most beautiful of the Soviet's nature films, *Earth,** by the Ukrainian Dovzhenko, love of life and the theme of the rain are mingled. (The Ukrainian studios had already concentrated upon legends such as *Taras Shevchenko* by Chardynin, or dramas such as *Two Days* by Stabovoi.) A simple story serves to support the documentation of *Earth*. We see the village with its young men and girls. At night, when all are sleeping, Vassili, a young man who symbolizes the new life of the country, goes to a love tryst, and on the road, alone, dances the Dance of Happiness. It is one of the most moving things the cinema has ever given us. Later, the whole village carries Vassili's bier shoulder-high through the bushes and growing things which cling to the magnificent body of the dead man as it passes. It is spring: life goes on. Warm rain falls and hangs upon the fruit trees and the tips of branches. Rarely has so much poetry been mingled with such simplicity.

Other directors have also brought nature, the plants and the animals to the screen, as in *The Yellow Pass* of Ozep and especially in the lovely *Peasant Women of Riazan* by Olga Preobrazhenskaya, a charming film full of dancing, the simple magic of folklore and the beautiful faces of women, plump and smiling under their embroidered and pointed headdresses. A somber

* Released in the United States as *Soil*.

enough plot served as the groundwork for the film—the story of a woman, seduced by her father-in-law, who bears a child by him. Yet it was not the naturalism which struck us, it was the pictures of the harvest in the midst of which suddenly tolls the bell of the war of 1914; the wedding of Ivan; the beautiful peasant women bundled up in their skirts washing in the river; and the Fete of the Assumption. The censors mutilated this film, leaving it only its simple charm, but we must not complain too bitterly—the images it provided are powerful enough without propaganda or antitheses.

In all these poetic documentations, men count less than the four seasons and the eternal earth, the collective effort, the beauty of the world. Here the Russian genius, independently of social and political forms, has expressed with magnificent amplitude a sort of grave good nature in which youth and hope are perfectly blended. They have put new life into the Sunday-school lessons because they have become a matter of life or death for these people; because they believe in them. They have carried us back, innocently, to the first age of the world and to Adam digging the fruitful earth, and this is the most extraordinary adventure that has befallen the cinema.

5. *The American Film*

After 1923 the American film enjoyed an untroubled prosperity. That happy time disposed it to all sorts of adventures: stars earned unheard-of salaries, fortunes were spent on sets, on landscapes created for a week or two, on orgies that were seen only for a moment. These were the whims of a *nouveau riche*, but what was their real value?

ART AND COMMERCE

Except for the comedies, it is astonishing to find how insignificant American production was during that period of prosperity which lasted until about 1926. After the death of Ince and the semiretirement of Griffith, little creative genius inspired it. Perhaps even Griffith had confined himself to discovering the best methods of expression, without ever having had a really forceful personality to express. Also, as few films were imported into the United States, the American film was not fertilized or renewed by what it might have drawn from French, German, Swedish or Russian experiments.* Working in a vacuum, the Hollywood directors tended to repeat the same formulas and to use the same stories, all the more confidently since the financial success of their product encouraged this. Two reasons strengthened this attitude.

One was of a purely commercial nature. In the fight waged by the big firms, by Paramount and First National in particular, the method most often employed was the wholesale purchase of theaters, which assured them of an outlet for their productions. Within a few years three or four big firms became the owners of nearly all the large theaters in the United States, or at least of first-run theaters, which present to their audiences films never shown before. The result of this strategy was practically to close these outlets to independent producers, who gradually disappeared or considerably reduced their output. Except for the special group at United Artists, which occupied a place apart, the independents slowed up and finally ceased work.

This situation, moreover, had repercussions on production at United Artists. During this period this group produced what was least mediocre among American films, but it more or less consciously underwent the influence of the ban on everything not resembling current productions. Men who did not lack ideas or initiative seemed paralyzed by the fear of seeming original and of beginning to displease.

* An enormous number of foreign films were imported at this period. Moreover, there has hardly ever been a Swedish, French, German or Russian film of interest that Hollywood has not seen and studied, often before the public saw it. As the authors suggest further on, if the same plots and same methods are repeated by the Hollywood people it is because they believe that this is the way to please the greatest number of people and to make the most money: it is not from ignorance of other methods and other ideas.

From then on, the only differences in American films were in actual content: Westerns were abandoned * when it was observed that around 1920 to 1922 the faithfulness of Bill Hart's public was abating. Films of the DeMille kind multiplied when it became apparent that movies based on sex appeal attracted the public; war films were essayed again after Vidor's *The Big Parade* proved that this market could also be speculated in profitably. The older directors had nearly all become supervisors, which is to say that they no longer worked.† After the success of *A Woman of Paris* Griffith essayed a simpler style, less fertile in technical experiments, but only achieved dullness—neither *The White Rose* nor *That Royle Girl* nor *Sally of the Sawdust* nor *Sorrows of Satan*, not even *Drums of Love* was of much value. There were fine things in them occasionally, but there was also the old, familiar moralizing no less irritating than before. *The Battle of the Sexes*, better constructed and more interesting, threw the two sexes into contrast in a series of simple situations; but the creative function had almost ceased.

Cecil B. DeMille had temporarily abandoned his social dramas to devote himself to vast Italianate spectacles of the type that his *Ten Commandments* had proved to be financially successful. *The King of Kings*, a religious film, and *The Volga Boatman* were among his emptiest and most eminent films. He was followed into that territory by Rex Ingram, director of *The Four Horsemen of the Apocalypse*, of *Scaramouche* and *The Magician*, who proved to be as good as his master. He was surpassed by the able Fred Niblo.

Niblo had been Fairbanks' director, notably in *The Mark of Zorro*. Then, after DeMille's example, he made a film with enormous sets, *Blood and Sand*, and finally in 1925 produced his masterpiece, the famous *Ben Hur*. This film best summed up all the ideals of the American public and still holds a record for success unequaled in film history. It marked the height of film production both in its mediocrity and in its demands. It is more

* Westerns have been made continuously since the war, though sometimes only as "quickies."
† This must be unconscious humor, but it is hardly true.

than an historical fact, more than a cinema success, for it concentrates the taste of a period, the standards of a public, the mentality of millions of spectators who went to see it again and again with endless satisfaction. In it Ramon Novarro proclaims the prestige of the actor, but it also reduced him to the horrid necessity of being nothing but a lay figure, handsome and curlyhaired, inexpressive and ordinary enough to figure in a store window. It appealed precisely to that degree of sentimentality that every average heart holds within itself, to that degree of religiosity that every average soul contemplates within itself with satisfaction. The love of spectacle, of dressing up, of history illustrated in pictures, of spurious grandeur and false archaeology, in short all the elements of movie trash, are here co-ordinated, heightened, legitimized and crowned by the agreeable feeling it gives the onlooker of living in an artistic world, and of displaying those faculties which are usually evoked only by the duet from *Robert le Diable* or the Meditation from *Thaïs*. Actually, five years later an American film historian wrote that "it is probable that it will stand permanently as the highest point of film production, and, if chemists should discover a way to preserve the photographic coating on celluloid, may be considered by future historians, together with Douglas Fairbanks' superb fantasy, *The Thief of Bagdad*, as noteworthy achievements of the American civilization which inspired them." We should not have dared to go to these lengths, but since it is an American who speaks, that harsh judgment may be allowed to stand.

Thanks to *Ben Hur*, Ramon Novarro took his place in the pantheon of stars, where he succeeded the handsome Valentino, for whose sake women killed themselves and whose funeral was the occasion for world-wide mourning. The power of the stars now attained its zenith. Future generations will be amazed that an entire globe should have attached itself to the picture of a good-looking boy or oftener of a pretty girl, who had only to appear in some foolish film to make hearts beat faster and induce hundreds of men and women to make involuntary gestures. The history of that extraordinary craze, to which America has contributed twenty examples, ought to be written down. The names of Valentino and of Novarro and of twenty women would not exhaust the list: the talking films were to extend it. We sometimes forget to what lengths the folly of the fans can go. There are actresses who owe their success not to their ability, but to a mysterious aura which sets them apart from humanity, like Greta Garbo, the young Swedish girl brought to Hollywood by Mauritz Stiller, who loved her and perhaps died because of her. A perfect model of the *femme fatale* or vamp, in Seastrom's *Divine Woman*, in Clarence Brown's *Flesh and the Devil*, in *Anna Karenina* she was both mysterious and alluring. Gradually she has emphasized both her faults and her qualities. It would be pleasant to see her in the hands of a good director who knew how to make use of those veiled eyes, those disquieting mannerisms, that sad, secret face with its undeniable power. But Greta Garbo appears in miserable films, and her real talent as an intelligent actress cannot be judged, not even by analyzing all the frightful literature about her which her admirers have poured forth.

FOREIGNERS

To ameliorate the visible dullness of American films, certain producers called in foreign directors. Some of them had been in America for a long time and were to make their whole careers there. The first of them was the German, Ernst Lubitsch, who began by directing Mary Pickford in *Rosita*, and afterwards Pola Negri in *Forbidden Paradise*. *A Woman of Paris* caused this canny businessman to prick up his ears, and *Lady Windermere's Fan* gave much promise. It was a rather trenchant picture of English society produced with surprising discretion and economy of means. Later it became clear in *The Marriage Circle** and *The Patriot* that Lubitsch was little more than a clever craftsman ready to make any concession, though he is evidently seized with remorse at times and then performs miracles by way of compensation.

* Presumably the Lubitsch films were released in France in this order, but actually *The Marriage Circle* preceded *Lady Windermere's Fan*, and showed the influence of *The Woman of Paris* much more clearly.

But the foreigner who did most for American films before Sternberg was not Lubitsch. It was the Austrian actor, Erich von Stroheim. He had started out by playing antipathetic German officers, as in *Hearts of the World*. The ability to be antipathetic was his most powerful and most original asset. His haughty bearing, his ugliness, his diabolic intelligence rapidly made him one of the most prominent actors in the United States. It is said that women adored him; he was "the man you love to hate," and he continued to be so even after he became a director.

His output was somewhat uneven. *Blind Husbands* was stamped with a prudent and not unpleasing brutality; von Stroheim as the officer-villain created a personality definite enough to make this repugnant character acceptable. This same personality appeared, more marked, in *Foolish Wives*, set in Monte Carlo—a bold study of morals in the German manner which aroused the anger of the censors. *Merry-Go-Round* so alarmed the producer that its direction was taken away from von Stroheim. Then he started upon Frank Norris' novel *McTeague*, written in the purest tradition of naturalism, and derived from it his most impressive film, *Greed*.

Von Stroheim began spending money freely: this made the film people realize that he was a real artist. With his monocle, his contemptuous manner, his Oriental savor, this man was an alarming emanation. *Greed* was made in an atmosphere of veneration, regarded from the time the first shot was taken as the masterpiece of masterpieces and crowning jewel of the cinema; it took months to make and cost millions. One fine day von Stroheim, haughtier and more Byzantine than ever, brought to the producer with great ceremony a film twenty-eight reels long which would have taken seven hours to run, and indicated authoritatively that he could permit no cutting or changes. Nothing could persuade him to alter this. Unfortunately we shall probably never know what that strange and powerful film was like: the portions of *Greed* which were shown in America and in Europe and which called forth the admiration of the best critics were formally disowned by von Stroheim.

The director had concentrated in that masterpiece of film

sadism every imaginable violence and brutality.* Several scenes, such as the wedding with a funeral passing by outside, and the closing scenes in which two men handcuffed together kill one another, showed to what an extent this pamphleteer could hate men and despise them. So much odium became magnificent. But von Stroheim has never recognized as his work anything but the immense negative—probably destroyed by now—which the unimpressed cutters adapted for the public's use. The firm escaped with the dead loss of a million dollars and the eternal suspicion of intelligent directors.

Later, in *The Wedding March*, a very uneven film, that rugged individuality attempted to come to terms with business necessity. Von Stroheim acted in it, exquisitely arrogant, and occasionally succeeded in evoking the memory of imperial Vienna with its slow waltz-time charm, its excesses and its miseries. *The Wedding March* is a work of hatred, but it is also a work of love and of imagination. This, rather than the concessions it made to the public taste (for which it is clear that von Stroheim has nothing but contempt), makes it occasionally disconcerting.

ATTEMPTS TOWARD ARTISTRY

Despite the failure of *Greed*, and the very relative success of the films entrusted to foreigners brought over from Europe on princely contracts, there were other attempts to make American films a little more intelligent. It was a formidable task. Miss June Mathis, who had just made a reputation with her work on *The Four Horsemen of the Apocalypse*, was put in charge of a whole series of films. She conceived the idea of submitting the scenarios and rough cuts of these films to a group of writers, artists, dramatic and film critics. This curious collaboration succeeded in eliminating the overromantic or overmelodramatic elements from them, but the public seemed little interested in Miss Mathis' films. Goldwyn met with no more success when he had his films supervised by a committee of critics and writers. Another producer chose the opposite method: he invited his chauffeur and

* He filmed the novel scene by scene with scrupulous accuracy.

his friends to collaborate with him, which was at least in the tradition of American production.

These experiments are to be explained by the conditions of film production. The director, usually overworked, no longer exercised complete control over his films. Actually there was a move to take away from him what authority he still possessed. Most of the producing firms were alarmed at the extravagance in the studios, but it was difficult to stop it. The heads of the firms usually lived in New York, which was their headquarters, and their visits to California were infrequent. They struggled for a long time with the situation before entrusting the control of all the various processes on each film to a supervisor endowed with absolute authority over the producing staff.

The industrial organization of the studios explains how it is that a director who has made one good film can make another which is not merely dull, but also without any individuality. Those who can continue to be creative are rare. Just as in making comedies special teams work on the story, the cutting, the gags, so for dramatic films there are teams, too. As a result, the real author of a film is as likely to be the star it features as the humble director. This is always true of the comedies of Buster Keaton and Harold Lloyd, and is sometimes true of dramatic films, too. But whereas a comedy can easily depend on the one actor who gives unity to the plot, it is difficult to achieve the same unity and the same effect in serious films. It is not surprising, therefore, if American films manufactured wholesale have little originality. They only display any when a director is strong enough to stamp his personality on them; almost always such a director is a foreigner, like von Stroheim or Sternberg in their early days. Otherwise the only original creations in America, because of the method employed, will be found among the comedies.

COMEDIANS

The American comedies grew less in number during the years under consideration. Douglas Fairbanks even, despite his success,

Al Jolson in The Jazz Singer (*1927*).

Edward G. Robinson and James Cagney in Smart Money (*1931*).

A scene from The Italian Straw Hat (*1927*), *directed by René Clair.*

was obliged to slow up production. *Robin Hood* had been the first of those pictures in which his jolly personality was combined with immense sets. He made a sequel to his most celebrated film, *Don Q, Son of Zorro*. Even better, he conjured up the Oriental legend of *The Thief of Bagdad*, about a young man who can steal everything he wants except love. His performance, never varying, was not as effective as the big cities, the flying carpet, the trick work and the whole gigantic machinery of illusion, which bore certain resemblances to *Ben Hur*, and in which Fairbanks almost succeeded in burying himself under the sets and the props.

Adolphe Menjou, brought into prominence by *A Woman of Paris*,* now assumed a special place among American actors, and appeared in a number of screen plays—*The King of Main Street, A Gentleman of Paris, The Grand Duchess and the Waiter*—but unfortunately he succeeded in being little more than a remarkable actor. It is a pity that he could not have been put to better use, for his subtlety, his admirable characterization of a man about town—at once skeptical, blasé, cynical and witty—deserved more than films in which they are merely sketched in. Once, in the role of a lovesick maître d'hôtel, he succeeded in carrying comedy beyond the purely theatrical form—it was that delightful film, *Service for Ladies*, directed by Henri d'Abbadie d'Arrast, who assisted Chaplin on *The Gold Rush*. But he never found another vehicle as good as *A Woman of Paris*.

Harry Langdon, the eccentric who for a time was set up as a competitor of Chaplin's, like Menjou was a newcomer. Langdon has since disappeared, which is a pity. An able student of Chaplin, he made at least one delightful film of a somewhat melancholy humor, *Three's a Crowd*, in which he used to good effect ideas from *The Kid*. One of his first pictures, directed by Sennett sometime before 1925, also deserves to be remembered. There was an admirable scene in it, where a madman in prison explains the difficulties of cod fishing to a figure drawn on the wall. Langdon, puzzled, joins in gradually, plays up to the characters and begins to take an interest in that disquieting dia-

* Menjou had been in films for some time: *vide The Sheik* (1921).

logue. It gave one the impression that one was going mad, too.

There is no doubt that the two names which dominated the field of comedy at that time were those of Harold Lloyd and of Buster Keaton. Lloyd had definitely perfected his technique, which is that of an accumulation of gags. Four gagmen were attached to him with the task of hunting up amusing incidents to adorn plots, usually ordinary enough, in which Lloyd fell in love with a girl and finally married her. Some of these gags were of an immense virtuosity, as for instance the white mouse hidden inside a white glove which walks, ghostlike, in the black of night in *A Rich Family*. Lloyd made many films at that time (*Grandma's Boy, Safety Last*), but the best of them is unquestionably *Speedy*, in which the old pattern of chases and races so dear to Sennett succeeded in giving unity to the whole picture. With the gags, unity seems to be lacking in Lloyd's films: they seem to proceed in fits and starts, and the good-natured hero is not always able to sustain our interest. That he is a gifted comedian there is no question. It was Jean Prévost who observed one day that all of Lloyd's expressions are arranged vertically: his hair sticks up, his eyebrows go up, the corners of his mouth come down. Often when one fancies that the story is slowing up, some excellent gag sets things going again; but though his pictures are gay and enjoyable, their complete lack of humanity and their emptiness always strike one. Lloyd will only be perfectly successful when he realizes that his salvation lies in an intensive accumulation of gags, and when he does not hesitate to insert one every thirty seconds. At the present moment he is too economical.

Buster Keaton has an attractive but quite different personality. He also works with gagmen, but he imposes his own will on them from the start and knows clearly what he intends to do. His full-length features began in 1924 with *Our Hospitality*, which set the model for a series of films which are perhaps rather mechanical and deliberate but extremely and subtly intelligent. This intelligence is visible in *The Navigator, Go West, The General, College, Steamboat Bill, Jr., The Cameraman*.

The actor himself is extraordinary: his head is quite rigid and looks as though it had been carved out of a chestnut; his eyes are large and staring and his face is immobile. The entire head appears to be an inarticulate organ, expressionless and calm as a foot and seems to have been stuck or grafted onto his lively and elastic body like some addition made of stucco or papier mâché. The body is never still, but skips and jumps about with enchanting suppleness. The head follows it, without really understanding the adventures it participates in. This master of acrobatics finds the basic element of his comic genius in this contrast. But there is something even more important: *The Cameraman, Our Hospitality, The General* and *The Navigator* all have one thing in common—their principal character is not a man but a machine. The drama lies in the relationship between the comedian and this machine. *The General* is about Buster being chased by a locomotive during the Civil War. *The Cameraman* has for hero a strange monster composed of Buster and his camera. *The Navigator*, his masterpiece, is about an engaged couple alone on a huge liner, making their coffee in pots big enough to serve five hundred people. When a central object is absent, Buster seems lost. *Our Hospitality* is only really successful in its delightful first part, about a journey on a train around 1850. In *Steamboat Bill, Jr.* he makes us laugh when he tries on the hats, but not so much as when he is struggling against the flood, a new kind of monster. In *Go West*, the monster is a herd of cattle. In this formula which he almost always follows we find once more the contrast between immobility and suppleness which distinguishes his own acting; it is the well-known comic device in which inertia counteracts action. In this, Keaton's comedy is perhaps even more deliberate than Chaplin's, but it is less human since he relies chiefly on exterior elements.

Every film of Keaton's seems to be at once an essay on bad luck and a mathematical problem. Granted the physical necessity which directs the machine, granted the means by which man controls it, what can be made of the contact between them? Keaton's power to observe the most grotesque as well as the most logical details imposes an inflexible line of action on his gagmen. In his films of that period, after having developed his technique through the wildest and maddest fantasy in the short comedies, Keaton really became a relatively abstract personality, a mathematician highly gifted in calculating laughter. That is what appeals to one in his films, and why towards the end of the silent era there was hope that he would produce a masterpiece by quite seriously opposing machine to man in a profoundly modern comedy whose underlying intent would have gone far beyond our laughter.

CHAPLIN

Definitely successful and completely independent of producers, thanks to the money he had made, Charlie Chaplin throughout the classic era of silent films produced only two pictures, *The Gold Rush* in 1925, after two years when nothing of his appeared, and *The Circus* in 1927. *The Gold Rush* is one of the most famous of all films and is perhaps the masterpiece of the whole cinema. It is not so much that Chaplin surpasses here what he had done in *Shoulder Arms*, but that this is his first really long picture. Everything that had been indicated in *The Tramp* or *The Pawnshop* is made use of in it, and carried to completion within a complex composition where we pass uninterruptedly from laughter to sympathy, where the various episodes do not seem like separate fragments but as the unified parts of a whole. When *The Gold Rush* made its appearance we had just seen *The Covered Wagon* and had not yet forgotten Bill Hart, so that the atmosphere of this gold rush seemed familiar, even if it were a parody. There was unquestionably an element of critical comment in it which added to its immense charm. Today this implication no longer exists, and *The Gold Rush* is simply a magnificent poetic-comic picture.

It presents a whole series of famous scenes: the long trail of seekers after gold in the mountains among whom suddenly appears a strange wayfarer, with a bear following him; the blizzard in the hut; Charlie on the verge of starvation devouring his boots, and his companion going insane and mistaking him for a giant rooster; the saloon where people far from home sing Irish or Scottish songs and Charlie falls in love with Georgia; New Year's Eve, when he awaits the girl he loves and, dreaming, makes two forks shod with rolls dance a polka; the return to the cabin swept away by the storm and perched on the edge of an abyss. That dance of the rolls is the crowning point in the art of pantomime which Chaplin had revealed in *The Pilgrim*, just as the eating of the boots is the crowning point of his gift for comical transpositions as revealed in *The Pawnshop*. Here his gentleness of spirit carries us further and further into a realm of tenderness and drollery.

The Circus is less well constructed, and not as good as *The Gold Rush*. Some of its incidents are rather labored, as when Charlie on the tightrope is pursued by monkeys who tear his clothes apart, or when he finds himself face to face with the lion. But there are some breath-takingly lovely and funny scenes which might have come from *The Tramp*—Charlie cooking an egg in an old can; Charlie chased by a donkey into the ring where the audience, bored up till now, bursts out laughing and clamors for more of the "funny man." Best of all is the admirable closing scene of Charlie in the center of the ring of sawdust which a circus leaves behind on the site it has occupied, as he picks up a paper star before going on to seek his fortune.

These two films, in the silent days, were most praised of all Chaplin's work, even if they were not, the last one particularly, the most characteristic. Hardly a breath of criticism was heard, though in 1925 André Suarès ventured to say: "I confess that Chaplin bores me to death. He is the sort of hero which that awful America *would* create and I should enjoy crushing that base heart of his as though it were a bug." Francis Carcot compared him to Villon, finding him more genuine and more authentic, but André Maurois probably hit the truth as well as the general opinion when he declared that "three hundred years hence Chaplin will have become what Villon is to us now, a great archaic artist."

In *The Gold Rush* and *The Circus*, Chaplin completed what he had begun in *The Tramp* and continued through *Shoulder Arms, The Kid, The Pilgrim*. He had bestowed a soul upon his marionette, had transposed the contrast between Charlie and the rest of mankind onto the plane of the sentiments and made of him a creature utterly touching and convincing who has gone astray in our world. The soul of a marionette is a delicate thing. It must be sincerely naïve, well-intentioned at every moment, must have immense confidence in life and faith in mankind, must wear its heart on its sleeve and think that everyone else does likewise. In this extraordinary creation (in which tougher characteristics which the wear and tear of life had conferred on the marionette are also to be detected) Chaplin follows the same rule of contrasts as guided him in his early films. Just as Chaplin's body apparently does not obey the same physical laws as the rest of the world, so now the soul which inhabits this singular body also belongs to some foreign world of the emotions; but where the first contrast aimed exclusively at creating laughter, the second one arouses in us a deep affection for the simple hero at whom we are laughing.

And so we shall always remember Charlie in the snow, so ingenuously brave, and that New Year's Eve when he has spread the table in his cabin with a fine cloth and his best cutlery, has put favors in the tumblers, prepared gay candles, written the names of the girls on each of their gifts and then sits dreaming of the gaiety and the success which he is about to enjoy and the happiness that is actually never to be. He is so trusting, so utterly charming. His sadness, even, is that of a child, as on the morning when he gazes at the big circle left behind by the circus which has gone away.

No matter how life belabors him, he is always an "innocent," one of those little boys who give their marbles and their candy to other children but who never make any friends. The only friend he ever finds is the Kid, for he alone is innocent enough to love him. Otherwise he is always out of luck, poor fellow. With that same simplicity with which he allows himself to be led away when he alights from the train in *The Pilgrim*, he accepts the fact that for some reason he is suddenly amid the snows of Alaska. He is astonished neither by his misfortunes nor by his strokes of good luck, but gazes with the same great doll-like eyes when climbing up to stake his claim in the opening scenes of *The Gold Rush*, as he does at the end on the boat which is taking him back to civilization, a millionaire. The fine and simple love that awakes in him is the sort of passion one experiences at the age of ten for some beautiful queen whom one will never set eyes on. When "she" has gone away, he makes for the hundredth time that gesture of resignation with which he accepts the inevitable, and sets off again on his journey, towards some other adventure of the same kind to which he will abandon himself with similar fervor and just as little result.

We must never forget that a period so lacking in poetry and in truth to life was nevertheless one which, thanks to Chaplin, gave birth to this hero, an unknown man of an extreme anonymity, without passport and without means, without nationality or friends. Because of his inner simplicity, he barely criticized this world which had no reality for him. He simply accepts the fact that he is not destined for success any more than, in glory or in love, the best and worst of mankind are destined to succeed. He typifies that wry but appealing destiny which is perhaps really the destiny of man. "What I wanted to do," he said once, "was to create an imaginative tramp." This tramp is a true hero of our times, despite the concessions which Chaplin may have made to public taste, or those which his background may have suggested to him, such as his love for clowns and that effective but undeniable vulgarity which creeps out in the least admirable parts of certain films, as for example in *The Circus* and in *City Lights*. It is almost always so sufficiently controlled as not to embarrass us seriously, and can be disregarded because of his completely human truthfulness.

THE END OF THE SILENT FILM

The last years of the silent film provided audiences with other films besides comedies. We can forget Clarence Brown's success with *Flesh and the Devil*, Victor Fleming's with *The Way of All Flesh*, for which Greta Garbo and Jannings were responsible. But Flaherty, the director of *Nanook*, created in *Moana* an admirable documentary film which gave rise to a whole succession: after it came ten other films celebrating the beauties of harpoon fishing, of paring *taros*, and the innocent lives of the poor Polynesians troubled by the advent of the white man. Few of them managed to do homage to this simple Rousseauism with as much skill as the man who assembled such lovely pictures while rejecting the enticements of a plot, contenting himself with composing a pictorial ode to the glory of the sky, of labor and of repose. Elmer Clifton in *Down to the Sea in Ships* made a romantic picture without great merit, though it was enlivened with fine scenes of mutiny, of fishing, of the sailing of a ship and a fight with a whale, creating a pleasing hymn to bravery and the ocean. Van Dyke in *The Pagan* followed the same model.

Borzage adapted a few skillful pieces before he became, through the talkies, a really excellent director. Vidor finally achieved a triumphant success with *The Big Parade*, actually a rather unbearable picture, and then made *The Crowd*. This opens charmingly with the story of two young people of modest means who fall in love and marry after meeting at a fair, but the contrast thereafter made between the one man and the crowd gave evidence of a singularly primary and dull imagination. No one would have guessed that soon Vidor was to make the masterpiece among talking films.

Now and then a picture appeared by some unknown director which seemed extraordinarily perfect, so well had the technique of film making been established. Howard Hawks gave us *A Girl in Every Port*, a simple story of sailors and their flirtations, admirably acted by Victor McLaglen, which took us to Amsterdam and Buenos Aires and Antwerp. Really an adventure story with lots of fun and fisticuffs, it employed such perfect economy of means and such admirable straightforwardness that this unpretentious picture was one of the best that came from America.

There was also *Lonesome*, which introduced us to the Hungarian, Paul Fejos. A young workman and a little telephone girl at a fair fall in love with one another, then meet again. Around this simple courtship blares the noise of the merry-go-rounds, the gaiety of the crowd. It exhibited a singular skill in camera angles and curious photographic foreshortenings, somewhat reminiscent of Epstein's *Cœur Fidèle*, but beyond its technical merits it possessed a fresh simplicity which permitted one to overlook certain romantic contrivances and even the occasional horrid passages in color.

Last we became acquainted with the name of the German * Josef von Sternberg, certainly the most interesting personality working in America at that time. *The Last Command*, which featured Jannings, did little more than exhibit the actor's resources, though this story about a Russian ex-general become a film extra who recovers his former spirit when he once more dons his old uniform, is not without an emotional quality. *Underworld* and *The Drag-Net* were both crime films, and launched a new fashion which was firmly established by *Dressed to Kill*, made at about the same time. Here were no mystery films, but tough, grim and surprisingly realistic stories about armed gangs of crooks. Unfolding smoothly and unsentimentally, they took murder and all sorts of adventures in their stride with a gradually accentuated rhythm that eventually rose to some terrific conclusion, such as a raid on a heavily garrisoned house. The introduction of sound was to increase their effectiveness, but *Underworld* and Bancroft's brutal and expressive physiognomy had set the model which benefited in this case by the almost mathematical precision and extreme care with which it was constructed.

It was *The Docks of New York*, however, which put von Sternberg in the front rank. Just as *Such Is Life* was the swan song of the silent film in Europe, so did *The Docks of New York* represent the logical conclusion of a whole range of technique in which American skill was combined for the first and last time with the pictorial perfection of the Germans. In this gripping tale, the characters were brought to life with rugged truthfulness. Bancroft saves a woman from drowning; she is accused of murder; he confesses that he is guilty. These two suddenly

* It seems uncertain whether von Sternberg is actually a native of London or of New York, but he is not a German. His name was originally Joseph Stern.

discover an abiding sentiment: they are no longer alone. Olga Baclanova lent to the role of the murderess a passivity and a hidden energy, a sort of parsimony of effort which made the character singularly real; but more than anything else *The Docks of New York* was notable because of its photography. Seldom have we seen anything more beautiful than the scenes with which the film opens, the glistening bodies of the stokers in the oily steam, the smoky port with its fog, or than the low bar where, as a joke, Bancroft decides to marry his drowned woman and, in the midst of an incredible uproar, sends for the clergyman. As in *Underworld*, American vitality is added to the beauty of misty outlines and of faces half-hidden in shadow. In *The Docks of New York* the silent film reached a kind of perfection evermore to be regretted, which gave hope that through this German the American film was about to become humanized. He created two or three stirring and powerful films and provided a dramatic model full of verve and vigor.

In a different realm some remarkable technicians outside the studios had perfected the animated cartoon: Max Fleischer had created Koko, and Pat Sullivan had given us Felix the Cat, whose absurd adventures, which seldom obeyed the laws of reason, transported us to Alice in Wonderland's world. These animals with their quaint bodies created a sort of grotesque poetry, half fable and half nonsense, which had the charm of a child's dream. These films had real value and were to have further uses.

6. *The Death of an Art*

It is impossible to restrain a feeling of melancholy when one comes to the end of reviewing the chief events in silent-film history. Between 1927 and 1930 this form gradually expired, first in America and then in Europe. It is difficult to regard what came to take its place as a sufficient consolation, despite any number of excellent films. Not everything about the silent film was perfect, but at the end of its short life it possessed an enormous number of resources and had attained that relative degree of stability without which no renewal-from-within is possible. In short, it had almost completed its technical development. No doubt the cameras could have been improved, subtler methods of lighting might have been found, but by this time the technical development of the film was so complete that there had already been a swing towards simplification. Here was something of real importance, for henceforward cleverness of technique could be concealed. The telling of a story was no longer marked by perceptible devices, as in *La Roue* and the expressionist films, and films as a whole now flowed smoothly. People had realized that the discoveries of which everyone had been so proud in 1923 were those which made a film age more rapidly; that double photography was not a remedy for every ill; that *La Roue* and *The Stroke of Midnight* were themselves rather old-fashioned, whereas certain very simple films like those of Chaplin, and *Berg-Ejvind*, and a few Bill Harts, seemed just as fresh, or almost as fresh, as the day they were made. This new simplicity was perhaps carried too far in some cases, but it was characteristic of the period.

Without question it was carried too far: it was inevitable that comedy, for instance, reduced to the capacities of one single actor in a burlesque situation, would necessarily become rigidly set in a pattern and would completely neglect the comedy of inanimate objects which the film alone can handle and which was so popular in prewar days. It was easy to foresee, too, that narrative films were in danger of becoming little more than polished exercises of an extreme technical ability, content to relate ably constructed plots by a series of exquisite photographs. Of course, there were always the Russians to fling themselves upon epic subjects, but they were far away and Abel Gance was intoxicated with his own success. There were dangers as well as virtues in the form that the medium had taken at the time it died a sudden death. Was the invention of sound and talking films to solve this problem? It was impossible to tell, but certainly when movies began to talk, all those who loved the cinema clung desperately to the past and expected no good of the future.

Even today it is questionable whether it is possible to love the film sincerely unless one knew it in the silent days, in those last years which are inseparable from the days of one's youth. The Germans, the Russians, the French, the Americans and the Swedes had etched unforgettable shadows on the screen. They had robbed the sunlight of its brightness and the shadow of its secrets. The faces of men and women had learned to be expressive in those mute dramas by the aid of no more than an eyelid, the flicker of a glance, or a shadowy flush which mantled their cheeks. We demanded emotions and dreams, passion and suffering of them, and felt no need for words. There were quite ordinary films in which the extinguishing of a lamp at some window, a figure emerging from the mist pale and formless as a drowned body, the bend of a river revealing a road between two rows of trees, furnished us with that unique sensation of shock which a glimpse of an unknown world provides. Those actors, so well adapted to express subtleties, those plots which were of necessity so clear and so brief, may all be forgotten in the future. But we who witnessed the birth of an art may possibly also have seen it die. Recalling all that it promised, we are left with the melancholy regret one feels for a thing foredoomed.

PART SIX

The Talking Films

1929–1935

1. The American Film

THE experiments which led up to the talkies had started almost immediately after the war. The development of electrical devices, the multiplicity of laboratories and the progress of radio had constituted a set of favorable conditions. By 1924 the principles that were to serve as a basis for sound-on-film recording, as opposed to the use of phonograph discs, had been clearly established and important solutions of the various problems had been discovered, though none of the results were capable of practical applications.* The electrical or radio concerns which had chiefly devoted themselves to these experiments were RCA, General Electric, Westinghouse and Bell Telephone Laboratories, as well as numerous private inventors. In the film world William Fox alone commissioned an engineer to pursue experiments of this kind.

At the beginning of 1926 the Bell Laboratories had perfected a synchronizing process called Vitaphone.† The inventors addressed themselves to Zukor and to his principal competitors, urging the purchase of their patents. These rulers of the American film world pondered, conferred and finally decided that the invention was of no interest. The Bell Laboratories approached

* The basic elements of sound-on-film recording were known to physicists, in both Europe and America, well before 1900. Due, however, to the infinitely small amount of sound energy available for audio reproduction, this knowledge was no practical use. It was not until the decade following the World War, when the vacuum tube amplifier was perfected, that the art of sound-on-film recording and reproduction became commercially possible.

† This was a method of sound reproduction utilizing the disc mechanically coupled to the film projector to insure synchronization with the audio output electrically amplified.

several other magnates of less importance but met with the same reception. During a demonstration in Hollywood, however, Sam Warner, a producer of secondary importance who, moreover, was in no very secure position, became interested in the new invention and made an offer to the firm, which, tired of the struggle, accepted. Sam Warner had started out modestly in partnership with his three brothers as Warner Brothers. By dint of energy and ingenuity they had managed to create a good position as independent producers by about 1921 or 1922. It was just at this time that Paramount and First National had gone in for the mass purchase of theaters, in order to assure themselves control of the industry. Warner Brothers soon found their market disappearing; their lack of capital prevented them from putting up a fight. Sam Warner was possibly no more enthusiastic about talkies than the other producers had been, but, on the verge of ruin, he thought he might as well take this final gamble. It was not the end of his difficulties. Banks advanced money only reluctantly. Theater owners displayed no eagerness to install the necessary equipment. The first sound recording, timidly reminiscent of the first dramatic efforts of the silent cinema, aroused little enthusiasm among audiences. The critics were entirely against them: even those who had had least praise for the "simplistic" technique of the silent films now suddenly became apostles of silence. And it is true that these first talkies fell far short of the vulgarest contrivances of the old movies. Newspapers and magazines continued to examine this new discovery and to condemn it. Sam Warner, overworked and unhappy, died during these months of struggle. The times, however, played into the hands of Warner Brothers. The public, intoxicated with sound by the radio, was coming to feel that noise was now inseparable from entertainment. The crude music-hall sketches of the earliest days were now followed by much better-made sound films, in which only the noises of trains, machine guns, airplanes and the like were recorded. The public took to these much more readily and the theater owners began to think about installing the new equipment. Success finally arose out of competition. William Fox, who had perfected his process of sound recording,

Movietone, in 1927, launched a campaign for popularizing the talkies at the same time as the Warners. For three years Fox, entirely reorganized, had been buying theaters after the example of Paramount and now controlled quite a number of them. After the entry of Fox into the new field, many theaters were wired for sound and the public acquired the habit of regarding films as an audible medium. As sometimes happens, the two systems instead of doing each other harm actually conspired to establish a new habit. What neither Fox nor the Warners could have done alone, Fox and the Warners achieved together.

Towards the end of 1927 the public began clearly to demonstrate its preferences. Now was the moment to strike a decisive blow, and the Warners conceived the most monstrous and devastating of ideas. They decided to catch the public interest by having some actor sing, and selected Al Jolson. *The Jazz Singer* was the first big talking film,* and the forerunner of many. Under infantile pretexts dignified by the name of plot, a colored man moved up into a semiclose-up and reeled off a ditty. Plaintive and mild as the songs which small children make up, the crooning of the excellent Jolson might have harmlessly charmed all those who enjoy a dreamy state of semiconsciousness, had this not been the source of a perfect flood of nonsensicalities, of blackface minstrels, of singing acts, love duets and relentless sopranos, which continue to work havoc even today. Be that as it may, *The Jazz Singer* scored a triumph which recalled the fortunes made by *The Birth of a Nation* and *Ben Hur*. The talkies had won a victory. Harry Warner, now head of Warner Brothers, became one of the richest men in the country. William Fox moved his armchair over, chummily, beside Mr. Zukor's throne, and the population of five continents was condemned out of hand to hearing the movies prattle.

The introduction of talking films had many results. On the commercial side, Paramount saw its absolute power vanish. Since Zukor owned the handsomest and biggest American theaters, he readily adapted himself to the new situation, but not before

---

* Actually it was largely a silent film with brief scenes in which Jolson sang and spoke a few words.

other competitors had challenged his supremacy. The remaining
independent producers had to abandon the field because of the
capital necessary to engage in this new contest. Big changes were
made in the larger firms. First National, which had been a
dangerous rival of Paramount's for ten years, now became the
property of the Warners. By 1929 most of American production
was concentrated in the four big firms, Fox, Warner, Paramount
and Metro-Goldwyn-Mayer.

There were even greater changes and upsets in the machinery
of film production. The first to suffer were the actors: more stars
came to grief than one would have believed possible. This was
no great loss, for many of the players in silent films were really
quite third-rate actors, and their disappearance hardly merits attention. A few survived. Newcomers quickly submitted themselves to the entirely different technique demanded by the talkies.
Acting became more flexible, more varied and much less conventional. Sweethearts no longer necessarily resembled fashion
plates. Characters with marked temperament and from broader
walks of life made their appearance on the screen, and the public
now began to bestow on character actors the favors they had
formerly reserved for leading ladies and gentlemen. One admirable actress, Marie Dressler, who had been one of Chaplin's earliest partners, scored a triumph with her loquacity, her air of authority, her abrupt and vulgar turbulence and her extraordinarily
powerful acting. She was one of the rare film players who was
more than a public idol.

It remained to be seen what the effects on the artistic qualities
of the medium would be.

NEWSREEL

Sound now began to be added cautiously to the newsreels,
just as in its early days the silent films had set out by filming current events and the celebrities of the period. We marveled at
certain amazing effects which were accidentally secured, as during some topical picture of horse racing when the thud of hooves
rang out, then vanished amid the clamor of the crowd only to

ring out again, sharp and distinct, on the turf. Vast possibilities seemed to open before us. Putting aside entirely for the moment all films that attempted a degree of artistry, it is possible still to recall vividly, as one of the most affecting things ever given in a cinema, a film about India in which Rabindranath Tagore appeared in black draperies with his white hair and immensely penetrating eyes, reciting a poem in praise of his country. We did not understand a single word, but somehow received the impression of having heard and seen a Homer.

Impressions such as these are so intense that it was not long before those in control of the public's destiny pricked up their ears. It may be all very well to see a dictator or a riot, but it becomes dangerous to hear them as well. Censorship, whether official or officious (in France, by some admirable hypocrisy, censorship is theoretically not supposed to apply to newsreels), got its claws on the producers of newsreels. So it came about that while the world was being shaken by catastrophes, the screen showed us only dull boxing or tennis matches, bicycle races, the cultivation of the grape in California, harvesting in Denmark and—in every country in the world—local beauty contests at the seashore, local dog shows, but never the truth. Occasionally some political figure appeared on the screen, whereupon as a rule he was vociferously hissed and the theater proprietor trembled for the safety of his hall. As it was not always possible to foretell how audiences would receive Mussolini or the President of the United States, such figures were shown less and less frequently and the newsreels were deliberately turned into a magazine for children. It must be admitted that in providing these perfectly safe items the newsreels are most successful today, and that it is occasionally agreeable to gaze upon charming girls, new fashions which will be forgotten tomorrow, or pretty children—but it will be even more agreeable to see them twenty years hence. They have succeeded in presenting time-as-it-flies in pleasant fashion; it is impossible to recall without pleasure certain shots of winter sports or summer sports, with their crisp hard snow or striped sands, even a mere fleeting pose or a frock as caught on the screen by some unknown artist. Yet we should have liked to see the tragedies as well as the pleasures of daily life. Even so there have sometimes been surprises for us: in years to come we shall gaze with considerable emotion upon the amazing scenes of the National Socialist ceremonies, the cyclopean architecture of New Germany, the removal of Hindenburg's ashes, Tempelhof and Nuremberg and harvest festivals where, over a plain where a million men are standing, airplanes trail swastikas across the sky.

SOUND FILMS

Compromises were already being reached, at first by simply omitting dialogue, as in Borzage's *The River*, a creditable film containing much natural poetry, which was shown in France as a silent picture. A little later on they essayed musical films largely composed of singing and dancing in the manner of a revue, which, it was supposed, no one needed to understand, like *Broadway Melody* and *Fox Movietone Follies*. Audiences hissed, and yelled, "In French!"—which brought great sadness to the hearts of theater owners.

Afterwards they made several versions of each film, in various languages, but this was horribly expensive and the method was gradually abandoned. Finally some ingenious person invented "dubbing," in which after the film has been made in one language, dialogue in another language is composed which calls for approximately the same lip movements, and is then spoken by another set of actors. There is always a faint difference and one feels somehow that the character who is saying "oui" really had said "yes" or "ja." Nevertheless, most foreign films shown in the provinces are dubbed. In Paris we have become accustomed to seeing films in the original version accompanied by (overprinted) subtitles which summarize the dialogue, but these did not appear for some time, and for a long while it seemed that only straightforward talkies would be accepted.

The success of Van Dyke's *White Shadows in the South Seas* seemed to justify those who were timid about using dialogue.

In this film, which Flaherty was to have made and had actually started, the sweetness of *Moana*, the unvarying Polynesian climate, dramatic incidents such as pearl fishing, and a rather pleasing Rousseauesque romanticism were again to be found, though it was less "pure" than *Moana*. Polynesian charm now met the public's taste for Hawaiian guitars and other trite elements. *The Pagan*, also by Van Dyke and starring Ramon Novarro, erred further in this direction. Yet a few years later Van Dyke was to make a beautiful film called *Eskimo* which again used the method indicated in *White Shadows*. The film is not without faults; it continually throws the natives and the white men into contrast, though less harshly. A tale of murder and of race antagonism, it contains scenes like those of the walrus hunt and the attack on the caribou which are as touching as the finest things in the *Georgics*. Under a pallid sky each man or animal stands out in sharp silhouette against the great expanses of white snow. The actors speak Eskimo, which does not disturb us in the least, for the dialogue is not meant to be understood but, like the music of *White Shadows*, blends with the images. The important thing about the film is the way in which sounds and images are thus blended and combine to create a definite rhythm. Right at the start of the talkie era, Benjamin Fondane wrote in *Bifur:* "Dialogue and sound should be content to fulfil the function formerly entrusted to double-exposure and to take its place." With Van Dyke this is what happened.

Flaherty, too, to whom we later owed the beautiful poetic-documentary film *Man of Aran*, also made a similar use of sound. (Van Dyke, a versatile person, has since made all kinds of films, including detective films and an enchanting picture, *Hide-Out*, in which a gangster made the discovery of the countryside, with its hay and chickens and rabbits.) A similar procedure was followed by the directors of the various nature films which appear now and then, among which the most delightful was *Sequoia* with its wonderful animals and the almost human friendship between a puma and a deer. In *White Shadows* the right way to make sound films had been indicated, though lightly, if charmingly. It was not followed for long.

KING VIDOR

In spite of appearances, the experiments which many directors made all tended towards the same solutions. Many an otherwise ordinary film indicated a new and appropriate way of using sound, as in *Broadway Melody*, where we heard an automobile drive off, though the camera remained on the heroine's face, or in *The Wolf of Wall Street*, where the roars of a crowd swelled or diminished as a door opened or closed. Films already had begun to use not a juxtaposition of sight and sound, but a contrast or counterpoint of the two. Of course there were dozens of screened plays and photographed operettas, but nevertheless we began to have faith in the talking film.

We believed in it utterly when the director of *The Crowd* and numerous rather ordinary films suddenly in 1929 produced a real masterpiece, one of the four or five most important films ever made—*Hallelujah*—which made Vidor famous overnight.* There is probably too much dialogue in the film, especially at the beginning; this constant fault with talkies was unimportant in view of the general richness and mastery of the whole. To begin with, it achieved pictorial miracles: the bodies of the Negroes seemed to give out a soft, rich light which contrasted with the light shimmering on the tufts of cotton. Rhythmically it was also quite remarkable: the slow-moving story of life and love and death is interspersed with Negro singing; scenes of violence and drama are alternated with quieter scenes. A silent film could have given us pictures as beautiful as those of the cotton picking, or of the colored children's bedtime and the saloon, but it could never have conveyed the strong emotions evoked by the death of the small brother, the most real death ever shown on the screen, with its accompaniment of hoarse, broken sobbing. The mood changes as the Negroes begin to pray and sing, and gradually attains a sort of savage ecstasy. No silent film could have possessed the terrifying quality of that baptism in the river, when the colored people adapt Christianity to the

---

* *Hallelujah* was much more warmly admired in France than in the United States. It ran in a Paris theater for two years.

laws of their own hysteria through a succession of frenzied scenes in which the collective soul of a people is expressed as even the Russians have never expressed it. The love story, so plausible and convincing, and the famous sermon about the two trains which leave daily, one for hell and one for heaven, are both fine, but they are mere incidentals in the turbulent swing of the whole film.

What was more important than all else was that Vidor made an essential contribution to the medium when this film brought us, for the first time, silence. Silence attained an emotional value here for the first time, because it was contrasted with sound: one *heard* silence. We are referring in particular to that extraordinary ten minutes at the end where one man follows another through the swamp. One hears hardly anything but, now and then, the rustle of a branch, the sound of water and, gradually, the labored breathing of the hunted man. In the midst of a silence more protracted than the rest, a bird utters three cries. The sound film has never come closer to its true function of creating a universe subject to the laws of music, where everything which is transitory and intangible (a flickering light, a sigh, a murmur) is caught for eternity. Vidor, apart from his other very considerable qualities, performed a service here as great as that of Gance in *La Roue*, but where *La Roue* was copied by others *Hallelujah* was an isolated masterpiece without posterity. Vidor never quite attained such heights again.

Street Scene was not without interest in spite of revealing traces of the play on which it was based. Now and again amid those protracted conversations through which it attempted to indicate the life of a whole house, Vidor sometimes recaptured the virtues of *Hallelujah*. What gave the film its merit was that he treated the film as a composition in which the voices, the faces of the characters, the glimpse of some wretched old woman sweeping were all blended to convey values less readily discernible because they were profounder than those suggested by the Negroes around their pastor. *Street Scene* in retrospect is seen to be a very strange transcription of a play into terms which are occasionally purely cinematic, though not very obviously so.

Later, after making a few disappointing commercial films through which he hoped to obtain independence, Vidor attempted once more to compete with the Russians in *Our Daily Bread*. It was rather sermonizing and oversimplified, particularly at the beginning, but once the colony had been organized, the wicked characters reduced to silence and the good ones become better than before, there followed fifteen minutes of pure film. Water bubbled up and coursed through the ditches, giving birth to a whole genesis of plants and men and natural elements which carried all before it in exultant joy. This conclusion of *Our Daily Bread*, composed as a triumphant fanfare of images and sounds, shows that the man who made *Hallelujah* had not entirely forgotten his masterpiece.

DRAMAS AND STORIES

Beside *Hallelujah* all the rest looks dim. Von Sternberg had gone to Germany and made a film on which high hopes were founded, *The Blue Angel*, bringing back with him Marlene Dietrich of the husky voice, magnificent legs and weary glance. He made a film about the Foreign Legion, *Morocco*, in which she was lovely and alluring, in company with Gary Cooper and Adolphe Menjou. There followed a succession of deplorable films, each one more lavish and stupider than the others, in which this magnificent creature, laden with feathers and jewels, became a mere clotheshorse. Von Sternberg made the welkin ring with his oaths and disputes as he continually vowed he would have nothing more to do with such a fiend, yet returned to her again and again, losing his skill at film making apparently forever. His imitators, however, were not easily discouraged. Even the end of prohibition did not put a stop to the making of gangster films, in which America continued to exploit an atmosphere familiar since the days of *The Great Train Robbery*. There were so many of these that it would be difficult even to list them, and one must admit that a great many were excellent both in construction and in acting. An Armenian, Rouben Mamoulian, in *City Streets* directed a film constructed with mathematical precision—slow, pitiless, stifling—which suddenly burst forth into a magnificent automobile chase. People hoped that he would fill von Sternberg's place. The absurd *Dr. Jekyll and Mr. Hyde* he made next proved that this was not to be the case, and Mamoulian's stock fell with a crash.*

An ambitious attempt was made in *The Big House*, of which George Hill directed the English version and Paul Fejos a French one. The attack on the prison with tanks and machine guns was extremely impressive, but an unfortunate sentimentality spoiled most of this picture. There was not, however, a trace of sentimentality in the masterpiece of gangster films, *Scarface*, which we owe to Howard Hawks. In this brutal fictionized story about Al Capone the gangsters are shown as they really are, coldly, as cowards and brutes. So truthful was it that in certain States it was forbidden exhibition, perhaps for fear of reprisals. For those of us who were in no position to judge of its truthfulness, *Scarface* seemed a magnificently constructed and splendidly acted film, a triumph of the American style. Its impressive monotony was relieved by human and ineffectual gestures, as when Guido, Scarface's friend and brother-in-law, is killed by the gangster under the mistaken impression that he has betrayed him. George Raft's last glance as he falls to the floor, gently shaking his head to signify "no," was one of the most affecting touches in that uncompromising film. This was our first encounter, in France, with an actor of great power, Paul Muni, who now succeeded Bancroft. This sterling actor has not always been successful, because of the unskillful direction of some of his pictures; but *I Am a Fugitive from a Chain Gang*, a film based on actual fact about an innocent man, unjustly convicted, who escapes from prison and is caught again through treachery, gave him full opportunity. It was a film of unparalleled brutality, almost as good as *Scarface*, to which the escape of the convicts and the scenes of cruelty lent an even more natural and striking accent. Then there were other films featuring James Cagney which showed us somewhat differently the war between gangsters and the law,

---

* As in the case of the authors' estimates of other foreign (to them) directors, criticism has been based on scattered and often unrepresentative works.

such as *The Public Enemy, Taxi,* and so forth. Moreover, it was the gangster films which revealed a personality even more striking than that of Muni, when Edward G. Robinson appeared first in *Little Caesar, Little Giant* and, thanks to the director John Ford, gave, in *The Whole Town's Talking,* a model of gay satirical comedy full of virtuosity. Granted a free hand and the opportunity, there was little that that sturdy and choleric figure could not do.

Among newcomers it looked as though John Ford * were one of the cleverest and one of the most dependable. In the same year as *The Whole Town's Talking,* with its deafening chatter and extraordinary misunderstandings, he also gave us *The Lost Patrol* and *The Informer.* The first of these, a simple film made without sets and avoiding all facile exoticism, was a finely heroic picture in praise of man, prey of hostile nature and of human enemies, yet it seemed a trifle deliberate and artificial, smelling somewhat of the workshop. *The Informer,* on the other hand, reminds one of von Sternberg at his best, as in *The Docks of New York.* That simple tale of shadowy houses and squalid streets, about a man who betrays another for money, is, despite an element of melodrama and an absurd ending, one of the most powerful talking films yet made. McLaglen gives an astonishing portrayal of a low brute, and we shall not soon forget his tearing down the poster which offers a reward of twenty pounds to anyone who will give up his friend, and which seems to pursue him and cling to him as though it were alive. Despite its rather studio-made air, it was as impressive as *Scarface,* or anything in the whole powerful literature redolent of fog and grime and dreariness which the Germans introduced to the Americans.

But if in the early days of the talkies these gangster films were the best that America produced, another vogue which also spread to Europe must be mentioned—a special type of period film, with late-Victorian settings and costumes. We now saw opulent creatures like Mae West in *She Done Him Wrong.* Set in a similar period was *Back Street,* a somewhat melodramatic affair about a woman who lives on the fringes of society because she

* Ford has been directing films since 1915.

is the mistress of a man much in the public eye. It was a bad film, theatrical and crammed with dialogue, full of errors of taste, but now and then it succeeded in being effective and it also brought to the fore Irene Dunne, equipped with a peculiar gentleness and convincingness. It was almost the first time one had the impression of seeing a real woman on the screen. Eventually this kind of period film brought us in 1934, with George Cukor's help, the extremely successful *Little Women*, which sanctified the baroque talent of Katherine Hepburn, launched a new style of hairdressing and brought tears to the eyes of thousands. Based on the Louisa M. Alcott story, it hardly avoided all the book's faults, for it was overpathetic and overmoralizing, but Cukor made an extremely effective use of the costumes of a touching period.

In reviewing the best of the dramatic films made in America after the introduction of sound, we come to one in which dialogue was of little importance, which introduced no novelties in the use of sound and which disturbingly resembled some of the best films at the end of the silent era. It was *One Way Passage*, which contained a fine feeling for pictorial narrative and the same restraint and delicacy as adorned *A Woman of Paris, Lonesome* and certain German films, and two admirable players, William Powell and Kay Francis. Its story of a condemned gangster and a dying woman, who meet and fall in love during a sea voyage, who bid one another farewell with a smile when the voyage ends, could, heaven knows, have turned into pure melodrama, yet it evoked a sort of melancholy of the most agreeable variety. There was not a single moment of bravura in the piece, which offers only simple, straightforward images rather in the manner of the Austrian film *Liebelei*. One wonders, however, what sound really added to it and whether it might not just as well have been a silent picture. Perhaps the films were really not making so much progress as we imagined.

COMEDIES

What was the effect in the realm of comedy? We may dismiss the innumerable filmed stage comedies and operettas which the new invention led to. They brought fame to Maurice Chevalier and Jeanette MacDonald, paired in *The Love Parade*. Lubitsch, who directed that sumptuous but inane piece, made several highly profitable pictures of the same kind. In screening Noel Coward's *Design for Living*, however, he produced something charming and exquisitely humorous, far superior to the play itself, for he avoided the use of extravagant settings and concentrated instead on small, amusing details which evoked a genuine bohemian atmosphere. Instead of recording conversations he told the plot pictorially, including the past of the principal characters, the way they had met and the whole background of their lives.

But how were the old masters of American comedy to adapt themselves to the talkies? Buster Keaton came to grief almost at once. *Spite Marriage*, which repeated some of the themes of *The Navigator*, was rather entertaining, but in *Hollywood Revue of 1929* the unfortunate comedian, surrounded by stars and babbling women, seemed quite dim and pathetic. *What! No Beer?*, though Jimmy Durante talked like mad in it, had something of the earlier Keatons: here he was at grips with a beer-making machine that could be worked only by a stuttering man who is prevented from explaining it, and so once again there is a glimpse of his mathematical genius. Unhappily, *What! No Beer?* was the exception rather than the rule.

Harold Lloyd, on the other hand, took gladly to the talkies and, after *Welcome Danger* (a repetition of *Safety Last*), made two irresistible pictures, *Movie Crazy* and *The Catspaw*: they are perhaps his most satisfactory films. *Welcome Danger* had certain bucolic elements which remind one somewhat of Chaplin. The high point of the story is a fantastic night spent in a Chinese bandit's cellar, where some quite extraordinary effects are produced by lighted candles stuck on the back of tortoises which crawl hither and thither, and by Lloyd's mistaking rockets for candles, to which he consequently applies a match. In *Movie Crazy* the big scenes are those in which Harold makes horrible mistakes while a scene is being shot for the twentieth time, and the one in which he accidentally puts on a magician's costume from which issue rabbits and mice. Not all the gags are first-rate, but there is a new gag every thirty seconds and it is impossible to withstand this aggregation to which the cheery smile of Harold, always fortunate amid the worst catastrophes, lends undeniable charm.

Chaplin hesitated to make a film and produced nothing for five years before making *City Lights*, which was really a silent picture. At the beginning, when the statue is being unveiled, Chaplin hit upon a delightful device: we saw the orator speaking but heard only inarticulate and ridiculous noises. This was rejecting realism with a vengeance in masterly fashion. Otherwise, except when Chaplin swallowed a whistle or had hiccups, *City Lights* used little sound. It was not Chaplin's best film by any means, and it lacks unity, seeming to be made up of independent segments—Charlie as a boxer, Charlie as a street cleaner, Charlie with the millionaire who adores him when he is drunk but fails to recognize him and chases him off when he is in his sober senses—all rather labored and ponderous. The emphasis in *City Lights* for once is not on comedy: the accent is deliberately put on the love story. It is charming; Charlie is in love with a blind flower seller, who thinks that he is a fine gentleman. At the end of the film, after he has contrived to have her cured, she meets him but naturally does not know who he is. Just for fun she gives the poor fellow a flower for his buttonhole. He gazes at her, and somehow, when she touches his jacket, the girl seems to realize who he is, looks up at him puzzled and disturbed. He gives her an extraordinary glance in which grief is mingled with joy: the scene ends before we find out what is going to happen or what they say to one another. Chaplin had never gone so far emotionally as in that closing scene.

If the comedy of *City Lights* is a little heavy, at least the romance does not obtrude. It seems to be true that fear of displeasing the public and respect for the character he has created have prevented Chaplin—at least in films in which he himself appears—from doing all that his own bitterness might have dictated. It appears that Chaplin, who is constantly trying out this or that, keeps these bits of film and sometimes shows them, though not publicly. So it was that in 1927 Robert Florey saw a little picture of his called *The Suicide*. A man is about to kill himself. Charlie comes along, tries to tell him how sweet life is, but the man, without paying any attention, ties a rope round a rock and prepares to fix the other end round his own neck. Charlie hurls himself upon the man and, in the struggle, gets tied onto the rope instead of the would-be suicide, who hurls the stone into the water; it naturally carries Charlie with it. Now this incident was remade and included in *City Lights*, but in the original it did not end with a rescue. The man first stared in bewilderment, then, realizing what had happened, burst out laughing and walked off, leaving Charlie to drown. Of course Chaplin would hardly kill off his main character in a film made for public exhibition.

After *City Lights* he began on another picture, said to be one in which he would not himself appear, a sort of talkie *Woman of Paris;* but meanwhile he has completed a new comedy rather along the lines of Clair's *A Nous la Liberté*. It may well be that his career will prove to have been confined to the silent films.

NEW COMEDIANS

Neither Buster Keaton nor Lloyd nor Chaplin made any change in their customary characterizations, nor did Fairbanks, who made a modern *Mr. Robinson Crusoe* and then a rather cruelly aged *Private Life of Don Juan*. Two new comedians, Laurel and Hardy, admirable in short comedies and disappointing in full-length films, attempted to arouse laughter by familiar means, but it was others upon whom devolved the necessity for finding fresh comic inventions. When people saw in *Animal Crackers* a professor in a top hat who shot at clocks and used canvases by great painters to keep himself warm they protested, yet the Marx Brothers with all their deliberate absurdity were only leading the films back to the extravagant atmosphere of pre-war comedy: what seems a novelty is often merely the revival of something forgotten. This quartet, who first appeared in *Co-conuts* and grew famous through the fight in the stable in *Monkey Business*, definitely became the champions of absurdity and nonsense in *Horse Feathers*. Buster Keaton might have fallen from the ceiling into a ladies' tea party, like Chico, but neither Keaton nor Lloyd would ever have exhibited Harpo's calm savagery when he tasted the telephone and finally devoured it entirely. None of the other comedians would have so calmly made use of trick photography or of improbability; no one had done so since the days before Max Linder and Mack Sennett. A certain degree of tolerance is needed before one can accept the Marx Brothers wholly. Their wisecracks are insupportable (Harpo alone does not speak, and he is the best of them), yet their type of comedy is really based on a technique of silence. What they say is mere foolishness, though unfortunately they talk a great deal and with considerable vulgarity.* In reality the Marx Brothers are clowns, as their costumes and their antics prove. In *Duck Soup* (these meaningless titles are charming) they were greatly praised for the scene in which two of the comedians in disguise meet one another and fancy they are looking into a mirror. People had forgotten that this was how a Max Linder film began and that, for that matter, it can be seen any day in the circus. Another circus trick is the scene in which one of the brothers, thinking that he is opening a safe, turns on the radio and cannot contrive to turn it off, much as Chaplin in *The Pawnshop* could not stop the alarm clock. Far superior are those sudden, all too rare touches of imagination, as when a shell passes the warriors courteously and circumspectly, slowly, knee-high; or as when one of them sets out to make his fortune and, next morning, the camera opens on his bedside, beside which are his riding boots, a pair of female slippers and the four horseshoes of his steed. Such conceits make up for a lot of tomfoolery, for hoary jokes and for all the flaws in these idols whom the snobs have taken to their bosoms.

Other actors and other directors were to push absurdity still further. In *Million Dollar Legs* we entered a mythical country where sprinters run faster than automobiles and W. C. Fields is the president. In *International House* this same W. C. Fields rides

* Apparently the French understand the Marx Brothers' dialogue no better than they grasp the significance of the "meaningless" titles of their films.

up a staircase in an autogiro; if he takes a pot shot at a picture of an armored cruiser, that cruiser immediately sinks. Now there was considerable promise in films of this kind, but unfortunately comic inventions of the sort were lost in a flood of dialogue. In *If I Had a Million* only the most tenacious fans could tolerate Fields when he called his plump lady friend "my bird" or "my chicken." Later on, he was to abandon this sort of thing and find better employment for his talents than in those mingled delights and errors. This leering, elderly man who resembles both Babbitt and the Mr. Micawber whom he has portrayed, gave a fine performance as a traveling showman in *Poppy;* most of his more recent films are excellent. They are lighthearted affairs full of raillery, occasionally quite witty and wholly lacking the vulgarity of his earlier vehicles. Fields has greatly changed.

Yet after these little excursions into the regions of insanity the American films generally speaking became more orderly. The celebrated *If I Had a Million*, a sort of hodgepodge of various ingredients, was far from meriting the success it obtained and has already been forgotten. There were happy things in it, but its verbal comedy was tiring, as was also the film about the English manservant in America, *Ruggles of Red Gap*, despite that remarkable actor, Charles Laughton. Comedy on the screen cannot depend on dialogue alone, though America, like France, has gradually forgotten this fact. Both seem unable to avoid using dialogue culled from ancient books of jokes, or from almanacs.

ANIMATED CARTOONS

Meanwhile, America had discovered new marvels. Animated cartoons had been popular before, but now for the first time we heard the sound that a mouse makes when it is caught in a trap, the yawn which a clock gives when its cuckoo wakes it by striking midnight. Sound in the animated cartoons became quite nonrealistic: a loud noise went with a small movement and a little one with a big gesture in the most absurd fashion. Pianos bared their teeth and laughed aloud, amorous elephants accompanied their love-making by twanging the tresses of their loved ones like a guitar. Mickey Mouse had arrived.

On the surface, Mickey was just another animal, a sort of mouse with certain doglike traits who walked like a man and was always good-natured. This offspring of Walt Disney's shortly made us aware that an artist was at work. Possibly Disney over-does the use of animal jazz and animal songs, as his rival Max Fleischer does too, but when he relates some familiar story or fairy tale he blends into it the most comical inventions and cre-ates something truly miraculous. He did not do his best work, however, until he began making colored films. Then he rediscov-ered Méliès' secret. The crude and simple colors of old-fashioned children's books lend his films an infinite enchantment. Some of them are world-famous, such as *The Three Little Pigs* in terror of the bad wolf. We personally prefer *Funny Little Bunnies* who paint the Easter eggs, while the blind rabbits in spectacles plait rush baskets, hens lay to a distinct beat, and paintpots are put under each stripe of the rainbow to collect the drops that fall. More than all of them we like the superb *Pied Piper*, where the children are led towards a mountain that opens just wide enough to let them through and give us a glimpse of the land of toys and of eternal holiday. Then the little cripple, always behind the others, halts for a moment on the very threshold before dropping his crutches and running in. It was one of the most adorable things the cinema has ever given us. *Noah's Ark, King Neptune* and a few of the others should be permanently pre-served as monuments to this art of Disney's, which promises so much for the future.

Before finishing with the American film we must also add a word about the English film, because it is difficult to tell the difference between them and certain films with a definitely Eng-lish character made in America. The English studios had been only intermittently in operation during silent days * and turned out only relatively mediocre pictures; they reorganized and are

* That is, since 1914. Until then London rivaled Paris as a film-producing center.

destined to become increasingly important. *The Private Life of Henry VIII*, which Alexander Korda directed with Laughton, launched a new wave of historical films conceived not as vast decorative frescoes but in intimate and even ironic vein. It was a well-made and well-acted picture, though less valuable than people imagined; Korda will in all probability become one of the foremost producers and is already making color films.

With the exception of *The Constant Nymph,* an uneven film but in its first sequences full of an enchanting freshness, the most notable are the films which extolled the greatness of England. *Cavalcade,* made in America by Frank Lloyd from a play of Coward's, is the story of an English family over a period of thirty years. Unfortunately films seldom represent the passage of time very adequately, but content themselves with doing up actors in toupees and white wigs. The first part of *Cavalcade,* however—the departure of the troops for the Boer War and the funeral procession of Queen Victoria, which is not shown, and the passing of which is indicated only through the expression of the spectators—had a quite remarkable dignity. The same blend of gaiety and heroism was to be found again in *Lives of a Bengal Lancer,** in which the officer who praises his country does so with feeling and sincerity but uses the words of his colonel, and the lancers who decide which of them shall undertake a dangerous mission do so by betting on a cockroach race. Whatever the faults of these films, they possess a natural bonhomie similar to the books of Kipling. Having managed to express such sentiments, we may hope for much from the English film in the future.

*

Despite the fine films it sent us, the American output on the whole proved somewhat disappointing. *Hallelujah* gave us the highest possible hopes, but they were not fulfilled. There has been too much mere talk, there have been too few experiments with the use of sound. Films remained static while conversations were carried on between two or three characters, until even the impression of movement was thrown overboard.

* *Lives of a Bengal Lancer* is also an American film.

As a result of the bewilderment into which the invention of sound threw the producers, all sorts of peculiar things happened. There were all sorts of peculiar practices, all sorts of dodges, quotas, dubbing and so forth, but this was not all. Even in the actual making of films, things much funnier than the screen has ever shown us were taking place. Films were made by wandering Slavic directors, Germans who spoke no English, Frenchmen who spoke no German, actors whose voices their own mothers could not recognize, singers with tiny voices whose songs were magnified by the microphone, Austrians who assumed Hollywood accents when making French versions of pictures. Just as Elmer Rice has written a satire on the silent films in *Purilia*, so Paul Morand has provided us with one on the talkies in *France la Doulce*. Here we see what becomes of a scenario by Joseph Bédier when it has been rewritten by d'Annunzio, edited by a German schoolmistress, put into dubious French by someone newly arrived from the Ukraine and from which all of a sudden it is necessary to remove every "b" which occurs in the dialogue, as one fillets the bones from a fish, because the leading lady from London pronounces them unpleasingly. Such things really do happen; they are actually a commonplace in every country, and if America indulged in them generously it was not without reason that Morand laid the scene of his satire in France, which, in films as in everything else, has become the concentration camp of the world.

2. The French Film

IF America resisted the sound and talking films for years, France resisted them even longer, and the new invention, regarded as a catastrophe, was the occasion for any number of stratagems, of dishonest tricks and dubious schemes. The idea was to delay as long as possible the moment when the producers would be compelled to make talkies. As the public violently refused to accept films in foreign languages, of course this moment was imminent.

Gaumont in 1928 produced *L'Eau du Nil*, in which he had brought up to date the old system of synchronized phonograph records * which he had already "perfected" before the war. Everyone now admitted the inevitable: André Hugon was asked to direct *Les Trois Masques*, based on a melodrama by Charles Méré which had already been filmed in the silent days. It was perfectly dreadful. Stairs creaked like a clap of thunder, glasses clinking together sounded as though armored giants were in combat, the gurgle of a bottle resembled the noise of a waterfall and the most absurd dialogue emanated like the crack of doom, not from the lips of the actors, but from the center of the screen. The three masked figures, their vengeance accomplished, went off down a pasteboard street singing "Carnival is dead!" So it was that the talkies came to France.

In vain the best writers and best directors besought the producers to be careful: the big French firms were determined that the talkies should become "the theater of the poor," which, as René Clair said, made pretty poor theater. Was something being done in America or in Germany? What did they care, nobody knew anyhow. Censorship and tariff laws were strengthened. It would never do for the French public to realize that *Les Trois Masques* and Henri Roussel's *La Nuit Est à Nous* were not all that the new invention had produced. *The Blue Angel* was banned; so, later on, was *Dreigroschenoper*; *Hallelujah* was shelved. Not for two years were we allowed to see those successful early sound films.

After it was too late to stop the foreign films coming in, quotas were established and dubbing started—these hideous words speak for themselves. Then the French film hurled itself into adaptations of plays and brought to the screen the whole of modern drama, distorting wherever possible both the characters and their interpretation. A few dramatists like Henri Bernstein and Francis de Croisset protested, but this did not prevent anyone from repeating the same mistakes. The commercial film became more abysmal

* See p. 26. This, of course, was the method used in *The Jazz Singer* and many of the early American talkies.

than ever. From this time on the French film seemed to be typified in the work of one director, René Clair.

RENÉ CLAIR

It may be admitted that the first French talkie of any real importance, *Sous les Toits de Paris*, displayed faults inevitable at that period, for it made use of music and also of silence in rather haphazard fashion. The introduction of the street singer, who keeps the film perfectly static while he sings his lines, was almost obligatory at the time. Clair, however, through the expression on Préjean's face (and he never gave a better performance), contrived to keep the action going to a degree even through the singing. These faults are so slight and so unimportant that even today we can look at *Les Toits* with the same pleasure we took in it in 1930. Préjean, accompanied by a blind accordion player, sings a delightful popular song which René Clair must have had the greatest fun in composing. Neither the general public nor the librettists suspected how ironical it was. Around Préjean our old friends group themselves—the fat lady sings out of tune, the policeman in plain clothes looks on, the old woman and the lovers gaze at each other. When evening comes, the thin clerk takes a foot bath in his Henri II dining room just as the deceived husband had done in *Chapeau de Paille*. Later on during the night we see the immense concierge buried beneath a comforter automatically turning over to pull the cord. Every detail is based on real life, the vulgarest incidents of real life. But if we compare this realism with that of the settings in German pictures we see that in them the realism was dignified by a loving care for lighting and by a prodigious use of the pictorial medium. Theirs was the realism of a painter; but René Clair's realism is, as before, that of the ballet. He puts his characters in fancy dress and provides them with the appropriate accessories, but at the same time he stylizes them, simplifies their outline and leads them into that world which is peculiarly his. At times, when we see a procession of clerks, or a too typical baker's wife, we almost feel that it is life itself which has copied René Clair, for here we come up against a real artist with a quite special manner of perceiving the universe. That is the real value of this truly creative worker. No matter how great their ability, neither Pabst nor King Vidor nor Eisenstein has created a world of his own. If there is a Chaplin world, it is the actor who created it. Independently of the actors there is a quite definite René Clair world.

Had Clair really been trying simply to tell us a story we should not come upon those sequences that drag, those moments when the plot refuses to develop. We are given a series of pictures rather than a true narrative, for just as in *Les Deux Timides* its technical discoveries were more important than the whole, so *Sous les Toits* introduces the ingenious *tours de force* to which Clair was to devote himself right up to the time of *Quatorze Juillet*. The quarrel between Albert and Pola in pitch darkness was a genuine invention in those early days: images and words no longer ran side by side but intersected one another in a sort of pattern. The magnificent fight with knives at night near the railway embankment, with the slow noises of freight trains and mist rising the length of the fence, owes its existence to a love of the medium alone: the main story is forgotten. In none of René Clair's films has the lighting been so perfect, and this extraordinary episode is therefore justified. He was much more concerned with beauty than with reality here. The tendency indicated in *Les Deux Timides* is continued, for the ballet no longer takes first place: it becomes an accompaniment as in Greek tragedy, where one by one the principal characters detach themselves from the group and the chorus is reduced to the role of commentator. It remains, however, as witness to the drama; and René Clair was never to abandon these onlookers, among whom his films had found their original inspiration.

Le Million affords striking proof of this. In turning again to an adaptation of a play, Clair created the most successful if not the richest of all his pictures. It derives from a whole succession of operettas which had followed Thiele's delightful *Drei von der Tankstelle*, though Clair was to perfect the formula, whereas Thiele relapsed into machine-made and valueless spectacles. The original model, however, provided an opportunity for all the indications in *Entr'acte* and *Chapeau de Paille* to be developed fully: the ballet troupe now takes possession of the entire stage in joyous tumult. The tale of Michel and Beatrice's love blends into the general movement, the lovers are now members of the ensemble—along with the grocer, the dairywoman, the policemen, the lunatic in running pants, the drunkard, the tenor, the lady singer—who run after each other in and out of the wings calling, "He went that way," and, "We can catch him as he comes back along here." It is the gayest of Clair's pictures, rich in minor characters conceived without a trace of exaggeration and seeming, against those luminous backgrounds, as fresh and unruffled as dolls in a shop window. As in *Le Chapeau de Paille*, the whole composition moves forward with appropriate animation, and there is also a similar technical experimentation and a similar tendency to chop the thing up into distinct sequences. Here creative invention has functioned completely, and we are as infinitely far away from everyday life as *Entr'acte* was. This world of police stations and of the Opera and its backstage life is an exquisite but purely imaginary realm. Even the characters have little real connection with the story: their movements inscribe a sort of cryptogram whose real meaning can be guessed if we hold the key to the cipher. Those characters in *Le Million* who are fighting over a coat suddenly take on the appearance of a football team whose play is accompanied by whistles, scrimmages, passing the ball and so forth, as the tubes in *Entr'acte* gently rise up to assume the form of the most celebrated Doric columns in antiquity. The madman in pants belongs to either film indifferently, and *Entr'acte* is clearly the key to all Clair's work.

Or rather it is the key to his technique, for the lovers from *Les Deux Timides* from now on will be constantly with us. In *Sous les Toits* a third one appears: Pola hesitates between Albert and Louis as Michel hesitates between Wanda and Beatrice, or as Jean hesitates between Anna and Pola. Delicious emotions now suffuse the marionettes. Who could ever forget that first glimpse of Annabella, or the lovers' duet in that stage landscape under the cardboard arbors as stagehands fill the air with a rain of artificial rose petals? Clair has abandoned the open air of *Les Deux Timides* and has returned to the artifice of *Le Voyage Imaginaire*, inventing freely and creating a new form of poetry such as others of his generation and the generation previous, Max Jacob and Jean Cocteau, had foreshadowed. The huge opera singer and the absurd tenor sing out of sight while the wooing of Michel and Beatrice lends reality to the factitious passions which they are screaming at the public. Beatrice can no longer resist, for the picture postcard décor itself becomes Michel's accomplice and even the spectator falls victim to the atmosphere of make-believe and garlands, utilized with unfaltering good taste and underlined with the most gracious and smiling irony.

The same gracious good nature suffuses the best part of *A Nous la Liberté*, unquestionably the most complete expression of Clair's genius and which a number of cinema theaters consequently suppressed. Here the subterfuges of the stage have vanished: we see, though only vaguely, the Luna Park where the workers from the factory are strolling. This setting, where Rolla France takes her sweetheart and where Henri Marchand will follow them, is clearly an unreal and enchanted place, a playground for birds that have flown out of picture postcards and figures from a merry-go-round. One is reminded of *Alice in Wonderland*, in which pretense and absurdity are presented with such naturalness, for this is the world on the other side of the mirror. Birds speak, flowers sing—but they are stuffed birds and celluloid flowers. Nowhere has the cinema brought us so perfectly created a world as in this imaginative and innocent dream inspired by some tune from a hand organ. The very thought of irony is barely possible, unless as the excuse for introducing us to this universe, vaguely ninetyish with its bridges of artificial wood like those in the Parc Montsouris and the Buttes-Chaumont, its artificial forests and artificial waterfalls. Henri Marchand, subtlest of Clair's lovers, looks around, smiling like a child in ecstasy. He seems a little clumsier than the others, for Clair knows very well how to interrupt a dream when necessary, and the disillusionment of the unfortunate fellow in this landscape of romance is one of the most delicately bitter moments imaginable. The traditional cruelty of the artist, who suffers with his characters yet enjoys making them suffer, which renders Clair akin to Racine and to Marivaux, is underlined by the mockery of the setting, by all this pasteboard world of simple happiness. When Henri, standing in the shadow, thinks that the girl is smiling at him though in reality she is smiling at someone else, this old trick borrowed from Chaplin affects us just as deeply as it did in the most famous scenes of *The Gold Rush* or *City Lights*.

A Nous la Liberté is rather imperfectly constructed, and it overstresses both the similarity between the factory and the prison as well as the numerous chases, but it is undoubtedly the film in which René Clair put most of himself. Memories of many celebrated pictures, such as *The Pilgrim*, *The Gold Rush* and *City Lights*, are added to the creative qualities of *Le Million*, to themes repeated from *Entr'acte*, to atmosphere borrowed from *Les Deux Timides* or *Chapeau de Paille*. Yet Clair had never before penetrated so far into the world of pure imagination. By the time we reach the magnificent confusion of the end, he seems actually to have risen above his subject, his characters, his personal experiences and even life itself. It would be an error to consider that extraordinary scene in which the breeze scatters a bagful of bank notes over the heads of the crowd as a mere piece of fertile invention, like that which suddenly suggested the football match in *Le Million*. If the members of the crowd at the inauguration were simply running after the bank notes, that would be the end of them: they would vanish along with their booty. As it is, they reappear, running here and there all over the factory without apparent aim but not without order, for they form skillful dance designs as they thread in and out; and in fact they *are* dancing. It is good, after the grief of Henri Marchand and the imaginary voyage to the land of tinted postcards, to be back again in a realm where pastime is your only king. With this penultimate scene in *A Nous la Liberté* Clair renews his youth and sings a hymn in praise of pure movement, just as he had in *Entr'acte*.

It is impossible not to like this ambitious and perhaps badly constructed film in which, twice over, Clair so fully expressed himself, both in delineating the sorrows of love amid the beauties of the make-believe landscapes, and in this game which has no other motive than play. He utilized everything, even his early novel *Adams*, in this satire on Americanism. Two or three minor characters escaped from other films link everything together, and the clear, lively music of Georges Auric preserves the unity which seems so often in danger of being broken.

What was left for Clair to tackle after this, unless he completely changed the very form and basis he had hitherto selected, and where would the ballet of dancing shapes lead him in the future? There have been those who said that *Quatorze Juillet* was a sort of turning back or period of repose in his work. His admirers and friends thought so. I do not feel that they were right. *Quatorze Juillet* is probably the most ambitious of any of Clair's ventures, only in this case instead of concerning himself with outward appearances he was concerned with inner content. "Nothing could be simpler at first sight," Alexandre Arnoux said, "than perfection such as this: it is as simple as writing a fable by La Fontaine." (It is extraordinarily difficult not to think of the classical writers when considering the work of Clair, for he is a member of their family, and makes it easier for us to understand them.) His avoidance of exterior shots, his wish never to surprise or astonish us (and he has traveled far since *Entr'acte*) enabled him now to make his best-constructed picture. There are richer things he has done, but none having greater internal unity. Even *Le Million* was a summing up of one particular cinematic method only: *Quatorze Juillet* sums up all the René Clair films.

It may well be that Clair will be compelled later on to abandon his most noticeable traits and much that lay at the roots both of his popularity and of his charm. But in this film it seems that he wanted to perfect a formula, to clear it of extraneous matter, to transmute it into classicism and to avoid all else. With a severity which must surely have cost him a good deal, he avoided all obvious technical tricks and set himself none of those problems which formerly interested us so greatly. There is not one single scene which stands out particularly, as the quadrille in *Chapeau de Paille*, or the fight in *Les Toits*, or the football match in *Le Million*, or the lovers' stroll in *A Nous* all stood out. This film is simple, almost unadorned, like certain German films and especially *Maedchen in Uniform.* The fete here is almost disappointingly brief, for we expected all sorts of delightful touches which his love of garlands and picture postcards might have suggested, as in the former film. But this fete is merely indicated, with a few charming and brief details. It was the first time he had not permitted details to over-burden the main body of the film. The simple, beautiful story develops quietly, smoothly, with infinite discretion, and the end comes without our having been particularly struck by anything, unless it is perhaps the few moments when the lunar M. Imaque cleans his revolvers in the dance hall, or the even briefer moments when Annabella weeps while wiping away the tears of the little boy who had fallen down, or the death of the mother. Nothing stands out, the film drags a little, all the gestures in it are a trifle overrefined and emphasized. Yet at the same time we are enveloped in a sort of harmony which carries us back to the joys and griefs of adolescence.

From the dance of inanimate objects to *Quatorze Juillet* is a long way, yet this development is a natural one. We have still not left the world of the dance. The love troubles of the earlier films are essentially choreographic, like those in so many folk dances. Watch M. Imaque as he goes by: he isn't walking, he is dancing. Paul Ollivier moves constantly to the rhythm of some unheard music, just as he did in *Le Million* and *A Nous la Liberté*. René Clair does not need music. His characters are ever ready to take their places in the dance, the prodigious concierge and the members of the provincial-Parisian family as well as the bistro owner, the taxi driver, the dance-hall managers and cloakroom attendants. It almost gives one the impression that he is holding them back, forbidding them to dance in order not to break the spell of this pitiful tale where Annabella laughs through her tears.

After *Quatorze Juillet* René Clair abandons Paris—Paris, the only thing in which he really believes. *Le Dernier Milliardaire* was quite a disappointment to his admirers, and with some reason. Just as after *Les Toits, Le Million* and *A Nous la Liberté* took refuge in an imaginary world, so after *Quatorze Juillet, Le Dernier Milliardaire* abandoned Paris for burlesque and satire. Unfortunately, principally because the actors are mediocre and theatrical, this ambitious farce hardly succeeds in making one laugh. The best things in it are again the dance figures and the two or three comedy inventions. Everybody was struck by the scene where, in this land without money where barter is the rule, a customer in a restaurant pays for his drink with a duck and gets back, as change, two little chickens, and an egg which he leaves as a tip; while the man who lets his gun fall onto the roulette table wins thirty-six revolvers. Nevertheless, even those who do not admire the Marx Brothers must admit that their films are much fuller of movement than René Clair's. What is more, it seems to me that in *Le Dernier Milliardaire* there is a dryness and overintellectualization which already threatened the earlier films and *A Nous la Liberté*. There is nothing here about love, unless it is something ridiculous, nothing of that poignancy which gave so much value formerly to backgrounds and to ballets alike. Clair this time offered us a feast of nothing but intelligence and irony: his touch is recognizable but it sometimes grates a little. If the future brings him back to imaginary worlds and music, bittersweet romance, ballets of lovemaking and anxious lovers we shall forgive him. It would be foolish to try to put limits on what he may do.

He was the only film man in France whose work displayed both purpose and progress. There is no other such group of films as these, apart from the work of Chaplin, Eisenstein and Pabst. His delicately shaded style with its thin but strong line suggests far more than it actually shows. Clair is one of the very rare directors of whom it can be said that their films gain by being seen twice and cannot be understood until that second time, like certain music and poetry.

FAILURE AND PROGRESS

Whereas the advent of the talkies helped Clair to develop, it proved a stumbling block for certain other directors. Abel Gance, who virtually ruined all his backers, managed to find money to make *Fin du Monde*, which he subsequently repudiated. There was little in this grotesque melodrama of the qualities which had outweighed the immense mistakes of this director. Only the mistakes remained, because, according to Gance, the film had been savagely cut, but they were undeniably his faults. Afterwards he made a sound version of *Mater Dolorosa* no better than the earlier one, supervised some undistinguished films and seemed to be floundering helplessly. Finally he had the idea of making a talkie of *Napoleon*, using bits from his earlier picture: the poverty of the new scenes only reminded us of the tumultuous vitality of the earlier version, of which he had not preserved the best portions. Yet he really hit upon something when he scattered microphones all over the hall so that the sound issued now in front, now behind, now from one side, mingling with the action and almost compelling the audience to join the Convention in singing the "Marseillaise." The idea was not perfected but it gave us faith in this modern Ucello, despite his faults.

Jean Renoir showed two or three times that the teaching of the German school had not gone unperceived. From an execrable novel by La Fouchardière, *La Chienne*, he made an excellent picture where a rare pictorial sense came to the rescue of naturalism and where Michel Simon, playing for the first time on the screen the role of an old man persecuted by his wife, recalled the admirable performances he had given with the Russian players. The use of sound, especially the little girl playing wrong notes on the piano whom one hears through an open window, gave further indications of intelligence and of integrity. *La Nuit du Carrefour*, based on a novel by Simenon, had one unpardonable fault in a detective film—it was incomprehensible. *Madame Bovary*, alas, was merely a careful and tedious illustration without a trace of creativeness. However, under the supervision of Marcel Pagnol, Renoir made in *Toni* a peasant film full of violence and of ability, with a remarkable feeling for nature though also with some very evident faults. He is a painter, a connoisseur of forms and of tones, who has perhaps not yet given us the best of which he is capable.

On the other hand, it seems that Jacques Feyder has given us of his best more than once: there is much to be hoped from him. Of the films he made in America he prefers not to speak; he repudiates them. *The Unholy Night* was a clever detective film, but neither *The Kiss* with Greta Garbo nor *His Glorious Night* (from

Molnar's *Olympia*) had much merit. It was on his return to Paris that he found himself again in *Le Grand Jeu*. On the surface it was simply a French film about the Legion with the customary marching, discontent, cafés, and a love story which might have been dreadful, about a man who thinks that he has found again in a singer the woman he once loved, though the singer is dark-haired and the other one was a blonde. Out of this rather absurd plot Feyder made a profoundly human film. To begin with, an ingenious device was employed. The two women were, of course, played by the same actress, but Feyder had the excellent notion of dubbing in a heavy, hoarse voice for the character of the singer, so that the hero's uneasiness at hearing a voice which does not seem to belong to the person it emanates from became really comprehensible. *Le Grand Jeu* is one of the few films to have made use of a new idea since talkies came in.

This might not have been sufficient to hold our attention but for a certain vulgar brutality which sustained the interest of the plot. Though the film was overromantic, we had the impression of seeing real people. The poor singer was a pitiful creature, wonderfully silly and touching: it was obvious that eventually she would be deserted by the hero, despite the public's love for happy endings. There is a rare quality of truthfulness which always saves Feyder, and his rather vulgar characters exude a strange atmosphere of destiny and of death.

Pension Mimosas came next, the story of a woman who has adopted a child and who, as he grows older, gradually comes to feel not the jealousy of a mother but something less admirable. It is not a faultless film but nowhere has the cinema given us a living human being so complex as the character that Françoise Rosay created here with extraordinary intelligence and skill. As a whole, the film aims too hard at pleasing the public but it is impossible to deny the real merit of Feyder. We meet again what so pleased us in *Crainquebille*, the difficulties that beset humanity, the difficulties which the major human sentiments create. Even with the best intentions in the world, it is difficult to love—that was *Le Grand Jeu*. It is difficult to be a mother—that's *Pension Mimosas*. Genuine tragedy is born of the antagonism between the grandeur of love, the grandeur of motherhood and the pettiness of human conduct. Under certain conditions there are people who though pure of heart degrade everything they touch, for, borrowing from theology one of its most mysterious terms, they are lacking in grace. How many people realized that the fate of this character, so much admired by the ignorant public, was dictated by this tragic lack? Inevitably as in a Greek tragedy, degradation awaited. It would be well, no doubt, if Feyder freed himself from the influence of these ideas borrowed from the prewar theater, but it is rarely that ideas on subjects like these are provoked by films.

DISCOVERIES

Among newcomers we must mention first the most gifted among them, Jean Vigo, that anarchic and vigorous spirit who died at the age of twenty-nine after making a film full of bitterness which the censorship banned, *Zéro de Conduite*—a work of true merit rich with youthful veracity. Then there was Pierre Chenal, who attempted to recapture a German atmosphere in *La Rue sans Nom*, which started off magnificently amid squalor the equal of anything in Pabst or Junghans, though as a whole it was not a success. *Crime et Châtiment*, in excellent taste and cleverly directed, was really nothing but an exercise in book illustration anything but Dostoevskian in spirit, though well acted by the admirable Harry Baur. Another young man, Marc Allegret, pleased many with his *Lac aux Dames*, a slow-moving, charming film which was too pretty, too slick, full of exquisite photographic images sadly lacking in cinematic movement and in which a lovely little girl with plump cheeks made her appearance—Simone Simon.

The most important director to emerge during these last few years was Julien Duvivier. He was by no means unknown, but had as a matter of fact made any number of undistinguished pictures which placed him definitely among the commercial directors. Then one fine day he made *David Golder*, not precisely a good film but a clever one, in which Harry Baur created an extraordinarily truthful characterization recalling and even surpassing anything by Jannings. Then came *Les Cinq Gentlemen Maudits*, which made one anxious to see what he would do next, whereupon he produced first *Allo Berlin! Ici Paris!* slightly long-drawn-out and reminiscent of both Wilhelm Thiele and René Clair, but having several excellent and original things in it, and then, much more important, *Poil de Carotte.* Now *Poil de Carotte*, which Duvivier had previously made as a silent film, was not, either, exactly what one means by a good film, and the acting in it was extremely bad, save for Harry Baur and Robert Lynen, the good-looking little boy with an artificial manner of speaking but enchanting gestures. Though the picture lapsed into melodrama occasionally, though it was marred by unimaginative music during the most pathetic scenes, it contained one really magnificent moment—the marriage of Poil de Carotte and his little five-year-old sweetheart. As Jules Renard had written it, the incident was a vile parody. Duvivier transformed it from something slightly questionable into bucolic poetry, as the two children wreathed in flowers walked through a lovely landscape with the retinue of animals following them. Such charm and such fresh air had never emanated from the screen since Clair's *Les Deux Timides.*

Duvivier's other films unfortunately seemed comparatively cut-and-dried: *Le Petit Roi* had little merit; *Marie Chapdelaine* offered us some pleasing landscapes and actresses from the Théâtre-Français; *Golgotha* displayed marked ability and a most disconcerting lack of faith. *La Tête d'un Homme*, an excellent detective film, was preferable to *Golgotha.*

Poil de Carotte itself was to be overshadowed by a film which though also somewhat uneven was so full of variety and of emotional force that it is unique; nothing else done in France can be compared to it. This was *La Maternelle*, by Jean Benoit-Lévy and Marie Epstein. There were people who refused to praise it, and perhaps they were right: the beginning is quite bad, the whole cabaret sequence is thrown in gratuitously with its dull song, and the scene with the drunkard is overstressed. Everybody agreed that the end of the film leaves much to be desired, where there is an effort to repeat the attempted suicide of *Maedchen in Uniform.* There is also an excess of sentimentality, and a trace of clumsiness here and there. This may all be true, but there is no

Groucho, Harpo and Chico Marx.

La Kermesse Héroique, *directed by Jacques Feyder* (*1936*).

Die Dreigroschenoper, *directed by* G. W. *Pabst* (*1931*).

denying that in comparison with the extraordinary vitality, the emotion and the intelligence of this film, its faults are unimportant. Compared to the hundred or more children in this film, it is evident that Robert Lynen as Poil de Carotte was only an attractive child spoiled by the Conservatoire. Little Paulette Elambert in the chief role exhibits what can only be called genius— her concentrated passion, her expression, her intelligence and her fire remind us of Ludmilla Pitoëff. Even she is less important, however, than the swift rhythm which makes this film so delectable— joyous and sad scenes succeed one another with magical simplicity and speed, there is a wealth of both touching and humorous incident and we have barely stopped weeping over the death of the little-boy-who-wouldn't-smile before we are laughing at the swallowing of the penny and the revolt in favor of saving the rabbit's life. There are also those extraordinary faces: the small colored girl, the child who had eaten rabbit before, the convict's son, little Marie (acted by Paulette Elambert) and—almost as childlike as Marie—the kindly Rose, played with extraordinary grace, subtlety and humanity by Madeleine Renaud.

What might the Russians have made of such a subject? It is a question worth asking. No doubt they would have shown us how evening classes and obligatory education brought happiness to the children at La Maternelle. We saw something of the kind in *The Road to Life*. This primary philosophy would have been set off by quite a degree of fire, of faith. Our French directors have no faith whatsoever. They know perfectly well that in this nice school (for it really is nice) where the teachers love the children, the children will nevertheless continue to be unhappy, and in a middling sort of way. Even little Marie gets over her great grief, which of itself is a bitter thought and a true one. I myself regret that in this film of little faith the bitterness was not more stressed, though it is sufficiently redolent of despair for us to recognize it, and restraint and discretion are rarely a fault. But I wish that there were no possible room for mistake, that people had been able to realize more clearly the profoundly skeptical and almost nihilistic character of the film, which is also a realistic film, since it resembles life as it actually goes on today in the world.

Here for the first time the French film, which previously had excelled only in fantasy and in interpreting humanity, attained success through simple, straightforward means in a film made for the masses. The few faults in this fine and tragic picture can easily be overlooked, since it surpasses anything that we had seen for a very long time.

CANNED THEATER

Imagination and artistry were not what the French film public wanted. It might be as well to recall that, long after talking films were introduced, there was a serious argument in which theoreticians got very excited over the merits and demerits of various simple ideas which did not possess even the qualities of novelty. Marcel Pagnol, a dramatist who had enjoyed three big successes, made up his mind to do something for the films. According to him, any kind of experimentation or research was so much hairsplitting. The theater, with its painted sets, was doomed to extinction, the cinema was a mere mechanical invention, a printing-works for the theater, and the future alone would decide whether the directors who had insisted on the autonomy of the film would not come to look as absurd as Gutenberg would have looked had he invented an art of typography without any concern for the copying of texts.

In their literal application there is nothing to be upset about in such theories. Why should there not be films for copying plays as well as truly creative films? At least they would preserve the teaching of a few good actors. It was certainly enjoyable to see Louis Jouvet in *Knock* and in *Topaze*, though they were not cinematic in the least. Marcel Pagnol photographed *Marius* and *Fanny*, and there was just as much dialogue in the latter as in the original play: the film, he said, merely permitted him to change the settings oftener. He also made *Le Gendre de M. Poirier*, and Courteline made *Les Précieuses Ridicules* with the Comédie Française. Unfortunately, badly acted or ineffectual, they had nothing whatever to do with cinema.

Pagnol realized this and tried something else. Though he always remained faithful to his text, he nevertheless attempted to give France some nature films in *Jofroi* and in *Angèle*. They were well worth seeing for the beauty of the landscapes, a certain fresh and hard sensuality, the way in which a horse, a house, a wall or a tree is photographed. Pagnol continued to contend that the most important thing in a film is its text and published the scenario of his next film in *La Petite Illustration*. It was all too evident that the text was without merit. He was responsible for the fact that we have almost forgotten how relatively unimportant dialogue is in a film. Otherwise, how would it be possible to enjoy films in a language we do not understand, such as Van Dyke's *Eskimo*? Nevertheless to this pass was France rapidly coming: it had been for forty years her secret ambition, and right through from the Film d'Art down to Pagnol the same desire is evident. What France wants on the screen is theater, and bad theater at that. We may well recall what Louis Delluc said: Good films will perhaps be made, but they will be the exception.

*

In 1935 something quite important happened: the French film industry practically disappeared. Controlled by Americans or crippled by the depression, neither Eclair nor Gaumont was any longer of importance. Pathé-Natan, already ruined by a thousand extravagances, finally vanished amid an obscure financial scandal: only its distributing system is left. The few French films which appear are produced independently. As the history of the United States teaches us that it has always been the independents who have carried on the development of the film in opposition to the big firms, perhaps some good will spring from so much evil.

3. *The German Film*

In Germany the early days of talking films were marked by the same hesitations as in America and in France. Ufa, under the powerful management of Erich Pommer, was chiefly anxious to guard against competition, tried to recall certain directors from the United States, compromised with synchronized scores and finally, like the rest of the world, took the final plunge. Almost at the very beginning the Germans had the good fortune to produce two successful films, *The Blue Angel* and *Melody of the World*.

The Blue Angel, adapted with considerable freedom by von Sternberg from a poor novel by Heinrich Mann, turned a heavily ironical story into a coarse melodrama. Jannings was rather theatrical as the professor who falls into the clutches of a wicked woman and ends up by strangling her while yelling, "Cockledoodle-doo." Its generous proportion of bad taste was redeemed by its lively dramatic sense, by an incomparable feeling for light and shadow (von Sternberg had not yet quite forgotten *The Docks of New York*) and, beyond all else, by Marlene Dietrich, so extraordinarily beautiful in her suggestive undress, with her lovely legs, her cigarette, her hoarse voice.

Melody of the World offered no such delights: Walter Ruttmann here carried through completely the formula he had experimented with in Berlin. To the careful editing of his images he added sound, which gave the film its real value. Paul Morand wrote in *Bravo:*

"It is said that Ruttmann is a musician. Had he not been he could never have woven into this headlong flight of images the hoot of sirens (I still hear their three mounting notes); the rattle of chains on the windlass; the screams of mechanical saws; the panting of railroad engines (notice the six locomotives waiting one behind the other, steaming and puffing, ready to set off round the world). The howling of dervishes, the throb of Negro war-drums, the flat voices of American orators, the thud of wrestling Japanese bodies, the hoarse cries of Arab riders, the lamentations of Jews, the thunder of waves against rocks, the hammering of engines in the bowels of a liner, the gunfire, the bugle-calls as Ruttmann orchestrated them held me and my nerve-centers in thrall every evening last week."

The associations in *Melody of the World* were at times rather elementary, but the film opened new vistas of film editing and of screen beauty. Unfortunately these new paths were not followed, for that is the fate of everyone who discovers something in this new art, whether Vidor, Ruttmann or the Marx Brothers. And the rest of the better German films of the period were really not very different from what they would have been without sound—except, that is, for the dialogue.

ADVANCES

There were a few directors, however, who found through the talkies a means to develop their talent. Fritz Lang was never to attain the power of *The Nibelungen* and *Metropolis* again, though *By Rocket to the Moon* was not uninteresting. It starts off like a good detective film, and the departure of the first interplanetary rocket is remarkably handled. Thanks to his direction of the crowd and to the admirable Gerda Maurus' acting, we really have the impression of taking part in it. The rest of the picture, with its amatory complications on the moon, was altogether ridiculous. *The Last Will of Dr. Mabuse*, a sequel to one of his earlier successes, was entertaining, rather Caligaresque and well constructed. His *M*, based roughly on the Düsseldorf murders, was far better, and had some magnificently grim things in it. We can still hear the murderer panting when he breaks the penknife with which he is trying to pick the lock. Not until *Liliom*, however, did he create a film of real worth. It is based on Molnar's beautiful play about a poor but charming crook. With the exception of a well-handled village fair, it remains ordinary enough until Liliom dies and ascends to Heaven. Now the screen spread before us a lighthearted picture-postcard sort of Paris, with clouds and stars and noisy choirs of angels, cherubs escaped from some circus who look rather like mechanical rabbits, and bells, more and more bells ringing out during this vertiginous ascension as lovely as the best things in Méliès.

If Lang's work was uneven, Pabst's robust and workmanlike talent enabled him to accept the talkies readily. *Kameradschaft, Westfront 1918, Dreigroschenoper, Don Quixote,* even *Atlantide* all make this quite evident. He had never done such good work in the silent days. Abandoning psychoanalysis for cinematography, he now developed only the simplest emotions and states of mind, while at the same time the socialistic tendencies evident in *Joyless Street* brought him to a concept of the film akin to that of the Russians. For a time it seemed as if he would rival Eisenstein.

Westfront 1918, appearing at about the same time as the American-made *All Quiet on the Western Front*, almost launched a new wave of war films. Though the American picture gave a greater impression of skill, the actual fighting in it often looked rather theatrical and orderly. Pabst's film was intricate, obscure, sometimes confused and perhaps only really excellent at certain moments, but these moments were extraordinary. Concentrating entirely on the desolation and asphyxia of war, he presented it naturalistically, yet with a feeling for composition and for lighting, in a mood of bitter pessimism which was almost magnificent. One became acutely conscious of the mud, the mist, the rain shrouding his anonymous heroes and of the deadly yellow cloud of gas creeping over the land like some living creature. Trivas, an excellent pupil of Pabst's, tried later to repeat *Westfront 1918* in his *No Man's Land*, but despite some excellent photography it was bombastic and nowise comparable to Pabst's somber and hopeless picture of war.

Kameradschaft, inspired by an actual catastrophe at Courrières during which German miners went to the rescue of French miners, is likewise a striking and provocative film. We can overlook the melodramatic incident where the old grandfather goes down into the mine to look for his buried grandson. Magnificent and utterly natural things are throughout followed by forced and even disagreeable things. There can be no criticism of the scene in which the Germans in trucks cross the frontier to come to the rescue of their fellow workers. It is a fine scene. But a little later a member of the rescue party, wearing a gas mask, makes his way towards one of the Frenchmen, who makes an involuntary movement of terror. It could not be clearer (for this is a film of modern times) that the buried miner momentarily fancies he is back in the war, that the Germans are advancing. It is a gripping moment. Unfortunately, Pabst spoils it completely by going on to add horrible and grotesque superimposed shots to remind us about the war, as if we had failed to see the point. Moreover, at the end of the film Pabst, the good Socialist, reveals that he is, before anything else, a German. Police come to the mines to re-erect the bars which, in this underground world, replace actual frontiers. On the bars is affixed a date, "Frontier 1919." In other words, Pabst is not concerned with frontiers in general but with the Versailles Treaty.* Despite his ideology, *Kameradschaft* is nevertheless a striking film. Pabst has never made use of more skillful lighting: all the scenes in the mine are extremely beautiful.

Dreigroschenoper was another attempt to make a proletarian film, and when Pabst introduced into this somewhat heavy fantasy his famous procession of beggars he achieved a kind of brutal power which was highly effective, though lacking the profound significance of the Russian epics. The rest contained too many songs and was too long, though the scenes of Mackie with the girls in the brothel were colorful, and the shots of misty old-time London with which it opens are very beautiful. A street musician is singing an extraordinary ballad (Kurt Weill's music did much to popularize *Dreigroschenoper*), pointing meanwhile with a stick at crudely painted pictures which also narrate the exploits of Mackie; we glimpse through him the ancestry of the talkies. Like that amazing quadrille in the Moulin Rouge in 1900 which is the one great moment of *Atlantide*, some invention of the sort constantly reminds us that Pabst is truly an artist.

Then came *Don Quixote*, which Pabst made in France; it was very badly received. True enough, the action is constantly interrupted to permit Chaliapin to sing one of his songs, and the way in which the episodes are loosely strung together is quite disappointing. The merits of the film lie elsewhere. It leads one to imagine that someday Pabst may make a film without a plot and without characters, a sort of hymn to the visible world. Each single shot in the film is admirable, perhaps a little too perfect, but the light seems to caress the sunny villages, the Spanish priest's hat, the gleaming jars, the grass in which each single blade sparkles, the pebbles in the roadway, the girl asleep in the straw, with her

---

* Pabst was deeply concerned with frontiers and that was the whole point of this scene which the authors seem to have totally misinterpreted.

firm breasts and torn bodice. It is impossible not to respond to such frank and manifest sensuality. This decorative obsession finally escapes from its too obvious kinship with painting, and becomes genuinely cinematic. From the moment Don Quixote is caught up by the sails of the windmill the story, which until now has done nothing to move us, suddenly becomes utterly convincing. Though there is the same care for pictorial composition, now it becomes transformed by emotion and by movement. At the end the books are burned and there is a long, a very long scene during which the screen is filled with the curious flowerlike form which the fire and the burning pages compose together. Slowly this striking image fades away, vanishes, as Chaliapin's voice sings the sorrows of Don Quixote. It is one of the most genuinely cinematic things ever achieved on the screen.

Thus far has Pabst's love for his craft carried him: by dint of obeying its technical laws, by honesty, by a passion for composition it is possible for a good workman, even if he is not a genius, to attain success, and that is his reward.

OPERETTAS AND VIENNESE FILMS

Films as serious as these were not to everyone's taste. Erich Pommer, master of the German film industry, realized this and having pondered the new invention decided that it was first and foremost ideally suited to deal with operetta. There is nothing wrong with this idea. When Wilhelm Thiele directed German, French and English versions of his *Drei von der Tankstelle* we were all delighted. This commercial film contained quite a few surprises as well as a lot of singing—among them the birdlike charm of Lilian Harvey, the four little notes which announce the arrival of her automobile, the dance of the furniture-movers, a sprightly view of life and an exceptional gaiety. The three friends in their gasoline station seemed to be the very symbol of carefree youth; there has never been a picture which aroused one's tenderness more effectively than this simple operetta which ended up by poking fun at itself, in the music-hall revue.

We were destined to be flooded with films of the kind, and they quickly became insupportable. *Drei von der Tankstelle* was a stylization of contemporary life, it was too original, so there was a wholesale departure for the artificial paradise of Viennese operetta. Among so much waste footage there was one film of interest, extremely lavish but never in bad taste, Eric Charrel's *Congress Dances*, in which occurred Lilian Harvey's enchanting drive through the market place and the washerwomen, as she sits in her carriage and sings of her happiness. It was a facile enough picture, but an exquisitely enjoyable one.

The fashion for period films soon made other uses of Vienna. First *Liebelei* and then *Maskerade* * attempted to touch our hearts. In the former, Max Ophuls really succeeded in doing so with his delicate, melancholy love story with its prewar costumes, its atmosphere of Imperial Vienna, and an unforgettably lovely sleigh ride in the snow touched with all the magic of youth and of winter. Here we found no technical innovations but instead a sureness in the narrative, a sort of recitative style which knew exactly how to catch one's imagination as well as tell a story. No other film in the Viennese manner, not even *Unfinished Symphony* nor *Maskerade*, had the same intoxicating quality. The original play by Arthur Schnitzler was subsequently staged [in Paris] and we realized then that the play is far subtler, for films always seem to coarsen everything. The point of the play was that it concerned only a light love affair, a *Liebelei* which only one of the characters takes seriously, whereas on the screen it was a question of mutual passion. Yet the film had its own charm, a sort of fugitive poetry, exquisite costumes and settings and an indescribable melancholy. It showed clearly what makes the cinema distinct from the theater, since it constantly links the ephemeral to the eternal.

YOUTH FILMS

Youth was the fairy godmother of *Liebelei*, and continued for many years to be the German film's guardian spirit. This trend was definitely affirmed about 1932 by a first-rate picture, *Maedchen in Uniform*. Here for the first time, if we except the experiments

* Remade in America as *Escapade*.

of Mme. Germaine Dulac and *The Peasant Women of Riazan*, we saw the work of a woman film director.* Made by a woman and acted by women and schoolgirls, the film depicts in extremely moving fashion the life of a German girls' boarding school, and achieves a curious perfection. It develops a difficult subject—the excessive affection which a too good-looking young mistress inspires in the hearts of these girls. In Leontine Sagan's hands it is treated with restraint, with tact, with a sense of proportion that contribute no small part of its merit. There is only the barest trace of the German mania for moralizing in the conversation between the headmistress and the young teacher, though, without being unduly censorious, it is difficult not to feel that the former was wrong in keeping so dangerous a young woman at the school. That apparently is not what Leontine Sagan thought, and it need not worry us unduly, borne along as we are by the magic of this romantic piece which makes the filmgoer feel sixteen years old and quite capable of taking up poetry again or of wanting to die of love. The adorable Manuela smiles through her tears; she and all these other children in their impossible uniforms, with their hair scraped back, transport us to an absurd and miraculous world. They hide photographs of actors in their bureaus, sing ridiculous songs; on Mademoiselle's birthday they perform Schiller's *Don Carlos*, with little Ilsa in a big beard as the friar. Manuela gets more and more worked up: when they decide to expel her from school she wants to die, and goes upstairs saying the Lord's Prayer to herself. Only her little companions can save her from flinging herself into the basement: what a joy to hear their terrified young voices calling "Manuela" all over the house. Tragedy is avoided only by a hair's breadth, but during that one hour we have been shown the very spirit of youth and of tragedy.

There are no technical originalities; the film flows along smoothly and simply through a succession of images each one of which is a masterpiece of delicate ingenuity—the girls going to bed, the conference in the headmistress' room with the giggling French teacher, the party where Manuela looks so pretty in her Don Carlos costume, the visit of the royal personage which would

* Dorothy Arzner, Lois Weber, June Mathis had all directed films.

have delighted Marcel Proust. The whole thing is acted by un-
tutored, natural girls who are genuinely convincing, and who
compose with total success a study full of utter grace and freshness, in which gaiety and sadness are wonderfully mingled.

Leontine Sagan ventured later to interpret life at Oxford with
her *Men of Tomorrow*, but it lacked the fire of *Maedchen in Uniform*. We were, however, to see the two principal actresses, Hertha
Thiele and Dorothea Wieck, again, especially in *Anna and Elisabeth*, made by Frank Wysbar, an unknown director—a far from
successful effort, though it indicated to what a marked degree
Germany has ventured to film the most difficult subjects, has
refused to admit that there are limits to what the film can do. It
attempts to treat the case of a little girl who is unconscious that
she has the power to perform miracles. He confines himself to
contrasting the tyranny of Dorothea Wieck with the young
Hertha Thiele, and once or twice (when the young saint's brother
is brought back to life, and when Dorothea is cured) this really
achieves the desired effect. This strange, unsuccessful film is one
of the most unusual that has ever been attempted.

The serious, gentle face of Hertha Thiele and of other fresh,
young German girls recur in any number of films—*Eight Girls in
a Boat, Reifende Jugend, Musik im Blut, Hermine und die sieben
Aufrechten* as well as in certain Czech films such as *Life at Eighteen, Reka* and the rather different one about youths in military
school, *Kadetten*. Maybe there is an excess of romanticism in these
films, and an even greater insistence on moralizing, but sometimes
this very moralizing is characteristic of the age of the characters,
is something they will lose as they grow older. We must remember
how at the end of *Eight Girls in a Boat*, one of the more charming
of these films, the little group of feminists who sincerely believe
that they hate men is completely bowled over when a man appears. This is delicious, quite touching and a trifle ironical. The
moment the man comes marching along, these girls betray themselves, betray how young they are. So the companions of Manuela,
too, will betray themselves someday—as is all very right and
proper. These films of youth are charming because they allow us
to perceive this fact, constantly to sense the brevity and evanes-

cence of time, the preciousness of each single, fleeting moment while these young girls are still young girls, before the fragile bark of youth gets shipwrecked amid the rocks of family demands, of human struggles and of life itself. All this is evident in the ending of *Reifende Jugend*, and much can be forgiven these films because of their romanticism, because they perpetuate this fleeting moment of bliss granted by the gods and reveal the beauty of human existence.

Sometimes they attempt to show us more than this: one or two of them stand out. *Kuhle Wampe*, for instance, a study of unemployment and distress, has certain qualities which remind one of *The Joyless Street*. Despite certain imperfections it is one of the best German talkies, and makes excellent use of the outdoors, of woods and the love of nature and healthy young bodies, though well aware that all these things are subordinated to the necessities of a world in despair. *Kuhle Wampe* is a film about Germany before Hitler. *Hermine und die sieben Aufrechten*, on the other hand, is a film about Hitlerian Germany. The young people in it build a house themselves, and when their class parades before the national gods they do it with such grave enthusiasm that we believe wholeheartedly in the virtues of hard work and of social reconstruction. One is not surprised that Herr Goebbels liked *Hermine und die sieben Aufrechten*. Finally, to these rather monotonously charming pictures must be added an extremely simple and really exquisite one—*Emil and the Detectives*, with a plot derived from a book for boys and a cast of schoolboys who give an astonishingly convincing performance.

NAZI FILMS

When Hitler seized power, he realized the important function that the film plays in our modern world. Now the German film industry was largely Jewish. When the anti-Semitic crusade was launched, the most famous German directors were gradually driven out. Fritz Lang found himself among them, but left his wife Thea von Harbou behind him as a hostage. Pabst went to France and then to America. Erich Pommer, even, was exiled.

There was a clean sweep, and at the same time Ufa succeeded in establishing itself firmly in foreign countries and especially in France.

Ufa, which had always been subsidized by the German government, by magnates such as Hugo Stinnes or by powerful industrial firms such as I. G. Farben, during recent years had fallen into the hands of the National-Conservative Hugenberg. Hugenberg not only controlled most of the big German newspapers (he owned more than sixteen hundred) but also the lion's share of radio and cinema. The Munich firm of Emelka, affiliated with the firm of Phoebus, had offered him strenuous competition, but the depression rid him of Emelka, and by the time the Nazis came into power Ufa was all-powerful. A few years previously this firm had produced a big propaganda film, *Behind the German Lines*, not seen in France but destined for the United States. It attempted to demonstrate pictorially that Germany was not guilty of causing the World War, the mistakes of the Versailles Treaty and the sufferings of the Germanic people. In Paris the A.C.E., a branch of Ufa, took over the distribution of German films and, more than that, the moment talkies came in also began to make films in French. It is estimated that one-third of Ufa's income was drawn from France and from Belgium and that it was therefore French money which financed anti-French propaganda films such as *Der Schwarze Husar* and *Die elf Schillschen Offiziere*. A particularly violent campaign, and really a perfectly justifiable one against dubbing, was carried on by Ufa, who hoped in this fashion to dominate the European market easily without even having to bother to make films in French.

Hitler placed Goebbels in charge of the film industry, as a division of the Ministry of Propaganda. He created the Reichsfilmkammer, one of the seven departments in charge of culture in Germany, and took over the daily film newspaper, *Film-Kurier*. Moreover, in order to belong to the Film-Fachschaft, a corporative organization which it was compulsory to join, it became necessary to prove one's Aryan descent. A credit of over four hundred million francs was allotted to purchase theaters abroad.

The films made before Hitler came into power and even those

made at the beginning of his dictatorship rather skillfully disguised the element of propaganda in them. For instance, *F.P.I. Does not Answer* (in three language versions), a good adventure film of Pommer's (he had not yet been exiled), bore the appearance of a simple straightforward advertisement for Lufthansa and its airplanes. Nevertheless, Germany had never ceased to make use of the direct propaganda so dear to her during the war and in 1920. During the Occupation of the Rhine the interallied commission listed fifty films whose exhibition was prohibited, beginning with *Black Shame*, which attacked the Negroes, down to *U-9* and *The Rhine*. Other films of the kind were made in France, like *The Dreyfus Affair* directed by Richard Oswald. Gradually the propaganda grew more outspoken. It was not merely a question of certain semihistorical films like those made around 1920, though Jannings in 1935 returned to the screen in *Der alte und der junge Könige*, an admirable and skillfully made picture to which there could be no real objection. Nor was it merely a question of films which extolled the prowess of Germany in the past or today, like *The End of the World* or *Morgenrot*, so markedly unamiable towards England. There now appeared definite propaganda for the new party, stamped with the new-fashioned ideology, such as *Horst Wessel, Blutendes Deutschland* and *Hitlerjunge Quex.*

The history of *Horst Wessel* was extremely complicated. Goebbels forbade its exhibition, the Nazi newspapers announced that it was unworthy of the hero whose life it attempted to recount. Actually the difficulty seems to have revolved around some obscure quarrel between Goebbels and Goering; not long afterwards the film reappeared—severely re-edited and under a new name—as *Hans Westmar.* Its scenario had been written by the mysterious Hans Heinz Ewers, a maniacal anti-Semite. Paul Wegener played the evil Bolshevik. Though the ideology of the film was quite summary, though the scenes of the horrors attributed to the Jews were both brutal and untrue, though technically it was clumsy, nevertheless there was about this film something of the rough vigor and stirring faith of the Russian films of 1925. So there was, too, about the film made to the glory (the very dubious glory) of Leo Schlageter, shot by the French in 1923.

Hitlerjunge Quex, an infinitely better film, tells the oft-repeated story of the son of a Communist workman who becomes a Nazi and dies for the cause. In his dying moments he sees the heavens diapered with swastikas. This film, so characteristic of new Germany in its fervor, has provisionally been banned in France, but it seems to be the most important of the recent pictures.

In 1935, rather as the Russians with Eisenstein and Dovzhenko ultimately discovered "the pacific front of labor" after the warlike fervor of the Revolution, so the Germans with a flourish of trumpets produced a very curious film, dedicated to the glory of the labor camps. Monotonous but often impressive, *Triumph des Willens* is a film without a narrative plot, a film of massed crowds and processions (some of which are magnificently handled) which presumably expresses the climax of mass emotion inspired by Hitler. Its ideology is opposed to that of Marx but produces a similar effect.

Goebbels has definitely taken control of the destiny of the German film. What will be the result? It is impossible to say, as yet. What we must hope is that Germany will not entirely forget what she owes to the Jews and to the Aryans who labored to create her industry. If German films lose their passion for morbidity, so much the better, but it is to be hoped that the films of the future will retain the best things of Pabst, of Lupu Pick and even of Fritz Lang—especially their sense of pictorial composition, their rare mobile and plastic qualities. We must hope that they will forget neither *Variety* nor *Such Is Life* nor *Maedchen in Uniform* nor —what was finest about the product of this country—their irreplaceable *humanity.*

4. *The Russian Film*

THE Soviet film industry because of its peculiar constitution underwent no crisis upon the advent of sound. Very few foreign films were imported, there was no danger of competition, and this state of independence made it possible gradually to replace silent films with sound films exactly as desired and to the public taste. Elsewhere the talkies became a necessity: in Russia they were a free gift from the gods of the Soviet paradise.

Physicists and engineers had by now constructed cameras as good as the American ones; and to the production of from one to two thousand silent films annually allowed for under the Five Year Plan until 1937, were now added almost as many sound or talking pictures. Naturally, the theoreticians set to work immediately, the state schools examined the various problems and it is interesting to reread a manifesto of 1930 signed by Eisenstein, Pudovkin and Alexandrov, who had been Eisenstein's assistant on *Potemkin* and was to make the film known in America as *Moscow Laughs* in the future. They stated:

1. In the future development of the film the only important factors are those calculated to reinforce and to develop the present discoveries about editing, in order to produce an effect on the spectator. In examining each new discovery from this point of view it is easy to demonstrate that color films and stereoscopic films are relatively of little interest in comparison with the immense significance of *sound*.

2. The sound film is a two-edged invention and will probably be used according to the laws of least resistance, which is to say simply to gratify the curiosity of the public. First we shall see the commercial exploitation of that merchandise which is easiest to manufacture and to sell, i. e., of *speaking films*—of those in which the record of the sound will coincide in the most exact and realistic manner with the movement on the screen, and will convey the "illusion" of people speaking, of the sound of objects and so on.

This first period of sensations will not prejudice the development of the new art, but there will be a terrible second period, which will come with the fading of the first realization of new practical possibilities, and in its place will be established an epoch of automatic utilization for "high cultural dramas" and other photographic performances of a theatrical nature.

Utilized in this way, sound will destroy the art of montage.

For every addition of sound to portions of the montage will intensify the portions as such and exaggerate their independent significance, and this will unquestionably be to the detriment of the montage, which produces its effect not by pieces, but, above all, by the *conjunction* of pieces.

3. Only utilization of sound in counterpoint relation to the piece of visual montage affords new possibilities of developing and perfecting the montage.

The first experiments with sound must be directed towards its pronounced noncoincidence with the visual images.

This method of attack only will produce the requisite sensation, which will lead in course of time to the creation of a new *orchestral counterpoint* of sight images and sound images.*

This theory of visual counterpoint was shortly illustrated by Pudovkin in *Life Is Beautiful* (*The Story of a Simple Case*), which took as its subject the crisis undergone by one household during the civil war. He aimed at making a highly stylized sound film in which he used not real sounds but imaginary sounds destined to suggest audibly the thoughts of the characters.† Thus, a mother mourns the loss of her son, a big strapping fellow who has long since attained manhood, but instead of letting us hear her sobs, Pudovkin conceived the idea of letting us hear the voice of a child in order to suggest by direct means that the man she mourns is still a "little child" for the mother. In another scene a woman leans out of a carriage window to bid farewell to her husband. Suddenly she remembers that she has forgotten to tell him something, but cannot remember what it is. What we hear is the noise of the train, quicker and quicker, though actually the train is still stationary and the sound is only the symbol of her anxiety. Unhappily, as one might have foreseen, experiments and aspirations of this kind were gradually abandoned by the Russians, as they were by everyone else who had not neglected them from the start. The history of the Soviet talking films is much less glorious than that of its silent films.

---

* *Close Up*, III, No. 4 (October 1928), pp. 10–13.
† This was Pudovkin's aim, but due to the quality of Soviet sound apparatus at this early stage, the film was released silently.

FROM SILENCE TO SOUND

Just as before, the impetuous Dziga Vertov led the way. In *Enthusiasm* (*The Symphony of the Don-Basin*) he mixed an accompaniment of traditional music, the magnificent Russian folk music, with sounds, and especially the sound of machines. Sound with him was seldom disassociated from imagery, certainly not in the richest parts of *Enthusiasm*, but incorporated with it. As always with this Delluc of the Russian cinema, his theories were much better than his practice, though he really contributed some ideas in 1930.

Fedorov in *House of Death* and Yutkevich in *Golden Mountains* attempted to follow his indications but made the mistake often committed by musicians when approaching the sound film —they tried to compose original music as an accompaniment. In *Rapt*, for instance, a French film by Kirsanov, storm music was added to pictures of a storm irrespective of the fact that, contrary to general belief, the two arts are incommunicable.* Visually a storm is necessarily realistic, while storm music is necessarily not, and there can be no real unity. Like the Germans, the Russians were reluctant to abandon the use of a musical accompaniment though it is almost always useless and, when the characters actually speak, seems definitely distracting and false. A musical accompaniment was used in *The Road to Life* by Nikolai Ekk, who recalled memories of the great days of the silent film. This picture about the reclamation of stray children was uneven and at times as boring as a Sunday-school lesson. None of the drama, the revolt of the children, the raid on the brothel by these young champions of virtue, was worth very much. What one remembers is the smile of the ringleader, and the charms of Russian faith and charity. Little Mustapha is sent to fetch provisions: will he come back or will he run away with the money? This was exciting. Mustapha returns, triumphant, with the provisions, and what is more, he also brings a sausage—a stolen one. That was genuinely delightful;

---

* Although Kirsanov was born Russian, his work, all done in France, was entirely divorced from the development of the Soviet film.

so was the installing of the children in the old convent, and the deeply touching ceremony of the locomotive's arrival at the end, bearing on its cowcatcher the body of Mustapha, who had given his life to the building of the line. Here was the old, familiar social lyricism, which the introduction of sound had neither increased nor diminished.

Patriots (*Okraina*), which came later, was a sort of proletarian *Cavalcade*—the prewar period, the war, the Revolution. Semi-symbolic figures pass—the soldier, the profiteer, the patriot, the well-behaved prisoner, the workman. Parts of it, especially the war scenes and the romance between the prisoner and the girl from the village, were both forceful and charming. As a whole, however, it was disappointing.

Some of the directors had abandoned the Soviet paradise for re-munerative capitalist purgatories. Ozep made a *Karamazov* abroad which was rather confused and quite ordinary. Then one day we learned that Eisenstein (we had seen a rather undistinguished little talkie of his, full of songs and leaves and springtime, called *Romance Sentimentale* *) had gone to take a job in the United States. Removed from the Russian atmosphere, what would he do?

EISENSTEIN

The tale of the difficulties he had with the American firm for which he worked soon echoed round the world. Like Griffith and von Stroheim, he had ruined his backers, he had produced a film sixty miles long which could never be shown anywhere, from which adroit specialists had managed to edit a reel or so which he solemnly repudiated. Finally we saw a mutilated version of the film in *Thunder Over Mexico*. No question about it, here was a masterpiece. The director of *Potemkin* had displayed no less talent in a capitalist country than he had displayed in the U.S.S.R.

It is evident that the subject matter of this film is stamped with the Bolshevik genius for propaganda—gentle and virtuous Indians are oppressed by pitiless white men. Except during the last three

* This was made in France by the Eisenstein group, Eisenstein himself having little to do with its making.

minutes of the film, when a proletarian revolution breaks out, the absurd theme does not really bother one. The adventures of Sebastian, the charming Indian who is the victim of greedy Spaniards, might have taken place anywhere—actually have taken place. Every colonization has similar crimes on its conscience, and what happens to Sebastian is sufficiently individualized to seem convincing. That, however, is not the essential thing. What is important is the plastic perfection of the photography of these temples, these stones which do not seem to be inanimate, these fleshy plants which lend the Mexican scene so funereal an aspect, in which man and nature are perfectly in accord. How theatrical, how melodramatic Lawrence's *Plumed Serpent* seems beside this gifted Russian's work! Beyond all else, how far such a film, overburdened as it is with beauty, carries us from filmed dramas.

We are quite aware that this is a wordless film with musical accompaniment, which carries us back to the silent technique out of which *Hallelujah* had delivered us. But at the same time it also carries us back to the autonomous reality of cinematography. Tormented by the thought of what has been cut out of this picture, everybody has regarded *Thunder Over Mexico* as though it were not truly a film, but a collection of stills. This is a profound injustice. The ideal thing would be to own this film, as one owns a book, so that its construction and its rhythm could be examined in detail. We only signalize the brief instant when Eisenstein, having just shown us the monuments of Pre-Columbian Mexico, then attempts to provide a rapid and bold synthesis of Mexico today, choosing only the most familiar elements, almost the clichés of that romantic land—a bullfight, beautiful women in mantillas fanning themselves and smiling, monks more hideous than those of Ribera, a grave in which a bunch of flowers lies beside a skull. Each one of these images is of a prodigious and sensual sharpness, boldness and color. Looking at the texture of the materials, the plaited straw, one has the impression of having touched them, just as in a painting of Manet's or in Pabst's *Don Quixote*. All these images, each so beautiful in itself, vanish and reappear—the señoritas smile at the skull, the gloomy monks seem to be watching the bull ring—in the mounting crescendo of a composition like music which is one of the purest things we have ever seen in the cinema.*

Many others could be quoted, such as the death of the wounded men among the dying and torn cacti, the hunt, the ghastly and almost unbearable sights which give birth to the whole genius of Spain, not through imitation but through kinship of inspiration. Here is Berruguette and his auto-da-fés, here when the young girl arrives in her jingling trap is Goya and his cartoons, here at almost every instant are Zurbarán, Valdes, Leal and—above all—Ribera. When Sebastian is being tortured against a background of stormy skies between two half-naked companions bound with ropes, the resemblance is so striking as to be overwhelming.

It is the peculiar quality of this novel, new-born art to evoke the memory of such names as these. We will not repeat here that the film stands at the crossroads between music and painting. After *Thunder Over Mexico* it is not necessary to repeat it: it is obvious. Eisenstein's plastic qualities are not isolated as Pabst's often are; they are combined in conformity to the rhythm. This, despite anything that may be said, is significant.

DRAMAS AND COMEDIES

While *Thunder Over Mexico* carried us back to the silent film, what was happening to the orthodox sound film in the U.S.S.R.? Some quite extraordinary things were taking place: the directors were heeding a popular demand for adaptations of the great Russian classics, among which they looked to find some condemnation of the bourgeoisie. These films were well made and well acted in the tradition of the Russian theater—*Thunder Storm*, after Ostrovski, *Judas Golovlev* (*House of Greed*), after Saltikov-Shchedrin, and of course *Petersburg Nights*, after Dostoevski—but one sought in vain for any glimmer of the former artistry.

* Curious praise for a film which Eisenstein regards as a travesty of his intentions and which from the context is being judged here largely from stills which bear no correspondence to any image in the film—such, for instance, as the skull.

Now and then, upon the occasion of a festival or a celebration, propaganda films were still made, such as *Chapayev*, in which there is an admirable scene where a woman is taught to handle a machine gun (all of a sudden this peasant woman smiles, nods her head and bursts into a torrent of words), and *Three Songs About Lenin*, in which the memory of the father of the Revolution is extolled in an heroic manner, and the story of his life is related by simple people, each telling what he did for them in the accent of his own province or craft and composing a symphony which is incomprehensible to foreigners, but which might well produce valuable results. But *Chapayev* and *Three Songs* are rare items in the bulk of production. Today the neonationalism of the Russians goes so far as to exalt the past of the holy land of the Czars, and the big film for 1936 is to be *Peter the First*, which can hardly be very proletarian but which one hopes will be extremely Russian.

It is a pity that the Russians demanded romance, for much of *Moscow Laughs* is unbearable since it is a hodgepodge of singing and flirting in the worst style of German operettas. Nevertheless, it is among these errors that we have to seek some genuine novelties. *The Czar Wants to Sleep* (which, like an excellent German comedy, *The Thirty Trunks of Mr. O. F.*, is about an imaginary person) was extremely heavy. The soldiers maneuvering in front of the Czarist Kremlin, however, moved like marionettes to a delicious little tune played on the fife. A little later *The New Gulliver*, a film with propagandist tendencies, though likewise heavy, contained some charming sets; there were pleasing elements in this puppet *Metropolis*. Realistic comedy was abandoned in favor of a puppet play in the spirit of an animated cartoon in which humor was intended to become fanciful—but this was no more than indicated. Alexandrov's film, despite its faults, its heaviness, its interminable romances, its overemphasized effects, was much better, and if about half of *Moscow Laughs* could be cut we should have a sort of masterpiece. It would be a masterpiece in which thirty years of film making were summed up in a bold synthesis. There is unquestionably something of the Marx Brothers and of Chaplin and Lloyd in *Moscow Laughs*.

There is a walk to music which might have come out of *Congress Dances*. It also displays a childish and delightful love of destruction, pitched battles which evoke the great days of 1915 with Fatty, Max Linder, the first Chaplin comedies and those of Mack Sennett. Here and there one is even reminded of René Clair. What is even more extraordinary, there is real imagination, too. A shepherd is mistaken for a celebrated musician—that's pure farce. But he plays his pipe, and lo and behold, his flock appears. The cow puts her nose in the powder box on the dressing table, the sheep lies down like a rug on the floor, the sucking pig arranges himself on a bed of parsley and herbs, oxen in pairs drink champagne nose to nose out of the ice bucket and guzzle water out of the fish bowl. Here was a frenzy of absurdity such as had never been seen. A little while before we had seen birds sitting on telegraph wires like notes of music on staves. The shepherd plays the tune which their little bodies make, and all of a sudden one of them flies up an octave and becomes a high note. Here we join hands with Méliès and the films of 1900 with their ingenuous illustrations, their side-show fantasy and their inventive fecundity. At the end, when the musicians want to rehearse their music without bothering the neighbors, they rent a hearse and walk singing behind it, knowing that no one will venture to interfere with them. This grotesque scene reminds us of both Méliès and of *Entr'acte*. Each time the cinema takes on new life shall we always meet with this vehicle coming to bury what is outworn and prepare for a new order of things?

5. A World Industry

FILMS are made as well as shown all over the world today. The United States, Germany, France and Russia have maintained uninterrupted production either from the very first days or at least since 1914. Other countries where production formerly flourished but afterwards declined, have also begun to make films again.

ITALIAN FILMS

Production in Italy, as we already saw, had virtually come to a standstill in 1925. The example of Lenin and of the U.S.S.R. soon suggested to Mussolini how important the cinema was, both socially and culturally. Once Fascism had been firmly established, the studios in Turin and Milan, almost shut down or only producing very sporadically, were reopened. At first they concentrated on dubbing films, particularly French films. That is still a major activity in Italy. At the same time, however, they also began actually producing. Carmine Gallone, back home again, directed *Casta Diva*, which failed to avoid all the faults of the older Italian product. Camerini on the other hand turned out an amusing, rather casual comedy somewhat in the manner of René Clair, entitled *What Fools Men Are!* Then followed some historical films, such as *The Hundred Days*, historically correct but slightly stiff, based on a scenario by Mussolini himself.

Italy was naturally anxious to provide a Fascist counterpart of *Potemkin* and *Triumph des Willens*. *Black Shirts*, celebrating the march on Rome, and *The Old Guard* thereupon appeared as monuments to national pride and the Fascist reconstruction. Neither of them possesses the turbulent beauty of the Russian films; both of them contain too much dialogue and both of them seem almost too restrained, too smooth, too anxious to avoid the emphasis of the older Italian pictures. This is particularly true of *The Old Guard*. This simple story contains some striking comedy scenes of village life, though the director's scrupulous desire to provide us with beautiful compositions somehow defeats its own ends—his pictures are so beautiful that one becomes bored by them, though the end of the film is fine. The concluding scenes show the men of the village leaving to join the militia on the march to Rome. We see only the profiles and the helmets of these men as they climb into the trucks. The headlights give out a small, pale beam in the rising dawn. Nothing is heard but the slow throb of the engines, interrupted now and then by the distant crowing of a cock. This chilly and silent departure is singularly impressive, with the long, pale road stretching out under the gray of a hesitant dawn—no songs, no triumph, no glory—only some trucks on their way to the city, and the leader's name printed in big type like an advertisement for patent medicine. We can still look forward with considerable hope, this film suggests, to Italy's providing us with its own epic of modern life and endeavor.

THE NORDIC COUNTRIES

Sweden, another country of which little had been heard lately, never entirely ceased producing films. *Men of Varmland*, a pleasantly countrified affair overburdened with trills and music, somehow suggested that the old originality had been lost. Its landscapes no longer emanated that national emotion which swept through the films of Seastrom and Stiller, and there were no innovations in the use of sound in this straightforward transcription of opera. What is important, however, is that a new outburst of activity had hit Sweden, Denmark and Norway and that Finland, a newcomer, had also started to make films. It is difficult to see how these countries with such restricted populations can afford to make talking films. Take the case of Holland, with a population of only eight million Dutch-speaking people, which nevertheless does not prevent it from making talkies, or from having its own Hollywood. Towards the close of the silent era Holland had produced a new director of real ability, Joris Ivens, who made *The Bridge* and the even better *Rain*—a simple documentary that achieved extreme photographic perfection and possessed a rhythm the equal of Germany's best pictures. Moreover, Ivens has since made a remarkably daring and impressive film, *New Earth*, though censorship did its best to ruin it.

AND ASIA, TOO

As seems natural enough, it is Germany which supplies Holland and Denmark with most of their films and takes into its embrace all the Central European cinemas. It is significant, however, that studios have been opened in Bohemia and in Austria as well as in Hungary and in Poland. Countries which have never gone in for film production before are now beginning to do so. Greece and Rumania have both entered the field. Perhaps someday we shall be allowed to see these too, as we have lately been allowed to see Czech films and those English films which so seriously rival the American films.

During the first six months of 1935 roughly four hundred new films were exhibited in the United States, of which 133 were foreign-made—44 German; 26 English; 24 Spanish; 16 French; 10 Russian; 7 Hungarian; 3 Swedish; 2 Polish and 1 Italian.

The spread of film production, which alone can counteract the monopoly now held by the United States, is undoubtedly destined to succeed less rapidly than it could have done in the silent days, because of the language difficulty. This need not be an absolute impediment, and before long there is little question that every country will have its own national production. It is to be hoped that by that time the various quota laws and import restrictions will have been adapted to permit of our seeing them.

We know virtually nothing of the Asiatic film, though everyone is aware that Japan produces an immense number of pictures and, throughout the Pacific, offers the United States the keenest competition. From the little we have seen and from what returning travelers tell us, it appears that Japanese films are of two distinct types. There are the purely national films, which bring to the screen national legends and old heroic dramas. Impeded by a highly stylized and traditional manner of acting, these seem, nevertheless, to be of great documentary value, and might ultimately give rise to an entirely new kind of film. There are also the very different films which are actually a free translation of the American films, with violent plots full of fights and chases, produced with that amazing genius for imitation that the Japanese have always possessed, and displaying undeniable cleverness.

If the figures are accurate, in 1929 Japan produced 780 films, whereas America produced 800. In 1933, out of the 2,100 films produced throughout the world, America only produced 510 as against Japan's 750. Some of the biggest Japanese firms produce as many as ten feature pictures a month.

Since 1930 the cinema has been largely taken over by propagandists. Nazi and Fascist films are welcomed cordially in Japan. *Hitlerjunge Quex* scored a tremendous success there. It is not surprising that, in a country where eighty-five per cent of the films shown are home-produced, the producers should attempt to imitate the films of those European countries which exalt race consciousness. A number of films have undertaken to recall the ancient Japanese virtues and to extol the deeds of the Japanese armies in China. Some of these were based on actual newsreels, such as *Three Heroes* and *Yamada the Soldier*. One of them out-Japanesed the Japanese—*The Wife of Lieutenant Yanoy*, made in 1931, in which the heroine commits hara-kiri in order that her lieutenant-husband may go peacefully off to war without any family responsibilities. This actually had occurred, however, and Montherlant has written a beautiful account of it.

Firms like Sotsikou, Mikadzou, Sinko are flourishing; famous actors like Nakano outshine the greatest American stars. Nakano as the very pattern of sailors in *The Pacific*, as a lieutenant in *The Parade of Manchuria*, is eternally brave and ever the patriot. Other films, which depict the feudal life of the ancient samurai in which hara-kiri plays an ever-important part, extol those self-same virtues. The Japanese learnt much from American technique: sword fighting and heroic chases enliven these historical reconstructions. Just like the more modern films, they too seek to preserve Japan from the contagions of the Occident and to restore it to the true spirit of the fatherland. Influential organizations and the press attempt to keep this spirit alive within the industry. As in Russia or in Germany, films are an instrument of government. It seems regrettable that we do not know more about all this.

But the Japanese are not the only people to love films. Shrewd businessmen armed with anything but the best type of equipment bore down long ago on China, on India and the Archipelagoes. There is far more film production in India and in Ceylon than is generally realized. Henri Michaux, author of *Un Certain Plume*, found the Indian films intensely interesting according to his own account. They appear to be based on ancient legends, badly photographed and extremely slow-moving. It does not sound as though European filmgoers would take much pleasure in them. According to Michaux the films of northern India display a most extraordinarily persistent, wanton and innate cruelty and brutality. This same writer found the films of southern India, populated by Bengalis (and we must remember that Tagore is a Bengali), entirely different in character. Despite their extreme slowness, they reveal the same gentleness, the same love of nature and of mankind as characterize the poetry of this region. Whatever the films of this land of monstrous legends and interminable dramas may be, one would like to see them.

PART SEVEN

Forty Years of Film

IN 1935 the film's fortieth birthday was celebrated. This seemed a good moment to examine the little-known history of this still embryonic art.

From *Arrival of a Train* to *Kermesse Héroïque*, from *The Great Train Robbery* to *The Informer*, from *A Bicycle Ride in the Forest* to *Triumph of the Will* the motion picture has progressed far. Contrary to the general opinion, however, it quickly discovered its own particular vocabulary and technique; its real difficulty was in becoming an independent art.

It is usually regarded as having found its true identity at about the time of the war. Chaplin's comedies and Sjöström's *Berg-Ejvind* lend authority to this opinion. It was in *Berg-Ejvind* that we first became aware of the beauty of its moving images; of the slow, flexible and vivid manner in which it presents characters and makes them materialize gradually from shadows; the importance with which it endows forms and all the common details of everyday life, whether inanimate objects or animals or the human face. It was *Berg-Ejvind* that made us conscious of the peculiar vocabulary of the medium and of the emotional content of its compositions in light and shade, where truth and beauty become one.

It was at that period, in fact, that the basic nature of the screen was discovered; that is to say, the peculiar manner of seeing, of feeling and of presenting scenes which differentiates it from the theater. It was through the Swedes that the autonomous character of the film was established. Yet in looking back over the history of the prewar film we perceive, too, that credit for the discovery of many of its original qualities must be attributed to the earliest workers in the field. There seems to be reason for believing that the highest achievements of this art, its richest and most vigorous creations, have lain in the realms of comedy; and that the most fertile, the most profound work of exploration was possibly that done in the earliest French comedies and especially by Max Linder, by the first French directors and in particular by Méliès. The experiments they made, though frag-

369

mentary, ill co-ordinated and ill developed, served as the foundation for Griffith's work. When Griffith built up a complete system of devices on which he relied for years to come, he reaped
the benefit of what they had already done. He had the merit of
unifying them and of developing them in a manner definitely
opposed to a theatrical technique. The Swedes enriched this
new method by contributing to it intellectual preoccupations unknown to Griffith—a love of the external world, a passion for
lighting, a care for the image itself—all of which conspired to
carry the film on from mere promise to near-mastery.

From then on the film, in the hands of the best directors, abandoned its futile rivalry with the theater. The fatal years of mis-
guided efforts on the part of the Film d'Art and of the Italians
were relegated to the past. By the end of the war, there had come
into existence a cinema which proclaimed its own independence
and proceeded to undertake its own creative tasks.

Then followed a great period, a period of immense hopes.
Outside the regular channels of production, individual experimentation was carried on from which the cinematographic art drew
its most precious treasures. Favorable financial conditions made
it possible to undertake experiments without regard for public
taste—the results were always fruitful. There came into existence
a small body of workers who had the support of a limited following—such as had recently rendered so great a service to literature and the drama. These men were boldly ambitious and
sufficiently independent of the current accepted technique to endow it with a copious, new vocabulary, to extend the new art
into realms which had seemed closed to it. The business of telling a story in pictures, which formed the basic material for all
films, was relegated to a place of secondary importance by some
of these men. Technique was made sufficiently flexible to translate into images, or into a sequence of images, subtle or delicate
concepts which previously had been the exclusive domain of
painters, musicians and poets. In this pioneering movement the
French had the good fortune to win a place in the vanguard,
side by side with the Russians, the Swedes and the Germans.

Only this had been lacking to give the film true dignity. Between 1920 and 1928 the most critical spirits paid it homage, considering it an art equal in promise to any. The film was in vogue among the intellectuals during this period. Similar excitement prevailed throughout the fertile era of the silent film. For some no doubt it was a snobbish enthusiasm, but for others this act of recognition had the value of a sincere act of faith in the destiny of a newcomer among the arts.

These experiments had a definite influence on the whole body of film production. More rapidly than one would have believed possible, technical discoveries peculiar to the work of the advance guard were adopted generally, and the very directors who had made a reputation by films which were daring, rather than remunerative, were hired by the producers. In more than one instance it is true that they afterwards ran into obstacles which completely changed the character of their work, but nevertheless there was a constant exchange between the advance guard and the commercial film makers, and it seemed obvious that such continual penetration must benefit regular production.

When the talkies came in, of the two opposed tendencies which inclined the film towards commerce on the one hand and attempted to bear it successfully through the early stages of its artistic development on the other, the second seemed to be prevailing. The new discovery was to change all that. It so radically affected the cost of production that independent effort now became quite impossible. In adding language difficulties to the film, it gave the advantage to the great Anglo-Saxon firms, which had always exhibited a marked dislike of innovations. Coming as it did at the same time as the world depression, it induced producers to concentrate on what would certainly make money, and to sacrifice quality to box office. It also revealed that, whatever illusions we may have to the contrary, the film was a slave to fashion and to the vulgarest of influences, whose dominance was suddenly made apparent by these new circumstances. In less than one year everything that had given the film its claim to be an art was thrown overboard. Once more the film was tied to the coattails of the theater.

It is also true that the film conceals within itself a hidden element whose effects have not been fully realized. More than any other medium, it appears to be inextricably linked with the ideas and the ideals of its time—and, moreover, with those which are the vulgarest, the most superficial, the most ephemeral. The fact that most films are dressed in contemporary costume which is cruelly outdated within a few years makes this weakness readily apparent. Nor is this confined merely to the cut of a coat or the length of a dress. In order to catch the popular fancy, films also limit themselves to sentimental and emotional fashions which become old-fashioned quite as rapidly, and just as hideously betray the year which gave them birth. Better than any fashion magazine or illustrated weekly, films provide us with an abiding record of their period. Future historians will no longer have to seek in novels and magazines for those characteristic details, often so hard to discover, which stamp each decade with its own peculiar quality. They will only have to look through a group of box-office successes, and will need little critical judgment for their work. There they will see our pitiful gestures, our current mannerisms, our false sentiments—an unmistakable reflection of the poverty of our era.

In its way every film is a documentary film. Film actors, almost all of whom are undistinguished and lacking in resources, rarely inject into their characterizations any personal truth. They are, all of them, little but "a girl of 1930," "a gigolo of 1923," "a society man of 1913," "an officer of 1916" and represent even these restricted types with a superficiality which amounts to caricature, like that of a fashion plate. Thus they bear witness to our social modality as unmistakably as a drawing room of 1927, a house of 1900 or an automobile of 1915 bears witness to the décor and spirit of a period. The basic material of the films themselves, their plots and the manner in which these are worked out, the very color of the sentiments they reveal, are unconsciously dated too, so that it is as impossible to mistake the film sentiments of 1920 for those of 1930 as it would be to mistake a model T Ford for a Packard straight eight. For this very reason, try as one may, there is always something shallow and even grotesque about film psychology.

The moment that a film attacks the subtler or finer emotions *
one is fairly sure to detect a distinctly commercial flavor, a sort
of compromise with current popular fashion or, at the best, a
coating of some equally objectionable modern sauce. The plots
on which the bulk of films are based bear a close relationship to
the stories printed in daily newspapers; emotionally they are
about as true to life as the popular magazines. Between the cheap
films destined for the small cinemas and the superfilms intended
for the big theaters there is really, all said and done, a difference
only of more skillful production and more care for details. The
inspiration in both is equally vulgar—in all but a very few ex-
ceptions.

In the majority of films made between 1918 and 1929 a rather
ingenious system was often adopted. It consisted in borrowing
from the experimental films in order thereby to disguise an underlying worthlessness. It all worked very simply. The producer
himself or his assistants retain absolute control over the scenario
and the main outlines. It is they who control the main thread of
the film and whatever ingredients are deemed necessary for the
sacred task of "pleasing the public." For the director, who has
little choice between agreeing with them or getting out, the
best solution is usually a compromise. He accepts the general
groundwork but eliminates as many as possible of the worst
stupidities. Upon such a compromise the director and his assistants, often men whose taste and talent are beyond question
but who entertain few illusions, attempt to create a film in which
technical brilliance and certain original ideas will assure success
with the public. Thus the big firms profitably diverted to their
uses the discoveries made by such directors as worked independently or for something more than mere money.

This had the unhappy effect of causing people to confuse the
really individual work of artists working with limited resources
and those commercial films which borrowed the methods and
sometimes the collaboration of these artists. The commercial film
became tainted with "art" to such a degree that it was impossible

---

* On this topic, too, Dr. Erwin Panofsky's article "Style and Medium in
the Motion Pictures" in *Transition* No. 26, 1937 is extremely revealing.

to tell where sincere encouragement of the arts ended and shrewd business instincts began. The critics, eager to applaud where they could, only added to this confusion. Everyone admitted that the film experienced certain difficulties when confronted with psychological problems, and that these difficulties were best overlooked. People formed the habit of not being too critical about something which was probably very important. From closing their eyes to these extremely evident failings, they then proceeded to hail as masterpieces all sorts of films which, though well enough made, lacked precisely those qualities that a masterpiece must possess.

The willingness of the public not to demand too much of the film during the silent era created a general tendency to exaggerate the potentialities of the medium and to overestimate its actual achievements. Only when dialogue was added did it become necessary frankly to face its deficiencies. Even if the first talkies had been as good as the last silent films, they would still have been a giveaway. What really happened was something far more serious. It became all too apparent that the spoken word is a formidable medium, and that it revealed in all its frightfulness the mediocrity which silence had hitherto disguised. Had one or two gifted artists come along at that time they might have found a remedy, but at that period, on the contrary, the ideas of the producers alone and unimpeded found expression.

There is little point in saying more. Itinerant carpet vendors, strange men from Poland and Rumania, adventurers of every sort who had already gained partial control of the cinema now made matters worse by methods which would have endangered the future of any industry and which orientated the whole of production, but particularly that of France, towards a permanent mediocrity. This aspect of film history has been referred to before; if we are to regard the film as an independent art and trace its gradual evolution we must never lose sight of the fact that it has so far been primarily an industry, and often the basest of them all.

THE MUSIC OF IMAGES

Incurable as the ills that arise from this false situation may be, it is now necessary to take thought and, in concluding a study in which we have traced the slow evolution of this art-industry from a peep show, to consider what it may bring us in the future and on what, in spite of everything, its value and its magic lie.

This is no place to outline an aesthetic of the film, for every art by its very development traces out its own aesthetic, and the works of art themselves are infinitely more valuable than any discussion of them can be. In the output of the cinema during the past forty years, everything that has seemed to possess the characteristics of a work of art has exhibited one of two tendencies—one of which is to accentuate the most realistic properties of the photographic image, the other to escape as far as possible from reality.

To escape from reality and give it a figurative interpretation —sometimes poetic, sometimes comic or fantastic—this was the direction along which Méliès impelled the budding film. In this he differed from his contemporaries. Influenced no doubt by circumstances as well as by his own instinctive preferences, rather than by any calculated plan, he inclined the film towards the unlikeliest impossibilities. He made us realize that this form of entertainment, since it is created in secret and remotely, is thus peculiarly capable of nurturing irreality and make-believe. What it is impossible for men to do, can be done and set before their eyes. The film sets no limits on the imagination of its creator, and the most rigid laws can be upset by it with impunity. This realm of utter freedom was limited only by the bounds of imagination. Yet Méliès shared the predilection common to most pioneers for the bizarre rather than for the impressive. The unreal world which he created differed little from that of stage spectacle and illusion.

Later on others were to follow this same path, within the limitations imposed by the development of the film industry and the new obligations which this entailed. So *Caligari* and the other fantastic German films came into existence. In France this tendency best adapted itself to the requirements of public and of producers alike in the work of René Clair. When he began with *Entr'acte*, Clair clearly displayed his desire to achieve the purest fantasy, to create a sort of visual poetry. When he afterwards made use of plot or narrative he also made free use of the director's right to interpret them according to his own peculiar vision, to interpose between reality and himself tinted spectacles which lend it an unexpected and personal aspect, expressive of his individual mood and fancy. In the simplest and most conventional plots, he sets into motion characters which might have stepped out of a family photo album, real human beings to whom, however, some skillful touch has added the old-fashioned or awkward or romantic look they will have acquired in a faded snapshot twenty years hence. We are far from unreality, because these characters, and the backgrounds they inhabit, are pictures of something actual; yet they form part of an interpreted or transfigured reality, idealized as memory can idealize it by preserving the exact details, while utterly changing the general impression and atmosphere. He had abandoned the desire to apply the film's resources to free fantasy, but created instead a new aspect of the world in some subtle fashion which often makes us think of the paintings of Henri Rousseau, though it is less labored and careful. He discovered a penetrating and photographic vision of the world, which is the exact antithesis of the vision furnished by "artistic" photography. We can hardly say that it liberates the film from reality, but it certainly subjects reality to respectful obedience.

Chaplin's method was markedly different and followed a much simpler line. His interpretation was based on the creation of a character so palpably free from the common necessities that it created round itself a new and different reality, unlike that of the everyday world. Once you admit the existence of this character, there is no question of expecting him to adapt his behavior to common, human logic. Chaplin's films are, perhaps more than any others, completely independent of reality. This is because they stem from pantomime and not from a careful imitation of the theater. Their origins lie in a singularly abstract and imaginative interpretation of human impulses and gestures. The world in which Chaplin dwells can, if necessary, limit itself to the purely figurative world in which a dancer mimes. That explains why Chaplin avoids dialogue, which has no place in his technique.

Chaplin's influence on the other comedians has been sufficiently strong to stamp all their work with a similar distaste for reality, though in this they followed him timidly and only because it made things easier for them. As comedians they had everything to gain by surrounding themselves with a crazy sort of atmosphere: both Buster Keaton and Harold Lloyd availed themselves of it but without much real imagination. Actually the most interesting experiments along this line occurred in the cycle of "absurd" films that made the Marx Brothers and W. C. Fields world-famous. When these first appeared it seemed for a moment as if comedy were taking on a new lease on life. Violent and tumultuous fantasy broke every known custom and even threatened the usual pious adherence to a more or less consistent plot. Confusion reared its head; fancy spread its wing. For a brief moment it seemed probable that comedy was about to join hands with the animated cartoons in joyous liberty, that brilliant and ludicrous inventions were going to free men and animals alike from all laws save those imposed by the director. Films, we fancied, will become like jazz music, gags will explode like rockets amid a veritable festival of ingenuity in which all the riches of the circus, the cock and bull fight, the municipal parade, music-hall farce and acrobatics will unite.

It was, after all, only a flash in the pan. We soon realized that this new type of comedy was only a framework for the multiple and individual stunts of the Marx Brothers, and that Fields' incoherence arose rather from an overabundance of material than from any intention to break with tradition.

There was something to be learned, nevertheless, from the appearance of these clowns on the scene. It pretty well demonstrated that the public is only too delighted to follow those who offer it fantasy, fresh and effective conceits, even if mixed with other elements of debatable merit. At heart, the public is always wishing that the film, and especially the film comedy, would rid itself of its bonds. Admirable instrument though the film is for overthrowing reality and drowning it in folly, it has never been used for the purpose except timidly. Anything *can* be shown on the screen: but all they have shown us is the same familiar story over again. The continued and highly significant success of Walt Disney is sufficient proof of the homage which the masses will always render to creative imagination, to powerful and unstinting inventiveness. There may, there must, someday be films which will make brilliant and masterly use of unreality and imagination: the public is sure to welcome them enthusiastically. Was it not towards this end that the most intelligent and most successful attempts of the first few decades of the cinema were directed, though confusedly and under the various compulsions imposed by commercial necessity?

The contrary trend can also claim to have produced some equally important films. The Soviet Union had produced pictures of a realistic order so powerful and so well balanced that they inclined one to the opinion, at first, that theirs was the only true approach. Their success was all the more disconcerting because there was no question here of the work of any particular director, but of the style of an entirely national output which differentiates it immediately from anything that has come out of any other European country, or from America. Germany and Czechoslovakia, two countries which may have had some influence on the Soviet films, also produced realistic films whose sincerity and power placed them in the forefront of contemporary productions. This distinct group of films does exist and has exhibited such incontestable superiority that only with difficulty can one prevent oneself from regarding it as the source of all sincere strivings after beauty. In this connection we must not forget the origins of this school—among the Swedes and in *Berg-Ejvind*.

Has the development of the film been confined, then, to two opposed currents, two irreducible methods of approach characteristic of two different creative temperaments? Certainly it would be impossible honestly to regard the work of Eisenstein and that of Chaplin as springing from the same inspiration or having the same point of view. The film is a medium of expression to both of them, but their methods of using it are different. Yet we must not overstress this difference; there is much in common between the realistic school's approach to the medium and the manner in which the imaginative school weaves far fantasy out of moving images.

When Eisenstein brings the Czar's troops marching so mechanically and grimly down the steps at Odessa he knows very well that actually they did not keep this cynical and lordly rhythm. He is well aware that the revolt at Odessa did not actually take the form of the huge, austere composition he shows us. His realism goes to the extent of using as actors people who had actually taken part in the real event, but it also permits him to invent when he composes and arranges the images which are to form his visual symphony. Realism carried to the utmost point in every photographic detail is relegated to a place of secondary importance in the actual conception of the film and in its final editing. There is no such thing as absolute realism in any art, because the artist imposes form on his material, and because this form is precisely his creative work. In the film more than elsewhere, the creative man is he who submits strict reality to the laws of his own vision. Eisenstein is not the servant of reality, but its organizer. He even organizes it twice over—first when he preconceives his film and afterwards when he orchestrates it during the editing period, blending fragments of reality together and arranging them in a certain order. Here reality, or the bits of reality, is like the frozen words that Pantagruel encountered. A true creator, be it Chaplin or Clair or Eisenstein, must make them undergo a process of transmutation. Epic transmutation in the case of Eisenstein comes in the long run to the same thing as the fanciful transmutations of Clair or the comic transmutations of Chaplin. All three of them are men who work with little pieces of photographic images. All of them have to start with a certain interpretation of the world which they wish to bring into being, and to photograph according to this interpretation. Afterwards,

while making this selfsame thing, they detect the hidden laws
that govern the construction of a film, which they apply no
doubt according to their own instincts but which they all possess, like some inner feeling for the music of images. Despite
appearances, the old, naturalistic definition is illustrated nowhere
better than in films—art is nature seen through a temperament. It
is the temperament which is all-important. Where it is lacking
we have a meaningless copy, mere photography, a total absence
of style. As in any other art, style is everything in a film, which
is to say the individual creation expressed according to the individual type. None of the innovations which the cinema has had
to undergo since 1929, nor those which still await it, will, we
think, make us change that opinion.

Editorial Postscript : 1935-1938

THE motion picture is so much part and parcel of contemporary life, reflects its inconstant moods so closely and draws so immediate and superficial a response from it, that any attempt to weigh and classify current productions accurately is almost impossible. It is true, of course, that any current evaluation of contemporary novels and plays, also, provides an unreliable measure of their permanent worth. But a lapse of several years is essential before any film can be "seen" properly, or assigned its place in the main stream of production. The most cursory survey of the history of the art-industry at least proves this. It was doubtless natural in 1916 that Sir Herbert Beerbohm Tree's "archaeologically correct" *Macbeth* should have been regarded as a worthy and momentous undertaking, but films of a very different and much vulgarer nature being made by Mack Sennett at the same time proved, as we can now see, to be working a richer vein. *The Phantom of the Opera* and *The Lost World*, two "big" films of 1925, made it a less memorable year in retrospect than did *Potemkin* and *The Last Laugh*. We already entertain a far keener and more affectionate recollection of *It Happened One Night*, *A Day at the Races* and *Black Legion* than of *Midsummer-Night's Dream*, which the future may come to consider as flat and unrewarding as the equally sincere and equally misdirected efforts of the Film d'Art, long ago, to elevate the motion picture.

In any attempt to bring up-to-date this lively but controversial history it follows, therefore, that a plain record of facts and of events would be more in place than theory or criticism. The temptation to comment on the text that immediately precedes this postscript is, however, too great to be borne in silence.

In translating the last few chapters of MM. Bardèche's and Brasillach's history I found myself, frankly, in almost total disagreement with them and particularly with their evaluation of American films. In reviewing, for instance, the last of the silent pictures which they praise so highly, one seeks in vain for the elements which their memory (for I think it can only be memory) cherishes. *The Docks of New York* and *Underworld* were really not so stupendously good as they fancy, though even at the time they appeared these two pictures had an exotic air and a bravado of toughness, as well as a fine but conscious photographic gloss, which combined to make them enjoyed abroad to a degree out of proportion to their merit.

The survey of the American talking film seems to me, likewise, equally at fault. Historically *The Assassination of the Duc de Guise* was an important film, though a bad one, and this their book appreciates. But the importance of *The Jazz Singer* is minimized, though it was also of the utmost account historically. It is perhaps inevitable that the language barrier should confuse critics in all countries when any account of the talking film comes into question. Certainly it is very difficult to understand the authors' enthusiasm for a film like *One Way Passage* on any other grounds. What is more important, however, is their inference that in some sort of way the best days of cinematography were over by 1930, and that the films of today cannot compare with those of the previous decade. Actual examination of the product suggests no such conclusion. There are many filmgoers who will always recall the 1920's with particular affection, but this need not blind them to the fact that little real justification can be found for the subtitles on which at that time the medium so largely depended for its expression. Spoken dialogue at its worst can hardly be a worse evil. Actually, a really vital medium such as the film can absorb (and throughout its history has absorbed) all sorts of apparently extraneous elements, of which in 1930 sound still appeared to be one. Yet we must remember that from the time of Edison's earliest experiments, on through the films of the Paris Exposition of 1900, mechanically reproduced sound and dialogue had constantly been on the verge of acceptance as an integral part of motion pictures.

It is difficult to reject the suspicion that the sad state into which the French film industry had fallen at the time this book was written may account to a very large extent for the pessimistic note on which the authors closed. Happily a new wave of activity has since broken over the French studios; and this alone might excuse a more cheerful outlook today.

During the past three years, as often during the previous forty, the film has been declared moribund and also said to be still in its infancy, while audiences in increasing numbers have gathered in cinemas and there enjoyed themselves. The film everywhere has meanwhile continued, as before, to draw heavily upon the stage and fiction, upon biography, history and musical comedy as well as upon contemporary occurrences, but in all of its products it has inevitably continued to reflect contemporary judgments and opinions and it has also created much that is spontaneous and original. American-made films continue to be shown all over the world, though under some difficulties and against considerable opposition. Some two hundred foreign films have been imported annually into America, a few with success, and all of them eyed sharply by Hollywood for signs of talent. Well-intentioned groups have endeavored to improve or reform the film on any of a hundred grounds and other equally well-intentioned groups have attempted to suppress its freedom of expression and exhibition.

Color films have grown more numerous and more pleasing. Popularized in its new form in skillful fashion by the Disneys in their Silly Symphonies and later in their Mickey Mouse films, color has been adopted more and more frequently by other producers, and today is discussed endlessly by critics and filmgoers. Russia made use of it in the not-wholly-admirable *Nightingale, Little Nightingale:* England contributed *Wings of the Morning* with France's own Annabella, who has since been imported to Hollywood. The manner in which color is used has continued to make us unduly conscious of it sometimes, as a slightly distracting presence, even in films as relatively restrained as Marlene Dietrich's and Charles Boyer's languid *Garden of Allah.* Nevertheless today we have arrived at a point when somehow we miss its presence in certain films, particularly in landscape shots, and take it almost wholly for granted in others, as in *A Star Is Born.* It would be quite impossible to conceive of the enchanting *Snow White and the Seven Dwarfs* in any other terms: for in this, as in their short subjects, the Disneys with their free and imaginative use of color continue to lead the way. The public was slow to accept the apparently unnatural appearance of human gait and of all living movement on the screen when motion pictures first appeared forty-odd years ago. It is possible that in the end we may come to correct our opinion as to the colors of the world about us, through the same medium.

There are some indications at the moment that film stars no longer rank quite so high in importance, in relation to the other ingredients of which a film is composed, as formerly they did. Many old favorites have disappeared, others have sacrificed a deal of their popularity: new figures have, generally speaking, failed to excite the frenzied admiration provoked by their predecessors. Many actors and actresses are obviously taking more pride in their work and less in their fan-mail: several highly paid stars today would rather interpret an interesting role than continue the vapid tradition of beauty and banality which at one time seemed to be imposed on the screen's favorites. More importance is being attached in many instances to plot and to a cinematic kind of plot-development than to the provision of "star-vehicles." Directors are once more being publicized: some of them have apparently won the full right to self-expression, for there are a dozen directors today well known to the public who possess so individual a style that it is easy to recognize their handiwork from internal evidence alone. Frank Capra, Alfred Hitchcock, Henry Koster, Fritz Lang, Mervyn LeRoy and W. S. Van Dyke are among them, though it is true that in the language of the industry Capra and Hitchcock would be described as producer-directors, and that the hand of David Selznick, Samuel Goldwyn or Darryl Zanuck is as a rule also clearly evident in the pictures they produce, although they do not profess to "direct" them. So was the touch of the late Irving Thalberg, whose death in 1936 was such a loss to the American industry. It would seem, in any case, somewhat of an advantage that larger and larger numbers of the public are inclined to go to see a film because it is about an interesting subject or made by an interesting director, rather than for the reason that it stars this or that personality—especially since experience over a period of many years has clearly indicated that a film actor is largely what his producer or his director makes him.

The American film industry continues to produce ever longer and costlier films—many pictures released during the past two years have been advertised as costing two million dollars or more. It is not true in all cases that "every nickel shows," for the cost of a film has never at any time been commensurate with its merit, and along with this high expenditure there have also been films which cost relatively little and nevertheless very rightly reaped a substantial reward. None has ever earned so huge a profit, of course, as D. W. Griffith's *Birth of a Nation.*

The trend in public taste which has been evident in the increased popularity of non-fiction, of biography, autobiography and books about "real" life of the past or present, has also expressed itself to some extent in the world of motion pictures. There has lately been an unusual number of biographical films of an unsensational and agreeably unromantic variety—*The Story of Louis Pasteur, The Life of Emile Zola, Rembrandt, Chapayev.* They have come from various parts of the world. Other films have reproduced historical events, usually minor ones, in straightforward fashion and, while not intending to instruct, have (despite some wrong emphasis and stupid compromises) agreeably reflected a graver and more intelligent approach to fact than in the past was customarily regarded as either acceptable or profitable. Yet other films, primarily imaginative in nature, have nevertheless touched, almost boldly at times, on topics of profound social importance such as hitherto the screen usually eschewed—films about lynching, or prison reform, or housing.

America has meanwhile seen the rise of a new type of light-hearted comedy of a rather novel kind, in the whole succession of pictures stemming from *It Happened One Night* and *The Thin Man.* Here a compound of slapstick and chase, of light social comedy and pleasantly colloquial dialogue has been blended with a shrewd and salty acceptance of human nature as it is, rather than as make-believe would have it be. Pictures like *Nothing Sacred* and their kind have reintroduced a breezy and characteristically American element that is as much to the taste of the day as Mack Sennett's diversions were a couple of decades ago.

Discussion about films of fact has been much in the air. In America *The March of Time* has brought a new liveliness to the jaded thing that our newsreels had become. The firm effected this revivification in part by a sharply journalistic approach to current events, and in part by a return to the methods of Méliès and other "news" makers of the early days—for (just as Méliès filmed the coronation of Edward VII in his greenhouse, and Amet created a naval disaster in a bathtub) what *The March of Time's* cameras cannot suitably record on the spot they have re-enacted for them in their studios, and so provide a lively if somewhat confusing view of the world about us.

Since the advent of sound, feature-length travel and documentary pictures produced commercially have been less evident than formerly. Instead, several governments have seized upon this facet of cinematography in order to set before their peoples a glimpse of government undertakings, and explain in some part upon what activities the ruling power is spending the national wealth at its disposal. Big business has followed suit, more particularly in the British Isles where government control of radio has prevented the major industries from seeking to build up good-will over the air. What results may accrue from this only a rash commentator would hazard to predict: it is remarkable, however, that many talented individuals in several countries who, otherwise, would presumably have been diverted into journalistic channels, have as a consequence entered the ranks of film production. Their influence is already considerable, and may become greater than we now realize. It has often been said that it is not the function of the motion picture to preach or to instruct or to spread opinion, but merely to entertain and distract. Actually, even while entertaining, the motion picture cannot help also preaching and instructing and spreading opinion, and few will deny that it may therefore be well, in cases where it is frankly and openly intending to do so, that it should employ alert and intelligent minds to direct its undertaking.

MM. Bardèche and Brasillach have regretted the decreased activity among amateur or experimental cinematographers during recent years. What has apparently happened is that the experimentalists have been drawn into the field of documentary propaganda. That was the road Vigo had taken in France before his untimely death. The Frenchman Cavalcanti in England, the German Ruttmann in Italy, the Dutchman Ivens on his trip to Spain, besides Grierson and Rotha in England and the promising young men along with them, have all been concerned with training the peculiar eye of the motion-picture camera on actual problems of the world of today. Highly significant, I believe, of this response of the motion picture to the public demand for reality are the two short pictures made for the American government by Pare Lorentz—*The Plow That Broke the Plains* and *The River*—for they have begun to do what the film industry of the greatest film-producing country had never quite succeeded in doing. They have begun to set before the Americans in non-romantic and therefore impressive fashion a glimpse of their own historical wealth with its full complement of grandeur and tragedy and hope.

Curiously enough, the U.S.S.R., which first made us alive to the peculiar propensity of the film for this kind of production, has lately seemed to be borrowing a leaf, in turn, from the American film industry and to have turned to a Hollywood-struck romantical vein. Of Eisenstein and Pudovkin and Dziga Vertov we hear no more: or they have sent us no films these last years. Films like *Peter the First* are hardly a substitute. Very recently, we learnt of considerable changes within the industry there, of charges of past extravagance, and of a new order of things to come.

Repressive influences have been at work, as ever, throughout the world industry. Censorship the film has known from its earliest days. It is curious to reflect that although it was children and very simple people who first enjoyed and popularized the movies, there has always been a tendency to protect simple people and children from them. The indictment of the gangster films, which was followed by an attack on the Mae West films and had the effect of modifying even the behavior and appearance of some of the animal characters in the Disney cartoons, proved (as censorship sometimes can) to be a blessing in disguise. Opposition sharpens creative wits, and the necessity to avoid what would distress influential if restricted numbers of persons, led to the discovery on the part of the film makers of newer and livelier ways of providing entertainment for the vast public which might perhaps grow accustomed to do without much, but hardly to give up its movies.

Since the general public has little occasion to compare the quality of sound-recording and sound-reproduction in current films with that of films made some years ago, it has not been fully realized how considerable an improvement has been achieved in this direction. The best films of 1937, as compared with those of 1933, are in this respect as superior as electrically recorded phonograph records are to the now generally obsolete variety of disc. It is readily apparent, however, that in many quarters a very considerable progress has been achieved also in the use of dialogue. In quite a number of films there is, today, far less talk, and what there is of it is infinitely less literary, far more spontaneous, colloquial and effective: moreover, it is delivered in considerably less elocutionary and much more natural manner. This has even applied occasionally to dialogue uttered by children and to libretto rendered by singers. And original music, used as a background for scenes whose primary interest is visual, has more often been written intelligently and modestly.

Technically, the film has always been somewhat in advance of its ability to harness new technical resources to the expression of more penetrating, funnier, or more significant subject matter than it has utilized at any given moment. This has never been truer than at the moment of writing and, in consequence, there has never been more hope for the future.

Index of Film Titles

General Index

CPSIA information can be obtained
at www.ICGtesting.com
Printed in the USA
BVHW010923100219
539745BV00018B/84/P

9 781163 196442